Praise for *The Invisible Emperor*

"A suspenseful, fast-paced account . . . Braude's prose glints with humor and humanity. We follow the fortunes of the bewildered citizens of Elba as their beautiful but poverty-ridden island becomes ground zero for international intrigue. We get poignant glimpses of a time when life was shorter and simpler."
—*The Seattle Times*

"An intriguing look at a still controversial public figure during an often overlooked historical period. For readers of French history, there is little about the Napoleonic legend that isn't fascinating, and as Braude proves, the time spent on Elba is no exception." —*Library Journal* (starred review)

"Braude renders Napoleon Bonaparte's ten-month exile on the tiny Mediterranean island of Elba and his brief return to power in 1815 in short, punchy chapters that read like an exciting novel or an episode of *Prison Break*. [Braude] has a talent for looking at history from a slant." —*The National Book Review*

"Magnificent history."
—Australian Broadcasting Corporation (*This Weekend's Recommended Reading*)

"A lively and insightful account . . . Braude has a wonderful eye for the striking image or scene, and establishes the peculiar world of Napoleon's Elba through vignettes by turns humorous and poignant."
—*The Times Literary Supplement*

"The improbable and riveting story of one of history's most celebrated jailbreaks." —*The Quarterly Journal of Military History*

"This is the story of how a man who had conquered a continent was transformed by an island. Defeated and suicidal, Napoleon departed France in disguise and was exiled to Elba with one ship, a small army, and his mother. He reformed Elban society, read voraciously, and cheated at cards—all while plotting his escape. *The Invisible Emperor* reveals the lesser-known Napoleon backstage from history and preparing his final act. Braude's thorough research and eye for telling detail breathe life into an incredible story of determination."   —Kevin Birmingham, author of *The Most Dangerous Book*

"Of the many chapters in the great 'Napoleonic novel,' few are more loaded with possibility and peril than Napoleon Bonaparte's exile to and escape from Elba in 1814. With vigorous prose and rich attention to detail, Mark Braude fashions a mesmerizing narrative about a former emperor caught between the fate the allied powers had assigned him and the destiny to which he surely was bound. *The Invisible Emperor* uncovers profound human drama in the story of a political creature who, defying reason and disregarding collateral damage, needed a historical stage to prove that he was still alive."

—Stéphane Gerson, professor of French and French studies, New York University; author of *Disaster Falls: A Family Story*

"In their haste to reach Waterloo and Saint Helena, Napoleon's historians habitually pass speedily over the three hundred days that the ex-emperor spent in 1814–15 as ruler of the principality of Elba. Mark Braude has had the ingenious idea of slowing down history, and indeed historians, and lingering thoughtfully over this neglected island episode. His careful and compelling microscopic reconstruction of this moment in Napoleon's extraordinary odyssey is a historical tour de force."

—Colin Jones, author of *Paris: The Biography of a City*

"The story of Napoleon's first exile, starting with his military defeat and failed suicide attempt, and ending with his return to France and to power, is one of the most dramatic in all of history. Mark Braude tells this story with the eye of a novelist and the sure hand of a seasoned historian. *The Invisible Emperor* is a brilliantly vivid account of the tiny realm of Elba, which the exiled monarch ruled for ten months; his captors; his entourage; and, above all, the extraordinary figure of Napoleon himself."

—David A. Bell, Lapidus Professor, Princeton University; author of *Napoleon: A Concise Biography*

"Mark Braude navigates complex motives and wavering loyalties to tell the intriguing story of the fall and rise—and fall again—of Napoleon. He offers an intimate portrait of the dethroned emperor, both his humiliation and his resilience, as the grand panorama of history suddenly comes to focus on a few rocky acres of island. A wonderfully readable evocation of a place and time— and of one of history's most eternally compelling figures."

—Ross King, bestselling author of *Brunelleschi's Dome* and
Michelangelo and the Pope's Ceiling

"One of the great mysteries of European history is how the fallen emperor Napoleon managed to escape his confinement on the Mediterranean island of Elba under the supposedly watchful eye of the Royal Navy. Mark Braude unravels this fascinating episode with all the skills of a historian and all the talent of a natural storyteller. Anyone interested in the amazing rollercoaster of Napoleon's road to Waterloo will find much enlightenment here."

—David Bellos, author of *The Novel of the Century:*
The Extraordinary Adventure of Les Misérables

PENGUIN BOOKS

THE INVISIBLE EMPEROR

Mark Braude has been a postdoctoral research fellow and lecturer at Stanford University and was named a 2017 Public Scholar by the National Endowment for the Humanities. His writing has appeared in *The Globe and Mail*, the *Los Angeles Times*, and *The New Republic*. His first book, *Making Monte Carlo: A History of Speculation and Spectacle*, was published in 2016.

The
INVISIBLE
EMPEROR

·———·

NAPOLEON ON ELBA
FROM EXILE TO ESCAPE

·———·

Mark Braude

PENGUIN BOOKS

PENGUIN BOOKS

An imprint of Penguin Random House LLC
penguinrandomhouse.com

First published in the United States of America by Penguin Press,
an imprint of Penguin Random House LLC, 2018
Published in Penguin Books 2019

The Invisible Emperor was supported in part by a generous Public Scholar Grant
from the National Endowment for the Humanities. Any views, findings,
conclusions, or recommendations expressed in the book do not necessarily
represent those of the National Endowment for the Humanities.

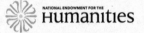

ISBN 9780735222625 (paperback)

THE LIBRARY OF CONGRESS HAS CATALOGED THE
HARDCOVER EDITION AS FOLLOWS:
Names: Braude, Mark, author.
Title: The invisible emperor : Napoleon on Elba from exile to escape /
Mark Braude.
Description: First edition. | New York : Penguin Press, 2018. |
Includes bibliographical references and index.
Identifiers: LCCN 2018031919 (print) | LCCN 2018044898 (ebook) |
ISBN 9780735222618 (ebook) | ISBN 9780735222601 (hardcover)
Subjects: LCSH: Napoleon I, Emperor of the French, 1769–1821—Elba and
the Hundred Days, 1814–1815.
Classification: LCC DC238 (ebook) | LCC DC238 .B738 2018 (print) |
DDC 940.2/7—dc23
LC record available at https://lccn.loc.gov/2018031919

Printed in the United States of America
1 3 5 7 9 10 8 6 4 2

Book design by Marysarah Quinn

Map illustrations by Jeffrey L. Ward

FOR

Eleanor and Jeremy

Paradise is an island. So is hell.

—JUDITH SCHALANSKY, *Atlas of Remote Islands* (2010)

· ————— ·

Lucky Napoleon! This is the most beautiful island. . . . There
is no winter in Elba; cognac is threepence a large glass;
the children have web feet; the women taste of salt. . . . The
Island I love, and I wish I were not seeing it in one of the
seasons of hell.

—DYLAN THOMAS, postcards and letters from Elba (summer 1947)

· ————— ·

The Island of Elba, which a year ago was thought so
disagreeable, is a paradise compared to Saint Helena.

—NAPOLEON, on Saint Helena (February 1816)

CONTENTS

· ——————— ·

SUMMER

FALL

WINTER

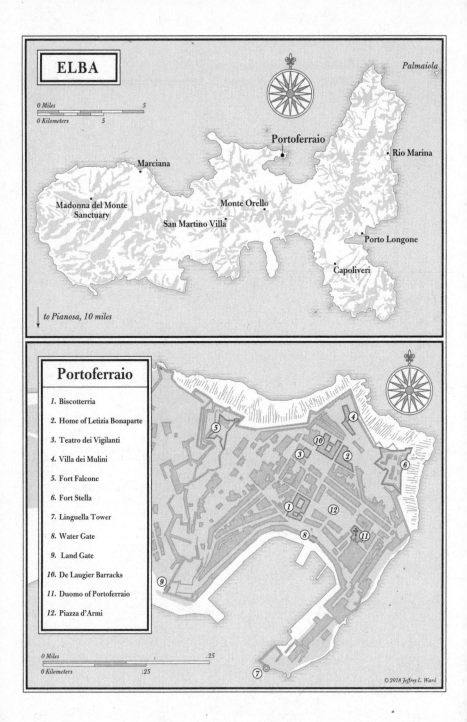

ELBA

0 Miles — 5
0 Kilometers — 5

Palmaiola

Portoferraio

• Rio Marina

• Marciana

Madonna del Monte
Sanctuary

Monte Orello

San Martino Villa

• Porto Longone

Capoliveri

↓ *to Pianosa, 10 miles*

Portoferraio

1. Biscotterria

2. Home of Letizia Bonaparte

3. Teatro dei Vigilanti

4. Villa dei Mulini

5. Fort Falcone

6. Fort Stella

7. Linguella Tower

8. Water Gate

9. Land Gate

10. De Laugier Barracks

11. Duomo of Portoferraio

12. Piazza d'Armi

0 Miles — .25
0 Kilometers — .25

© 2018 Jeffrey L. Ward

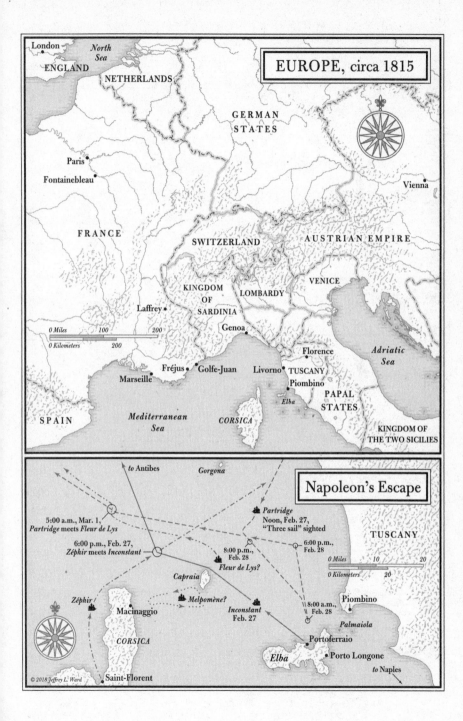

EUROPE, circa 1815

London
North
Sea
ENGLAND
NETHERLANDS
GERMAN
STATES
Paris
Fontainebleau
Vienna
FRANCE
SWITZERLAND
AUSTRIAN EMPIRE
KINGDOM
OF
SARDINIA
LOMBARDY
VENICE
Laffrey
Genoa
Florence
Adriatic
Sea
0 Miles   100   200
0 Kilometers   200
Fréjus   Golfe-Juan   Livorno   TUSCANY
Marseille   Piombino
Elba
PAPAL
STATES
SPAIN
Mediterranean
Sea
CORSICA
KINGDOM OF
THE TWO SICILIES

Napoleon's Escape

to Antibes   Gorgona
5:00 a.m., Mar. 1,
Partridge meets *Fleur de Lys*
Partridge
Noon, Feb. 27,
"Three sail" sighted
TUSCANY
6:00 p.m., Feb. 27,
Zéphir meets *Inconstant*
8:00 p.m.,
Feb. 28
Fleur de Lys?
6:00 p.m.,
Feb. 28
0 Miles   10   20
0 Kilometers   20
Capraia
Melpomène?
Zéphir
Macinaggio
Inconstant
Feb. 27
8:00 a.m.,
Feb. 28
Piombino
Palmaiola
CORSICA
Portoferraio
Elba
Porto Longone
© 2018 Jeffrey L. Ward
Saint-Florent
to Naples

INTRODUCTION

·———·

IT ALL FELL APART quite quickly. From the towers of Notre-Dame and some of the higher rooftops, people watched through telescopes as invaders breached the outskirts of Paris on the night of March 29, 1814. Cossacks crouched round their campfires atop Montmartre, the sounds of their eerie music drifting down into the village below. They were toasting the death of the miller of the Moulin de la Galette, whose ravaged body was tied to one of the mill's sails, or so went the rumor.

Parisians had good cause to be terrified just then. Fearing the populace's revolutionary potential as much as any foreign force, French officials decided against distributing arms en masse, even after troops failed to hold the enemy beyond the gates. This left the city's defense to the twelve thousand members of the Paris National Guard, facing a force nearly ten times larger.

Though the result would have been obvious to everyone going in, the spectacle was played out just the same. A British artist who lived in Paris, Thomas Underwood, recalled passing that bright spring day among "fashionable loungers of both sexes" at a popular café on the boulevard des Italiens, "sitting, as usual, on the chairs placed there and appearing almost uninterested spectators of the number of wounded French and prisoners of the allies which were brought in." Each side suffered roughly nine thousand casualties, making this the deadliest battle of 1814.

Napoleon's subjects wouldn't soon forget his failure to appear in the capital alongside his generals. After a year and a half of fighting across much of Europe, an allied coalition led by Britain, Austria, Prussia, and Russia had driven French soldiers out of German territory and crossed into France. Instead of falling back to Paris, the obvious target, Napoleon had opted to dig in by the Aube River about a hundred miles east of the city, thinking he could cleave the attacking forces in two and defeat each half in succession. This had freed other allied troops to reach Paris largely unchecked.

Allied and French representatives had been trying to arrange Napoleon's surrender for months. Joseph Bonaparte warned his brother that people would turn against him as soon as they realized he preferred prolonging war to making "even a disadvantageous peace." But aside from a few brief moments of armistice, Napoleon had kept fighting, forever seeking the one dramatic victory that would allow him to negotiate from a position of strength. Having risen from artillery officer to general to First Consul to Emperor of the French on the promise of constant and glorious triumph, he feared he would be overthrown at the first sign that he was even considering bending to an opponent's demands.

Napoleon had ridden for Paris as soon as he realized his mistake, switching out his exhausted horses for fresh ones borrowed along the way at intervals. But by the time he reached a posthouse just south of the city, around midnight on March 30, he was too late; a column of French cavalry had already arrived with news of the capitulation signed hours earlier by representatives of his trusted general and confidant, Marshal Marmont.

Realizing they could avoid a wider massacre by surrendering, Parisians had rushed into the streets to welcome the occupying soldiers with shouts of "Down with the Emperor!" and "Death to the Corsican!" Imperial eagles and N's gave way to fleurs-de-lys, the stylized lilies of monarchy. People waved handkerchiefs of white, the traditional color of the Bourbon dynasty that had once ruled France. They brought down the statue of a laurel-crowned Napoleon that had topped the Colonne de la Grande Armée in the Place Vendôme, built from melted-down cannons seized in the battle of Austerlitz, his gift to the city he had promised to make the most beautiful that ever existed.

After a short sulk by the side of the road, Napoleon retreated to the castle complex of Fontainebleau, nearly forty miles to the southeast, sending his aide-de-camp Armand de Caulaincourt to negotiate in Paris on his behalf.

At Fontainebleau, surrounded by his marshals, with soldiers bivouacked on the lawn and injured men recuperating in the outbuildings, he spoke of launching a counterattack on the occupied capital. He had about forty-five thousand troops at his disposal. But while his harangues drew cheers from the members of his Guard, beyond the castle confines such talk would have been dismissed as madness. Every village and town in Europe had been marked by the two decades of nearly perpetual war, with estimates of the death toll in the major conflicts since 1803 ranging from one to six million. Most of these deaths came not in the quick of battle but from festering wounds, or from dysentery, or from frost, or from being marched past the point of exhaustion. It was common to see mental patients forced out of asylums to free up space for incoming injured men.

"Nothing but abdication can save us!" said the esteemed Marshal Ney, not quite to Napoleon's face but loud enough for him to hear. And then he made a joke with ominous undertones, telling Napoleon he had no reason to worry since nobody wanted "to act out a scene from Saint Petersburg," a reference to the assassination of Tsar Paul I masterminded by two of his generals.

Napoleon began drafting the document of his abdication. At its height, his empire had spanned half the European continent and beyond. He had directly or indirectly governed the lives of some eighty million people. Soon he would be sent to a place with less than a hundred square miles of territory and a population of just over twelve thousand.

NAPOLEON'S POWER had rested largely on his ability to tell a compelling story, both about himself and about the historical significance of his rule. "What a novel my life has been!" he supposedly said, looking back on his accomplishments. The Napoleonic novel promised all those who consumed it that they were participating in a glorious adventure simply by doing so. Napoleon and his supporters crafted this seductive lie through images as well as words. Their story depended on the right costuming (the famous hat, the hand in the greatcoat), the right heraldry, the right painting, the right sculpture and architecture. It depended on grandiose ceremonies and lavish processions. But while Napoleon presented himself as a sight to behold, the living embodiment of some abstract notion of greatness, the viewing was always meant to be done from a distance.

Which is what made the Elban exile such an unusual moment in this most unusual life. On Elba, Napoleon was seen by more people at closer range than at any other point in his career. Stripped of his wealth, abandoned by most of his family and all but a few members of his coterie, he was made to interact daily with men and women from different social stations. One afternoon might find him sharing a meal of hard-boiled eggs and crusty bread with the laborers preparing his hilltop villa for a much-delayed visit from his wife and child; another might find him serving as a kind of tourist attraction for a humble copper-master from Wales who showed up unannounced asking to see the Emperor of Elba and was granted an hours-long interview with the man who only a few months earlier had wielded more power than anyone else on the planet.

What follows is the story of Napoleon's disappearance from the main stage of global power in the spring of 1814 and his reappearance the following winter, when he and a few hundred followers landed on a beach in southern France to begin their ultimately disastrous march on Paris. But rather than focusing on how Napoleon was rendered invisible during the ten months separating those two points, this history instead traces how people started to see him in new ways during that same stretch of time, precisely because he'd been banished to such a seemingly remote place and into unprecedented intimacy with others.

SPRING

THE MORNING OF THE POISON LUMP

THROUGH THE THIN WALL of the closet he lately called his bedroom, the valet Pelard heard liquid being poured into a glass, and then a gulp followed by a long silence, and he knew the emperor had poisoned himself. Another attendant had hidden his pistols, but this had been insufficient precaution. Only its creator, the physician Yvan, knew of the poisonous concoction of opium, belladonna, and white hellebore stashed in the silken bag Napoleon had taken to carrying around his neck ever since the Moscow campaign two years earlier.

Now the chamberlains were shouting for the same Yvan. It was three in the morning, April 13, 1814, in the royal bedchamber of the sprawling castle complex at Fontainebleau, two days' hard ride south from Paris. Napoleon was forty-four, and had a wife, an ex-wife, a mistress, two stepchildren, and two young sons, one legitimate and one not.

In his fever he spoke several names: his betrayers. He called for the red morocco portfolio that held letters from his wife, Marie Louise, so it could be given to their son, Napoleon, the King of Rome.

Yvan ordered hot drinks to be brewed, administered cold compresses, and made the patient swallow vomit-inducing ashes from the fire. By sunrise the doctor had confirmed his initial suspicion that two years and its dilution in water had drained the poison lump of any real potency. Still, the task riled him, and as soon as it was completed he collapsed into a chair and had a delirious laughing fit, after which he ran outside, grabbed the first horse he could find, and rode off, leaving his hat behind in the mud.

Napoleon was left to sleep for a few more hours. Later he rose and signed the final document of his abdication:

> The allied Powers having declared that the Emperor Napoleon is the sole obstacle to the restoration of peace in Europe, the Emperor Napoleon, faithful to his coronation oath, declares that he renounces for himself and his successors the thrones of France and Italy, and that there is no personal sacrifice, even that of his life, which he is not prepared to make in the interests of France.

In Paris, people were meanwhile reading copies of a declaration signed in the name of the Russian tsar, Alexander, though actually penned by Charles-Maurice de Talleyrand-Périgord, Napoleon's former foreign minister and now the chief diplomat guiding the French surrender. The declaration stressed that while the allied sovereigns no longer recognized Napoleon's rule, they pledged to "respect the integrity of ancient France as it existed under its legitimate Kings" and that people should consider themselves under Alexander's personal protection until a provisional French government could be established.

Talleyrand—brilliant, elegant, reptilian—had invited Alexander to stay at his town house at the corner of rue de Saint-Florentin and the bustling rue de Rivoli, one of Napoleon's few great achievements in urban planning, meant as a modern triumphal way and named for his fame-making victory in his First Italian Campaign. Talleyrand and Alexander had been colluding since 1807, after Talleyrand resigned as Napoleon's foreign minister to protest his policies, though staying within the imperial fold as vice–grand elector, prompting the joke that this was the only "vice" he didn't yet possess. While Napoleon dismissed the higher-born Talleyrand as no more than "shit in a silk stocking," he valued his counsel and Talleyrand remained privy to military and diplomatic intelligence, much of which he passed on to the Russians and later to the Austrians. Though he was compensated for doing so, Talleyrand seems to have been largely driven by the belief that he was saving the French people from their once promising but now disastrous ruler and that an alliance with Alexander offered the best chance for a lasting peace. This was the man who was famously quoted as defining treason as "only a matter of dates."

Talleyrand gently helped convince Alexander and the other allied sovereigns and ministers that France should be ruled by a member of the Bourbon dynasty: the Count of Provence, Louis Stanislas Xavier, younger brother of the guillotined Louis XVI, who would return from exile to lead a constitutional monarchy as Louis XVIII. Talleyrand predicted that the French Senate, stocked with his cronies, would grant institutional legitimacy to a Bourbon monarchy and that Louis, "having always had more liberal ideas and having lived in England, would return with the desired opinions."

People knew little about the exiled Louis aside from his famous name, and no one under the age of twenty-one had known a France that included a Bourbon. Yet his appeal was clear. He offered a living link in a dynastic chain that led back to the sixteenth-century grandeur of Henri IV and further to the very roots of the Capetian dynasty that had been established before the turn of the millennium. A Bourbon on the throne promised not only a definitive end to the Napoleonic age, but a return to order—just as Napoleon in coming to power as First Consul had declared the French Revolution and with it years of civil strife to be finally at an end.

The allied leaders had never actually formulated a clear idea of what they would do after Napoleon's fall, if they did manage to defeat him, just as they had never publicly called for the absolute destruction of the Bonaparte dynasty while fighting France. A Bourbon restoration appeared to many of the principal diplomats to be the least terrible option from which they now had to choose.

To stave off any chance of a desperate rally, the allies granted Napoleon light terms of surrender. He was allowed to keep his head, for starters, since it was feared that executing him would throw France into civil war. He still inspired feverish devotion in some circles, especially among those who killed and died by trade, and with so many public squares still bearing the stains of a guillotine's work, no ruler wanted to suggest a beheading as the way to cap a victory. Napoleon also escaped heavier punishment because Europe's sovereigns still thought of themselves as a band of equals, "cousins," as he liked to call them, bound despite internecine conflicts by blood, history, and protocol. They alone understood the heavy task of ruling and they alone understood that a defeated emperor must be treated with the deference due his title, even if in this case the ruler in question had invented that title for himself.

The question now was where to put him. If the point of banishment was to render a threatening person invisible and ineffective by removing him from a place of power, Napoleon presented a strange case in the history of exile. He'd "not simply been at the center of the world," as one biographer put it, "but [had] *been* that center." Before sending Caulaincourt off to negotiate his surrender, Napoleon had told him to push for asylum in Great Britain, where he imagined a kind of country-squire existence as guest of the empire he claimed to respect most after his own. When Caulaincourt proposed the idea to the British foreign secretary, Castlereagh, the latter said he was shocked and embarrassed at even being asked.

Napoleon meanwhile wrote to Marie Louise, telling her to send "a very strong letter to your father commending yourself and your son to his care. . . . Make it clear . . . that the time has come for him to help us." Her father was the Austrian emperor, Francis I, who four years earlier had arranged for his then eighteen-year-old daughter to marry the newly divorced Napoleon. At forty-two, Francis had been only two years older than the groom at the time of the wedding, though with his ash white hair, frail frame, and timid bearing he looked much older than his age. The marriage forged an uneasy alliance between Europe's oldest dynasty and its newest. The Habsburg archduchess Maria Luisa became Marie Louise of the house of Bonaparte, empress of France. But Francis now had nothing to gain by his association with his defeated son-in-law. "The principal thing is to get Napoleon out of France," he wrote to his foreign minister, Count Klemens von Metternich. "And, please God, as far off as possible."

Alexander was meanwhile toying with the idea of a Russian exile. "I am more his friend than he thinks," he told Caulaincourt when they met in Paris to negotiate the aftermath of Napoleon's abdication. Even while speaking of himself as a crusading "Angel" who had finally completed his quest to defeat the French "Antichrist," Alexander still admired his enemy's military brilliance and statesmanship; if Napoleon had sometimes acted ruthlessly it was only because he understood, as Alexander did, the value of unscheduled brutality. Napoleon had been similarly impressed by the tall and imposing Romanov. "If he were a woman," he once told his first wife, Joséphine, "I think I would make him my mistress."

The tsar eventually recognized that the other sovereigns were unlikely to favor Napoleon living under his protection, a setup that would have paired the two most dangerous men on the globe in relatively close quarters. His negotiations with Caulaincourt for an alternate solution weren't as tense as might be imagined; the two men had established a camaraderie from Caulaincourt's years as ambassador to Saint Petersburg. After ten days of talks the tsar devised an only slightly less eccentric solution than a Russian exile.

How Alexander came to choose Elba as the site of Napoleon's banishment remains a mystery. He and Caulaincourt fixed on the strategy of an island exile early in their discussions, floating Corfu, Sardinia, and even Corsica as options. There was a certain symmetry in casting this upstart islander back out to sea, a warning from this most hereditary of sovereigns and ruler of Europe's largest landmass to any other parvenu daring to step out of place. Alexander may have thought Elba a wise choice because it lay only a day's sail from Piombino, isolating Napoleon from the continent while keeping him close enough to observe. He might also have wanted to grant Napoleon dominion over a small and relatively well-secured bit of land surrounded by water out of genuine concern for his safety, reinforcing Alexander's religious convictions, which championed forgiveness and generosity. Or it may be that the tsar found the most insignificant territory he could think of and sent his fallen enemy there to humiliate him. Not that he gave his confederates much choice in the matter, one way or the other. He simply announced the decision as a fait accompli one night in Paris, as though testing out his newfound status as the globe's most powerful sovereign and daring anyone to oppose him.

The other sovereigns and their ministers were shocked by how boldly

Alexander had acted on their collective behalf. The British contingent wondered if Napoleon might not seduce the Elbans into forming the hard core of
an army that could come to wreak havoc on the continent. Castlereagh
thought this was all just more of Alexander's acting with too much emotion
when it came to Napoleon, unconcerned by the ramifications of his deeply
personal and quasi-mystical quest to defeat the French emperor. But Castlereagh recognized that separating Napoleon from his soldiers and warding off
civil war trumped all other concerns for the time being. "The whole nation is
released from their oaths to Buonaparte, but bound to *no one*," he wrote to his
prime minister. "This is a dangerous state." He saw no advantage in challeng-
ing the ruler of a nation seventy times larger than Britain and so went along
with the tsar's strange fancy, though he refused to sign any treaty codifying
the terms of surrender.

The Austrians interpreted the tsar's choice of Elba, which lay close to their
Tuscan territories, as a direct insult. "They give to others what belongs to my
family . . . and Napoleon remains too near to France and Europe," Francis
wrote to Metternich. The new setup forced Austria to dedicate extra resources
to help make sure Napoleon stayed put, which left fewer men to deploy as a
check against Russia's westward maneuvering. Metternich claimed that if he'd
only reached Paris a few days earlier he would have stopped Alexander, "the
biggest baby on earth," from acting "like a schoolboy who has escaped from
his teacher." He predicted they would all be back on the battlefield before two
years were out, but he knew that the weakened empire he represented lacked
the ability to counter Russia.

Talleyrand, knowing Napoleon better than anyone, had the most reason to
feel unnerved by Alexander's decision. Privately, he feared putting Napoleon
so near to Napoleon's brother-in-law Joachim Murat, still the key force in
southern Italy as he clung to his rule in Naples. (After months of furtive negotiations Murat had signed an alliance with Austria that January, strengthening
his claim in Naples and making him an enemy of the French.) But Talleyrand
sensed that the time had come for impetuous warriors to give way to orderly
diplomats, of which he thought himself the shrewdest and most civilized of all,
and that the real currents of power would now flow not on the battlefield or

the grandstand but around tables and behind closed doors. He stood to gain a great deal by shuffling Napoleon offstage, and quickly. "I see Talleyrand has been naturally taking as much care as possible of himself," wrote one British official to Castlereagh during the negotiations.

However odd the idea sounded, there were some practical advantages to an Elban exile. The French held it as a subprefecture under the jurisdiction of the Département de la Méditerranée, meaning that it technically formed part of metropolitan France, as was the case with much of northwest Italy. Napoleon had sent detachments there in 1802 to make it a base from which to block British trade in the region. And while it had some value from a naval point of view, handing it to Napoleon hardly constituted a huge economic loss. Across the Atlantic, islands were so valuable that a half century earlier the French had thought themselves wise for retaining sugar-rich Guadeloupe instead of swapping it with the British for all of Canada, but Elba, by contrast, had little by the way of natural resources or industry. And any island, even one as close to the European continent as this one, could serve as a kind of blank slate, terra incognita, a place that very few people involved in the matter would have known intimately, if at all, and so an empty space onto which to project all sorts of best-case scenarios. Such mysteriousness was what made islands such ideal rewards for would-be adventurers. Elba could be transformed overnight into Napoleon's fiefdom without much fuss. There is no evidence of the allies' giving any thought as to how this recoloring of the map might affect the lives of the roughly twelve thousand islanders.

Representatives of the allied powers (save for the British) put their names to what became known as the Treaty of Fontainebleau, though it was signed at Talleyrand's town house in Paris. Napoleon would retain his title of Emperor and would possess Elba as a separate and sovereign principality for the rest of his life, without the right to pass it down to any heirs. The Russians had almost single-handedly shaped the treaty's terms, though the British had devoted more men, time, and money to fighting Napoleon than anyone else, while the Austrians had arguably suffered the most humiliation at his hands, and the French were expected to foot the bill of two million francs to be paid yearly to their former emperor in return for his surrender, another key term of the treaty. In the end, the signatories were united only in agreeing that they had crafted an imperfect solution. A British general who was following the peace negotiations closely wrote in his journal, "Napoleon in the Isle of Elba has in this case only to be patient. His enemies will be his best champions."

Why weren't Napoleon's enemies sufficiently terrified by the prospect of having the most fearsome general in recent history a day's sail from the Italian coast? The answer had much to do with water. For centuries, Europeans had thought of the sea as a boundary between order and chaos, and islands as places distinct from the realm of the everyday, worlds apart and unto themselves. Islands were for refuge and rites of passage, resting places for demigods, hermits, martyrs, knights-errant, pirates, and smugglers, and dream-spaces for seekers of sex, treasure, and utopia. For the same reasons, islands offered readymade holding pens to which to send anyone deemed dangerous to orderly society. Napoleon would be following in a long line of island exiles, real and imagined, from the Roman general Metellus Numidicus studying philosophy on Rhodes, to John wrestling with apocalypse on Patmos, to the mysterious masked convict on Île Sainte-Marguerite whose life Alexandre Dumas would turn into the stuff of fiction.

The ten-kilometer strip separating Elba from the Tuscan coast may as well have been an ocean by people's mental maps. The Elbans referred to the landmass across the water as the *continente*, the continent, rather than as *terraferma*, the mainland. The allied leaders, then, were following seemingly sound logic: that on this tiny island Napoleon would feel more distant from the centers of European power than if he were sent to the farthest tip of Siberia.

A Lodger in His Own Life

While arrangements were being made for Napoleon's travel south, Colonel Neil Campbell lay staring at the ceiling of a small and dingy room in Paris. He had a broken arm, a punctured lung, a bandaged eye, and a ringing in his ears. His face was a mess of purple and red framed in gauze.

The pain of his wounds was compounded by the embarrassment of how they had been acquired. A few weeks earlier he'd been in the fray at Fère-Champenoise near Vitry. Some Russian cavalrymen heard him calling out to their shared enemy to stop firing and surrender, shouting in French to be understood. Along with his blue surtout and red sash this made him look like a French officer giving orders, reason enough for a Russian hussar to ride up and pierce his lance through Campbell's back. Though as he fell Campbell opened his coat to show his Russian decorations, his comrades, those "wild sons of the desert," as he called them, missed seeing them. A second hussar slashed the prone Campbell across his head and went in for the kill, but Campbell saved his own life, thanks to the same facility with foreign talk that had been his undoing. "I cried out lustily, 'Anglisky Polkovnick' [sic] (English Colonel)," he recalled in his journal, and "a Russian officer succeeded by the use of better language in preventing the infliction of a third wound."

Tsar Alexander was stationed a quarter mile from the battle and sent his personal surgeons, who were Scotsmen like Campbell, to dress his wounds. Campbell had been serving as military attaché to the tsar's headquarters, fighting alongside a Russian corps through much of Europe, and his eastern allies had named him a Knight of the Imperial Order of Saint Anne for valorous duty the previous summer.

At the Vitry infirmary someone stole his luggage, which held all his clothes, decorations, and army records. The worse news, from Campbell's view, was that his doctors advised him to stay in bed for several weeks, which would have kept him from the final push on Paris. After a few days he ignored their counsel and headed for the French capital, determined to be close to the action even if he could not fight. One of the tsar's surgeons trailed after him so he could continue treatment. By the time they reached Paris the fighting was over.

Campbell's first days in the city were quiet and lonely, but things brightened with the delivery of an unexpected letter. "Being still unable to undertake any duty or to mix in society I had no knowledge of the important arrangements in progress regarding the future destiny of Napoleon, except through the channel of the daily newspapers," he wrote. "I was therefore quite unprepared for a message from Lord Castlereagh, which I received on the 14th." The foreign secretary invited him "to accompany, in a day or two, the *ci-devant* Emperor from Fontainebleau to the island of Elba" in the role of commissioner, representing the British contingent of the allied coalition.

The next morning Campbell met with Castlereagh, who presented him with a second letter, formally outlining his duties, and crafted with all the tact of a seasoned diplomat, looking as much to posterity as to the present situation and opting for the abstract rather than the specific. The letter directed Campbell "to attend the late Chief of the French government" (Castlereagh was still unsure of Napoleon's proper title) to Elba and to help secure his "asylum" there. He was to tell Napoleon that he'd been "directed to reside in the island till further orders, if he should consider that the presence of a British officer can be of use in protecting the island and his person against insult or attack."

The looseness of the language could help Castlereagh make the case that he had assigned someone to Elba only as an ad hoc response to Alexander's single-handed decision to determine the terms of the exile, rather than as part of some strategy meant to advance British interests in the Mediterranean. The letter's final instruction, that Campbell exercise "discretion as to the mode of communicating with His Majesty's Government," was a way of telling him to consider this a clandestine assignment. Campbell was never actually shown the Treaty of Fontainebleau and only learned of its terms much later through a newspaper item. He was to appear as no more than an impartial observer of Napoleon's banishment rather than as its chief enforcer, which was what he effectively was. All the better lest the exile go awry, as Castlereagh and many of his colleagues feared it would.

Campbell must have wondered why he specifically had gotten the call, though he had some obvious merits. He was a Highland gentleman of Duntroon in Argyll and a rising field officer. At thirty-seven he'd already traveled the far reaches of the empire, from the Caribbean to northern Africa, putting his dark good looks to work as attaché to several European courts, where he developed a feel for the pomp and protocol of royalty. He was an able commander and he spoke French, the international language of diplomacy, if too fluently for his own good. He was smart enough, well liked, and upright.

Castlereagh would have wanted someone clever enough to finesse this strange assignment, but not so devious as to hide anything important from the Home Office. A solitary type was needed for such a secretive solo mission, which had no real end date, an ambiguous set of duties, and little chance for public acclaim. With no sign of a fiancée and no deep ties to any place aside from the family plot in Scotland, Campbell would have presented an especially appealing candidate. And Castlereagh knew loneliness well enough to spot the affliction in others. Born just a few weeks before Napoleon, in Dublin, he was a former Irish volunteer who had gone on to oversee the dissolution of the Irish parliament, a Presbyterian who had remade himself an Anglican. He'd once cheered for the revolutionaries in France and even admired the American rebels for breaking away from their English rulers, but buried those youthful and romantic notions as he rose in the diplomatic corps. Such an enterprising outsider may have had a special affinity for an ambitious Scottish officer trying to make his way in a system ruled from London.

The following night, April 16, Campbell rode up to Fontainebleau's imposing iron gates of green and gold. A palace guard led him to Henri Gatien Bertrand, grand marshal of the palace. They chatted about the island they were both soon to call home. Campbell realized that Bertrand knew Elba no better than he did. He spoke about it "in most melancholy terms," saying only "that it was very small, very barren, part of it extremely unwholesome from the exhalation of the salt-ponds, and that there was very little wood or good water to be had."

Campbell had breakfast the next morning alongside some surprisingly friendly French generals and the three other allied commissioners who would escort Napoleon toward Elba: General Waldbourg-Truchsess of Prussia, Baron Koller of Austria, and Count Shuvalov of Russia. He struggled to focus on the meal as he waited to meet the man whose armies he and his countrymen had spent so long trying to destroy. If he thought then about his older brother James, killed while leading an attack on the French, and the son "on whom," as one Campbell relation wrote, "the hopes of the family had fondly rested," he didn't record it in his journal.

Campbell described the

> strange feeling that came over me when the aide-de-camp, after announcing my name, retired shutting the door, and I found myself suddenly closeted with that extraordinary man whose name had been for so many years the touchstone of my professional and national feelings and whose appearance had been presented to my imagination in every form that exaggeration and caricature could render impressive.

He had seen Napoleon once before. Surveying enemy lines at the battle of Bautzen the previous spring, he spied through his brass telescope a smallish man with a black two-pointed hat, hands clasped behind his back, striding back and forth, haranguing his troops. Now the emperor was close enough to smell. It turned out he smelled of heavy cologne and stale tobacco. "I saw before me a short active looking man, who was rapidly pacing the length of his apartment, like some wild animal in his cell," wrote Campbell. "He was dressed in an old green uniform with gold epaulets, blue pantaloons, and red topboots, unshaven, uncombed, with the fallen particles of snuff scattered profusely upon his upper lip and breast."

Long and lanky, Campbell towered over Napoleon. They spoke in French, with Napoleon rendering his name as "Combell." He wanted to know at which battles he'd fought and what honors he'd received. Commenting on Campbell's arm in a sling and the silk kerchief covering his scarred forehead and damaged eye, he asked how his wounds had been received. Campbell's journal makes no mention of how he answered. Learning that Campbell was a Scot, Napoleon waxed rhapsodic about the epic works of Ossian, his favorite poet, which he praised as "very warlike." He commended the military skills of the Duke of Wellington, under whose command Campbell had fought. Still holding on to the chance he might be sent to Britain, he likely hoped Campbell would report on his Anglophilia to Castlereagh, which Campbell did, quoting him verbatim. "Yours is the greatest of all nations," Napoleon told him. "I esteem it more than any other." Next he peppered him with questions about his specific orders concerning the exile and "expressed satisfaction at hearing that I was to accompany him to Elba, if he so desired, and to remain in the island so long as my services might be required."

To Campbell he seemed a broken man, resigned to his fate. He spoke of living out whatever years were left to him in quiet retirement, "studying the arts and sciences," surrounded by family. "I have been your greatest enemy— frankly such; but I am so no longer," he said. "I have wished likewise to raise the French nation but my plans have not succeeded. It is all destiny." By this point Napoleon had worked himself up to tears and closed their talk with a subservient bow, saying, "I am your subject. I depend entirely on you." Campbell noted in his journal that his fifteen-minute interview with Napoleon was the longest of any of the commissioners.

Napoleon would have seen much in Campbell to flatter his view of the new social world of which he saw himself chief architect, wherein reward was meant to be based on merit rather than birth and careers were opened to talent, "or at any rate to energy, shrewdness, hard work and greed," as one historian put it. Campbell's making colonel before forty was perhaps not as great a feat as becoming a general at twenty-four or an emperor ten years later, but impressive nonetheless.

IF, AS NAPOLEON CLAIMED, surviving his weakened dose of poison had renewed his resolve to live, many people still wanted him dead. Earlier in his life he must have felt invincible, as on Christmas Eve 1800, when he hailed a cheering audience at the Paris Opera just hours after a would-be assassin's bomb hidden in a cart missed him but killed eight bystanders. Now he spoke openly and often of his impending murder, predicting that it would take place on Elba or on the way there. He gave away cherished objects—swords, guns, coins, books, and decorations—to favorite officers. He fixated on the threat of Barbary corsairs, pirates who sailed out of ports along the north coast of Africa, whose crews seized trading ships at will, marauding points along the Italian coast and its islands. It was said that either slavery or a gruesome death awaited any sailor caught by these profiteers. Over dinner one night at Fontainebleau "the subject of punishment by impaling, as practiced in the East, was mentioned," recalled Campbell, which prompted a French officer to joke that those headed for Elba might soon get a chance to witness the practice firsthand.

The allies had granted Napoleon permission to establish a military presence sufficient to control his subjects and defend himself against attack. Four hundred veterans from his Old Guard were allowed to join him on Elba. The French also pledged to give him an "armed corvette," meaning a warship with a single tier of guns, which was to be the main asset of a small naval force. He would have to pay for these defenses out of his savings of three million francs, at least until he could collect the two-million-franc pension that the French Provisional Government had promised to pay him, according to the Treaty of Fontainebleau.

He tried delaying his departure by issuing formal written complaints to Campbell about various small matters pertaining to his transportation. In this time of limbo, Countess Marie Walewska, known as "the Polish mistress," his sometime lover, arrived at the castle. She never connected with Napoleon, either because word of her presence was kept from him or because he'd fallen too deeply into depression to bother. Later, he wrote to apologize for not having called for her, saying that if she found herself on the Tuscan coast he would greet the chance to see her, and telling her to think of him "with pleasure."

He wrote to Marie Louise to tell her how the terms of his surrender would affect her. While most of their property would revert to the French state, she would be granted three small territories south of Milan, the duchies of Parma, Piacenza, and Guastalla, which had once been Habsburg holdings before being occupied by the French. While his dominion over Elba would end with his life, she would be able to pass down her duchies to their son. "This means 400,000 souls and an income of 3 or 4 millions," he wrote. "You'll have at least one mansion and a beautiful country to live in when you tire of my island of Elba and I begin to bore you, as I can but do when I am older and you still young." He failed to mention that it had been Metternich, and not his own representative Caulaincourt, who had pushed for Marie Louise to have her own lands. He closed the letter with a promise to meet her in the town of Briare, about a hundred kilometers south of Fontainebleau, from where they could complete the trip to Elba as a family.

He sent a troop of cavalry to Orléans, where the most recent reports placed the empress, with orders to "liberate" her from the allies. But she was already on the move to Rambouillet, escorted by Austrian soldiers following Metternich's command to have her brought to Vienna as quickly as possible. She was feverish and coughing blood. Emperor Francis wrote his son-in-law a terse letter informing him that Marie Louise would be returning home to regain her health, safe from harm and surrounded by family and friends.

Napoleon wrote again to his wife, telling her that while Francis had treated them very badly, "he'll be a good, kind father to you and your son." He added that he'd sent a copy of a document signed by Caulaincourt, "for ensuring a safe future to your son." He closed by saying that "my misfortunes only affect me in so far as they grieve you. As long as you live you'll be lavishing your affection on the most devoted of husbands. Give my son a kiss. Goodbye, my Louise. All my love."

She never got the letter. Metternich's band of spies was well versed in unsealing, transcribing, and then resealing private messages; when it came to the archduchess, Metternich often had Napoleon's letters destroyed before she even learned of their existence.

CAMPBELL WANDERED the castle corridors alone. One night a palace concierge offered to serve as guide. He pointed out the room where ten years earlier the empress Joséphine had begged her husband to spare the life of the duc d'Enghien, a Bourbon prince charged with plotting with the British to overthrow Napoleon and whose ruthless killing sent shock waves across Europe. Next, he showed him some upper-story apartments from where Pope Pius VII had recently been released, after being prisoner there ever since France had occupied the Papal States five years earlier.

Indicating the hallway by the royal bedchamber, the concierge spun the tale of Roustam Raza, Napoleon's bodyguard, kidnapped as a young boy and sold into slavery in Cairo, where he was integrated into the martial caste of the Mamelukes after becoming the favorite boy of Sheikh El-Bekri, who presented him to Napoleon as a victory gift during the French invasion of Egypt. Roustam had guarded Napoleon ever since, sleeping on a mattress outside his bedroom wherever he traveled, a dagger at his side. He'd fled Fontainebleau a few nights before. The concierge told Roustam's story as one of abandonment rather than escape, saying that Napoleon had arranged for him to join the exile with a substantial wage and had given him leave to go to Paris so Roustam could have his wife and children accompany him, after which he disappeared. Roustam later claimed that he fled Fontainebleau because he thought Napoleon would try again to kill himself and that he would be framed as the murderer if he succeeded.

BY APRIL 20 the allied leaders had run out of patience and ordered Napoleon to quit Fontainebleau for good. At six in the morning, dressed in his worn royal uniform and two-pointed hat, he walked down the castle's main staircase and into the Cour du Cheval Blanc, where he addressed some of the veterans of his Guard, telling them, "Do not lament my fate; if I have decided to go on living, it is to serve your glory. I wish to write the history of the great things we have done together!"

He kissed the eagle standard carried by one of his favorite generals, mounted his carriage, and shut the door. His entourage followed suit. The horsemen had been told to set the beasts off at a gallop for a dramatic exit. Trumpeters and drummers played the party off with an imperial salute that mixed with the sounds of shouts, most of them genuine, of "Long Live the Emperor!" Napoleon later said that when he left Fontainebleau he didn't expect to ever return to France.

For the rest of his life, save for the brief interruption of the Hundred Days, other men would control where he went and when. Working together in an uneasy coalition, the allied sovereigns and their ministers forced Napoleon to feel something he'd avoided for half a lifetime: the sense of being someone to whom things happened.

NAPOLEON IN RAGS

A DOZEN CAVALRYMEN RODE out from the gates of Fontainebleau, followed by a few carriages, Napoleon's in no way decorated to distinguish it from the pack. Then came sixty cavalrymen and four more carriages, each hosting one of the allied commissioners. Eight berlins brought up the rear, carrying a physician, an apothecary, a secretary, a steward, two chief farriers, various valets, lackeys, and grooms, two assistant paymasters of the household, and the imperial paymaster Peyrusse, never out of sight of Napoleon's chest carrying just under three million francs in gold and silver plate, which he'd spirited out of Paris a few days earlier. The young paymaster later said that he hadn't followed the emperor into exile so much as his cashbox; yet it held only a fraction of Napoleon's reputed two-hundred-million-franc fortune, which had been seized by the French Provisional Government.

Napoleon had once employed a staff of three thousand. On Elba the number would be just under forty. Those joining the exile knew they would be marked for having declared themselves for the deposed emperor and they risked losing their standing as citizens if they stayed beyond French borders for more than three years, as stipulated by the Treaty of Fontainebleau. Most of these followers were young and unmarried, but others left families behind.

Whether or not they still felt loyalty to Napoleon, most of the highest-ranking officials under the empire had refused to join the exile. The devoted Caulaincourt, for instance, preferred retirement in the French countryside.

More than a few minor functionaries traveled to Elba thinking it could lead to unprecedented chances for advancement. If Napoleon remained there permanently, one could try to make oneself an indispensable part of his small staff, and if he somehow returned to power in France, those who had joined the exile would surely be rewarded for their loyalty. A twenty-four-year-old Corsican named Giovanni Natale Santini, who had been a courier at Fontainebleau at the time of the abdication, petitioned Grand Marshal Bertrand for a job on Elba but was told no room could be found for him in any of the carriages. He kept pestering until Bertrand told him he could sail with them so long as he made his own way down to the coast at his own expense and arrived in time to meet the ship that would carry them to Elba. He made no promise of a position. Santini scrounged up as much money as he could and headed south.

The two most senior French officials heading to Elba were men who had been relatively minor figures under the empire, General Antoine Drouot and Grand Marshal Henri Bertrand, both just into their forties. By giving up the comforts of home they progressed from being two more members of the imperial entourage to forming the whole of Napoleon's inner circle. Defeat had rooted out so many others who had once competed for the emperor's attentions.

Neither man was particularly distinguished or especially brilliant, but they were both loyal, in their own ways. The third of twelve children born to a relatively poor baker and his wife in the northeastern town of Nancy, Drouot had risen to become the "sage" of the French army. He was a stern man with a prominent forehead and thin silver hair, renowned for a boldness on the battlefield proportional to his shyness and sobriety away from it. His colleagues said that nothing made him happier than poring over verses in the small Bible he carried everywhere. He looked forward to the exile as a time for quiet contemplation. Napoleon had offered him a gift of two hundred thousand francs as a reward for joining him on Elba, but Drouot refused, saying he didn't want people to think he was following him for any other reason but love for his emperor.

Bertrand was the higher born and more handsome of the pair. Early in his career he'd been an engineer, and the pivoting bridges he designed for the famous battle of Wagram, which allowed troops and supplies to cross the Danube, were fêted as one of the era's most brilliant feats of ingenuity. Fussy, stubborn, and prone to depression, he'd put his love of detail and etiquette to use while overseeing the daily operations of the most opulent court of the age, at least by French opinion, which was the only one that mattered. As grand marshal of the palace he was also charged with the security of the Bonaparte family, making him something between a majordomo and the head of the secret service. (Drouot had thought that *he* would be the one to be named to that position after the previous grand marshal was killed at the battle of Bautzen a year earlier.)

Napoleon had requested that the allies allow him to make the bulk of the journey through the Italian peninsula so he could sail to Elba from the port of Piombino. He may have wanted to rally Italian support for his eventual return, or it may be that he figured the Italians were less likely than the French to try assassinating him. But the allies ordered him to sail from the French port of Fréjus. Campbell suspected that Napoleon had only wanted to avoid that point of departure because he expected the portmaster there to cause a scene by denying his request to embark. To be insulted by a portmaster would have embarrassed any sovereign, but for one from Corsica, a society built on the twin bedrocks of pride and shame, the sting would have been especially strong. So Napoleon would take the straighter shot down through Provence to the coast.

The deeper this retinue traveled into the countryside, the fouler the mood and more violent the reception. Royalist and Catholic currents flowed stronger in the south than elsewhere in France, and conscriptions and taxation had hit the region particularly hard, while trade at the ports suffered under Napoleon's embargoes. Southern royalists were also fired by the antirevolutionary rhetoric newly unleashed in pamphlets and papers. People with known republican sympathies were threatened with violent reprisal. "The countryside," wrote a prefect for the Loire valley, "is in full revolt. Against whom? They don't know, but to shoulder a gun is one way of expressing their thoughts."

When the carriages passed through the town of Orange at three in the morning of April 24, villagers climbed onto them until being fought off by allied soldiers. Napoleon, terrified, remained hidden. Approaching Avignon a few hours later, he heard cries of "Down with Nicolas!," a southern name for the devil, and his coachman was forced at saber-point to shout, "Long Live the King!" In the following town Napoleon saw himself swinging from a tree in effigy, smeared in butcher's blood, a noose around the neck, from which hung a placard reading "Here, then, is the hateful tyrant! Sooner or later crime is punished!"

Napoleon continued the journey in disguise, wearing a tattered blue great-coat and a simple round hat decorated with a Bourbon cockade. He borrowed a horse to ride ahead of the group posing as a courier, accompanied by another rider. When the rest of the procession caught up with him just south of Saint-Cannat, they found him in the back room of a run-down inn whose walls were draped in Bourbon white. The Prussian commissioner claimed the innkeeper, not recognizing the emperor, had asked Napoleon if he'd seen the "scoundrel Bonaparte" on the road and said she hoped he would be drowned on the way to his puny island. Napoleon begged off his food for fear of poison and drank only wine from his personal supply.

He changed costume again, leaving Saint-Cannat in international mufti. An Austrian officer had given him his jacket while the Russian commissioner wrapped him in his cloak. Only at Aix-en-Provence did the procession pass in relative peace, as cautious officials shut the town gates while Napoleon wheeled by, keeping the ferocious crowds at bay.

Momentary relief came at the medieval Château de Bouillidou just west of Fréjus, where Napoleon reunited with his favorite sister, Pauline, the Bor-ghese princess. They hadn't seen each other in two years. "Paulette," as he preferred to call her, teased him by saying she couldn't embrace him until he removed his ridiculous coat, that "enemy uniform," and then she kissed his hands and cried, all under the watch of allied officers. She promised to visit him on Elba, but compulsively seeking the cure to various mysterious ail-ments, said that she first had to take the waters on the island of Ischia. That night she gave her brother and the allied officers run of the chateau while she found quarters nearby.

· · ·

CAMPBELL HAD by then broken off from the group, riding alone to Marseille to arrange for an English frigate, *Undaunted*, to meet the party at Fréjus to serve as allied escort, protecting the French *Inconstant* from attack on the open sea. In Marseille he found Captain Thomas Ussher, a jocular Dubliner then acting as the town's civil authority until the French Provisional Government established its control. Despite only recently being promoted to the command of the *Undaunted*, after having worked his way up the ranks of the Royal Navy that he'd served since age twelve, Ussher carried himself as a born gentleman and took pride in his gallantry. With the close of the war he was looking forward to retiring from military life.

Campbell presented him with a mission that sounded so bizarre he could hardly believe it. "It has fallen to my extraordinary lot to be the gaoler of the instrument of the misery that Europe has so long endured," Ussher wrote to a friend in London. "It appears to me like a dream when I look back eighteen months and see all Europe prostrate at his feet—and he now absolutely my prisoner. It is a glorious finish to my services and leaves me nothing more to wish for."

WHEN NAPOLEON ARRIVED at Fréjus on the morning of April 27, Campbell, Ussher, and the crew of the *Undaunted* were already waiting. At the harbor Napoleon saw the rickety and humble French corvette *Inconstant*, which had already been stationed there, and which the allies had hoped would fulfill the terms of the treaty that promised him control of a ship for his protection on Elba. Napoleon told *Inconstant*'s captain, Montcabrié, that it was beneath his dignity to board a vessel of such poor quality, and the humiliated captain mounted his horse and rode off for Toulon. Campbell suggested that Napoleon and his staff should sail aboard the better-armed *Undaunted*, and the *Inconstant* could be sent to Elba a little later and would then be left there for his use. The arrangement satisfied Napoleon, and that night at dinner he was all charm.

The *Undaunted* was loaded to sail that evening, but Napoleon tried again to delay, holding out for some miraculous change of events that could keep him on the continent. He presented Campbell with a formal letter declaring that he now refused to board the British ship unless its crew hailed him with a twenty-one-gun salute. Though it wasn't customary to give such a greeting when boarding a vessel in the evening, Campbell yielded to Napoleon's request, seeing it for the silly gambit it was. While no last-minute change of fortune arrived to keep him from sailing, Napoleon had at least scored a symbolic victory against the allies, a small victory, but not one to be dismissed in an era when political power and the minute details of etiquette and display were so closely tied.

Lack of wind still kept the ship in port for a few more hours. This was a lucky chance for the eager courier Santini, who reached Fréjus just in time to find Bertrand and secure a place on board. The delay also allowed Captain Ussher some time up close with Napoleon. They dined together at an inn near the docks. Napoleon had by then dashed off another letter to Marie Louise. "My health is good, the weather is fine and I shall have a smooth passage," he wrote. Bertrand meanwhile wrote to his own wife, Fanny, telling her that they had had "happy travels" down from Fontainebleau, aside from a few minor "insults" at some villages they had passed.

The last time Napoleon had sailed the Mediterranean from the south of France was as the ascendant commander in chief of the French Army of the Orient, sixteen years earlier, nearly to the day. An armada of fifty-five warships and more than a hundred transport vessels had left for Egypt and the promise of glory, with General Bonaparte aboard the flagship, the three-decked, 118-gun *Orient*, at the time the largest vessel of any navy in the world. Under his command were more than fifty thousand men, including leading "savants" of France—engineers, naturalists, artists, astronomers, and other scholars charged with studying (and looting) the wonders of Egypt, many of which were eventually housed alongside his other pillaged war trophies at the Musée Napoléon in the Louvre.

He would now be sailing from the same jetty where he'd docked on returning from that grand, failed campaign. The small inn near the docks where he enjoyed his first meal on French soil after the time abroad was the same inn where he dined with Captain Ussher. Absence had been his ally then, as talk of his Oriental adventure spread across Europe, helped largely by Napoleon's own growing propaganda machine.

As he ate with Ussher, a crowd gathered outside. "His sword was on the table and he appeared very thoughtful," wrote Ussher. "There was a very great noise in the street and I said to him, 'The French mob are the worst I have seen.' He answered, 'They are a fickle people.' He appeared in deep thought, but, recovering himself, rang the bell and, ordering the Grand Marshal to be sent for, asked if all was ready. Being answered in the affirmative he turned to me and said in his usual quick way, 'Allons.'"

They boarded the *Undaunted* at eight to wait for favorable winds. It so happened that a fourth lieutenant Smith, nephew of the British admiral Sir Sidney Smith, one of Napoleon's chief naval foes during the Egyptian campaign and beyond, was the man to take him out to the *Undaunted* in a shore boat. The young Smith had just been freed from seven years as a French prisoner. Ussher introduced him to Napoleon, mentioning his lineage and the details of his captivity, and thought for a moment that Napoleon felt "his conscience prick him." But Napoleon only muttered, "Nephew to Sir Sidney Smith. I met him in Egypt."

Twenty-one guns saluted Napoleon as he boarded. Ussher described "bugles sounding, drums beating, horses neighing, and people of every nation in Europe witnessing the embarkation of this man who had caused so much misery to them all." The *Undaunted* left the harbor at midnight, brightened by a large moon.

4

THIS NEW COUNTRY

FROM HIS LEAKING CABIN, Paymaster Peyrusse wrote to his father about being rocked so violently by the waves that he fell out of bed and smacked his head on the wet floor. The sounds of overnight hammering had him convinced the ship wouldn't survive the crossing. When he voiced his concerns about the rough weather to some midshipmen on watch, they laughed and told him winds ten times stronger could hardly be called a storm by their reckoning. He spent the rest of the trip sulking in his cabin, trying to soothe his seasickness with ham, tea, and sweet Málaga wine.

Napoleon enjoyed a more comfortable night than did his paymaster. Ussher had given him the run of the captain's quarters, which spanned the *Undaunted*'s stern, while he shared a smaller night cabin with Bertrand and Drouot, the Frenchmen's beds separated from his own by a flimsy screen.

Out on the bridge the next morning with a cup of black coffee in hand, Napoleon said that he'd never slept so soundly and that he felt in excellent health. The ailments from which he was silently suffering (gallstones, hemorrhoids, urinary infections, stomach cramps, and swollen legs—not an unusual list for that era) would have been exacerbated by the sea journey, and Napoleon wasn't a great sailor, yet the farther south he traveled, the happier he seemed to be. Campbell overheard some French officers saying they had never seen the emperor looking so relaxed.

Away from France on a thirty-eight-gun ship he no doubt felt safer than he had in months, even if his current protectors had until very recently been among his fiercest enemies. And so long as the *Undaunted* sailed, he still occupied the unsteady space between departure and arrival, where the past felt not quite real and somehow reversible and the future could still be shaped to suit his needs.

The *Undaunted* passed within "a cannon's shot" (Peyrusse's words) of the northern tip of Corsica on May 1. Peaceful salutes were exchanged with a squadron patrolling the coast, which cheered the passengers, still unsure if anyone in the region knew whom their ship carried or how they might react to that information. Perhaps prompted by seeing the island, Napoleon sought out the young Corsican messenger, Santini, and asked about his family history and career ambitions. He assured him that Bertrand would find a place for him on his staff once they were all settled. When Santini started to cry, Napoleon wandered off to some other part of the ship.

Accustomed to commandeering any ship in his sight, Napoleon demanded that the captain of a passing brig be brought aboard to give news from Corsica, but Ussher, laughing, denied the request. In his letter to London, Ussher gloated about these kinds of intimacies with the emperor. As they had sighted the Alps from the bridge, he wrote, Napoleon "leaned on my arm for half an hour, looking earnestly at them" and then smiled at Ussher's remark that he'd "once passed them with better fortune."

A few months earlier the captain had cut out a newspaper rendering of Napoleon and pinned it to a wall above his table so he could advise guests aboard the *Undaunted* to study the image and commit it to memory. The word back then had been that Napoleon would try to escape across the Atlantic rather than surrender. The Royal Navy might require their help to spot this enemy in disguise, Ussher would tell his dining companions.

Now he shared the same table with the man from the picture, whose likeness he would have seen in so many different forms: in pen, oil, clay, silver, stone, wax. With the relative freedom of the British press, he might have seen

Napoleon as the snub-nosed imp who pestered John Bull in inky caricatures, or as Gulliver, helpless in the palm of a Brobdingnagian King George III. Perhaps he'd seen some version of Jacques-Louis David's famed painting of the general as a modern Hannibal astride an enormous charger subduing the windswept Alps, or of Ingres's severe, laurel-wreathed emperor, all ermine and purple velvet. His face would have come to Ussher head-on, at three-quarters, and in profile (the subject increasingly preferring this last angle as his features softened with the years), with the penetrating blue-gray eyes never meeting the viewer as an equal but always looking off to some luminous future he alone could see. "He laughed at the idea of our being caricatured, and said 'the English had a great passion for caricaturing,'" wrote Ussher, who answered that "John Bull caricatured and abused people when they deserved it" and joked that he himself would likely be victim to this same treatment and that someone would probably draw him nursing Napoleon's son.

Only natural, then, that when describing the real man, the best Ussher could do was compare him to a representation. "The portrait of him with the cockaded hat and folded arms is the strongest likeness I have seen," he wrote to his friend, adding that Napoleon's pudginess suited him finely, saying that "he looks uncommonly well and young and is much changed for the better, being now very stout." In the letter's postscript Ussher wrote that "someone said I was like Bonaparte, but not so well looking. It was a Frenchman and he thought even with that amendment that he paid me a great compliment."

As they sailed near the west coast of Corsica a storm front moved in and it looked as though they would be waylaid overnight. Napoleon asked if they could be anchored at the harbor town of Ajaccio, his birthplace. He and the rest of clan Bonaparte had been expelled from the island in 1793, branded as traitors for sympathizing with the nascent French Republic above championing Corsican independence, though Napoleon had initially hoped the two causes could be compatible. He hadn't visited his birthplace since an unpleasant five-day layover during the journey back from Egypt, waiting for winds to carry his ship home to France, and to the end of his life no epithet apparently riled him so much as being called "the Corsican." Ussher felt that the poor weather made an anchorage too dangerous, but as a sop Campbell told

Napoleon he could write letters to friends on the island and he would make sure they were delivered. Instead, Campbell had the letters sent to Corsica's commanding officer with orders they be opened and destroyed.

Before sunset, a passing tartane instigated contact with the *Undaunted* and Campbell and Ussher allowed its Corsican shipmaster to come on deck, seeing it as a way to pass the time. The sailor spoke of how eagerly his fellow islanders had declared themselves for the restored Bourbons and, unaware that Napoleon numbered among his listeners, praised the new state of affairs somewhat too enthusiastically for the emperor, whose loud sigh caused the shipmaster to observe him more carefully. He continued his report, now even more bold in his support for the Bourbons and throwing in a few choice oaths for emphasis. Napoleon walked away while he was midsentence and asked Ussher to tell the man to return to his ship.

The skies cleared the next morning and the *Undaunted* sailed on, eastbound. Campbell passed his thirty-eighth birthday. His diary makes no mention as to whether the anniversary was celebrated. Napoleon spent much of the day reading. He'd taken nearly two hundred works from among the thousands of books at the Fontainebleau libraries. Among them was a travelogue he'd spotted just before leaving, Thiébaut de Berneaud's *Voyage to the Isle of Elba*. Berneaud advised that on approaching Elba one should expect to see nothing more than a few "roads rugged and uneven, cottages deserted. Ruins scattered over the face of the country, wretched hamlets, two mean villages, and one fortress." Napoleon would have read that "the mountains of the Isle of Elba . . . together present only a mass of arid hills which fatigue the sense, and impart to the soul sensations of sorrow."

Despite the descriptions of supposedly barren landscapes, Berneaud's book was an odd sort of love letter to Elba. He was one in a long line of writers who believed they had discovered something enviable in an island people somehow spared from the miasma of civilization. The Elbans, he wrote, were "endowed with a certain sprightliness of imagination that renders them capable of receiving the strongest impressions; thence proceeds their excessive predilection for extravagant and romantic tales. . . . They are unacquainted with the monstrous luxury of cities." Berneaud claimed that these islanders possessed a "vital current . . . of pure quality. The old men are not decrepit. I have known many of them who had reached their ninety-fifth year without experiencing the slightest ailment." They had none of "the cunning, the laziness, or the listlessness so natural to a southern people," and though Elban women were "not in general beautiful," there were "pretty girls in the western mountains and at Rio [a mining town on the east coast]. They press their swelling bosoms under enormous busks laced tight with ribbons."

Though the Elbans seemed insular and primitive to outsiders, they looked out on the world with a broader perspective than that of most mainlanders. Seafaring people had their minds opened by always being on the move, fishing, sailing, and trading. They were among the globe's most cosmopolitan souls, forced by geography and economic necessity to regularly do business with strangers. Being such rich economic prizes, capable of sparking wars among powers thousands of miles away, islands were forever being conquered, colonized, and traded, leading to polyglot populations. Elba had its share of outdated customs, parochial thinking, and isolated villages, but many of its men and women, especially in its capital, Portoferraio (the "Port of Iron"), on the island's northern end, would have met daily with travelers from afar.

UNKNOWN TO ANYONE on the *Undaunted* was that reports of the allied victory had thrown Elba into open revolt. A British naval blockade had kept the island cut off from the continent since December and starvation loomed. Troops remained under the nominal charge of the French governor, Dalesme, but just barely. He'd once controlled a force of five thousand men drawn from France, Corsica, and the Italian peninsula, but by early 1814 so many soldiers had deserted that Dalesme was left with only five hundred Frenchmen garrisoned at Portoferraio.

West of Portoferraio, in Marciana, the townsfolk flew crude versions of the Union Jack and had tried unsuccessfully to get the captain of a passing British ship to land and take control. They burned Napoleon in effigy, singing and dancing around the flames. To the south in Porto Longone (present-day Porto Azzurro), a mutiny that started with villagers tearing tricolor flags had escalated to their shooting the French commanding officer and hacking his body to pieces. Porto Longone had been Dalesme's key southern stronghold, with its imposing hillside citadel, a remnant of Spanish occupation centuries earlier. Farther along the coast some villagers openly declared allegiance to Napoleon's brother-in-law Joachim Murat, while a few hard-liners around the island saw this as the time to throw off the rule of all masters forever and urged a total revolution. The French commander in the rural northern and eastern regions beyond Portoferraio managed to quell some of the uprisings but only through the most brutal means.

Still, it was a celebratory time on the island. On the first day of May, following a centuries-old tradition, unmarried men wandered the villages to sing *serenatas* in praise of springtime love and the charms of the local maidens, who rewarded them with little *corollo* cakes as syrupy as the lyrics being sung. No one wanted to abandon a tradition that had led to so many marriages, and so the sounds of protests and politics were made to compete with poetry and guitars.

Adding to the confusion, Dalesme had no idea whether or not Elba was still a French possession. A British ship had landed under the flag of truce late in April and its messenger presented Dalesme with an order to relinquish control to the British, and had shown him French newspapers detailing Napoleon's abdication. But Dalesme dismissed this as a ploy to lure him into surrendering and the ship sailed back to the mainland. It was replaced the following day by another British vessel, this one carrying a representative from the French Provisional Government who finally convinced Dalesme that Napoleon was in fact en route to Elba.

Armed with this latest intelligence, Dalesme told his men to be on the lookout for the French corvette *Inconstant*, which, as the French official had told him, would be carrying Napoleon and flying Bourbon white. Any ship not fitting this description was to be treated as an enemy.

THE *UNDAUNTED* WAS BECALMED near the island of Capraia on the night of May 2. The ship gave a salute, answered by the island's battery, after which some officials were invited on board. They told the crew about how things stood on Elba. The *Undaunted*'s passengers could just make out the fortifications topping the rocky ridge of Portoferraio, a shadow against the bloodshot sky. They took turns on the telescope. "Each of us," recalled Peyrusse, "looked eagerly at this new country."

They reached Elba the following afternoon. A crossing that in fine weather could be done in two days had taken them nearly a week. As rowers pulled the tall ship toward the small horseshoe-shaped harbor tucked south behind Portoferraio's main town, away from the open sea, watchmen at the edge of the quay sighted the well-armed ship flying the Royal Standard. Dalesme ordered them to aim their heavy cannons at the *Undaunted*, but after some minutes of standoff Ussher gave the signal for parley and the case of mistaken identity was solved.

Campbell, Drouot, and a few other officers were brought to the quay. "The inhabitants," wrote Campbell with his typical understatement, "appeared to view us with great curiosity." Santini also disembarked, with a private mission to sound out the mood among the Elbans, who might more easily let their guard down around a fellow islander. He returned with a positive report, telling Napoleon that the people were overjoyed that such a great man was to be their sovereign. Bertrand stayed behind, so weakened by the sailing that he could hardly get out of his chair.

On a bluff overlooking the harbor, Campbell and Drouot entered Fort Stella, named for its star-shaped footprint, where they met with Governor Dalesme. He was still struggling to make sense of this surreal change of events and later said he was only convinced that the handover wasn't a ploy when he saw General Drouot, "whose integrity was a byword in the French army." Drouot signed some documents to officially take possession of Elba in the name of the emperor Napoleon, who remained out of sight on the *Undaunted*.

Also present at the fort was André Pons de l'Hérault, who as administrator of Elba's mines oversaw the bulk of the island's economy. While obscure by the standards of the French Empire he was the nearest thing Elba had to a Napoleonic figure. He went by Pons, though to the thousands of islanders depending on him for their livelihoods he was simply *Babbo* (Father). Born in the Occitan village of Sète to innkeepers of Spanish ancestry who had wanted him to go into the priesthood, he'd escaped that fate by going out to sea at the age of ten, becoming the master of a merchant ship while still a teenager, and later rising in the French military. Pons strategized with Campbell, Dalesme, and Drouot about how to smoothly transfer control of the island. He fought the urge to ask for a document confirming the unseen Napoleon's claim, since, as he later recalled, "It would have been too insulting to make any demand that might show that we doubted anything said by the Emperor."

The landing party sailed back to the *Undaunted*, with Pons in tow for a reunion of sorts, as he and Napoleon had crossed paths in different military and political settings over the years. When they first met, in Toulon in the fall of 1793, both were ambitious artillery commanders of the Revolutionary Army engaged in taking back the harbors of that port town from the British. Napoleon and his family had recently landed at the small beach of Golfe-Juan as political refugees from Corsica. It was in Toulon that the twenty-four-year-old Bonaparte received his first significant public notice for orchestrating a clever barrage that broke the British siege and resulted in his promotion to brigadier general. In the battle he received a wound from a bayonet to the thigh that nagged him for life, and he suffered chest injuries after his horse was shot out from under him. It was also in Toulon that he tried, on Pons's urging, his first taste of bouillabaisse, the traditional Provençal fish stew.

Pons described himself in his memoirs as "republican before there was a Republic" and had remained faithful to France over the years, pleased to serve its government in whatever form it took. But by 1814 he was disillusioned by what he saw as Napoleon's corruption of republican values in his search for personal glory. As with many sons and daughters of the Revolution, he couldn't forgive the former General Bonaparte for crowning himself Napoleon I. The opulent coronation at Notre-Dame, where Napoléon had snatched the crown from the pope to place it on his own head; his marriage to an Austrian archduchess; his placing three brothers and one brother-in-law on foreign thrones; his reinstating slavery in the Caribbean colonies: all were abhorrent to Pons.

"Now I was to appear before the great hero who had voluntarily thrown away his glorious halo!" he wrote. "I was to appear before the extraordinary man I had so often found blame with, even while admiring him, and on whose behalf I had so often prayed that he might win his holy struggle on our sacred soil! I was to present myself to the emperor Napoleon, but aboard a British frigate! It all seemed like a dream, a painful dream, a frightful dream."

On greeting Pons, Napoleon would have seen his own aging process reflected back to him. The mining administrator had grown plump and wore thin wire spectacles, which he attributed to too many nights poring over ledgers by lamplight. He practiced the bald man's trick of growing out his meager tonsure of hair into long strands to be deployed at various angles. Though Napoleon's junior by three years, he carried himself like someone who had already seen six or seven decades, if restful ones.

To Pons, Napoleon no longer even closely resembled the long-haired, rake-thin officer he'd known in early adulthood. His face had gone puffy and pasty. And yet aboard the *Undaunted,* "carefully dressed" in his pristine green coat, white breeches, and red boots, he looked to Pons like "a soldier ready for an official reception." His bright eyes offered little sign of shame and retained a trace of the ineffable glimmer that for the past two decades had helped to make him the focus of any room he entered.

Campbell, in the background, tall and silent, put Pons on edge with his "artfully bandaged" head, his forced smile, and his searching gaze, "the perfection of the British type." Their instant dislike was mutual; in his own journal, Campbell later referred to the unassuming Pons as "a violent intriguing fellow."

Napoleon said little that night. Pons recalled that when he spoke of the events that had brought him there he talked as if he were detached from the action and had only read about it in the papers, and that he managed with a few fatherly nods and grave looks to convey that he understood everything these excited children wanted to tell him, even as they tripped over their words. He pledged to do right by the people of Elba who were now his only concern. It was agreed that he should debark the next morning so that a suitable reception could be arranged overnight.

Dalesme and Pons rowed back to the quay, where all sorts of rumors spread among the gathered crowd. Children stayed up late, trying to make sense of the story of the Corsican brought from France on a British ship to become Emperor of Elba.

Across the water Napoleon paced the bridge of the *Undaunted*. He would have seen a constellation of flickering lights. Most, though not all, of the three thousand inhabitants of Portoferraio had placed candles in their windows as a sign of welcome.

{ 5 }

GILDED KEYS

THE WALLS OF PORTOFERRAIO had been littered for weeks with proclamations promising penalties for any rebel Elbans. On the night before Napoleon's landing these were pasted over and replaced by copies of his official message of greeting. Napoleon had "chosen" their island for "his sojourn," it said, because of the kindness of its people and the mildness of its climate.

Men and women worked into morning to build a stage of painted plaster that would host a sofa-chair-throne decorated with gold paper and scarlet rags. As the sun rose they were still busy lining the streets with ribbons and myrtle garlands. Portoferraio's mayor, Traditi, had the keys to his cellar gilded overnight so they could be given to Napoleon as ceremonial keys to the city. Following Bertrand's request that a large crowd be on hand at the quay, he called for representatives of all notable island families to come to Portoferraio for the landing, as though anyone needed encouragement to witness the arrival of the most famous man in the world. Some of the more prosperous Elbans sent along a few sticks of furniture for the unoccupied top floor of the town hall, formerly a bakery and still dubbed the Biscotteria, which was being cleared of cobwebs to house the emperor.

On the *Undaunted*, Napoleon put the finishing touches on the flag he'd designed for Elba, which would be solid white, cut by a diagonal red stripe emblazoned with three golden bees. When proclaiming himself Emperor of the French a decade earlier he'd chosen this industrious insect as part of his imperial symbology, an antique motif connecting him to the past while signifying the immortality of his line. The white with red diagonal theme he borrowed from the standard of Cosimo de' Medici, who had served as Elba's protector from his base in sixteenth-century Florence, during which time Portoferraio had been known as Cosmopoli. The ship's tailor crafted two flags from some extra canvas, to be hoisted when Napoleon reached the shore. "What a childish vanity!" wrote Ussher of seeing good sailcloth put to such use.

Before breakfast Napoleon asked Ussher for the use of a rowboat to surreptitiously slip across the harbor so they could take a closer look at a farmhouse he'd seen at the edge of a small beach there when they sailed in. Crossing on the rowboat, beyond the protection of the *Undaunted*'s guns, Napoleon joked about being without his sword and wondered aloud if the Elbans were known to have any special taste for assassinations. "Evidently he is greatly afraid of falling in this way," wrote Campbell in the day's journal entry.

After waiting two hours for someone to find keys to the farmhouse, Napoleon inspected the property, which left him unimpressed. None of the locals realized that the small man in the greatcoat and round hat was their emperor. "The peasants, considering us all as Englishmen, cried 'Long Live the English!'" wrote Ussher.

Back on the *Undaunted* for a light meal, Campbell said that Elba reminded him of the colonies. Several small craft were by then circling the ship, some near to sinking under the weight of curious bodies. Bright bouquets littered the bay. Napoleon heard people in the boats singing serenades and shouting vivas. After breakfast he presented each member of the *Undaunted*'s British crew with a bottle of wine and a gold coin. He'd always been good at keeping his troops well stocked with food and alcohol, and these Jack Tars were to be no exception. They in turn sent "Boney" off with a raucous toast to "good health and better luck next time!"

The yards were manned and royal salutes fired from the *Undaunted*'s guns. Napoleon crossed to shore standing at the bow of a rowboat, while others carried officers, fifers, and drummers. The harbor was so clogged with rowboats and debris that this last leg of the trip took a full half hour.

Shots from the battery and clanging bells greeted the landing. On Napoleon's request, Campbell had arranged for some of the British marines to surround him as he stepped onto the quay. He took the keys from the pewter plate held by the mayor, who bumbled through a speech until Napoleon cut him off to make a brief impromptu address, which he capped by kissing a cross held by the local vicar. Out of the mass of people Napoleon spotted and called out the name of a sergeant he'd decorated years earlier; the man wept at being recognized. This was an old trick of Napoleon's, whose skills of memory were legendary, though often aided by preparation and whispered help from his aides. After the speech, bread was distributed to the poor. The quay was full of "pretty little faces," as Peyrusse described in a letter home, all wide-eyed and smiling. Napoleon had a crowd; he seduced it.

Pushing against the multitude, Napoleon and his retinue passed through the Water Gate dividing Elba's port from the main town square and on to the parish church. There they heard a Te Deum, the traditional ceremony combining thanks to God with prayers for a monarch, typically chanted at coronations and royal births, or to mark a military victory. French kings had used the Te Deum as a way to make their royal presence felt intimately though they were physically distant from their subjects. In Napoleon's case the ruler being celebrated as though he were divine sat in the same small room where the hymns were being sung. He kept his head down, moving his lips in prayer, paying no attention to the other congregants. A wheezing beadle, short and round, presided. There were N's of silvery paper on the whitewashed chapel walls.

After the service they returned to the town hall, slowed by the pressing throng, everyone illuminated by the heavy glare of the high sun. In the ersatz throne room on the top floor Napoleon met with subprefects and magistrates and landowners, who heard his conversational voice for the first time. They could have reached out and touched him. A string quintet played in the corner. Vantini and Balbiani and Talavo and Traditi of Elba could now say they had shared something intimate with the man who until a month ago had been master of the world.

Pons noticed that Napoleon spoke about places on the island with the familiarity of someone who had seen them all firsthand. He remained standing throughout, perhaps unwilling to dignify the sofa-cum-throne by actually sitting on it. "What is a throne?" he'd said a few months earlier in Paris. "A piece of lumber covered with a velvet rug. But in the language of monarchy, *I* am the throne!"

Following the luncheon he was given a tour of Portoferraio. There wasn't much to see. The fortifications, the church, the ramparts, the bay, the rectangular tree-lined Piazza d'Armi with its inn and a smoky café called the Buon Gusto where they specialized in *aleatico*, the local red wine, sweet and fruity and sometimes cut with fresh ginger to mask a poor-quality vintage: all lay within a few minutes' walk of the town hall.

"Anyone who thought Napoleon's day was finished by this point didn't know the man," wrote Pons. "His day was only starting." Next he went out riding to survey some of the surrounding territory, accompanied by Campbell, Ussher, and a few other officers. They went out through the Land Gate, Portoferraio's main entrance, built into a tunnel and protected by a drawbridge spanning a narrow canal. It gave onto the Via della Porta a Terra, the lone road out of town.

At sunset the riding party returned for a celebratory dinner capped by illuminations and fireworks, after which Napoleon went up to his slapdash bedroom on the top floor of the Biscotteria. It was musty and reeked of rotting fish. On a thin mattress splayed out on the hallway floor lay a British sergeant selected for the task, fully clothed, sword at his side, just as the long-gone bodyguard Roustam had done so many times before.

Napoleon was more than six hundred miles from Paris. He had the night to make sense of his new surroundings since the townspeople kept him up with their singing and chattering below his window. He wrote to his wife, telling her his crossing had been smooth and the weather calm:

> I've arrived in the isle of Elba, which is very pretty. The accommodation is middling but I'll have a home fitted up in a very few weeks. I've had no letter from you. It is my daily sorrow.

6

ROUGH MUSIC

BEFORE MARRYING HIM, the archduchess Maria Luisa had only ever known Napoleon as the enemy. She was four months old when France declared war against her father, and just short of two years when revolutionaries beheaded her great-aunt, Marie Antoinette. As a teenager she'd congratulated her father on his supposed victory at the battle of Eckmühl, writing that it "was with much joy that we heard Emperor Napoleon was there in person, for as he has lost such a battle he can lose his head as well." After the victory report turned out to be false and the French occupied Vienna, she'd fled the city along with her stepmother and siblings. The Habsburg empire lost more than forty thousand square miles of territory and was made to pay an indemnity so heavy that the palace plate and silverware had to be melted down to help cover the immediate costs. Napoleon had presided over her family's summer palace at Schönbrunn, enjoying operas and ballets from the comfort of the imperial box.

On the heels of his Austrian triumph, late in 1809, Napoleon had sought a younger replacement for Joséphine, who was six years his senior. Though he claimed to still be very much in love with her, the divorce was necessary "for the welfare of the nation." Or at least this was how he explained it to Joséphine, and only after having dodged being the first one to inform her of the break, leaving the task to his minister of police, who had told her the emperor needed to produce an heir for "the cohesion of the dynasty." Napoleon had already conducted a successful experiment with his mistress Marie Walewska, who was by then pregnant with his child. The split with Joséphine had been finalized in a candlelit ceremony in Fontainebleau's throne room, after which she took up residence at Château de Malmaison, their estate west of Paris (each had contributed half of the purchase price), which would be hers from then on. Napoleon sent her a new Sèvres dinner service and money to upgrade the gardens.

Napoleon wanted to combine finding a new mate with some alliance building and had calculated that more political value lay in marrying a Habsburg than a Romanov, though he briefly considered Tsar Alexander's fourteen-year-old sister, Annette. When the archduchess Maria Luisa learned that the newly divorced emperor wanted to meet her, she told a friend "that to see this creature would be for me a worse torture than all the martyrdoms." She read the papers, hoping to find news of his engagement to anyone but her. "I'm only sorry for the poor princess he will choose," she wrote to a friend, "for I'm sure I won't be the victim of politics. . . . Napoleon is too much afraid of a refusal and too bent upon doing us further harm to venture upon such a request. And Papa is too kind to coerce me in so important a matter."

She told her father that learning about Napoleon's search for a wife had compelled her to reveal a secret: she'd fallen in love with her cousin, Archduke Francis. "I'm certain he has all the qualities that would make me happy," she wrote. "I've confided in Mama and she shares my unbounded confidence and has had the kindness to suggest that I write to you about my sentiments." Though she pledged to respect his final decision on the matter as "a loving obedient daughter," she reminded her "dearest Papa" of his promise never to force his eldest and favorite daughter to marry against her will.

Francis was unmoved by his daughter's newfound interest in her cousin, which was likely an invention prompted by "Mama," her stepmother, Maria Ludovica, who was not much older than the archduchess, who had recently turned seventeen. He had Metternich advise Maria Luisa of the political advantages of a match that would simultaneously cement an alliance with France and stop Napoleon from marrying a Romanov to strengthen Russian ties that could threaten Austria. He told his daughter that she alone was in charge of deciding her fate. But given her time, place, and station, she would have known that any talk of freedom carried no weight. "I desire only what my duty commands me to desire," she told Metternich.

A few days later Napoleon sent Maria Luisa his first letter, which he'd handwritten (terribly, the letter is barely legible) rather than dictating, as was his usual practice. This was, after all, a marriage proposal. He said that her "brilliant qualities" had inspired him to approach her father with "the request that he shall entrust us to the happiness of your Imperial Highness. May we hope that the feelings which prompt us to take this step will be acceptable to you? May we flatter ourselves with the belief that you will not be guided solely by the duty of obeying your Parents?" He promised to care for her and please her in every way, "with the hope of succeeding some day in winning your regard."

He'd never met her, but an Austrian ambassador had told him that she was in good health, had a light complexion, and was pleasant to look at. She could play the piano and the harp and liked to paint. Her mother had given birth to thirteen children, her great-grandmother twice that number. "When I heard Louise was fair I was very glad," Napoleon later remembered.

Maria Luisa received a second letter two days after the first, this time dictated. In an elaborate ceremony at the Hofburg palace, the French chief of staff, Marshal Berthier, handed her the message along with a diamond-encrusted portrait of Napoleon:

> Madame my Sister, the successful issue of my request to His Majesty the Emperor, your Father, to be joined to you in marriage is a most precious token of the esteem and regard in which he holds me. I highly appreciate the consent you yourself bestow upon a union that fills me with the most heartfelt joy and which will embellish the whole of my life. I look forward with the greatest impatience to the moment when its conclusion will be in sight.

Maria Luisa asked Berthier if he thought she would be allowed to keep a garden in Paris, and also did Napoleon have any great love for music. A proxy wedding took place three days later, with a Habsburg uncle standing in for Napoleon and Berthier serving as witness, eating the post-wedding feast on the groom's behalf.

A few days later, Marie Louise (as she was known from then on, though Napoleon, who liked to alter the names of the women in his life, preferred to call her Louise) reached Compiègne in her golden berlin to meet her new husband, who'd been trying to master the waltz to surprise his Austrian bride but had abandoned the lessons given by his stepdaughter with Joséphine, Hortense, after two nights, saying that he wasn't "meant to excel as a dancer."

For many observers the union was a debacle, the kind of inappropriate match that in a more rural society might have been met by the clanging pots and disapproving horn blasts of *charivari,* rough music. At court in Vienna they were already saying that Austria had been humiliated by a foreign rival, just as the archduchess would be despoiled by the Corsican ogre in the marital bed.

Yet according to the later recollections of the bride and groom, it was a happy honeymoon. Marie Louise painted Napoleon's portrait in oil. He liked to pinch her cheeks and smack her backside in front of the staff. Marie Louise had grown up in a household where naked bodies had been cut out of her books and she had been given only female pets so that no one would have to explain to her the mechanics of sex. In his final exile, Napoleon boasted about their first night together, saying that "she liked it so much that she asked me to do it again."

A few months later the family physician, Corvisart, told the couple to expect a child sometime around the first day of spring. Another Napoleonic offspring had recently entered the world, as Marie Walewska had given birth to a son, Alexandre, on her ex-husband's estate outside Warsaw that May. Count Walewski, nearly eighty years old, had recognized the boy as his own. Napoleon sent some Brussels lace as a gift.

Marie Louise went into a difficult labor on the last day of winter. Though any birth at that time was dangerous, one "by irons," as forceps were known, was especially risky. Napoleon advised the doctor to "save the mother, it's her right. We can have another child." The baby that arrived showed no apparent signs of life, but then cried out seven minutes after delivery. The commandant of ceremonial artillery gave the sign for the 101-gun salute to celebrate the birth of Napoléon François Charles Joseph, the new King of Rome.

"Never would I believe I could be so happy," Marie Louise wrote to her father while recovering from the labor. "My love for my husband grows all the time and when I remember the tenderness I can scarcely prevent myself from crying. Even had I not loved him previously, nothing can stop me from loving him now."

THREE YEARS LATER, in the spring of 1814, Marie Louise was again following her father's orders concerning her husband, though now Francis wanted to break the union he'd helped to create, since it no longer served Austrian purposes. Citing her recent fevers, Francis told her that if she rushed off to join her husband in her condition it would only cause her and Napoleon more anxiety. He promised that after regaining her strength in Vienna she could travel to Parma to establish her rule there and then, if she wanted, could go on to Elba.

Just before Marie Louise left the chateau at Rambouillet for Vienna, Tsar Alexander visited her to pledge his friendship. "Would you ever have believed I should still have to face meeting the man chiefly responsible for all the ill that has befallen us?" she wrote to Napoleon just after their meeting. She wanted him to know that her "heart was dead" when she received the tsar.

In her letter she outlined her "plan of campaign," advising Napoleon not to mention any detail of it in his replies since his letters were no doubt being read by others before they reached her. She said she would stay in Vienna as briefly as possible and would then travel to the French resort of Aix-les-Bains, under the pretense of taking the waters there for her health. Once out of her father's reach she would go on to set up her rule in Parma and then, along with their son, would be reunited with him on Elba. "I'm hoping to be able to join you in July," she wrote. "I haven't mentioned such a thing to these gentleman [at

Rambouillet] but I've set my heart on it. My health is going from bad to worse. I'm so wretched that I just don't know what to say to you. I beg you again not to forget me and to believe that I'll always love you and that I'm deeply unhappy."

Her letters never revealed how badly she was treated after fleeing Paris. In notes omitted from his published memoir, Napoleon's aide-de-camp Caulaincourt alludes to Joseph Bonaparte's trying to force himself on Marie Louise once or more during this time. Though she'd earlier sworn to Caulaincourt that she would join the exile, she told him "that she was willing to die with him, but not to go to Elba with him because of his family."

7

THE ROBINSON CRUSOE OF ELBA

CAPTAIN USSHER WOKE TO drum rolls and shouts of "Long Live the Emperor!" The sun had yet to rise on what would be his first full day on Elba. Napoleon was already up and eager to inspect some of Portoferraio's fortifications and storehouses. The two men toured the town on foot, escorted by a dozen soldiers. They visited with some veterans of Napoleon's campaigns at the barracks, who traded battle stories for his benefit: Cairo, Jaffa, Marengo, Austerlitz, Moscow, Leipzig. "He liked every bit of vulgar chit-chat," wrote Pons of Napoleon's fondness for soldierly scuttlebutt. "All kinds of foolishness."

Hoping to spot a building worthy of an imperial residence—the existing governor's house was deemed too small—Napoleon rode out with Ussher to survey some of the island. They returned to Portoferraio that afternoon having seen no more worthy candidate than a run-down structure just a few hundred feet from the town hall from where they'd started. The structure was actually two squat buildings that were being used in tandem as a mess hall. They sat on the ridge above Portoferraio's main settlement. The locals called the site I Mulini, for the two windmills that had once stood there. Decades earlier, the governor's gardener had made the place his cottage; now grain was being stored in what had been his outhouse.

It was a modest property, better suited to a provincial lord than to an emperor, and it would put Napoleon near enough to his subjects to hear the clinking of their dishes and smell the frying of their fish. But it had clear military advantages, sitting as it did atop a sea cliff with a face sheer enough to discourage anyone brandishing grapple and hook, a hundred feet above the shoreline. The guns of Fort Stella stood just to the east, abutted by a lighthouse, while to the west stood another citadel, Fort Falcone, and some batteries. Along with a hexagonal watchtower guarding the harbor, Forts Stella and Falcone had formed the "three backbones" of Portoferraio's defense since the time of Cosimo de' Medici, who had funded their construction to protect his maritime trade, and for a time Elba had been one of the most secure places in the Mediterranean. Napoleon thought the two buildings comprising the mess hall could be connected and made livable in a few weeks. By the end of summer it could be transformed into a proper palace, with a second story added for his wife and child. Bertrand was to draw up plans and figure out how to complete renovations at the least possible cost.

After surveying the grounds, Ussher thought Napoleon had "made a better bargain than most people imagine and may be comfortable if his imagination will allow himself to be so." From his back garden he could survey the open sea and from his front door he could wander out and look down at the town and marina. His subjects, in turn, only had to look up to see where power resided on Elba. Portoferraio was all zigzagging muck-strewn lanes, winding, disjointed staircases, and shadowy corners, the product of an architecture of fear, designed to misguide outsiders. The best a ruler could do was to perch himself at the top of that wild maze.

Having secured the site of his main residence in the closest thing Elba had to a metropolis, Napoleon next wanted to find a country house. He set off again with Ussher on another long ride, "about two leagues into the country," wrote Ussher, "over mountains and precipices, but nothing is impassable to him." They stopped at the shop of a village wine merchant for lunch, where there were fresh strawberries for dessert. When Ussher commented favorably on the wine, Napoleon ordered two thousand bottles to be sent to the crew of the *Undaunted*. Years later, Napoleon recalled the pleasures of Elban wine, which he claimed the people of Tuscany preferred to all the other wines of Italy.

They returned to Portoferraio after sunset, unimpressed by any of the houses they'd seen. Following a starlit stroll around the grounds of what he'd taken to calling the Palazzo dei Mulini, Napoleon returned to his room in the Biscotteria. He sent a messenger to summon the mining administrator. It was just after midnight.

On approaching Napoleon's bedchamber, Pons heard his name and the sounds of arguing. Entering, he saw General Dalesme, who with a nod indicated that he should answer yes to whatever question would be asked of him, while Bertrand signed that he should answer no. Napoleon, oblivious to the pantomiming taking place behind him, asked Pons if he could arrange a tour of the iron mines in Rio for nine in the morning and if he could tell him where to find a good breakfast somewhere in town before the visit.

Pons said he would be honored to guide the tour himself and to host him at his own table, so long as he could be forgiven for the sorry state of his house. He'd deserted Rio a few weeks earlier after deciding to shut down the mines until it was clear who was in charge of Elba, moving his family to Portoferraio, which he thought safer than a town full of out-of-work miners. Pleased by the answer, Napoleon turned to Bertrand and chastised him for having doubted that Pons would be willing to grant such a reasonable request. Watching Bertrand leave in a sulk, Napoleon told Pons that the grand marshal suffered from the affliction of thinking everything impossible.

Pons woke his wife and asked her to sew two Elban flags to be sent overnight along with any food she could scrounge up to add to whatever they'd left in their larder in Rio. He rode alone ten miles through the darkness. Arriving in Rio, he found no meat in his house and went out in the half-light to try his luck in the waters. He caught a whopping porgy right away, prompting some fishermen who witnessed this little miracle to call him a "conjurer" who cast his nets like spells.

At seven, Pons rode up into the hills of Rio Alta to meet Napoleon, Bertrand, Drouot, Dalesme, Koller, Campbell, and Ussher so they could all ride in to Rio Marina below. As with other twinned towns on the island, Rios Alta and Marina evolved out of an ancient practice of splitting coastal settlements into a fishing village at the shore and a fortified town above to which coastal dwellers could flee in the event of an attack by sea. Over the centuries the two Rios had developed into separate towns, each with its own customs and communities, who, as Pons put it, "have never agreed and . . . never will."

Following instruction from Pons, the mining families had lined the red foothills bordering the road into Rio Marina. Two Elban flags that had arrived just in time care of Madame Pons flew at the main gate to town. A cortege of young girls presented Napoleon with flowers and took turns kissing his hand.

Despite the day's encouraging start, it soon turned into one full of "gaucheries," to use Pons's term. First there was an uninspiring church service led by a bumbling priest, who struggled through even the most basic rituals. Next, while showing Napoleon and the others his office at the mines, Pons realized that his gardens were dominated by three-petaled lilies, fleurs-de-lys. Though they had been planted without malice months earlier, Pons was furious that no one had thought to pull up these Bourbon symbols. Worst of all, from Pons's view, was the boisterous reception he received from the townspeople wherever he and Napoleon went. While there were customary cries of "Long Live the Emperor!," the vivas for Pons were far louder. "Babbo! [Father!]," shouted the workers and their families, who hadn't seen Pons in weeks. Napoleon bristled at the word, perhaps because it reminded him of Corsica, where a generation earlier the peasants had referred to their beloved patriot Paoli with the same epithet. He told Pons that it seemed that he and not Napoleon was the true "prince" in Rio. Pons demurred by saying he was no sovereign but merely cared for his workers the way a father would for his children.

At lunch Napoleon asked detailed questions about the mines but directed them to everyone but Pons, even turning away from him as he spoke. Cut by the gesture, Pons made as if to leave, until Dalesme persuaded him to stay with an entreating tilt of the head. The meal went on for a while until it was

Napoleon who left abruptly, standing up and exiting the dining room in silence before coffee had been served.

A few hours later he called on Pons for a private talk and now they had their coffee. "He asked if I wanted to stay with him," wrote Pons. "I answered that nothing would please me more than to be useful to him. He misunderstood my words, thinking that I was trying to tell him he needed me." Napoleon sipped his drink and glared. He said he didn't care whether Pons thought he could be useful but only wanted to know if he wished to keep his job. "An old soldier must get straight to the point," he said. "Are you staying or are you going?" Pons misinterpreted his tone as playful and so answered in what he thought was the same lighthearted manner that he would do whatever was wished of him. Napoleon said nothing, stood up, and left the room.

Unspoken but at the heart of this joust was the fate of roughly fifty thousand francs in mining profits that had accrued in the months since Elba was put under British naval blockade. As new owner of the mines, Napoleon felt entitled to what was in the coffers, while Pons thought it wrong to disobey his existing written orders, which dictated that the money should be sent, as it always had been, to the French treasury, where it helped provide pensions for soldiers decorated with the Legion of Honor. Napoleon had been the one to arrange this system in the first place, which was why Pons had been sent to revitalize Elba's modest mining industry five years earlier. Pons had been so good at his job, introducing bonuses, an emergency medical fund, and a retirement program on one hand, while rooting out theft and corruption through brutal disciplinary measures on the other, that the mines were putting around three hundred thousand francs a year into the treasury.

The day ended with the two men taking a conciliatory walk along the edge of the ironworks, only to be interrupted by some miners who pressed a petition into Napoleon's hands asking that Pons be kept on as their overseer. The people of Rio weren't known for their delicate manners; a local saying held that "it was easier for a Moor to become white than for an inhabitant of Rio to become polite." Pons begged Napoleon not to think he'd arranged this ambush and got so flustered that he slipped into calling the emperor Monsieur, rather than Sire. Napoleon laughed off the breach in etiquette, never having been overly concerned with honorifics, especially after his time as an officer taught him how easily he could ingratiate himself to subordinates simply by letting them address him with the informal *tu* or by the nickname the "little corporal," which he encouraged. Despite Napoleon's assurances, Pons thought this tongue slip marked the fitting end to a disastrous day.

The next morning at his Rio home, he and Napoleon shared biscuits dipped in Málaga wine and Napoleon seemed to be in a better mood. But just as Pons started to relax, Napoleon struck, saying out of nowhere, "But you've written against me," in the same casual voice with which he'd just praised the wine a few seconds earlier. Pons understood the meaning right away. Fifteen years earlier he'd authored a short tract in praise of republicanism and harshly critical of Napoleon. He explained that his brief experiment with political pamphleteering had been a mistake, a not-so-youthful indiscretion. Napoleon only nodded. They never discussed the matter again. Remembering their exchange years later, Pons still had no idea how Napoleon had learned about his obscure pamphlet.

They rode back to the Land Gate of Portoferraio, where Pons left Napoleon so he could join his wife and daughters at their home near the quay. Later, from Dalesme, he learned that his apparent hurry to get away had upset Napoleon since manners dictated that he should have first seen his riding companion all the way to his own door. "He was right," wrote Pons, "but one must have some sympathy for an old republican who found himself suddenly transplanted into a new world."

Pons received a letter from Bertrand officially endorsing his continued employment as chief administrator of Elba's mines. A few months later, Paymaster Peyrusse would record the transfer of 50,349 francs from the accounts of the mines into the Elban treasury.

8

My Island Is Very Little

NAPOLEON SAID THAT ELBA was to be an "isle of rest," but Campbell had yet to see anything to convince him that this would be the case. After only a few days with Napoleon he wrote:

> I have never seen a man in any situation of life with so much personal activity and restless perseverance. He appears to take so much pleasure in perpetual movement and in seeing those who accompany him sink under fatigue, as has been the case on several occasions when I have accompanied him. I do not think it possible for him to sit down to study, on any pursuits of retirement, as proclaimed by him to be his intention, so long as his state of health permits corporeal exercise.

Napoleon's reputation as a relentless dynamo was by then already well established, so much so that his critics pointed to his fierce energy as the cause of all the recent destruction. As Talleyrand once quipped, "What a pity the man wasn't lazy."

Napoleon wanted to see Monte Orello, which stood at the center of the island, about a thousand feet high. He and Campbell rode up to its peak on May 10. They discovered a small chapel that had been built by a hermit, long since dead. The climb had been grueling and Campbell joked that it would take more than "common devotion" to get people to attend services in such a setting, to which Napoleon agreed, adding that "here the priest can talk as much nonsense as he likes." And then, as Campbell recalled, Napoleon went quiet for some time and looked around in all directions. To the north was the Ligurian coast. Corsica, nearly forty times larger than Elba, was near at hand to the west. Below that was Sardinia, dwarfing Corsica, and beyond that lay the western tip of Sicily and the unseen Tunisian coast. Napoleon smiled, shook his head, and said, "Eh! My island is very little!"

Returning to Portoferraio along a sunbaked country road, they met a finely dressed young woman who spoke to Napoleon "with great ease and gaiety," simpering that she'd been invited to a ball a few nights back but on hearing the emperor wouldn't be there had decided it wasn't worth going to at all. Campbell could tell how much Napoleon enjoyed these rides around the island, ambling along deserted mule paths and humming "Italian music, which he does very often, and seemingly quite in spirits." He liked to suddenly veer off from a main path and into some thicket buzzing with insects, playing at shaking off the officers who tailed behind him wherever he went.

Each new bit of the island seemed to spark a fresh memory of some other place. Napoleon told Campbell during one hillside trek that it reminded him of crossing the Great St. Bernard Pass in the Alps, more than eight thousand feet above sea level, early in his Italian campaign. Back then he'd chatted with a young peasant who had no idea who he was and who talked of how wonderful life must be for those who possessed a decent house and a workable number of cattle and sheep. He asked the peasant to "enumerate his greatest desires, afterwards sent for him, and gave him enough to purchase all that he had described." He told Campbell the man's happiness had cost him sixty thousand francs, which he considered money well spent.

Napoleon's tours were as much about having people see their new ruler as they were about his sizing up the island's commercial and military potential. He understood the importance of maintaining appearances, doubly so in this place where he lived so near his subjects. Even the most casual wanderings were preceded by detailed instructions on protocol from Bertrand to the village mayors, and each new stop meant another reception, as people vied to outdo their neighbors in making grand displays. Campbell soon adapted to the routine, the "firing of musketry and cannon, triumphal arches with inscriptions, processions of priests bearing a canopy and accompanied by young girls and children strewing flowers who led him into the church." Always a church. At the close of a day spent at four services in four separate towns, Napoleon asked Campbell if he worried he might be turning "devout."

The Elbans could sometimes annoy Napoleon with their rustic ways. Near Porto Longone he was repulsed by some villagers who knelt in the muck and prostrated themselves as he passed, an unthinking obsequiousness he blamed on their "education at the hands of the monks," as Campbell wrote. Wherever he went people pounced on him with all sorts of requests. Some begged alms, some just wanted to kiss his hand. To the Elbans he appeared to be forever in motion, spotted all across the island (often in two or more places at once) on foot, on horseback, in his carriage, in his rowboat, but never alone.

On such surveys Napoleon would have seen cypresses, heather, and chestnut trees, bright violets and purple cyclamen, aloes and agave, myrtle and tamarisk and lilies of the Nile. He would have passed limestone hills sloping down to the shore and craggy ranges of granite, their peaks usually wrapped tightly by clouds. Terraced vineyards dotted the hillsides, as did yellow broom and lupine shrubs, the hallowed *macchia* of the Mediterranean. Along the coasts were men worrying the salt pans and tending huge nets bearing tunny and anchovy. Others carted mineral hauls to tall ships waiting at Portoferraio. To the west, across the island from Rio's iron mines, were quarries for granite and marble, the point of origin for the Parthenon's columns, the walls of the Pisa cathedral, and the Medici chapel in Florence. Along the ragged shoreline Napoleon would have seen sandy beaches and rocky bays, so numerous that no one had yet to properly count them.

Like many Mediterranean populations, the Elbans cherished the power and mystery of their island's mythic past. Elba had been a landing point for Jason and the Argonauts on their way to seek the golden fleece, and according to Virgil the "isle renown'd for steel, and unexhausted mines" had supplied three hundred soldiers to fight the Trojan War. But though rich in legend and mineral deposits, Elba was hardly a self-sufficient Eden. Due to its relative isolation and small size (223 square kilometers), the island had passed through many hands over the centuries. Ligurians, Carthaginians, Etruscans, Romans, Visigoths, Ostrogoths, Vandals, Lombards, Turks, Genoese, Pisans, Spaniards, Florentines, the English, and the French had all laid claim, while all sorts of pirates and marauders, including the notorious Barbarossa, would sack each new settlement as soon as it went up.

So much back-and-forth meant that no single power had stayed long enough to set up much by the way of infrastructure. When Napoleon first sent men over to improve fortifications, in 1802, the detachment had more than its share of "deserters and robbers picked out of a colonial depot," as one French commander recalled. Along with the first wave of French settlers, more than a few outsiders had come in the ensuing years, eyed warily by locals claiming lineage that spanned back several generations. After twelve years the French had little to show for their labors aside from two primary schools, two hospitals, a few narrow unpaved roads, a main artery to connect Portoferraio and Marciana, and a small armed force.

Elba remained riven by long-standing regional divisions. Each village was like a smaller island within the larger one. Pons wrote that he'd lived for years in Rio without meeting anyone there hailing from Marciana, and had never heard of anyone from Rio moving to Marciana. The people of Porto Longone lived like "prisoners" in their own town, he said, while the people of Campo (present-day Campo nell'Elba) were indifferent to anything beyond their front yards unless it related to their meager wine trade. Portoferraio was populated mainly by Tuscans, while Porto Longone was mostly Spanish-speaking. Neapolitans dominated the fishing trade, while Corsicans were dotted all around, having infiltrated nearly every industry.

What united all of them, save for a few estate owners, merchants, and financiers, was poverty. The mineral-rich ground was too rocky to grow decent-sized crops. Soil tended to run from sulfurous yellow to sun-bleached beige, and only rarely did one see truly black earth. Citrus, fig, and olive groves occupied what little flat ground could be found, but their yields were slim and harvests difficult to plan, as long stretches of drought would be suddenly broken by mammoth thunderstorms, leaving the land as confused as its tenders. With so many men conscripted there were never enough laborers to work the fields, and the population hadn't really grown in the past twenty years. Bouts of typhus, dysentery, and malaria hit every so often and spread with fierce speed because the infrequent rain bursts weren't sufficient to wash away the waste that piled up in the gutters that ran down the middles of the sloping streets. It was a landscape that bred reliance on strangers, and most years the Elbans imported the bulk of their grain, wood, and meat.

Now Napoleon could imagine himself a modern Augustus, finding a city of bricks he would leave as one of marble. As much as it would benefit his rural subjects, "civilizing" the island could also serve as testament to his reign. After all, his "passion for monuments nearly equaled his passion for war," as his personal secretary and childhood friend Bourrienne once said about him.

Before two weeks on Elba were up, Napoleon boasted to Pons that he already "knew his island by heart." Surveying the place in its entirety, or near so, would have marked a kind of victory for a man who had tried to extend his gaze so much farther than anyone of his time had thought possible. From now on he would spend his days looking mostly at weary faces, sun-faded uniforms, cramped rooms, leather-bound books, his furniture, his garden, looping cobblestoned streets, horses, carriages and ships, the ocean, and stars. But he could still point to some place on the map and say that there he alone was master of all he could see.

9

LOUIS THE GOUTY AND THE WEATHERVANE MAN

WHILE NAPOLEON HAD BEEN traveling down from Fontainebleau to begin his exile, the restored Louis XVIII was embarked on his own southern voyage, in his case returning from banishment. He'd fled France in 1791 at the age of thirty-five, disguised as a British trader. From then on he'd been on a strange sort of Grand Tour, traveling from place to place across Europe, sometimes staying in the grand chateaus of fellow nobles proud to host a man they regarded as a rightful king-in-absentia and other times holing up in less luxurious surroundings, including a brief stretch in Verona, where he lived above a shop in a tiny apartment.

The past five years Louis had lived at Hartwell House in bucolic Buckinghamshire. Gout-ridden and obese, he indulged his appetites for rich food and lively company while the British and Russian governments covered the bulk of his expenses and helped to distribute royalist propaganda calling for his return to the French throne. When a marquis rushed to Hartwell to tell him of Napoleon's abdication, saying, "Sire, you are King of France!," Louis reputedly answered, "Have I ever ceased to be?"

He left Hartwell accompanied by his niece and two Bourbon cousins, the elderly Louis-Joseph, prince de Condé, and his son, Louis Henri, bound for Paris but first stopping in London for his first official state visit with the prince regent at Carlton House. Lord Byron described the scene to a friend:

> At this present writing, Louis the Gouty is wheeling in triumph into Piccadilly in all the pomp and rabblement of Royalty. I had an offer of seats to see him pass, but as I have seen a Sultan going to mosque and been at *his* reception of an ambassador, the most Christian King "hath no attractions for me."

London had just passed through its worst fog in more than fifty years, though the skies had cleared on the day of Napoleon's abdication, as though victory had been heaven-sent. People rushed out to the streets to celebrate the fall of "the usurper," ringing bells, singing songs, and lighting off crackers. Over a roast beef and plum pudding banquet for eight thousand in the coastal town of Great Yarmouth, whose port had so often teemed with battleships outfitted to fight the French, revelers hanged, burned, and buried their fallen enemy in effigy. "Nap the Mighty is *gone to pot*," wrote the young Thomas Carlyle to a friend, twice underlining the sentence.

At a time when the major British papers boasted annual print runs in the millions, any edition promising new details of Napoleon's defeat promptly sold out. Caricaturists competed to dream up the most pathetic scene of his surrender: Napoleon in handcuffs, shoeless and in tatters, being dragged to the ocean's edge where the devil waits to ferry him off to his island hell; Napoleon and his brothers pressed into a chain gang and whipped by a Cossack; Napoleon grasping for his crown as it's lifted from his head by a black eagle while imperial bees fly off his red robe; Napoleon brandishing a broken sword, faced backward toward Fontainebleau while his pathetic donkey follows a sign for Elba; Napoleon being smacked by Talleyrand's crutch while soldiers shout, "Bone him, my tight little Tally!"

Some detractors thought Napoleon's unwillingness to fall on his sword like defeated emperors of old revealed the weakness of his character. "He is deserted by all and called a craven for not putting an end to his degraded existence," wrote the young baronet and diarist John Cam Hobhouse to Byron from Paris, adding that he'd heard the emperor's own supporters had left pistols and poisons on his table. At one time both young men had idolized Napoleon, but his inglorious fall lacked the panache of the dramatic career that had so captivated them. Napoleon might have agreed. Years later, on Saint Helena, he said he "ought to have died at the Battle of Moscow," meaning the bloodbath at Borodino in 1812, the deadliest battle in the history of warfare until the First World War, which had opened the road to Moscow and ruin.

LOUIS XVIII AND HIS RETINUE sailed from Dover to Calais aboard a yacht borrowed from the prince regent, escorted by eight British ships of the line. On May 2 they reached the chateau of Saint-Ouen, north of Paris, where Louis signed a declaration guaranteeing a liberal constitution, a bicameral legislature, and freedom of the press. He dated the document "the nineteenth year of his reign," as though he'd been king ever since the death of his young nephew, who would have been first in line to inherit the throne as Louis XVII had he not died of illness at the age of ten. Talleyrand had begged Louis not to include that turn of phrase, knowing that people still thought of the recent past with some pride and would never accept the pretense that during the years they had followed Napoleon the exiled Bourbon had been their true ruler all along. Talleyrand also hoped that Louis would take the title of King of the French, rather than styling himself by his preferred moniker, King of France and Navarre, which would send a signal that the new regime's power emanated from the people rather than the sovereign, but failed to convince him.

The English artist Thomas Underwood was among the thousands in Paris who crowded around the Porte Saint-Denis, remnant of the city's medieval fortifications and northern gateway to its heart, to witness Louis's entry. Under "a cloudless sky and the temperature of the dog-days," Underwood had the bad luck to be pressed in next to a roadside burial mound containing the rotting corpses of a few hundred victims of the recent fighting. The smell "was most horrible." He spotted one of Napoleon's magnificent carriages drawn by eight white horses. It had been repainted Bourbon white and emblazoned with fleurs-de-lys, and it carried Louis XVIII squeezed into a blue overcoat with gold epaulettes, his head bedecked with an oversized hat. His niece, the duchesse d'Angoulême, accompanied him, as did the future and current princes de Condé, with hair curled and powdered in the style of the ancien régime. Louis's relatively more athletic younger brother, the comte d'Artois, rode on horseback alongside, escorted by his two sons, one of them wearing an English uniform because he hadn't found proper dress in time for the ceremony.

The family pierced the city center to the sounds of pealing bells and cannon shot. There were flowers and Bourbon flags. Underwood was struck by the quaint English bonnet worn by the stiff-backed duchesse d'Angoulême, the opposite of the oversized ones that were then fashionable in Paris. The crowds cheered, if somewhat mechanically, as Louis bowed, smiled, and put his hand to his breast in salute. His movements were stiff and forced. "There was but little demonstration of joy on the occasion," wrote Underwood, "either on the part of the royal personages or on that of the people."

Passing down the rue Saint Denis the marshals trailing Louis XVIII tried to rouse the crowds with cheers for the Bourbons. While some people joined in their hailing, others tried to shout them down with "Long Live the Guard!" and a few daring cries of "Long Live the Emperor!" There were still many men in the army, especially in the officer ranks, who felt a strong allegiance to Napoleon, though for now most of them were more interested in ending their fighting than anything else. To spare Louis the sight of foreign troops, his carriage was escorted by foot soldiers of the Parisian corps of the Imperial Guard, who did little to conceal their rage and humiliation. Chateaubriand described how they

> brought their great busbies down over their eyes, as if to avoid seeing anything; others turned down the corners of their mouths in angry contempt; others again showed their teeth through their moustaches, like tigers. When they presented arms, it was with a furious movement, and the sound of those arms made one tremble.

Satirists were quick to skewer the monarch's big moment. Parisians were soon passing from cloak to cloak copies of a crude engraving of a porcine Louis XVIII brought into the city on the back of a Cossack, whose overwhelmed horse wades through bodies of fallen guardsmen, burnt villages dotting the background. Another caricature showed a crazed-looking writer handing a dedicated copy of a thick and beautifully bound book to the beaming king; the tome is titled *A History of the Nineteen Glorious Years of the Reign of Louis XVIII* and all of its pages are blank.

A few hours later, at a crowded mass at Notre-Dame, Louis XVIII gained a deeper approval than he had when bouncing along the rue Saint Denis in Napoleon's old carriage, as people now saw him up close and in a hallowed setting. He could play the role of stern and paternal monarch with skill. Shouts of "Long Live the King!" overpowered the roaring organ. Following the mass a giant balloon festooned with white flags was released into the skies above the cathedral. A few hundred meters away at the other end of the Île de la Cité, royalists put the last layers of paint on a plaster equestrian statue of the first Bourbon king, Henri IV, replacing the original that had stood by the Pont Neuf until it was toppled in the Revolution. The replacement statue bore the legend *Ludovico reduce, Henricus redivius* (By Louis's return, Henri lives again).

While Napoleon was passing his final night aboard the *Undaunted* in the harbor of Portoferraio, Louis XVIII would spend his first at the Tuileries palace after nearly a quarter century away. Imperial bees still dotted the drapes, and the furnishings bore the mark of eagles and N's. The new king slept in the former emperor's bed. No one could say for certain how long his reign would last. As Napoleon himself had remarked several years earlier, "To be at the Tuileries is not all. We must stay here."

FOR TALLEYRAND, the Notre-Dame mass had been just one more in a long line of similar rituals. He'd watched over the coronation of Louis XVI decades earlier, just as he'd witnessed Napoleon's ascension as Emperor of the French in 1804, and just as many years later he would be present to see Louis XVIII's eventual successor installed on the throne. Not for nothing was he known as *l'homme girouette,* the weathervane man. An 1815 bestseller titled *The Dictionary of Weathervanes,* a kind of proto–Michelin Guide to political flip-flopping, would rank Talleyrand as the man who had changed his mind more than anyone else in France, for which he was awarded twelve weathervanes.

Now, by promoting a regime based on the idea of legitimacy, Talleyrand showed a keen understanding for what the French people wanted at that moment: another grand idea around which they could rally after the failure of Bonapartism. As Talleyrand had told the allied representatives just after the fall of Paris, Napoleon's empire could only be replaced "by invoking a principle." Nothing else but "a right hallowed by tradition . . . could vanquish one based on conquest and reinforced by glory." The returned Bourbons offered not the wild dreams of the Revolution, nor a strongman on a horse, but an embodiment of the very history of France itself.

10

Pretty Valleys, Trees,
Forest, and Water

IN EXILE NAPOLEON COULD shape his days however he wished. He was free in a way he hadn't been since adolescence, but that freedom seems to have terrified him. In his first week on Elba he issued a flurry of minor directives as though trying to ease his unquiet mind by busying it with procedure and protocol. As Bertrand later said of the first exile, Napoleon "dictated letters about fowls, ducks, meat and all eatables as if he was dealing at Paris with matters of the greatest importance."

His first written order was a rambling letter to Drouot:

> On Sunday hoist the new flag in every village and make a kind of holiday of it. . . . Call a meeting of the naval commissioner, the harbor master, the commander of the French ships in the harbor. We will make a count of how many ships there are and who owns each one. . . . Arrange for me to see anyone who can brief me about the civil administration, customs, taxes, sanitary matters and the management of the port. . . . Find a reliable man in town who can take charge of the stores and supplies. . . . By Sunday I want to know how

many of the French garrison wish to stay with me. . . . It is urgent that the gendarmerie be efficiently organized. . . . See the sub-prefect about a store of grain that he says belongs to the Grand Duchess of Tuscany. . . . Take it over as Crown property. . . . Make sure we have disbanded the coastal artillery companies. . . . They cost too much, and are useless anyway.

Next, in a three-page "constitution" dictated to Bertrand, he explained how Elba was to be organized. He named Drouot the new governor and head of military while Bertrand would handle matters of court, civilian issues, and Napoleon's personal affairs. Peyrusse was treasurer. There would be a comptroller of the household and a master of ceremonies, a chief cook and a chief baker. A former veterinary surgeon of the imperial stables was promoted to court physician. Footmen, valets, grooms, bailiffs, and polishers were also named.

Positions were invented for as many Elbans as there were who needed flattering. Repeating his well-worn strategy of breeding loyalty by bestowing titles, Napoleon posted four influential Elbans to the newly created sinecure of imperial chamberlain. "I defy you to show me a republic, modern or ancient, that did without distinctions," he once said. "You call them 'baubles,' but let me assure you that it is with baubles that men are led!"

Pons found the quartet somewhat lacking. The first man, Dr. Lapi, a former commander of the Elban guard, had a fine reputation but had "gotten by more on charm than talent." The second, Vantini, chief prosecutor, had burned through his family's fortune "by indulging in inexcusable excesses," and made too much of his flimsy claims to noble lineage. The third, the blind Gualandi, mayor of Rio, was "less than nothing, and should never have crossed the Emperor's door." The final chamberlain was Portoferraio's beloved if absent-minded mayor, Traditi, about whom Pons could find nothing bad to say.

Along with a few landowners and magistrates these four men formed a Sovereign Council overseen by Drouot and Bertrand, giving Elba the appearance of a constitutional monarchy. But in reality, the daily running of the island fell almost exclusively to Bertrand and Drouot. Napoleon did manage to make use of an Elban judge he named to this council, Poggi di Talavo, who had a knack for drawing people out and hearing their stories, and became one of his main informers.

Bertrand arranged a ball for Napoleon to meet some of these notables and their families. The evening started slowly. The women sat silent on wooden chairs while their men stood behind, everyone waiting for the emperor to appear. The guests had dressed elegantly, if inexpensively. "A hat of black straw, a white bodice, a short petticoat of red or blue, is the whole attire of the women," Berneaud had written in his Elban travelogue. "A flower, ribbons, a huge ring, large ear-rings, a gold chain (of which the precious metal is lost in alloy): these are the objects of a female coquetry, which is not destitute of charms." (Pons added in his own memoir that Elban women had "the most beautiful hair in the world.") Late into the night Napoleon finally appeared, in full military regalia. He "went round the whole party, asking a question of each female after her name was announced—if unmarried, as to her father; if married, how many children she had," wrote Campbell. "After this farce was played off he spoke to two or three of the gentlemen who were nearest him at the end of the room, and at last walked off, apparently impressed with the ridiculous nature of the scene." Among the guests Campbell spotted three sisters he'd hired a day earlier to embroider his coat.

DROUOT SETTLED into a spartan cell in the officers' barracks by Fort Stella, not far from the Mulini palace, furnished with little more than a bed, a desk, a lamp, and a few straw-backed chairs. He welcomed this chance to contemplate, pray, and wait. He had no wife or children. Before leaving Fontainebleau he'd written to the incoming minister of war to say that while his personal attachment to Napoleon was taking him away from France, he would never cease "to wish for its happiness and its glory," and that "regardless of the circumstances," he was always ready to "file in alongside her defenders, ready to spill blood for her." He closed by asking that the minister formally accept his allegiance to the new Bourbon government.

A few days after landing at Portoferraio, Drouot described his situation to a friend, a French general who had retained his position under the new regime:

I've been ordered to take provisional control of the island's government, and I've only accepted on condition that I can leave this post after fifteen days, when the troops will have arrived from France. I've entirely renounced the great things of this world, and I want to devote the days of my exile to study. When I have the good fortune to return to my country it will be to enjoy a sweet and homey retirement, among family and friends.

In his letters, Drouot often said he was just about to leave his post so he could finally study full-time. "I'm still the governor of Elba," he would write in early June. "I haven't yet obtained my demission. I'll insist again, and more forcefully once everything here is more organized." He mentioned that he'd already found a few hours for study, which had given him "inexpressible pleasure."

Drouot did have his pleasure-seeking side and briefly courted the Elban woman hired to tutor him in Italian, Henriette Vantini, who came from a respected island family. He was set to propose until a letter from his mother citing the complications of a marriage in such a "far off" country quashed the match. Napoleon was disappointed by the news. "You should get married here," he told Drouot. "I want to keep you near me, I'm waiting to see you form a tie that will bind you permanently to the island."

Bertrand was meanwhile taking over Napoleon's apartments in the Biscotteria. The rooms would be large enough to accommodate his wife and children when they arrived, as well as a few servants. At Fontainebleau he'd told Napoleon he would follow him to the ends of the earth, but in the first weeks of April he and his wife had considered his quitting his service altogether. "I would love to believe the Revolution is finally over," he'd written to his wife, Fanny, "and that the return of the Bourbons will restore calm and give our sad homeland the rest it so badly needs." He told her he saw his service to Napoleon as separate from his identity as a Frenchman and that his true loyalty would always be to his family. Madame Bertrand, described by a contemporary as carrying herself like "a young queen," hated having to trade the gilded lives they had made for themselves in Paris for an aimless existence in some

Italian hinterland, where the educations of her children would suffer. She was pregnant with her fourth child.

In the end, Henri Bertrand was compelled to join the exile by a sense of duty and an equally strong sense of fear that if he abandoned Napoleon he would be doubly marked as a traitor to his past master and a threat to the new regime, and that his family might be left stateless as a result. Before he left Fontainebleau he sent a letter to a brother-in-law to be given to Louis XVIII. It contained his pledge to be as loyal a subject to the Bourbon king as he'd been to the emperor, and stated that he held no obligations or debts to Napoleon and was accompanying him freely of his own initiative. He wanted it known that he believed Napoleon when he claimed to have renounced all desire to return to France, and that while he couldn't assure Louis XVIII about Napoleon's state of mind one way or the other, he could promise that he himself would no longer become involved in "political affairs," for he wasn't a man "of revolution or intrigue." He closed the letter by asking permission to visit his family in Châteauroux for a few months at some later date.

After a few days on Elba, Bertrand wrote to tell his wife that it was more pleasant than he'd thought it would be, even if he could only describe it in the most banal terms: "pretty valleys, trees, forest, and water." No property on the island was anywhere near as brilliant as their family estate in France, but the houses were "passable." He assured her that life would be easy and uneventful once she came to join him, since Napoleon could no longer claim any more right to the French throne than could Bertrand and so was no longer capable of "playing the adventurer." They assumed Fanny would soon be traveling to Elba alongside Marie Louise, after which she would serve as the empress's lady-in-waiting. Henri promised that once she reached Elba they would be free to travel at their leisure. "We'll go see Naples, Genoa, and Livorno, Rome and Florence."

LESS THAN A WEEK after Napoleon's landing, Portoferraio's harbor welcomed an unexpected British ship, the *Curacoa*, which had sailed from Genoa. One of its officers presented Napoleon with a copy of the preliminary peace treaty that would soon be codified by the allies and the French Provisional Government. Napoleon read the document aloud with Bertrand, Drouot, Campbell, Ussher, and Koller in earshot. He returned it to the officer with a curt thank-you, as though he'd given up caring about such things.

The *Curacoa* was to leave the next day, carrying the Austrian commissioner, Koller, who felt he'd completed his duty in escorting Napoleon safely into exile and leaving Campbell as the last allied representative on Elba, as the Russian and Prussian commissioners had ended their missions at Fréjus. The ship would also carry one of Napoleon's valets, bound for Milan to organize furnishing for the Mulini palace. Campbell asked Koller to make sure the valet was tailed after landing.

Just before the *Curacoa* sailed, Napoleon handed Koller a letter for Marie Louise and asked him to send back any word of his family's whereabouts and health. "I'm having fairly nice quarters fitted up, with a garden and in very good air," he wrote. "My health is perfect. The island is healthy, the inhabitants seem to be of a kindly disposition, and the countryside is fairly pleasant. All that's missing is news of you and the reassurance that you're well." Napoleon gave Koller a final ribbing before he left, telling him that Austria had been foolish to join in a coalition against France that would only make Russia more powerful and threaten Austrian safety.

Campbell had also passed Koller a letter, a request to Castlereagh to extend his stay on Elba indefinitely. He wrote that he wanted to "obtain information of the intercourse which Napoleon or his agents hold on the opposite coast of Corsica" and added that the emperor himself had asked him several times to stay on as his personal guest. Campbell was transforming himself from a mere military escort into a kind of spymaster.

Napoleon would have known that Campbell was reporting to Castlereagh about everything he heard and saw on Elba, but the arrangement evidently pleased him. Campbell's presence was the closest thing he had to diplomatic recognition of his reign, and he understood that the threat of British naval power was the only thing that enforced his claim to sovereignty in the region.

The night the *Curacoa* sailed, Napoleon treated Campbell to a three-hour discourse on military matters. He dissected the methods the allies had used to defeat him and then explained how he should have outmaneuvered them. Campbell paid close attention. His summary of Napoleon's talk took up seven pages of his journal:

> His best information led him to believe that, instead of retreating to Langres . . . in the affair against the Prussians near Chateau Thierry . . . it was not for the sake of a crown that he had continued the war, but for the glory of his country. . . . Barricade all the streets with casks, and it would be impossible for the enemy to advance. . . . They took from 1500 to 2000 prisoners. . . . He knew all the workmen of Paris would fight for him. . . . That Marmont, a man who owed everything to him—who had been his aide-de-camp and attached everything to him for twenty-one years—should have betrayed him! . . . Three battalions of his Guards, in reserve against double their number. The instant these old soldiers showed themselves, the affair was decided.

A few days later, deep into another dinnertime sermon, Napoleon told Campbell of an abandoned plan to invade Britain, which he could have done despite being outnumbered at sea because he would have outflanked the Royal Navy "by leading our fleet out to the West Indies, and suddenly returning." He seemed to Campbell to be a total novice when it came to naval strategy; he had no idea of the kinds of risks involved in "movements upon a coast, nor of the difficulties occasioned by winds and tides, but judges of changes of position in the case of ships as he would with regard to troops upon land."

Campbell also noticed that when Napoleon talked about "public affairs" he often lost his composure and talked "so openly as to leave no doubt of his expecting that circumstances may yet call him to the throne of France. . . . If opportunities for warfare on a great scale and for important objects do not present themselves, he's likely to avail himself of any others in order to indulge this passion from mere recklessness. His thoughts seem to dwell perpetually on the operations of war."

11

THE EMPEROR IS DEAD

WHAT DOES AN EMPEROR do if he's banished to a small island? Finds an even smaller island to conquer. Nine miles to Elba's southwest lay an uninhabited, triangle-shaped rock known as Pianosa. The ancient Romans had once made it a bustling colony, but its size and relative distance from Elba made it difficult and dangerous to maintain over the centuries. By the time Napoleon arrived the Elbans had long since abandoned it, though they sometimes came over to run wild horses on its flat fields.

Napoleon sailed to Pianosa in late May with Campbell and a few soldiers to claim it as a possession. "All of Europe will say I've made a conquest already," he told Campbell. They shared a picnic in the long grass, using a sail to shade themselves. Campbell noticed that Napoleon kept his hat on throughout the meal and sat far away, as though the moment might otherwise feel too intimate. Napoleon spoke of bringing settlers over to make the place farmable, with a small garrison to defend them. They would plant Black Forest acorns that would become towering oaks, he told Campbell, and there would be citrus orchards and vineyards as well.

Before returning to Elba they made a detour to another islet just east of

Pianosa, whose lone peak housed some old cannons. Campbell wrote that Napoleon rushed to climb to its top but "after getting up half-way, although assisted occasionally both by the lieutenant of the Navy and myself, was obliged to desist. Indefatigable as he is, his corpulency prevents him from walking much and he's obliged to take the arm of some person on rough roads." On another occasion, a stocky Elban soldier, who had seen Napoleon hesitate before mounting his horse, had picked him up and put him in the saddle while he squirmed against his help. When the man was promoted to second lieutenant, Pons, who witnessed the scene, said it was so that no one could say the emperor's body had been handled by a common foot soldier.

BACK AT PORTOFERRAIO, Napoleon slept at the Mulini palace for the first time, occupying the central room on the ground floor. There were still large holes in the pink-white, dust-powdered plaster, the second story remained unfinished, and the garden was a mess. There were hardly enough linens, tableware, or furniture to host guests, since whatever household goods hadn't been seized after's Napoleon fall were still packed away in a chateau in Blois, where Marie Louise had deposited them after fleeing Paris.

One thing Napoleon didn't need was a new bed. He liked to sleep on the small collapsible one he'd taken with him on campaign; it was simple and light and could be put together in five minutes, perfect for a soldier on the move. Weeks later, after his workmen had uncrated a larger and more comfortable frame, he still liked to pass some nights on the camp bed, entombed in a shroud of thick green curtains. "The Emperor is very happy here and seems to have forgotten that only a very short time ago he was in such a different position," wrote Bertrand to Napoleon's former secretary Baron Méneval, who was tending to Marie Louise. "He's very busy getting his house in order, furnishing it and looking out for the site of a pretty country house."

But Napoleon still felt unsettled. He'd yet to receive reliable intelligence on the whereabouts of the battalion of his Old Guard meant to be bound for Elba to form the core of his defense, and it was possible Louis XVIII or Talleyrand had persuaded the allies to renege on the pledge to let him have these soldiers, leaving him vulnerable to assassination by some third party who would do the job they couldn't be seen to do themselves.

If and when the battalion of the Old Guard arrived, there would be horses and carriages needing housing. Bertrand handed some money to the man who oversaw most of Elba's tuna trade and told him to vacate some warehouses near Portoferraio, which would become the imperial stables. They would eventually house nine carriages, eight baggage wagons, two post-chaises, two hunting carts, a landau, a cabriolet, and more than a hundred horses and mules, all tended to by a chief saddler, three assistant saddlers, a harness maker, a veterinary surgeon, a farrier, a head groom, a stud groom and his assistant, a coachman, eight postilions, ten stablemen, two troopers, two locksmiths, two carpenters, and a tailor to make the uniforms.

Commandeering warehouses for the use of horses was an especially excessive act on an island with few proper roads and whose narrow passages were so steep and winding they hardly fit a single rider. Campbell wrote that this showed "how little Napoleon permits reflection to check his desires." Yet the Elbans seemed to love him. Campbell thought that any initial apprehension had faded after only a few days, which he attributed to the seductive power of royal spectacle:

> The *éclat* given to him on landing by the salute of his Britannic Majesty's frigate, and other marks of attention and protection which he's evidently sought for all along on purpose to make an impression on the minds of the people, have contributed materially to the change of feeling.

Campbell also figured that the Elbans assumed their lives would only improve by their new association with Napoleon, even if he was no longer a real force and only there against his will. They had already seen Portoferraio teeming with ships offloading soldiers and diplomats; it was logical to expect a boost in trade as well. From his pulpit, the local vicar-general promised that wealth would pour into the island, and he called on his flock to pray for the man "who is more your father than your sovereign, and exult with holy joy in the bounty of the Lord who has marked you out for all eternity by this auspicious event."

LATE IN MAY, Captain Ussher sailed for Fréjus to pick up Napoleon's sister Pauline, who was supposed to be there waiting. As they watched the departing *Undaunted* from the terrace of the Mulini, Campbell listened as Napoleon slipped into another nostalgic reverie. "Smiling, with an air of triumph," he told Campbell that the Russian army had never truly recovered from the battle of Borodino, where he'd killed fifty thousand of their troops. Recalling former strength offered momentary relief from his present weakness. Though the *Undaunted* would soon return, Napoleon knew he couldn't rely on its guns forever. The British navy, while the largest in the world, floated less than a thousand ships and each one had to be sent where it was most needed. The *Undaunted* was sure to be called away on some more important mission, eventually.

Shortly after the *Undaunted* sailed, a French frigate, *Dryade*, reached Portoferraio alongside an escorting corvette, the *Inconstant*, the same ship Napoleon had refused to sail on when leaving Fréjus a few weeks earlier. Montcabrié, the captain he'd insulted with that gesture, now brought orders to return to France with all of the troops who had originally been stationed on Elba under the governor's control. This returning party would sail aboard the *Dryade* and the *Inconstant* would be left behind permanently for Napoleon's use.

The allies had honored their pledge to furnish him with a ship, but to Napoleon the modest *Inconstant* fell well short of being the "armed corvette" specified by the treaty, and he interpreted this bit of bait-and-switch as evidence of a plot to leave him open to attack while maintaining the appearance of protection. Yet while it only had a single deck and sixteen guns, the *Inconstant* had its merits. At three hundred tons it was fairly fast and maneuverable and could be quickly outfitted to sail should it ever need to leave port in a hurry. And it was large enough to carry a full battalion of troops, at least for a short crossing.

The same day the *Dryade* and *Inconstant* arrived also saw the *Undaunted* returned from the continent, but without the Princess Pauline. She'd already sailed from Fréjus a few days before Ussher reached the port, where he'd heard she was heading for Naples under the protection of the Neapolitan navy.

Ussher and Campbell climbed the 135 steps up from the main square to the Mulini. They found Napoleon playing chess with Bertrand. Campbell wrote that he sympathized with the "sulky" chamberlains watching the game and trying to stay awake, "interrupted from attending their private affairs or being with their families, for 1,200 livres a year."

Ussher told Napoleon that the battalion of the Old Guard had safely reached the coast under British escort and that he was sure they would have pushed off in time to miss the gale that had recently pummeled the region. He added that in Fréjus he couldn't convince anyone that he'd actually taken Napoleon to Elba, rather than to America, Gibraltar, Dover, or some other secret place. The papers had made much of his being conveyed into exile aboard a British ship, especially since people had seen the French corvette in port just prior to his sailing. The talk on the mainland, he said, was that the British "had seduced him." Napoleon laughed and said, "What! Did they say I had now become an Englishman?" Ussher next reported that he'd seen on this recent trip back to France just how many supporters Napoleon still had there. Campbell wrote that Napoleon answered, "Oh! the Emperor is dead. I'm no longer anything."

That evening Napoleon sat in the Mulini's garden until sunset, scanning the waters in the hope of spotting the flotilla carrying his reinforcements. After dinner he invited Campbell and Ussher back out to the terrace to join him in his vigil, by which time the sky had gone purple-black and rainy. They took turns looking through Ussher's night-glass, stubbier than a standard telescope, with a larger objective lens to make night viewing possible, while lacking the added glass to correct inverted images as an extra lens would block too much light. Meaning that when some faint shapes at the horizon line finally came into focus, just before midnight, they would have appeared to Napoleon as the lights of several ships floating upside down in the darkness.

12

AND EVERY TUNA BOWS TO HIM

FIVE BRITISH SHIPS DOCKED at Portoferraio. They had sailed from Savona carrying eighty Polish lancers, eight Mameluke mercenaries, a ten-man military band, and another fourteen drummers. Most important, the ships carried guns, horses, and eight hundred elite veterans of the Old Guard who had volunteered to serve in exile. Though the battalion's size doubled the four hundred soldiers allotted by the Treaty of Fontainebleau, allied officials had granted it free passage to Elba. Talleyrand had figured that if Napoleon could still persuade a few more zealots to sign up for the drudgery of defending his little island, so much the better for him; the loss of a few hundred men of poor judgment dealt no great blow to France.

Napoleon came down to see the boats putting in, the glint of bayonets and the sunlit water making the morning shine silver. It took some time for each ship to find its berth and for the men to be processed, so Napoleon wandered onto the *Dryade*, which was being loaded for its return to France. Technically this was an act of hostility against an opposing power, since the *Dryade* flew Bourbon white and Captain Montcabrié hadn't invited Napoleon to board, but the crew greeted his breach of naval etiquette with boisterous cheers. Montcabrié wasn't actually available to invite anybody on board, as he'd been ashore since the previous night under the impression he would be taken to the Mulini at any moment to pay court to the emperor.

Campbell watched how Napoleon made special effort to chat with the low-ranking men, often ignoring senior officers in the process. He heard how the shouts of "Long Live the Emperor!" from the *Dryade* sparked more shouts from soldiers waiting on the ships still to be unloaded, so that soon so many voices were bouncing off the hills that make Portoferraio a natural amphitheater that it sounded as though the whole town were cheering. In his journal he wondered if Napoleon's impulsive dash up to the bridge of the *Dryade* had in fact been carefully planned, right down to keeping Montcabrié on land the night before, so that he would have a chance to "try the disposition of the [French] Navy, and to keep up a recollection of him in France." Napoleon knew the value of public opinion and especially how mutable a force it could be; nothing, he once said, was "more unsteady, more vague" than this "mysterious, and invisible power," adding that public opinion was also "truthful, just, and reasonable more often than one might think."

The *Dryade* was only the first stop on his morning tour. He next boarded the *Undaunted* and thanked its crew for their ongoing service with a florid speech and the promise of another thousand bottles of wine. He presented Ussher a snuffbox decorated with his portrait set in diamonds. "Napoleon speaks most gratefully to everyone of the facilities which have been granted to him by the British government," wrote Campbell in the day's journal entry, "and to myself personally he constantly expresses the sense he entertains of the superior qualities which the British nation possesses over every other."

Napoleon boarded another of the just-docked British ships and went down to the hold to see some of his old horses. He found Wagram, a gray Arabian, named for the battle in which he'd carried Napoleon so deftly, who whinnied and stamped on seeing his master, who gave him some sugar and a kiss, saying, "There you are, my cousin!" He visited with Montevideo, a huge bay, and Emin, chestnut and black, veterans of his Spanish campaign. Then with Gonsalvo, another bay, who had had his bridle split in two by an enemy ball while Napoleon rode him at Brienne, as well as the hot-tempered Roitelet, a French and English cross, who had gained Napoleon's love ever since trying to throw him during a review in Vienna. He ended by seeing his two favorites: Intendant, a white Norman, used mostly for parades, and Tauris, a silvery Persian gifted by Tsar Alexander during a peace conference, who carried Napoleon for part of the retreat from Moscow until he was abandoned in favor of a sleigh.

Back up from the hold at quayside, Napoleon welcomed his men as they came down the gangplanks, sunburned and restless, and lauded the British sailors for having ferried their former enemies with such discipline and decorum. By late morning all the troops had disembarked, as had their commander, the redoubtable Pierre Cambronne, known as "protector of widows and orphans," and terror of the barracks. He was prone to unleashing ferocious barbs on enemies and friends in equal measure, and the troops whispered that the reason he no longer partook of alcohol was that he'd killed one of his best friends in a drunken duel. His face was a map of crosshatched scars. In the last days before the surrender he had suffered blows to the head in three separate battles and the wounds had yet to heal by the time he reached Elba.

Cambronne and his troops pressed into the cramped Piazza d'Armi, sweating under their bearskin hats. Napoleon addressed them, urging them to live in harmony with the Elbans, who "also had French hearts." Afterward, the soldiers regaled him with stories about their monthlong march to the coast, telling him how they had defiantly waved the tricolor in territory under allied control. While they were crossing the Alps, at Mont Cenis, heavy snow had forced them to shed some cannon, but they had refused to abandon his beloved chargers and so carried the horses along by hand, cosseted, through the icy pass. Cambronne told of the Austrian mayor who had tried denying them quarters until he said, "Very well, your men shall stand on one side and mine on the other, and we will see who the quarters will belong to," which had quickly changed the mayor's mind.

That afternoon Napoleon took one of his horses for a long ride inland, "to tire myself out," as he told Campbell. By evening he was back to see that all the new arrivals were lodged within a mile radius of the Mulini. Infantrymen occupied the old San Francesco monastery and lancers, Fort Falcone, where they would be retrained as artillerymen since such a small island had no need for cavalry. The *grognards*, or old grumblers, as the grenadiers were lovingly known, went to Fort Stella, along with Cambronne, who moved into the apartment next to Drouot's. Their windows looked out onto the emperor's garden. Napoleon and his defenders now occupied the whole top third of Portoferraio.

DROUOT TRIED TO BOLSTER the island's forces by covertly recruiting troops from Corsica and the Italian peninsula, and he formed a battalion drawn from the existing Elban guard. The soldiers wore French uniforms adorned with the new Elban three-bee insignia. To complement the *Inconstant*, he requisitioned two lateen-sailed transport feluccas that had served the Rio mines, the *Mouche* and the *Abeille*, and converted them into patrol ships. He bought a six-gunned xebec, the *Étoile*, from a merchant in Livorno, and a small Maltese ship with a single gun, the *Caroline*, which was used for running mail between Elba and the mainland. Ussher helped out by gifting a ten-oared barge from the *Undaunted* for Napoleon's personal use, duly baptized the *Ussher*. Despite his notoriously nasty attitude and undistinguished career, a sailor named Taillade was promoted to lieutenant and given command of this motley fleet. Pons claimed that Napoleon had only chosen the "insufferable" Taillade because he'd recently married an Elban woman and it was thought this promotion would please the locals. The ships were never properly outfitted, and their crews consisted mostly of career soldiers, poorly versed in maritime matters.

The entire armed and naval forces of Elba numbered around 1,750 men, enough to feasibly guard Portoferraio against attack, so long as they stayed clustered there atop the ridge. The rest of the island would have to be left undefended, save for a small garrison at Porto Longone and a few batteries scattered along the coast. Drouot calculated that defense costs would run up to a million francs for the year, eating up half of Napoleon's yet-to-be-seen pension from the French government.

Campbell was nonplussed by this ragged army. As he watched them at their drills, he thought the Elbans especially ill equipped for military work.

They soldiered without enthusiasm and had the habit of losing, or more likely, Campbell suspected, selling, their guns and uniforms. Few islanders joined the corps after the first round of recruitment. "The organization of the military force does not keep pace with Napoleon's wishes," wrote Campbell.

It would have been a difficult army to command. There was no chance to win glory or promotion through bravery on the battlefield, unless someone attacked Elba, no foreign enemy to conquer, meaning no way to add to one's pay through pillage, and no real sense of collective purpose. While its core consisted of veterans of the Old Guard and Polish lancers who had shared long histories together, the force as a whole was made up of Elbans, Corsicans, and other volunteers from farther abroad. A polyglot army was not in itself unusual. Of the six hundred thousand men Napoleon commanded in the Russian campaign, for instance, likely over half hailed from beyond France. But on Elba any divisions stemming from differences in background were exacerbated by the lack of any common tradition, ideal, or clear goal around which to coalesce aside from Napoleon and the promise of steady pay.

People on the continent were already swapping jokes about the fearsome army of Elba. One Florentine illustrator pictured a parade of tuna enlisting for military service at the edge of a desolate marsh, with Portoferraio looming in the background. Fish-soldiers stand on their tails and hold bayonets with their fins, balanced against their fish-shoulders, while a human Drouot, seated next to a human Napoleon, enlists more tuna by drawing lots. Human officers measure one tuna to see if he meets the minimum height requirement, while another less fortunate fish carries a note in its mouth, begging off service due to epilepsy. The caption reads:

> *New tuna soldiers draw your number*
> *Bonaparte says in a loud voice,*
> *You will get for me new conquests*
> *Transmitting the lightning bolts of my avenging sword*
> *The Magistrate presents himself at the sea shore*
> *And every tuna bows to him*

Now that Napoleon had his Old Guard garrisoned and the *Inconstant* moored in the bay, Campbell had achieved his mission of seeing him safely installed and defended against attack. He'd received no further word from the Foreign Office since leaving Fontainebleau more than a month earlier. With the British ships from Savona unloaded and set to return to their normal duties, it was a logical point for him to leave the island for good. But he felt compelled to stay. His journal offers no specific reasons why. His entry for the day the ships arrived with the Old Guard tells only of how he told Bertrand "that in case either Napoleon himself or others might ascribe any underhand motive to my remaining here, I was ready to quit the island at once should such be his wish."

If declaring his readiness to leave had been a gambit, it worked. Bertrand relayed Napoleon's message that the emperor deemed Campbell "indispensable for his protection and security . . . even after the arrival of his troops and baggage." Campbell asked Bertrand to put this in writing so he could send it to Castlereagh and the next day was handed a letter formally asking him to stay. It explained that a British officer would be helpful in dealing with all the ships that were sure to make contact with the island, and since it remained to be seen if Barbary pirates would try to attack Elba, having a representative of the Royal Navy on hand was vital to its continued defense. The letter closed, "I can only reiterate to Colonel Campbell how much his person and his presence are agreeable to the Emperor Napoleon."

Campbell gave a copy of the letter to Ussher, who was preparing to leave, without any orders to ever return. There is no record that they discussed whether Campbell, too, might quit the island the next time a British ship came in. For now Campbell was acting entirely on his own initiative, still unclear if he was Napoleon's jailor, companion, both, or neither.

{ 13 }

A Death, a Treaty, and a Celebration

In Paris, the hawkers were back on the boulevards pitching their wares with cries for hotcakes, potatoes, big wheels of cheese from Champagne, rabbit skins, and milk. Metternich remarked that people in the city were already speaking of Napoleon "as if he had ruled in the fourteenth century. . . . Everything is as peaceful as if there had been no war." Allied diplomats and soldiers capped days of parading with wild nights at the gaming tables and rides in carriages with courtesans, and people joked that the occupiers were spending more in Parisian brothels, shops, and *enfers* ("hells," as the city's gambling dens were known) than the French would ever have to pay out in war reparations. "This capital is as bad as any other big city for business," a Bavarian prince reported to his king. "We eat, we drink, dance, see the sights and the women, but affairs do not move forward as one would desire."

On May 29, Empress Joséphine died suddenly at her Malmaison estate, just short of what would have been her fifty-first birthday. Scandalmongers pinned her passing to the failure of her muslin wrap to protect her from an unseasonable chill during a flirtatious walk with Tsar Alexander in the Malmaison gardens during a ball she hosted to celebrate the peace. A few days earlier she'd sent what would be her last letter to Napoleon:

> It is only today that I can calculate the full extent of the misfortune of seeing my union with you severed by law. It's not for the loss of a throne that I mourn for you . . . for that there is no consolation, but I'm saddened by the grief you must have felt in separating yourself from your ancient companions in glory. . . . Ah! Sire, that I cannot fly to you to give you the assurance that exile can only frighten vulgar minds and that, far from diminishing a sincere attachment, Misfortune lends to it a renewed force.

According to one of her friends, Madame Junot, Joséphine had been sincere about wanting to join Napoleon in exile, and told her she wished her ex-husband would "permit my accompanying him to the island of Elba, if Maria Luisa should keep away." Junot wrote that she talked Joséphine out of going to Elba by asking what kind of reception she expected from her former in-laws, who had always been so cruel to her and were surely heading off there themselves.

The final words from Napoleon that Joséphine would have read, closing a letter he sent to her in late 1813, were, "Goodbye, my friend, let me know you're well. They say you're fattening up like a good Norman farm wife. Napoleon."

THE DAY AFTER JOSÉPHINE'S DEATH, representatives of the allies and the French Provisional Government signed the Treaty of Paris that officially ended the war. The terms were good for the losing party. Rather than trying to enforce any major territorial changes, the allies saw France restored roughly to its borders as they were in 1792, returning it to the limits of its old continental territory before these wars. To show how much they wished to distance themselves from the recent past, the allies chose not to seek major war reparations or the return of looted artworks. The French would not have to endure the humiliation of a permanent occupying army, and while they had to demobilize and yield possession of roughly fifty fortresses, they were not forbidden from rebuilding a military force. With the redrawing of borders and some territorial exchanges, more people and land would be put under French control than there had been in the time of Louis XIV.

Talleyrand was happy to let his king take credit for the treaty that he'd done so much to help draft. "No sooner than did our monarchs appear than we had peace," proclaimed the *Journal des débats* after the treaty was signed. A few days later, a long line of carriages snaked east out of Paris. Headed by Tsar Alexander, the cortege carried the last of the allied soldiers away from the French capital, save for a few Russians still convalescing in the southern suburb of Bicêtre, whose hospital's most notorious inmate had been the Marquis de Sade. The Russians had left their mark on the city. Their word for "quickly," *bistro*, for instance, had become the label for any restaurant serving the fast and simple fare that these occupying soldiers preferred.

Castlereagh also left France, sporting a rich tan acquired during the campaign. He carried a copy of the new treaty whose contents were still unknown to the British public. Guns were fired in his honor as he passed each village on his way to London, accompanied by his wife, Emily (who had shocked the other allied diplomats and their wives with her outré outfits in Paris), and their pet bulldog, Venom.

Though he received a standing ovation when he tabled the treaty in the House of Commons, the actual terms of the peace he'd helped to craft proved divisive. His opponents skewered him for allowing the French to maintain a relatively strong military presence and for failing to secure reparations or push France forcefully toward the absolute abolition of the slave trade. Castlereagh's supporters countered that Britain needed to avoid meddling in French affairs for the sake of future diplomatic and trade relations, and that the lenient treaty terms helped them make the case that the French people had called for a Bourbon restoration independently of British influence. They should congratulate themselves for their generosity in having helped their former enemies to come out of the Napoleonic wreckage stable enough to bring order to Europe and prosperity to their respective overseas empires. As one London journalist put it, "England is never so powerful as when France is strong. When the Continent trembles, her voice is heard. In her true station, she is Captain of the watch."

For a few days in June, London's diplomatic work was put on hold so that the peace could be celebrated with a massive festival, which touched every section of what was then the largest city in the world, having just passed the one million mark in population. The entire route from Dover was lit up for the visiting allied sovereigns who went in procession toward London, trailed by thousands of the war wounded, who were cheered and handed drinks by locals along the way. There were fireworks and the dancing of Scottish reels. On the Strand in central London stood an illuminated model of Napoleon at a table making a house of cards, while Wellington, looking over his shoulder, blows them down.

The allied sovereigns and their ministers agreed that they would gather in Vienna that autumn to hammer out the many issues left unresolved by the treaties of Fontainebleau and Paris and by their own internal negotiations prior to Napoleon's abdication, from the fates of the territories in present-day Germany, Italy, and the Netherlands, to islands from the Caribbean to the East Indies of Southeast Asia, to the future of Poland, at that time partitioned between Russia, Austria, and Prussia, and the Duchy of Warsaw created by Napoleon as a client state.

There was also the matter of Napoleon himself, and whether his exile on Elba was tenable. Representatives from all nations that had fought in the wars, on either side, would participate in a set of general meetings, and people were confident that all lingering diplomatic matters could be resolved by an intense burst of hard work, and that this Congress of Vienna would last no longer than a few weeks. That the conference would take place in the Habsburg capital signaled how drastically political power in Europe was shifting from Paris to the three "northern courts" of Vienna, Berlin, and Petersburg, as the French never tired of complaining.

. . .

PEOPLE ACROSS EUROPE MEANWHILE waited for bulletins from France as the Bourbon government was left to firmly establish its control. The French had shown themselves capable of great antimonarchical violence, and after Napoleon's fall, anything was possible. This wasn't a generation accustomed to any feeling of permanence. In the fiery years since 1789, France had seen an absolutist monarchy give way to a constitutional monarchy, followed by a First Republic with its National Convention backed by terror, and then on to the Directory with Napoleon as its "sword," which after Napoleon's coup gave way to the Consulate and finally the empire. "This quarter century," wrote Chateaubriand, "equaled many centuries." Now with the Bourbons, France would be stepping backward and forward at once.

In the event, the transition of power went fairly peacefully. Though some royalists engaged in scattered outbursts of score-settling, the Bourbons themselves pledged to never persecute anyone for past political actions. The columns of the official *Moniteur* once reserved for praising Napoleon were now devoted, in the same supercilious language, to praising Louis XVIII and his family. As during the Revolution, people found order in a time of transition by coming up with new names for old things. The Lycée Napoléon was reborn as the Lycée Charlemagne; the rue Impériale became the rue de la Paix; the *Journal de l'Empire* returned with a variation on its pre-Napoleonic name, as the *Journal des débats*. Writers once censored under the empire now enjoyed relative freedom to unleash their vitriol against the man no longer referred to as Napoleon, but only as Bonaparte, or even better because it was not French, "Buonaparte." Some people, rather than giving him even the slightest acknowledgment by uttering his name, preferred to talk of the usurper, the ogre, the tyrant, the Corsican, or simply "that gentleman at Elba."

14

A Ridiculous Noise

THE DAY JOSÉPHINE DIED in Paris was a festive one in Portoferraio. Townspeople gathered at the parish church for a morning prayer in honor of Cristino, their patron saint. Napoleon arrived in a golden coach, passing through twinned lines of soldiers on the short ride down from the Mulini palace. He left the service in equally theatrical style, hailed by members of the Guard who had formed a battalion square outside the church doors. Drummers beat a tattoo while shots from the forts matched the clang of church bells.

That evening by the harbor front more carriages, guards, and firepower greeted Napoleon for his reappearance. Ashamed at not having hosted a grand enough occasion to mark his landing in May, the Elbans had elected to turn their customary San Cristino feast into Napoleon's official welcome banquet. It was a pleasant night except for a bit of tension when Pons toasted to "Liberty, sun of the universe," a veiled call for Napoleon to return to his republican roots, which had once been genuine, even if he'd embraced that cause out of political pragmatism as much as ideological fervor. On her husband's signal, Madame Pons capped the speech by firing some small and until-then-ornamental bronze cannons decorating their garden patch not far from the quayside. There is no record of how Napoleon responded to Pons's jab.

Napoleon complained that his beloved "Paulette" had missed the party. Since the feast was doubling as his official welcome, he'd thought it could be trebled to include a celebration for his sister as well. By Ussher's report she should have arrived by then, but, unknown to anyone on Elba, a squall had delayed her sailing. Napoleon had considered postponing the banquet but decided that asking his subjects to reschedule their saint's day was a step too far, even for an emperor.

Conducting a postmortem on the event with Bertrand, Napoleon admitted that while logic dictated that he should have arrived at the chapel on foot alongside his general staff, he'd felt it necessary to make a "ridiculous noise" of his entrance. As he once said of his French subjects, people didn't want to see their rulers "walking in the streets," and the Elbans should be treated no differently. If he failed to show the Elbans the kinds of splendor expected from a sovereign, how should they be expected to continue believing in his sovereignty? He once defined greatness as the ability to make a "big noise. The more noise you make, the farther it will go. Laws, institutions, monuments, nations, all this passes—but the noise it makes continues to vibrate through other generations."

Pons heard that the locals had judged Napoleon's show of pomp inappropriate, especially at the solemn morning mass, though in his defense Napoleon had chosen to sit in a pew among the congregants rather than on the throne they had prepared for him. Yet Pons had seen that the Elbans, too, were capable of making their own ridiculous noise. He'd never seen them compete so fiercely with one another as they had at the banquet, where the women vied to display the most opulent silks and brightest jewels and the men made sport out of who could consume the greatest amounts of food and drink, as though Napoleon's presence had freed them to unleash their own inner emperors. While allowing that the occasional show of wealth could be good for the local tradesmen, Pons counted no more than six island families who could afford such displays. There were plans to mark Napoleon's birthday in August with a party that would make this one small beer by comparison. Pons worried that to cover the predicted expenses, Elba "would have to have produced not iron but gold."

. . .

CAMPBELL MISSED the San Cristino feast, having borrowed the brig *Swallow* to sail out into open waters in the hope of connecting with a British ship that was reportedly bound from Genoa to Sicily and carrying two senior officials. He thought that if he could make contact, these officials would have the authority to endorse his unanswered request to Castlereagh to extend his stay. But if the British ship did in fact pass on its way to Sicily, then Campbell failed to spot it. Dejected, he returned to Portoferraio on the last day of May.

As he pulled into the harbor he saw a Neapolitan sloop, *Letizia*, named for Napoleon's mother. A few hours earlier Pauline Bonaparte had disembarked, along with some members of her household staff. She'd brought her custom-built carriage aboard the sloop, and the islanders followed alongside as it carried her and her brother up the hill. "Ah! Madame," Pons overheard Napoleon telling his sister, "you might have thought that I was in some desert island with a bunch of half-savages. But look again and tell me if anyone could be better set up than I am!" The next day, on a tour of the island, Pauline told Napoleon of her ideas for improvements. She would have mirrors, clocks, and candelabras sent from Paris and some orange trees sent from Naples. She gave him a diamond necklace with which to buy another property for her sole use when she returned.

Pauline had been Napoleon's coconspirator and source of comfort since childhood. She shared in his earliest military triumphs in Italy, around the same time she married her first husband, one of Napoleon's officers, following his advice. She'd gone out of her way to make her former friend Joséphine feel unwelcome in her own home after Napoleon decided to divorce her, hosting dinner parties at Fontainebleau without inviting the chatelaine herself. When Napoleon hid himself away for a week at the Grand Trianon at Versailles after the divorce, Pauline was installed nearby at the Petit Trianon.

Following the abdication, Pauline had written to tell her mother that they should both get to Elba as soon as possible. "He seems to want [you to come] very much and he told me to tell you that," she wrote. The Bonapartes had all been granted passports and free passage to Elba. Joseph, Louis, and Jérôme

Bonaparte were then in Switzerland, and Lucien was in Rome. But Pauline would be the only one to make use of the privilege, while the others made their excuses. She complained of such behavior to her mother. "One mustn't leave the Emperor all alone. It's now when he's so unhappy that one must show him affection."

Possessed of the same quicksilver energy as her brother, she left Elba after only a single full day on the island, heading for Naples. She couldn't even be persuaded to stay for the celebration of George III's birthday that officers of the two British ships still moored at Portoferraio had planned for June 4, a curious decision for someone as fond of sailors as she was of parties. When Campbell asked about his sister's quick leavetaking, Napoleon told him Pauline had only happened to be in the area because of existing plans to visit their other sister, Caroline, in Naples. Her visit to Portoferraio was only meant as a quick stopover on the way, he said, though he was sure she would return soon.

Campbell suspected that Pauline had come carrying correspondence from family and friends, and that she might also be carrying letters to Naples from Napoleon. Their brother-in-law, Joachim Murat, knowing he couldn't hold on to his kingdom without allied support, had put on a good show of breaking ties with Napoleon and had halted all customary shipments of cattle and wheat to Elba. But Campbell recognized that Murat and Napoleon could easily be in covert contact and that Pauline might be their intermediary.

ON JUNE 4 THE CREWS of the *Curacoa* and *Swallow* invited Napoleon, his generals, and a few Elbans aboard to celebrate their king's seventy-sixth birthday. It was a tricky thing to pull off. Mindful of not upsetting anybody in port, the British officers flew the Royal Standard at mainmast, the Bourbon white at foremast, and the new Elban flag at mizzenmast. The crew of the *Dryade* returned the favor by flying the blue, red, and gold of the Royal Standard, and the magnanimous spirit spread to the crew of the *Inconstant*, which was soon flying British colors as well.

Napoleon arrived late in the proceedings, accompanied by Bertrand, Drouot, and Cambronne. Apart from lifting his hat to the captains of the

British ships, he made no ceremony of his entrance and spent much of the hour he attended the party off on his own, inspecting different parts of the boats. Before dinner he sought out Pons, who had shied away from making the first contact since they were still the middle of what Pons called their "great quarrel," prompted by his speech at the San Cristino feast. Pons presented his wife, and Napoleon praised her as an ideal mother, so singularly devoted to her "saintly duties" of childrearing. He chatted with the couple's young daughter, tickled by the fact that she had no idea who he was and spoke to him as she might to a bootblack.

Napoleon signaled to Pons that they should talk privately and asked if it was true that he objected to the party and had considered boycotting it. Pons answered yes, he thought it in poor taste to celebrate a foreign ruler in the backyard of the sovereign he'd just defeated. Napoleon countered that for now the British sailors were part of Elba's community, making this a "family gathering," and that they should respect any enlisted man's duty to celebrate his king's birthday regardless of where he happened to be stationed. But he allowed that maybe Pons was right in being wary of the British, and that the night might just have been Campbell's way of taunting him. He told Pons they must never forget that Campbell was not their friend but the representative of a government with "evil intentions" and that whatever his surface actions might be, his duty was to do harm. The British would never forgive him, Napoleon went on, for having challenged their supposed supremacy, and they still dreaded his influence, which was why they wouldn't let him be exiled in England.

It was the first time Napoleon had spoken so openly to Pons and the latter was eager to keep talking, but Napoleon said he felt rude keeping everybody waiting to start the meal. The menu's highlight was roast chicken, served on a dining table stretching the entire length of the *Swallow*. Some flags and sails had been arranged to section off the quarterdeck as a makeshift ballroom, a lone chair up on a platform at the edge of the dance floor reserved for the emperor. Pons wrote that the rest of the evening was uneventful aside from some drunken dancing and the "improprieties" of a few British officers, which scandalized some of the local women.

. . .

THE FRENCH SHIP *DRYADE* was set to sail back to the mainland the next day, carrying any citizens from the original detachment of soldiers who wished to be repatriated. The former governor Dalesme understood that he no longer had a place on Elba and decided to return to France. Napoleon assured him he would have kept him on as commander of the army if it weren't for the arrival of the more senior Cambronne, and promised that if he couldn't find suitable work with the French government he would see him placed into Marie Louise's service. Dalesme, touched by the gesture, told Pons that he would gladly "be killed a hundred times" for Napoleon. Watching him board the *Dryade,* wrote Pons, "one would think he was the one going into exile." By contrast, Dalesme's second in command, Colonel Vincent, was less sentimental about his exit. He told Pons that Napoleon could hardly disguise how little he cared about their departure and that anyone stupid enough to stay on that wretched island just so they could serve so callow a man was in for a "hard time."

That afternoon a court herald caught Napoleon on the terrace of the Mulini following the *Dryade* with his eyes as it sailed north. Once the ship was beyond the view of the naked eye he didn't bother to watch it through his spyglass but only gave it a little salute with his hand before going back inside to bark orders for his carriages, his horses, and his rowboat. He went off on another aimless ride.

That night there was a fine meal, the palace lit blue and gold by another setting sun. After dinner Napoleon paid his courtesies to his guests and retired to his room. The court herald whispered to Pons that he pitied the emperor, who seemed to think they couldn't all see him "suffering through his smile."

SUMMER

15

THE MORE UNFAVORABLY DOES
HE APPEAR

THE SUMMER STARTED WITH a series of small crises. The first had roots dating back to before Napoleon's arrival. Months earlier a privateer had seized a British merchant ship sailing from Malta and brought it into Portoferraio to wait out the wartime blockade. After taking control of Elba, Napoleon had exercised his sovereign rights to claim the seized ship, and its cargo was kept under armed guard. Now Board of Health inspectors were calling for the ship to be brought to Livorno, where it would undergo the standard quarantine. Livorno served as the region's main lazaretto, where people and cargo sailing from ports prone to plague could be purified before being cleared to trade at other ports. But Napoleon refused to send the ship to Livorno, so the inspectors retaliated by putting Elba under a twenty-five-day quarantine enforced by all surrounding ports.

Napoleon was certain this protest would end quickly, and in any case, as he told Campbell, Portoferraio would eventually replace Livorno as the main lazaretto, now that it was under his control. He boasted that he would also make it the region's key port of trade as well, and said that the jealous health officials had only attempted this bit of "commercial intrigue" to punish him for wanting to establish Portoferraio's primacy. Campbell failed to make sense of Napoleon's rejection of "long-established practice although it cuts off his communication with every other part of the world except by clandestine means, to his own loss and inconvenience as well as that of every other person in this island."

At Napoleon's request he sailed to Livorno to play peacemaker. The quarantine restrictions kept him from landing, so he met with the health officials on his own ship. They confirmed Campbell's suspicions that they actually had no interest in punishing Napoleon, nor did they want to be cut off from trade with Elba. They saw no threat of Livorno's ever being surpassed, since its economy was so much stronger and its harbor was far busier and better located than that of Portoferraio. They explained that they were only following protocol and trying to avoid an outbreak of plague. They warned Campbell that the "mercantile world" wouldn't put up with Napoleon's selfishness, and by working in tandem they could easily starve out Elba, which was so dependent on foreign grain and other imported staples.

Campbell relayed all of this to Napoleon, and within days he quietly dropped his grandiose plans for Portoferraio's harbor. The health inspectors lifted their quarantine, the seas reopened, and although the bounty of the seized ship remained in Napoleon's possession, the little lazaretto war was over. It's possible Napoleon orchestrated the dispute to momentarily stop ships from coming in and out of Elba while creating an excuse to get Campbell away from the island, either as a test run for an eventual escape or because he planned an *actual* escape before losing his resolve. But there's no evidence he was seriously contemplating leaving Elba at that early stage of the exile.

The second crisis involved the miners of Rio and started when Napoleon asked Pons to assign his workers to clearing some of the island's roads, telling him that they should tackle this work after finishing their days at the mines. Pons refused. Such a workload would only exhaust people to the point where neither mining nor roadwork could be done effectively. But word of Napoleon's unreasonable request reached the miners nonetheless, and they took it as an insult. Morale was already low in Rio, where miners were on course to produce far less in the second half of 1814 than they had in the same period over the past two years. The town teetered toward outright rebellion after its mayor, looking to ingratiate himself with Napoleon, suggested that some rotten flour stored at Portoferraio, which the soldiers refused to eat, could be mixed with unspoiled flour to make bread for the miners. Napoleon liked the idea, which resulted in a few hundred miners sick with food poisoning.

The worst of the summer crises stemmed from the fact that taxes hadn't been levied on Elba for nearly a year because of the war. Drouot sent criers from village to village to announce that all back taxes were now owed to Napoleon and that anyone failing to pay by July 1 would face heavy consequences. The island's contributions to the French treasury had always been steady if meager, amounting to about thirty times less than what other departments might pay, and French tax officials had never encountered resistance from the Elbans. But the islanders had never had to come up with such a large payment in so little time.

To Campbell this was another of Napoleon's selfish and poorly conceived ideas. The announcement of the tax deadline "occasioned unusual outcry and supplications, but without avail. Such is the poverty of the inhabitants that most of them will be obliged to sell their houses, furniture, and clothing in order to raise money." Riding past a village one day, Campbell witnessed a tax official being shouted down by the inhabitants, and screaming that he would return with a hundred soldiers of the Guard to be quartered among the population until all taxes were collected.

The miners of Rio refused outright to pay any taxes. Napoleon sent Pons to deliver a proclamation on his behalf, which said that anyone failing to pay would be immediately fired from the mines. Following Napoleon's instructions, Pons told his workers that just as he held a father's affection for them, so did he feel "all the devotion of a good son" for the emperor. Napoleon had quietly granted him authority to draw from the treasury to front funds to anyone who needed help meeting their tax requirements, so long as they agreed to have the amount deducted from future paychecks. In the end only twenty workers applied to Pons for loans and the Rio taxes were collected without issue.

But a much fiercer rebellion took place at the hilltop village of Capoliveri, which already had such a reputation for intransigence that a dozen policemen were dispatched to escort the tax collector. Pons described the people of Capoliveri as "the dregs of the Elban population." The villagers greeted the arriving official and his policemen with horns and clanging pots and a representative announced their refusal to pay, citing as their reason that it could not be legally proved that the tax collector wasn't an impostor working independently of Napoleon to line his own pockets. Then the villagers chased the collector and the overwhelmed gendarmes down the hill and out of town.

The next day two emissaries chosen from the local population returned to announce that Capoliveri had twenty-four hours to pay. They said that Napoleon demanded a list of the rebellion's chief instigators. But the twenty-four-hour deadline came and went. Pons thought that Napoleon chose the wrong two men to serve as his emissaries, since they lacked the experience and "public esteem" to handle the situation. For the time being Napoleon took no further action against Capoliveri.

Campbell thought that after only two months of Napoleon's rule, Elba already lay on the verge of a general uprising. "Napoleon appears to become more unpopular on the island every day, for every act seems guided by avarice and a feeling of personal interest with a total disregard to that of others," he wrote. "The inhabitants perceive that none of his schemes tend to ameliorate their situation and that while the blessings of peace have restored to their neighbours commerce, a ready sale for the produce of their labours, exemption from contributions and from military service, they derive none of these advantages by Napoleon's arrival among them."

He no longer heard the hails for the emperor as he once had, despite Bertrand's obvious efforts "to give popular effect to every movement." All around the island people were railing "against his oppression and injustice. . . . The more he is brought upon a level with others and the more the opportunities of observing him, the more unfavorably does he appear." Campbell worried that unless Napoleon acted with more "discretion" going forward, only "the military force of his Guards" could keep him safe from total revolution, and he wondered if Napoleon was in danger of losing the loyalty of his soldiers as well:

Even the attachment of his Guards to him diminishes daily. They will soon tire of having expatriated themselves, and as all the officers were confident of his being called to the throne of France in a very few months they perceived daily that there's less prospect of realizing the expectations formed upon these grounds.

He'd heard a soldier comparing Elba to a foxhole, and a second to a desert, and a third, after being assigned to settle Pianosa, had privately told Campbell he would rather "blow his brains out" than stay there.

With his ears already pricked for any troubling talk, Campbell would continue to hear similar grumbling from the locals and low-ranking soldiers throughout the summer. And some of his men did desert, while those who stayed endured occasional abuse, especially at the hands of Cambronne, who, lacking action, had sunk into a depression and would vent his frustration by slapping clumsy troops with the edge of his saber. But Campbell underestimated the loyalty that Napoleon inspired in his soldiers, especially the veterans of the Old Guard. Even after the Russian disaster and its half million casualties, they still loved him. A slap or two during drill in some sunny square on a Tuscan island was nothing compared to the things they had seen. As another famous general once said of Napoleon, "Those he made suffer most, the soldiers, were the very ones who were most faithful to him."

{ 16 }

UBICUMQUE FELIX NAPOLEON

RENOVATING THE MULINI became an obsession. At five each morning
Napoleon would wander the grounds to supervise the work, dressed simply in
silk stockings and shoes without buckles. If he felt like dirtying his hands he
would play for a while at hammering, sawing, or painting and enjoyed the occasional noonday meal alongside his laborers, sharing hard bread and boiled
eggs. Many summer nights found him still occupied with his tinkering. He
grew a large garden on the Mulini's craggy cliffside terrace, as though heed-
ing the advice of that other famous exile that the best way to make life support-
able was to tend one's garden. He had a giant N done in heliotropes trimmed
with military precision. Among the hedges visitors would sometimes spot a
mischievous monkey, nicknamed Jénar, who served as the palace mascot.

Drouot was tasked with shielding the Mulini from the realities of island
life. *Bada di sotto!* (Look out below!) was a common refrain in town, as people
emptied their pots out their windows through webs of clotheslines and linen.
Drouot imposed a fine for anyone caught continuing the filthy custom and
gave property owners two months to dig latrines that would be emptied each
night at a far-off location, warning that failure to comply would result in a
"sanitary tax." He had the barracks whitewashed and fitted with proper

drainage, the thin path from the main square paved, and he arranged for a crew to clean the Mulini's lanes eight times a day. He instructed his officers to claim any of the town's public gardens to tend as they saw fit.

From outside, the boxy and unadorned Mulini gave the appearance of modest prosperity. Inside, visitors were greeted with a bit more color and flair. The walls were pink, highlighted by bright green shutters. Napoleon had sent some soldiers to Piombino to raid the palace there, which had been occupied by his sister Elisa and her husband, the former Prince of Lucca, until their reign had fallen alongside his own. He assumed that they had left in a hurry and packed lightly. His men pilfered whatever they thought looked good, and no one in Piombino felt bold enough to stop them. Napoleon added to that expedition's haul after a shipment of goods belonging to Pauline Bonaparte and the Prince of Borghese happened to be held up in poor weather at the docks at Livorno on its way to Rome. Napoleon sent troops to seize the cargo, joking to Pons that this way things would stay "in the family." Even with this booty and help from Ussher, who drew from the *Undaunted*'s provisions to outfit the Mulini's larder, Napoleon's palace was still relatively bare and sparsely furnished. Elba lacked for fine materials and luxury craftspeople. The effect was underwhelming. One valet wrote that the sofa in the main salon had "so little stuffing that one could feel the cross pieces and the straps."

The villa did have one great jewel. Before sailing from Fréjus, Bertrand bought a multivolume collection compiled by the famed linguist Baron Silvestre de Sacy, one of the first scholars to try deciphering the Rosetta Stone. The Mulini library's holdings multiplied as more cases full of books arrived with the battalion of the Old Guard, while others were sourced on the cheap from libraries and estate sales around Europe. Aside from the floor polisher, only Napoleon's secretary Deschamps was allowed to enter this sanctuary. Deschamps had to verify that each volume had arrived in good condition before Napoleon would allow Drouot to send payment for a shipment. The approved books were rebound and stamped with an imperial eagle or an N.

Napoleon's way of apprehending the world was inherently literary. He fed on books like food, reading for pleasure, but always looking for some insight that could help guide him to bettering himself and his world, which was why he was so fond of history and the lives of rulers. He grew up in a house with a thousand-volume library that likely numbered among the greatest collections on Corsica. Among his collection at the Mulini he prized a forty-volume set of fairy tales. There were books of English grammar and a few study guides that placed French stories side by side with their English translations. He amused himself by seeking out works that had been censored during his reign and later said he usually failed to see why the police had suppressed them in the first place.

In his letters to Marie Louise, Napoleon claimed that all the work on the Mulini was being done solely for her comfort and for that of the child he persisted in calling the King of Rome, although with his abdication the boy could only technically claim the title of Prince of Parma. But Campbell was already doubtful that there would ever be a happy family reunion. "He has not made any such arrangements as evince any expectation of his being joined by Marie Louise," he wrote, "nor has he mentioned her name in any way." The laborers stopped calling the rooms they were working on the empress's quarters and switched to calling them the princess's, anticipating that Pauline Bonaparte would be their occupant.

With the renovations nearing completion, Napoleon turned his attentions to Porto Longone. He'd been charmed by the seaside village after admiring a hillside villa where two huge carob trees had provided shade for a table laid for sixty guests. He thought of setting up his own tree-lined aerie nearby in the former chambers of the garrison commander at the old Spanish citadel. It was a tough climb up to the fortress, so Napoleon had a zigzagging road laid that allowed him to enter the grounds by carriage. But he dropped the Porto Longone project, telling Pons he wanted some place farther out "in the country."

He and Pons traveled to Monte Capanne, high above the northern town of Marciana. There they met the hermit who occupied a small dwelling next to the centuries-old chapel devoted to the holy virgin of Montserrat perched up in the rocks, its grotto fed by the crystal waters trickling down from the peak. The hermit had planted a few trees and some vines. He showed Napoleon and Pons a fig tree whose tentacular branches grew back down into the ground and took root there, so that a circle of smaller fig trees now surrounded it. He pointed to a peach tree yielding fruit so huge that each one seemed a small miracle. He motioned to the mountain of Cape Calamita in the distance and described its magnetic properties. Napoleon ventured that the place must look wonderful in a storm, surrounded by heavy clouds and lightning. The hermit answered that thunderstorms were frequent but with the protection of the holy virgin the hermitage had never been struck. Pointing to the surrounding peaks, Napoleon countered that these "splendid lightning conductors" might also have been of some help. They went over to the church to light a prayer candle. After lunch Napoleon drifted off for a few hours in the open air. Later he went to sit by himself on a large rock at the edge of a sloping hill, from which he would have seen Corsica.

Down at Marciana that evening he told Pons that these had been among the happiest hours he'd ever spent. He had plans drawn up for a mountain retreat, demarcating where his house would sit in relation to the hermitage and specifying how it would look. But he soon abandoned this project as well, telling Pons, "I'm not rich enough to achieve such a fantasy."

For a moment he eyed Pons's own house in Rio, which overlooked the ocean and had a gorgeous garden. It was the finest dwelling on the whole island, at least by Pons's own estimation, but Napoleon eventually elected to "deprive himself" of this house for the sake of appearances, telling Pons he didn't want the Elbans to think he was "persecuting" the mining administrator. Next he turned his attentions to a mildew-stained farmhouse in San Martino, a valley with oaks and brushwood climbing the foothills, where there were a few vineyards and the high ground provided views of Portoferraio and the ocean. Napoleon paid 180,000 francs for the house, likely with substantial help from the proceeds of some of Pauline's jewelry collection. Pons thought he overpaid.

A sculptor brought over from Carrara to set up a school of art was told to abandon that project so he could dedicate himself to decorating the new property. An illustration of two doves joined by a string whose knot threatens to tighten the farther the birds fly apart adorned the drawing room ceiling and was said to represent the emperor and empress. The walls of Napoleon's bedroom were painted to make it look like a tent, and the hallways were plastered with engravings taken from illustrated books on Egypt. The villa centered on a large hall, the Salle des Pyramides, made in accordance with Napoleon's orders for a central room "paved with marble, having an octagonal basin in the centre with a fountain in the middle, as in Egypt." The ceiling was painted with signs of the Zodiac and the walls with wild scenes of the desert, full of pyramids, columns, hieroglyphs, minarets, palm trees, and charging Mameluke warriors.

The Egyptian campaign clearly loomed large while Napoleon was in exile, perhaps because in the desert he'd experienced a similar sense of solitude and removal from French affairs. He was sent there in 1798 in part as a kind of banishment, a way for the five directors then heading the government to keep him far from the center of power just at the moment that people across France were reading more regularly about this young upstart and his military exploits, thanks to the increasing spread of print media. Ever since that campaign, Egypt had served as Napoleon's fantasy space, a focus for his romantic imagination. It was where, as he wrote, "I found myself freed from the obstacles of an irksome civilization. I was full of dreams. I saw myself founding a religion, marching into Asia, riding an elephant, a turban on my head and in my hand a new Koran that I would have composed to suit my need." To the veterans of the Old Guard the San Martino house prompted memories of another distant locale; they dubbed the property Saint-Cloud, the name of the suburban chateau overlooking the Seine west of Paris that had been the site of Napoleon's 1799 coup and later one of his main seats of power.

Napoleon found a job for a young Elban woman of limited means, who became the property's gatekeeper during the renovations. As a valet described, she was "sort of a Napoleonic fanatic, and as such was wholly devoted to His Majesty," and each time Napoleon arrived at the gates she sang him a new ditty composed in his honor. He called her "his madwoman."

Napoleon pushed his soldiers too hard on the Saint-Cloud renovations and after a few days of heavy work some of the grenadiers refused to continue, complaining that it was beneath their station. Napoleon understood that he'd insulted them and reworded his directive in the form of a personal request to his soldiers in a time of need, rather than an official order. He pushed back the deadlines to give the men more time for rest. The work resumed without further issue, but for the sake of appearances Napoleon sent a few of the insub-ordinates to Pianosa and the ringleaders back to France.

Napoleon lost interest in the San Martino property almost as quickly as he had the others and slept there only a few nights in all. He showed the same restlessness in France, where he'd once overseen as many as forty-seven pal-aces, and was shuffling between his main residences at Malmaison, the Tuile-ries, Saint-Cloud, Fontainebleau, and Compiègne (but never Versailles, tainted by its Old Regime associations), as though away from battle he needed to mimic the flurry of a campaign. The results were invariably disappointing. "I've seen no chateau, no palace, that can please me," he once said.

And yet it was at San Martino on a painted column on the wall of the Salle des Pyramides that someone, presumably the emperor, scrawled *Ubicumque felix Napoleon* (Napoleon can be happy anywhere).

SIROCCO

ON CERTAIN DAYS WHEN high Saharan winds blew in from the south, a note of despair seeped into Campbell's journal entries. He busied himself by blackening pages, "keeping my journal to assist my memory, writing my despatches and taking copies of them, obtaining information from a variety of parties in Italy." But he found even these simple tasks difficult because of his wounds. "I have no one to assist me, and when I write long there is a wearisome feeling which becomes very unpleasant from the muscles in my back not having yet acquired their tone." That summer was the hottest anyone on Elba could remember in years.

Campbell still hadn't received any word from Castlereagh giving him more insight into his role on Elba or to say whether the Foreign Office would devote any more resources to supporting his mission. A single British ship, the sloop *Partridge*, had been assigned to patrol the region, but it was based out of Livorno and only included Elba as one part of its longer regular cruise between Genoa and Civitavecchia. Any ship that came to Elba was subjected to quarantine and passport inspection, but once cleared its passengers could move about however they wished, and Napoleon was free to receive visitors as he liked. Campbell could hardly keep track of the emperor's meager entourage, let alone anyone else who might be roaming the island.

It was his French neighbors on Elba who often updated Campbell about pertinent developments on the continent, though sometimes they passed along false or misinterpreted reports. "Bertrand showed me in one of the French journals a paragraph wherein it was stated that the rank of colonel on the continent and in Elba has been conferred on me," Campbell wrote in June. "I am induced to believe that this may have been copied from the *London Gazette* and that therefore my remaining here is the pleasure of the Prince Regent, although I have not received any orders to that effect." In fact the *Gazette* had only included Campbell's name among a long list of officers and had given his existing rank, "Colonel in the Army." There was no mention of Elba.

Campbell's insecurities prompted him toward all sorts of speculation. "I have reason to believe that a Neapolitan officer has been here privately," he wrote in his journal. "A person in that uniform was seen to enter Napoleon's house about two weeks ago, and from my not being able to trace him it appears that pains have been taken to conceal the circumstance." He wondered if his own servant might be a spy in Napoleon's service.

In some ways Campbell would have felt his exile more painfully than Napoleon did. Whenever he visited the Mulini he was viewed with suspicion, and the Elbans never really understood why he was on the island in the first place. Ussher's departure left him no countrymen with whom to commiserate, and there weren't any officially accredited British diplomats nearby, as none were yet posted to Italy. Campbell dealt mostly with agents and go-betweens.

Most frustrating of all was that he still failed to see any real logic, pattern, or overarching goal driving his counterpart's actions. "Napoleon continues in the same state of perpetual movement, busy with constant schemes, none of which, however, tend to ameliorate the condition of his subjects," he wrote. He didn't seem to have any grand plan but was instead preoccupied with pursuing several pet projects at once. He had peasants smoothing out the roads where he liked to ride in his carriage; he had soldiers knocking down old houses to gather materials with which to improve his various properties; and he had plans to plant three thousand trees in Portoferraio to make a leafy promenade from the city gates. There were rumblings that he was going to triple the tax rate to pay for all his new projects. None of it made any sense to Campbell.

A FIRST DETACHMENT of soldiers sailed over to Pianosa on the *Inconstant*, bringing cannons, mortars, and ammunition, two cows, and thirty chickens. They had been given enough biscuit, brandy, and wine to tide them over for a few weeks and were told to slaughter all the wild goats they found to make way for future crops. The goal was to establish crops in soil more fertile than on Elba, which would be helped by the building of an irrigation works.

Napoleon wanted this first round of settlers to spend their first days on Pianosa in some caves that had been used as tombs, figuring it would make them work harder on building their barracks. His orders specified that the sappers should have the caves "cleaned out, first lighting some fires to burn the insects." This was hardly the limit to his level of specificity when it came to colonizing Pianosa. He wrote orders naming the priest of the Elban town of Campo as curate of a newly created Pianosa parish. "He will take his vestments and holy vessels and say mass in the open air until the church is ready," Napoleon ordered. "The village will be built according to designs submitted to my approval."

Napoleon declared that Pianosa now belonged entirely to him since there was no specific landholder on record. And although it was already too late to plant for the year's harvest, he set strict rules for future yields, which would be transported to Elba to be sold at prices set by himself. He subjected the Neapolitan coral fishermen who traditionally worked around Pianosa to a new tax, which was to be paid toward an "office of public works" that had yet to be built.

Having brought his wife and child over with him and not very keen to have them sleep in a cave full of interred bodies, Pianosa's new commanding officer, Major Gottmann, ordered his lieutenant to have the sappers build him a house before seeing to any other work. The lieutenant answered that Napoleon had made clear that arming the battery was the first order of business and had specified that they should complete this task no more than forty-eight hours after landing. He added that it was common sense to make this a priority since they could all be killed by pirates if they failed to set guns up before nightfall. Fists were raised, but eventually Gottmann yielded.

The next few days brought fierce storms that kept Pianosa cut off from Elba while supplies dwindled. The soldiers made due with a few slaughtered goats and shellfish scraped from the rocks. They ran out of wine. When the weather cleared, Drouot sent over some sheep, cows, chickens, and pigs, as well as a few doors and locks and hourglasses he found in a junk heap at Portoferraio. When Napoleon heard the first discouraging reports from Pianosa he told Drouot that he couldn't understand "what all the complaints are about," and so they sailed across to see things for themselves. Another storm kept them on board their ship overnight.

Napoleon would soon lose interest in seeing Pianosa properly settled. A short while later, Major Gottmann suffered a breakdown in Portoferraio, standing in the middle of a main road and raving complaints about Napoleon and Pianosa until Bertrand came and threatened him with arrest. Pons thought that Napoleon had actually conceived the whole Pianosa debacle solely as a make-work project to keep the unstable Gottmann away from Portoferraio after several complaints about his conduct.

IN THE EARLY YEARS of Napoleon's career, conquest, expansion, mobilizations, and reinforcements had been his most pressing concerns, but in the second half, dynastic rule, monuments, and a young second wife expressed his need for legacy. On Elba, denied any chance for territorial gain, he focused on the building of things and institutions and homes and laws that would survive him, a tremendous effort to fill his limited space with as much time as possible.

{ 18 }

SULTRY CONFINEMENT

IN EARLY JULY, Campbell left Elba for a short trip to the Tuscan coast. He gave no warning to anyone in Napoleon's entourage and the only person he told about his plans was a man named Ricci, who had been the island's British representative before the French annexation years earlier, and managed to stay on despite the regime change. Campbell asked him to write if anything important happened while he was away. He made no other arrangements for keeping watch over Napoleon.

No one officially controlled Campbell's movements. But he wrestled with his decision to leave nonetheless, arguing with himself in his journal that the travel was necessary because it would

> relieve my mind and prove a very acceptable release from the sultry confinement of Elba, besides assisting me in my public duties, which luckily do not require my banishing myself entirely in that island. . . . The evident restlessness of Napoleon's disposition, his plans for sending out officers to various parts of Italy in order to recruit soldiers clandestinely, there being no British Minister in Italy, and indeed scarcely a public and recognized agent between Vienna and

Sicily—all this made me anxious to compare my suspicions with what information I could obtain on the Continent.

After docking at Livorno, Campbell traveled to the thermal baths at Lucca, seeking relief from his wounds and treatment for his "increasing deafness." Next, in Florence, he met with an Austrian general, Count Stahremberg, who commanded forces throughout much of northern Italy. He showed Campbell some letters from Napoleon to various relatives that his agents had intercepted. The letters were unremarkable, which Stahremberg thought was the point; he was, wrote Campbell, "convinced they were sent merely to blind their other correspondence, carried on through more direct and clandestine channels."

In Florence, Campbell was watched closely by a French diplomat, Jean-Guillaume, baron Hyde de Neuville, a devoted royalist who had returned to France after nearly a decade in exile in the United States. Louis XVIII had posted him to Florence to gather information about Napoleon's conduct on Elba, though his official mission was to oversee "the suppression of the Barbary pirates in the Mediterranean." Before leaving for his post, he'd met with his old friend the British admiral Sidney Smith in London. "Don't you think that before Napoleon left Fontainebleau he looked at a map?" Smith had asked him. "Is the distance between Elba and the southern coast of France of any significance to a man who has marched from one end of Europe to another?"

Hyde de Neuville's memoirs reveal that Campbell's trip to the mainland offered more than medical treatment and work. He saw Campbell several times at soirées hosted by the Countess of Albany, who had set up in Florence after the death of her husband, Bonnie Prince Charlie. On one of these nights, a mysterious Italian noblewoman, the Contessa Miniaci, captured Campbell's attentions. Hyde de Neuville wrote that no one ever learned much about the "ravishing" contessa's origins. She spoke many languages and seemed to know everyone in Florence worth knowing, but no one could say where she came from. Campbell was especially attentive to Miniaci. "Each time he came from Elba he brought her the latest news," wrote Hyde de Neuville, who hinted in his memoir that Miniaci was a Bonapartist agent and that she seduced

Campbell to recruit him to that cause. Little is known about her. She could have been working for any one of the allied powers, or for the Bourbons, or for Napoleon, or for no one at all.

Campbell requested a change of assignment shortly after meeting Miniaci, writing to a senior officer to ask if he could be posted in a diplomatic capacity somewhere on the Tuscan mainland from where he would be available to travel to Elba as needed. He tried to convince himself of the soundness of this request in his journal, writing that Napoleon's

> schemes begin to connect themselves so openly with the neighbor-
> ing continent, and my information from Elba is so very detailed and
> correct, I think the spirit of my duties will for the present be better
> fulfilled by not shutting myself up in quarantine.

Campbell's association with Napoleon made him an object of fascination on the mainland. Playing at cards one night in Florence with the grand duke of Tuscany and his daughters, he fielded "some questions of curiosity about Napoleon," as he recalled, and passed along the emperor's respects to the duke. Hyde de Neuville thought Campbell showed an unusual and dangerous enthusiasm for Napoleon. He could tell that Campbell would have made a capable enough commander in the field, but in the salons and ballrooms of Florence, among Swedish consuls, Russian generals, and Austrian counts, Campbell struck him as a man out of place, "mixed up in major diplomatic affairs."

Campbell's tour then took him to Rome to meet with Pius VII, who received him lying in bed with a pillow propped behind his back. He told Campbell that with all the turmoil in the Kingdom of Naples and the closeness of Bonaparte family members to Elba, these were uneasy times for the Holy See. His officials were working furiously to overturn all inroads made by the French, suspending the Napoleonic Code and reinstating feudal rights and traditional tribunals. They had even stopped street lighting and vaccinations in their bid to return to old ways. Italian clergymen were reclaiming properties and resuming their former practices, and most days of the week saw some kind of procession, church festival, or religious illumination. Church officials had resumed banning books, including the work of Machiavelli, which had once circulated freely, and innkeepers were pressured to supply names of anyone seen violating fast days.

Campbell was disturbed by what he saw and heard during his Italian travels. Many people felt that whatever progressive gains had been made in the past years now risked being undone because of the power vacuum left by Napoleon's fall. Campbell wrote that

> the public spirit in this part of Italy is not tranquil. For, notwithstanding there was an universal and violent dislike to the government of Bonaparte, the people view it now, when past, with less horror. . . . All possible means are taken to disseminate the idea of Bonaparte's future return to influence and power, so that the impression becomes only too general.

Campbell learned that Murat had added fifteen thousand men to his army since returning to Naples and that all sorts of demobbed soldiers, deserters, and adventurers were heading south to join him. An agent informed Campbell of the arrest of a family in Livorno whose members had been carrying lists of men pledging to serve Napoleon, six hundred names in all, and of an Elban officer caught recruiting soldiers in the same town. Campbell now suspected that another officer who had recently made a big noise about quitting Elba because he missed his family in the Piedmont region had in fact been sent there for recruiting purposes. For now, all he could do in his position was hope Napoleon's agents would be watched "until sufficient proofs can be obtained of their employment," as he wrote in his journal.

He sailed back to Portoferraio and had a quick talk with Bertrand but then set off again for Livorno because Bertrand had told him Napoleon's mother had just arrived there, bound for Elba, and Campbell wanted to get there in time to offer his services to ferry her across. He borrowed the British ship *Grasshopper.*

A few days later in Livorno he connected with Letizia Bonaparte, known as Madame Mère. He liked her right off, finding her "very pleasant and unaffected . . . handsome, of middle size, with a good figure and fresh colour." One of the Mulini's valets would add that Madame Mère "must have been a beauty of the first rank in her youth," for she had wonderful cheekbones, he thought, though now rouged to a level that "did not harmonize with her age." She'd traveled from Rome incognito, but by the time Campbell walked with her from her inn to his waiting ship the townspeople had guessed her identity and hooted and whistled at her as she passed. She hadn't helped her cause by stiffing some local musicians who, following the tradition of greeting any notable arrival to town with a song, had serenaded her at the inn; custom dictated that she return the gesture with a small gift of money, but she seemed to care little for the practice.

A courier handed Campbell a letter as he was about to set sail, dated two weeks earlier. It was a brief message from Castlereagh to say that he'd received all of his dispatches and had shown them to the prince regent and that Campbell should

> continue to consider yourself as British resident in Elba, without assuming any further official character than that in which you are already received, and that you would pursue the same line of conduct and communication with this department.

Campbell dined alongside Letizia Bonaparte during the crossing, seated on plush couches that had been arranged for them on deck. She was keen to talk about all of the Bonaparte siblings. She'd given birth thirteen times before being widowed at age thirty, and eight of her children were still living. "Louis [the fifth oldest] seems to be a great favourite of hers," wrote Campbell. "His picture is on her snuff-box. She said he'd written several romances, which she admired, and was sure would be generally esteemed, such as would be fit for young ladies to read. She spoke of his fortune as being small although he did not spend money either on play or women."

When Campbell asked after the health of the young empress, Madame Mère spoke of her daughter-in-law with "many sighs and expressions of great regard, as if her separation from Napoleon was not voluntary on her part."

19

THE ONE-EYED COUNT

MARIE LOUISE PASSED THE first weeks of summer shut away in the Schönbrunn Palace. She'd arrived in late May after a winding, monthlong journey from France by way of Switzerland, which nearly mimicked her bridal route in reverse. At one point she passed within eight miles of Paris, close enough to see the golden dome of the Invalides church. On reaching Vienna she'd gone to her bedroom in the west wing of Schönbrunn, where a portrait of her husband still hung. "What a heartrending fate mine is!" she wrote that night to a friend. "To slip out of the Emperor's hands and leave poor France! God alone knows how great is my sorrow! How weak and powerless I am in this whirlwind of plotting and treachery!"

She suspected that many of Napoleon's letters weren't reaching her and knew to use subterfuge when writing to him. Early in June she employed the help of a Polish officer attached to her court, who promised he could get a message through undetected. "I only wish your letter could come by means which seem as safe as these," she wrote to Napoleon. "I need them so badly." She said she was certain that a plot was being hatched to wrest Parma from her rightful possession and that her father was trying to keep her from leaving

Vienna. She promised that she would find some way to get to Aix-les-Bains by feigning illness and that she would take their son as well.

She kept mostly to herself at Schönbrunn, just beyond the city proper. Her attendant Baron Méneval was never far from her side, and she could also rely on her ladies-in-waiting, as well as her son's governess, Madame de Montesquiou. When she tired of this cloistered company, Marie Louise would visit with her sympathetic grandmother Queen Marie-Caroline of Naples, who listened patiently to her complaints. The older woman considered Napoleon her worst enemy, a villain who had once taken all her property and was the inheritor of the revolution that had killed her sister, Marie Antoinette. But she also believed in the sanctity of marriage and told her granddaughter that she must fight to keep hers intact. "If I were in your place," she said, "I should tie my sheets to a window and escape."

IN THE END, a daring midnight escape wasn't required. Instead, Marie Louise simply wore her father down, persuading him to let her travel to Aix-les-Bains for the good of her health, although he insisted that his grandson remain in Vienna. Francis secured permission from Louis XVIII for her safe passage through France by promising that she would be under strict medical supervision, that her convalescence would last no more than six weeks, and that she wouldn't bring her son with her into French territory.

Before leaving the castle, Marie Louise received a letter from Bertrand that gave her the first real details of her husband's life on Elba. She replied directly to Napoleon, alluding to Bertrand's letter, and telling him the update had pleased her immensely. She was thrilled to hear he was looking for a country house to complement his main residence. "Do please keep a little corner in it for me," she wrote. "I hope you'll let me be your agent for the plants and flowers; people declared it was most unjust of them not to let you have such things sent from Paris." Because Bertrand's letter said they were planning to send horses to meet her at Parma (where they assumed she would soon be headed), she told them to hold off on that for now. She wasn't sure she would be able to feed them all, she said, since she was trying to "live as economically as possible."

She adopted a conciliatory tone when it came to family matters, telling Napoleon that Francis had

> anticipated my every wish. He told me there was not the least diffi-
> culty about my going to the spa, but advised me leave my son here
> for the time being . . . as I was going on to the French frontier it
> might be thought that I was wanting to disturb the peace, which
> might involve both me and my son in a certain amount of
> unpleasantness. . . . I know that he couldn't be in safer hands than he
> is here. . . . I can't tell you often enough how good my father is being
> to me.

Around this time, a popular French caricature showed a mean-faced boy, the King of Rome, wielding a hangman's noose in front of a shadowy Napoleonic bust adorned with what could be the ears of an ass or the horns of a cuckold. "It's papa's necktie," reads the caption.

On the first of July, Marie Louise traveled toward France, under the name of the Duchess of Colorno, which she took from the site of a royal summer residence in Parma. It was hardly possible for her and her thirty-three attendants to travel unnoticed, but she wanted to sidestep the political implications of still calling herself empress as she ventured into Bourbon lands, and she hoped a lower profile could save her from too many social engagements. "Receptions weary me so and are so boring," she wrote to Napoleon from the road.

Yet she made a point to visit her Bonaparte relations on the way down to Aix-les-Bains. In Munich, she dined with Napoleon's stepson Eugène de Beauharnais and his Bavarian princess wife, Augusta, who had quietly withdrawn from public life after Eugène's nine-year tenure as viceroy of Italy ended shortly after Napoleon's abdication. At Payerne she visited the unhappy Jérôme Bonaparte, the former king of Westphalia, whose wife had just been robbed of the jewelry collection meant to ensure their future. And at the Château de Prangins on Lake Geneva she shared a meal with Joseph Bonaparte, who according to Caulaincourt had tried to rape her the last time they had seen one another.

When she reached Aix-les-Bains at midmonth she set up in a villa nestled above the thermal springs whose previous guests had been Napoleon's first wife, Joséphine, and her daughter, Hortense, a visit that ended tragically when one of the ladies-in-waiting had slipped on a little bridge above a waterfall and fallen to her death.

Marie Louise was joined at the spa town by an Austrian general named Adam von Neipperg, who had left a cushy position at Pavia to serve as escort to the archduchess. He'd come on secret orders from Metternich:

> With all necessary tact, the Count von Neipperg must turn the Duchess of Colorno away from all ideas of a journey to Elba, a journey which would greatly upset the paternal feelings of His Majesty, who cherishes the most tender wishes for the well-being of his well-loved daughter. He must not fail therefore to try by any means whatsoever to dissuade her from such a project.

The roguish general, a champion duelist and brilliant musician, had ample means with which to dissuade the duchess from hurrying to see her husband. He wore a black silk patch to cover the loss of an eye, but, as Marie Louise's majordomo Méneval wrote, the wound "rather suited the *ensemble* of his face, which had a martial character," and was framed by thick locks of curly blond hair. He could be equally charming in a host of languages. Not yet forty, he was already the father of five children with his former mistress, who had recently become his wife after the death of her first husband, who happened to be Neipperg's best friend. Before leaving for Aix-les-Bains, Neipperg had bet his wife that within a few months he would have a new mistress, the archduchess.

He quickly pushed Méneval out of the way to establish himself as Marie Louise's main handler. He saw to it that her apartments were comfortable and orderly and had her piano tuned by an expert. Mornings he would row her out on Lac du Bourget and afternoons he would take her for walks around the town's main square under the benevolent spirit of Diana, the huntress, to whom a small temple in the square had been devoted. Nights he accompanied her on the keyboard as she sang Mozart.

A French spy assigned to watch Marie Louise was convinced that all of the frolicking was mere distraction from the fact that she'd come to Aix-les-Bains to stir up popular sentiment for Napoleon. She had, after all, arrived at the resort in a carriage still bedecked with Bonaparte arms, and the spy had yet to see her actually taking the cure. "I just can't believe it's solely for the sake of her health that she's come to France," he wrote to his superiors in Paris. "If one is in poor health one doesn't spend the day walking about, going out on carriage-rides or on horseback."

In late July, Marie Louise wrote to tell Napoleon that she planned to go to Parma as soon as possible and assured him she was only taking so long between letters for the sake of security, just in case he might think her "capable of forgetting" him. She said she suffered from not hearing more news from him. "Nevertheless, Darling," she wrote, "I feel certain that you *have* written, and that you think about me sometimes." She said that she still thought it best for their son to stay in Vienna, and that she was pleased to be away from there, especially since the upcoming peace conference would have forced her to be "in the same city as the allied sovereigns." She told him she was drinking the waters and "taking plenty of exercise" and that her health was improving. She'd sketched some nature scenes under the watch of her art tutor, who was thinking of sending one of his pupils to Elba to do Napoleon's portrait. "I am living in the strictest incognito here," she added. "My father has sent me General Neipperg, he's quite nice and speaks well of you."

20

A PERFECTLY BOURGEOIS SIMPLICITY

APPROACHING PORTOFERRAIO, Madame Mère mounted one of the *Grasshopper*'s guns to get a better look at her son's palace. The crew left her alone, having seen how confidently she handled her small, powerful frame. But when the ship docked on the night of August 2, no one was at the mole to greet her. Napoleon had expected her the day before, and when she'd failed to show, he'd figured she must have met with some long delay and had gone off riding without arranging for a greeting party.

Campbell suggested that Drouot or Bertrand could be brought to the harbor to formally announce her disembarkation. "She seemed greatly agitated and mortified at no one coming to her on their part and gave her assent with great violence, turning around quite pale and huffed," he wrote. Drouot and Bertrand rushed down to the dock, with the mayor and an honor guard in tow, while the staff tried to gather a sufficient crowd along the marina. Meanwhile, a messenger found Napoleon riding at Marciana and he hurried back to his mother, trying to gain time by switching from carriage to rowboat so he could bypass a curving road, despite choppy seas.

She was soon set up in a small but comfortable house close to the Mulini, which Napoleon had rented from the local magistrate, Vantini. It wasn't "a handsome house," as Bertrand wrote to Méneval, but "she has plenty of room and certain comforts." She'd planned to stay for a month, but after just a few days she decided to live there permanently, with two ladies-in-waiting and a retired French general as her chamberlain. She crowed in a letter to a friend that "the emperor has set me up in a pretty house next to his own. Every night we take a carriage ride or walk in his garden."

She sent for the rest of her baggage and ordered renovations. "It pains me to see that work continues at the Vantini house, worse still because it doesn't belong to me," Napoleon wrote to Drouot. "A bill detailing all of Madame's spending on the project should be presented to her: it's the only way to get her from ordering any more work to be done." In truth, she was much more of an economic help to Napoleon than a hindrance. By the time of the empire's collapse she'd quietly set aside as much as three million francs in cash and about half that in jewels and property. She lived relatively humbly in Portoferraio, at a level of luxury not much different from what she would have enjoyed if the family had never left Corsica.

And as on Corsica, she once again held the role of proud matriarch of a notable island family. "I've seen eminent people more intimidated in front of her than in front of the Emperor," wrote Pons. Though Napoleon sometimes chided his mother, he respected her advice. He was critical of his father, Carlo, a man he thought was "too fond of pleasure," who died of cancer when Napoleon was fifteen, but his mother, he said, "could govern a kingdom; she has excellent judgment and never makes a mistake." He dined at her house once a week and on Sundays she received palace guests in all her finery, accented by a feathered hat and her best diamonds.

Under her watch a sense of routine set in at the Mulini. Napoleon typically rose at seven, after having slept about six hours, far more sleep than he'd ever enjoyed during the height of his career. He started his day with a consultation from his personal physician and then dressed, usually in his uniform of a chasseur of the Guard with white cashmere culottes and silk stockings. His valets would have placed a snuffbox, reading glasses, and a little box of aniseed licorice in the pockets of his clothing. As he left his bedroom he would be handed his two-pointed hat, and he liked to start the day with a sip of broth and a nip of Constantia wine imported from Cape Town. Most mornings he headed to the harbor in his carriage, accompanied by a few of his officers. He might then survey the Guard as they presented arms, or stop for a quick chat with Bertrand.

In the early afternoon he downed a quick lunch, usually alongside Bertrand, Cambronne, and Drouot. The fare was simple and not too different from what he ate on campaign: lentils, white beans, or potatoes, accompanied by some Chambertin wine, followed by black coffee. Sometimes they went to a nearby beach for a picnic. In the open air Napoleon seemed most at ease. Pons remembered one carefree outdoor meal featuring an excellent bouillabaisse. "We ate, we drank, we sang," he wrote. "It was the strangest thing. . . . We saw the emperor . . . happy." During these trips outdoors Napoleon liked to practice his particular brand of ear-tugging, name-calling slapstick, the height of which he might have achieved on the day he slipped some live herring into Bertrand's coat pocket and then asked if he could borrow a handkerchief. Once, on a ride down a country road with Pons and Bertrand, he told the two men to go ahead of him and race. Both men begged off, saying it would be no contest since Bertrand's powerful charger, Euphrate, a gift from Napoleon, was four times the horse of the mingy Corsican that Pons rode, but Napoleon insisted and in the end Euphrate stumbled in a ravine and Napoleon declared Pons the winner by default. Pons recalled that Bertrand appeared to take the emperor's taunts in his stride and seemed well accustomed to his playful abuse.

Following lunch Napoleon would usually draft letters and orders. After the initial burst of the first few weeks he slowed to handling one or two pieces of paperwork a day, a pace of work about a tenth of what he'd maintained in previous years. Unlike Robinson Crusoe, he kept no journal of his time as a castaway, which may be evidence that he anticipated from the very beginning that he wouldn't be marooned there forever.

He took long salt baths in the afternoons, often while reading or dictating to his secretaries. During one of these baths he challenged his young valet to calculate the volume of water displaced by his body in the tub, and after the valet pled ignorance showed him how to do so. Following his baths he drenched himself in eau de cologne, usually some mix of bergamot, citrus, and lavender or rosemary. He obsessed over his appearance and shaved daily.

In the early evenings he would take a carriage ride or row out into the roadstead to watch the sunset. He liked to see the ships passing through the channel separating Portoferraio and Piombino, which he later recalled as being "in continual movement; not a day went by when there weren't several hundred boats passing through, of all sizes and of all nations." Sometimes he stayed in to take a nap, which members of his staff noticed was the option he chose with increasing frequency. Occasionally he and Drouot played at pétanque, a game the latter man dominated because, as he told Napoleon, it was one at which it was impossible to cheat. Some evenings were spent hunting or fishing. A valet recalled a trip in the company of some local fishermen on the search for tuna, from which Napoleon returned, laughing, covered in seawater and blood.

Nights at the Mulini unfolded with what Pons called "a perfectly bourgeois simplicity." After dining with family, his generals, and a few guests, Napoleon would press some lackeys into being conquered at cards. The favorite game was *réversis*, similar to hearts, or they played at the ivory dominoes Napoleon had specially made for the palace. Peyrusse was a regular tablemate, but best of all was if Madame Mère could be persuaded to join. Unlike his retainers, she was unafraid to confront Napoleon about his frequent misdeeds at the table. "Napoleon, you're cheating," she would say calmly, and he would put his hands on the green felt, curl them around the napoleons lying there, and then carry off the haul to his bedroom, barking his protests. A valet would come to collect the money to be redistributed among its rightful owners the next morning. There were variations on this little drama: sometimes instead of stomping off, Napoleon would meet the accusation of "You're cheating, son," with "You're rich, mother," and they would laugh it off before play resumed. Napoleon had never shown himself so wild for games of chance as he did on Elba, perhaps because the freedom of the unknown result is one of the few that can be enjoyed inexhaustibly and regardless of location.

When ready to retire, usually around ten, Napoleon would wander over to a little piano and play a few clumsy measures from Haydn's Symphony No. 94, nicknamed the "Surprise" symphony for some abrupt fortissimo chords that sneak up on listeners during the otherwise peaceful second movement. This was the signal for bedtime preparations.

Sometimes the household staff would hear Napoleon in the early hours of the morning pacing his garden, which was lit through the night by two giant alabaster vases with candles placed inside. He sang to himself, emphasizing unlikely syllables in his lilting Corsican accent.

21

TALL FANNY AND THE TWO
EMPRESSES BONAPARTE

FANNY BERTRAND REACHED ELBA in August with her three children. In their letters, she and Henri had wavered about her making the journey at all, fearing that she and the children might lose their standing as French citizens if they joined the exile, and that the sadness of the separation from her grandchildren might kill Henri's elderly mother. They had even briefly considered leaving one of the children behind, so she would at least have one grandchild to care for.

Most of the family's income had come in the form of rewards from Napoleon that were pegged to public funds in a complicated setup, which left them with little ready cash. The bulk of their wealth was eventually seized by the Bourbons. Henri kept close watch on Fanny's spending, complaining in one letter that she'd spent more in the past three weeks than he had in three months. He pressured her to sail to Elba not from Piombino, which was a shorter and easier journey, but from Marseille because it was cheaper. Before leaving home she fired nearly all the members of her household staff.

On the way to Marseille she was stopped in the town of Bourges by a French prefect who was following a tip that she would be passing through and carrying letters for Napoleon. After riffling through her trunks and searching her carriages, he found twelve letters, which he kept, and then freed Fanny to go while her maid and coachman repacked her trunks by the side of the muddy road. The prefect had missed finding a copy of the Treaty of Fontainebleau, which no one on Elba had yet seen, and a letter concerning Marie Louise's finances that Fanny had socked away more carefully than the others. Word got round of her shabby treatment at the hand of the royalist official, which got rougher with each telling, and in the taverns of the Bertrand hometown of Châteauroux someone made up a sad and secret song about the exile of "Tall Fanny" (she stood nearly six feet), which eventually spread across the country.

The moment Napoleon saw her in Portoferraio he took Fanny for a private ride in his carriage so she could tell him of the latest developments in France. Later, on Saint Helena, she told Baron Gourgaud that she'd been the first person to inform Napoleon of Joséphine's death. She was a distant relation of Joséphine's, who along with Napoleon had orchestrated her engagement to the older Henri, a union to which she'd at first objected, saying to Napoleon, "What, Sire! Bertrand! Why not the Pope's Monkey!" When she told Napoleon about Joséphine's death, as she later recalled, "his face did not change; he only exclaimed; 'Ah! she is happy now!'" Gourgaud wrote that he was sure Fanny would have handled the task with great sympathy and tact, because she was the only person on Saint Helena with "humane instincts and a feeling heart." (That she seemed to him so tenderhearted during that final exile was all the more impressive, given how much she hated Saint Helena, which she described by saying, "The Devil shit this island as he flew from one world to another.")

Napoleon shut himself away at the Mulini and called for two days of mourning. Later, he said that divorcing Joséphine had marked the start of his slow and steady decline. He told Baron Gourgaud:

> I think, although I loved Louise very sincerely, that I loved Josephine better. That was natural: we had risen together, and she was a true wife, the wife I had chosen. She was full of grace, graceful even

in the way she prepared herself for bed, graceful in undressing herself.

As with Napoleon, Joséphine was both an islander and an outsider. She was, he said, "the wife who would have gone with me to Elba." On his own death (another island, another camp bed) her name was his final word. The full sentence, whispered, was "France . . . the head of the army . . . Josephine."

While shut away at the Mulini, Napoleon wrote several times to Marie Louise, apparently feeling her pull strongly in the wake of Joséphine's death. He'd collected all her letters, which were numbered, and had spotted gaps in the sequence. He could tell by their wear that they had passed through many hands before reaching his. He admonished Marie Louise for not having written to him since leaving Vienna, though she had in fact written, and it was only that some of those letters were intercepted and destroyed, while others would only reach him much later. He told her that her rooms were ready and that he wanted to see her "in September for the vintage," adding that Pauline was due to arrive around the same time. He reminded her that

no one has any right to stand in the way of your coming. I have written to you on the point. So mind you come. I am awaiting you with impatience. . . . Complain of their behavior to you in preventing a woman and a child from writing to me. Such behavior is despicable.

22

TAKING THE CURE

As July gave way to August, Marie Louise waited for her father to advise her of the date she should leave Aix-les-Bains to take up her reign in Parma. "I'll never consent to return to Vienna before the departure of the sovereigns," she told Méneval, "and I'll try to have my son back." She was tiring of the thermal baths and told Méneval that she knew the multiple treatments she'd taken so far must be having some effect, but that her sadness kept her from feeling any better. "There are some moments," she said, "when my head is so troubled that I think the best I could do would be to die."

Her letters to Napoleon from this time contained little other than complaints of loneliness and the details of her medical regime, including one in which she copied out her physician's diagnosis: "Her complexion is good, her colour natural, her appetite quite regular, and her sleep would be sound were it not interrupted by hot flushes." She told Napoleon that she'd heard their son was recovering from a toothache and she described the Austrian officer who had lately joined her retinue. In one letter she devoted nearly the whole of the closing four paragraphs to describing his positive influence on her:

I am very pleased with General Neipperg, whom my father has appointed to attend on me. He talks about you so pleasantly and in a
way which goes straight to my heart, for I *need* to talk about you
during this cruel absence.

On August 18 she wrote Napoleon a long letter, perhaps finally writing in
detail because she was confident that this one was sure to get through undetected. An officer had stashed the letter among his luggage and promised to
take it personally to Elba, which he did. She told Napoleon that she was "surrounded by police and by Austrian, Russian, and French counter police" and
that "General Neipperg told me he had in his pocket orders to intercept every
letter I might write you." She swore she'd been writing to him regularly and
that she'd begged for their son to be sent to her, but that her plans had been
foiled and that her father now ordered her "back to Vienna for the congress,
where my son's interests are to be discussed." She hinted that being back in
Vienna would at least give her a better chance of fighting for her rights to
Parma, anticipating that the Bourbons planned to take these lands from her
during congress negotiations. "I wanted to go to Parma, they refuse to let
me," she wrote. She claimed that there were French officers at Aix-les-Bains
who had orders to arrest her if she even headed in the general direction of
Elba. She also said that "taking the waters" had "improved my health most
wonderfully." The letter closed with, "Remember me to Madame. I send you
a kiss and love you dearly. Your loving and devoted Louise."

The next day she wrote to her father to say she would soon be leaving Aix-
les-Bains to go home to Vienna, as he desired. Her pace would be leisurely but
she would try to time her arrival to coincide with the Feast of Saint Francis of
Assisi on October 4, his name day. She asked if Neipperg could accompany
her, for "he may be extremely useful to me on various occasions."

Four days later, a French captain named Hurault de Sorbée arrived at Aix-
les-Bains. Napoleon had sent him to Genoa on the *Inconstant* with orders to
collect his wife and bring her immediately to Elba and in the meantime had
tried to get letters through to Méneval to advise him in advance, though none

had reached him. Hurault's wife, an Austrian, was Marie Louise's personal reader, so he arrived at Aix-les-Bains under the pretext of a conjugal visit. He found Marie Louise and handed her a letter from her husband explaining the plan: they must leave the spa town at once for Genoa, where the *Inconstant* waited to take them to Elba.

Marie Louise asked for a moment to think in private. After the captain left her, she went to Neipperg, who had him arrested. He was sent to prison in Paris, but was later quietly released, as Talleyrand wanted to avoid stirring up any romantic Bonapartist spirit by publicizing the captain's failed adventure. Reporting on the incident to Metternich, Neipperg wrote that "the idea of the journey [to Elba] seems to inspire more fear than a desire to be reconciled with her husband." But whether Marie Louise performed such fearfulness specifically for Neipperg's benefit remains unclear.

A few days later she wrote to her father, "Be assured that I am now less than ever desirous of undertaking that voyage [to Elba], and I give you my word of honor that I will never undertake it without asking your permission." Next she wrote to a friend about her husband's "thoughtless" and "self-centered" demands, saying that the idea of a daring "escapade" aboard Hurault's waiting ship was ludicrous. "Really, the Emperor is so casual, so unreliable," she wrote, complaining that the revelation of his failed plan could have

> no influence on the Court in Vienna except to make them keep me away still longer from Parma. I shall give my ministers my most sacred word of honor that I shall not go to the island of Elba at the moment, that I shall *never* go (for you know better than anyone that I have no desire to do so).

{ 23 }

TOURIST SEASON

NAPOLEON SUMMONED CAMPBELL TO the Mulini palace to ask about his Italian trip. After keeping him waiting for several minutes while he finished a card game with his mother, Napoleon "came up tripping and smiling. Asked me how I did? Said I had got fatter. Was I quite well? Where had I been. 'What news? You are come, then, to stay some days with us?'" He wanted to know every detail of Campbell's travels, down to whether he'd "applied the water in a stream through a pipe" at the Lucca baths. After a barrage of questions and answers, during which Napoleon tried to learn as much about the political situation on the mainland as possible, Campbell revealed that the prince regent had officially approved his continued stay on Elba. Napoleon only nodded. And then he smiled, said he looked forward to seeing Campbell again soon, turned around, and left the room.

Campbell was left confused by this relatively cold reception. Not knowing what else to do, he sailed the next morning for Livorno. In his journal he justified the decision by noting that most Elbans had still yet to pay their back taxes, defying Napoleon's July 1 deadline, and that he thought it would be better for him to be away when that situation finally came to a head. As he readied to put out to sea, a village priest pressed a document into his hands, asking that he pass it along to his superiors. It was a request to the British to come intervene on behalf of the Elbans to keep them from having to pay unjust taxes.

Campbell traveled through Tuscany for much of August. He went to dinners and balls, returned to the baths, dined again with the Contessa Miniaci, bet on the horses, played at cards, and pored over letters intercepted from various Bonapartes. He traded information with a few other officials and learned that while he was away Napoleon had boarded the *Inconstant* escorted by fifty men and stayed there for two hours. The agent who supplied this report suggested that Napoleon was preparing to fetch Marie Louise, but Campbell thought it was more likely a routine check of the ship's weapons prompted by some recent sightings of Barbary corsairs. One night in Livorno, a strange man presented himself to Campbell, claiming to be the nephew of Ricci, Campbell's Elban contact, and looking for work on the island. When pressed about his background the man changed his story to say that he was only a distant relation of Ricci's. "He told me he was going to Pisa, in case I did not hire him, on account of a wound in the head received while serving in the French army," wrote Campbell. "He said he had been a soldier for many years and had a passport signed by the Mayor of Portoferraio. I think he has been sent to me as a spy!"

During this time Campbell finally received his first clear directive from Castlereagh, though it was far from a major one. Castlereagh had written to say he was heading to Vienna for the upcoming peace congress and advised Campbell to continue sending his dispatches to London; he could send duplicates to Vienna, but should only incur the expense of using a courier for reports significant enough to "require immediate dispatch." That was the whole of Castlereagh's instruction.

Late in the month Campbell sailed back to Portoferraio, but while he was docking, someone told him that they were about to mark Napoleon's birthday, which he thought he'd avoided since it had fallen on August 15, but the man at the dock explained that the festivities had been delayed two weeks out of respect for the late Joséphine. Campbell turned back immediately for Livorno, writing in his journal that he "did not wish to be present at the formal celebrations of Napoleon's birthday."

. . .

NAPOLEON'S FORTY-FIFTH BIRTHDAY party proved to be the biggest event Elba had ever seen, a costlier and more raucous affair than even the San Cristino feast. There was dancing in a wooden ballroom erected in Portoferraio's main square, races that pitted stallions from the imperial stables against others ferried across from Italy, fireworks displays, and cannon salutes from the ships and forts. Pons won a prize for the evening's finest display, having spelled out NAPOLEON in the windows of his home: a letter capped by a star in each window framed by lamps in republican red, white, and blue. Napoleon, somber and subdued, occupied himself by distributing gifts. The night could hardly have matched the birthday celebrations of his heyday, when he'd managed to have the day fêted as a national holiday as the Feast of Saint Napoleon, which, thanks to some finagling by the pope, technically commemorated a little-known Christian martyr of the same name.

The morning after his birthday feast, Napoleon left Portoferraio for the mountain retreat next to the chapel of the Madonna above Marciana. He'd arranged to borrow it from the hermit for a few days. He wrote again to Marie Louise, thanking her for a letter containing a lock of her hair she'd sent for his birthday:

> I am here in a hermitage, 3834 feet above sea level, overlooking the Mediterranean on all sides, and in the midst of a forest of chestnut trees. Madame [Mère] is staying in the village, 958 feet lower down. This is a most pleasant spot. My health is very good, I spend part of the day shooting. I long to see you, and my son, too. . . . There are some very fine landscapes to be drawn here. Goodbye, my dearest Louise. All my love.

And then, a few nights later, Marie Louise and her son were seen landing at a desolate beach at the edge of the village of San Giovanni, the site of the farmhouse Napoleon had inspected and rejected months earlier when first landing on Elba. Someone had seen a brig anchored far from Portoferraio's harbor and then, after going down to take a closer look at the boat, had seen soldiers setting a small fire on the sand. At this signal two women and a small child were rowed to shore by a man. They walked to one of Napoleon's berlins waiting at the top of the beach. Escorted by several riders lit in profile against the moon, the carriage traveled quietly through the night of September 1 and up to Marciana, where soldiers stood watch at the bottom of the steep rocky path lined with stations of the cross that had beckoned generations of pilgrims up to the hilltop chapel.

By the next morning, people were making preparations for welcoming the empress. They traded reports of how dazzling her jewels had been as they reflected the firelight at the beach. They speculated that the other woman seen in the rowboat must have been her lady-in-waiting, and that the man who had rowed them in must have been her stepson, Prince Eugène. The mayor of Marciana decided to organize an illumination so the villagers could properly pay their respects to the empress and the King of Rome.

Napoleon, however wasn't holed up at the hermitage with his wife and the King of Rome, but with his mistress Marie Walewska and their young son, Alexandre. The other two people who had been seen in the rowboat were Marie Walewska's sister and her brother, Teodor Łączyński, a Polish officer in Napoleon's service. Colonel Łączyński had served as intermediary for the correspondence between Napoleon and Countess Walewska over the summer, and with Napoleon and Bertrand had carefully arranged her visit. They had planned for her to leave fairly quickly, before anyone learned of her arrival, but they hadn't counted on being spotted landing at the beach so late at night.

Some of the more curious villagers had climbed up unmarked paths to hide in the ancient chestnuts near the chapel, trying to get a glimpse of the woman they still believed to be their empress, until guards shooed them away. Napoleon decided that Marie Walewska should sail home right away before the winds calmed. Having shared only two evenings with the Walewska sisters, he rode them half of the way down to the edge of Marciana and said his good-byes, leaving them to finish the rest of the night's seventeen-mile ride to Porto Longone, which he'd decided was the best place from which to sail on account of rough winds at Marciana. Walewska's visit may have been about business as much as pleasure. It was later revealed that she left with a letter from Napoleon to Murat asking to help her with some details concerning their son's property, and shortly after the visit she hinted that she'd played the role of courier, claiming that Napoleon "considers his exile temporary, and the information he demands is what he needs to choose the most propitious moment to bring it to an end."

CAMPBELL RETURNED TO ELBA just after Marie Walewska left. He brought news that the dey of Algiers had declared war against Naples, Genoa, and Elba and had ordered his cruisers to seize all ships sailing under those flags. The dey had also publicly declared that he would capture "the person of the Sovereign of [Elba] also, should any opportunity happily offer of getting hold of him," a piece of information Campbell withheld from his official written report to Bertrand, who was already jumpy, since two Barbary corsairs had been spotted off the coast a few days earlier and were only scared off after the *Inconstant* went out on patrol, manned as fully as possible, guns at the ready.

Napoleon sent for Campbell to visit him at the citadel of Porto Longone. Campbell figured he was hiding out there because of the corsair sighting and some new rumors of an impending assassination attempt, but Bertrand had set the Porto Longone itinerary long beforehand so that Napoleon could attend the town's feast day. Still, the soldiers were on the alert, after a report circulated that someone had paid a one-eyed Jew from Leipzig a huge sum to murder Napoleon and that the man had already landed at Portoferraio. The mayor of Rio Alta, who had lost an eye, was subjected to harsh interrogation, but in the end the spectral one-eyed Jew was never sighted.

Campbell and Napoleon had a three-hour interview in the citadel, the first time they had talked in several weeks. Napoleon paced back and forth, quizzing the colonel in his rapid-fire way: What were the allies planning to do about Murat in Naples? Had the British set up a regiment in Nice? Were they hanging on to Corfu? Where was the queen of Sicily at the moment? Was the king of Spain still visiting Rome? How was the pope's health? Campbell wrote that Napoleon laughed off the recent threats from the dey of Algiers and claimed that "the Algerines were well inclined towards him and related with good humor that they had ridiculed the crews of two vessels belonging to Louis XVIII near Elba, calling to them with reproaches, 'You have deserted your Emperor!'" The dey's subjects, he assured Campbell, praised him as "the enemy of Russia and considered him the destroyer of Moscow."

He also dismissed Campbell's revelation that allied officials knew all about his recruiting efforts along the Tuscan coast. He admitted that some Corsican officers had indeed gone there to recruit on his behalf, but reasoned that he hardly had soldiers enough to guard more than a few Elban villages, and it wasn't as if the island offered a huge supply of skilled men for him to draw on. He asked Campbell whether the allied powers were "so weak as to be alarmed at this," and added that it was a good thing Campbell was there as a witness to "dispel the notion." He told Campbell that he thought of

> nothing beyond my little island. I could have kept the war going for twenty years if I had wanted that. I exist no longer for the world. I am a dead man. I occupy myself only with my family and my retire-ment, my house, my cows, and my mules.

He spoke "with warmth and in strong language" about his continued separation from his wife and child and said that Marie Louise was "now abso-lutely a prisoner," wrote Campbell, "for there was an Austrian officer (whom he named and described) who accompanied her, in order to prevent her from escaping to Elba." He asked Campbell to write to Castlereagh to ask for help in bringing his family to Elba, to which Campbell answered that he only cor-responded with the foreign secretary about official matters. Napoleon pressed, suggesting that maybe he could ask someone other than Castlereagh. "I bowed and told him that I should be happy to do anything agreeable to him and at the same time consistent with my duty," wrote Campbell, which Napo-leon, evidently less well versed than he was in the art of British subtlety, mis-interpreted as a yes.

Napoleon next tried to feel out what level of support he enjoyed in France, but Campbell gave him only abstract and equivocal answers to his questions.

Then came more reminiscences about past battles, especially the final campaign:

> Enlarging for some time upon the influence which he possessed over the minds of French soldiers in the field, he said that under him they performed what no other chief could obtain from them. . . . With soldiers it is not so much the speech itself as the mode of delivering it [he said]. Here he raised himself on his toes, looked up to the ceiling, and lifting one of his hands to its utmost extent, called out, "Unfurl the eagles! Unfurl the eagles!" . . . It's like music, which either speaks to the soul, or, on the contrary, gives out sounds without harmony.

This speech ended the seven pages Campbell devoted in his journal to describing their talk at Porto Longone, which he closed by writing, "It strikes me there was something *wild* in his air throughout this last visit."

A FEW DAYS LATER an English colonel named Montgomery Maxwell traveled toward Elba, solely, as he put it, "with the hope of getting a peep at the great Napoleon, at present cooped up in that island." With his young companion, a Cambridge student named John Barber Scott, and some British officers, Maxwell sailed over from Piombino in a small felucca crammed with passengers, mostly French and Italian. With the lifting of blockades, people (mainly young European men with ample means and social connections) were free to resume the practice of embarking on Grand Tours, usually through France and Italy, and sometimes Greece, as part of their cultural formations. Napoleon on Elba had become a new tourist attraction. "I'm an object of curiosity; let them satisfy themselves," he said to Pons when he pointed out some travelers gawking at him. "They'll go home and amuse the gentlemen by describing my acts and gestures."

As with anyone disembarking at Portoferraio, Maxwell's party first had to endure the initiations of the broiling lazaretto, where they were held until their passports and bodies could be properly inspected for plague. "A more hot unwholesome locale I had never before visited," wrote Maxwell.

Eager for the company of his countrymen, Campbell called on Maxwell and his friends the next morning at breakfast. He told them that Napoleon was at Porto Longone and receiving no visitors but that they might be able to meet him "by accident." He meanwhile introduced them to Bertrand and Drouot, who offered a tour of the island's barracks and fortifications. Maxwell wrote of seeing the soldiers of the Old Guard, who "whiff their cigars and drink beer under an olive tree, and vote Portoferraio their little Paris." While discussing Napoleon's supposedly boundless energy, one soldier let slip that he was no longer the dynamo of past and "now took a nap in the forenoon, and gave himself up to the pleasures of the table," but Campbell countered that any man who tried to keep up with Napoleon would surely die from fatigue.

Maxwell and his party conspired to meet Napoleon as his carriage traveled from Porto Longone back to Portoferraio. They stayed at an inn near the citadel and hired a boy to stand watch on the terrace. That evening Maxwell saw Napoleon on horseback, about five hundred yards off, winding his way down a hill. He was in uniform and wearing his trademark bicorne hat. Maxwell recalled seeing him "pointing and giving directions to his attendants, offering to our now heated imaginations the idea that this was one of his celebrated reconnoissances on the eve of some great battle, such as Austerlitz or Borodino."

The romance faded when Napoleon drew alongside Maxwell and his fellow travelers, astride a horse whose dirty red saddlecloth and worn bridle gave the impression that "his majesty had a very indifferent groom." Maxwell wrote of feeling disappointed, as

> the film seemed to fall from my eyes and the man who had been the idol of my imagination for years stood before me with a round ungraceful figure, with a most unpoetically protuberant stomach. . . . The countenance, in which I expected to behold a unison of the demon and the soldier, appeared soft and mild in the extreme; there was nothing striking in it. . . . His complexion, too, though sallow, was not near so dark as I expected to find it.

Only when hearing Napoleon speak did he detect the hints of greatness. "I now became enraptured with his lively bewitching air, with his astonishing memory, his information, and the fertility with which he kept up an easy and agreeable conversation," he wrote. "No wonder French soldiers adored him, for he instantly proved to us all how well he knew how to tickle the human heart." They spoke of Maxwell's military service, his uniform, and of Genoa, where he was based. According to Maxwell, Napoleon "asked if the Genoese were civil to us and in a rather sly way inquired how we like the ladies, adding that they were *tres complaisantes* and that the men were all rogues. He then condescended to explain his meaning by informing us that one rogue made a Jew, but that it took nine Jews to make a Genoese!" Maxwell found it funny when Napoleon, on hearing that one of the British officers hailed from Kent, said, "We're neighbors!," forgetting "that he was by birth a Corsican and now banished from France."

Napoleon repeated the kinds of performance he'd so often staged for Campbell, saying that he'd totally renounced the ways of war and was of no harm to anyone. Maxwell and the British officers in his company were left so charmed by the interview that they spent the whole of dinner and well into the night talking about Napoleon and toasting his health. Maxwell left the next day, much impressed by his time with the "hardy highlander" Campbell, while his traveling partner, Scott, was less taken with the colonel, whom he allowed was "most polite" but adopted a haughty air whenever they discussed Napoleon, as though he held some special insight to his character that somehow made him superior to the emperor. "Campbell," he wrote, "thinks Bonaparte a man of ordinary talents who has had a great deal of luck."

Not long after Maxwell and Scott left Elba, Campbell sailed from Portoferraio as well for another trip along the Italian coast, ostensibly to compare information with other agents. He landed at Livorno on the last day of summer and went straight to Florence, where presumably the Contessa Miniaci was waiting.

24

THE POLITICS OF FORGETTING

TO THE FRENCH, NAPOLEON was far away and out of sight, yet the man who replaced him was hardly more present. Louis XVIII spent many hours that summer in his bathtub, soaking in acrid eaux de Barèges to ease the pain of his arthritis and gout. Occasionally he listened to summaries of the more troubling reports from around the country. In one, from the northeastern town of Nancy, an agent wrote that people were speaking as though France had somehow betrayed Napoleon:

> It seems that his reverses and mistakes have served only to soften public judgments on him. His follies, his outbursts of temper and the ridiculous side of his behavior have only slightly undermined the blind confidence that the people and the soldiers have in his capacities. No one exactly conspires for him, but this stupid infatuation is itself a kind of conspiracy which must be a cause of concern since he can dream of profiting by it.

The head of police, Beugnot, distributed a memo on the growing "tavern war against the administration." Soldiers on inactive duty were seen gathered at cafés where they rehashed former glories and complained about how much livelier and better paying their days had been under Napoleon. Some even spoke about his return, or "resurrection," as they worded it. Louis XVIII and his ministers knew better than to dismiss this kind of talk as idle chatter; French public opinion was shaped in the country's roughly three hundred thousand drinking establishments as much as it was in its salons, newspapers, and pamphlets.

Officials were also concerned by the "multitude of English who inundate Paris," as one prefect wrote, "and whose obscure station occasions uneasiness as to their destination and intentions." While financial markets had reacted favorably to the Bourbon restoration, prices for goods and services remained seductively low due to inflation, prompting many people to cross the newly reopened borders to reap the benefits. So many British visitors came to the capital in the first months after Napoleon's surrender that the city's Protestant church scheduled a regular Anglican service.

Added to this influx of travelers were royalist émigrés, returning from the provinces and beyond, who tended to congregate in the tony Faubourg Saint-Germain, traditional den of the aristos and a key royalist beachhead in the city. Napoleon's longtime rival Pozzo di Borgo disdainfully referred to these returned émigrés as "new" Parisians, despite their ancient names, and indeed many of them would have felt out of time and place after so long away. The émigrés were so quick to "watch, judge and tear each other to pieces," wrote Pozzo di Borgo, that life in the Faubourg Saint-Germain was like being trapped in some sly play by Beaumarchais, where everyone *without a single exception is discontented.*" Royalists back from exile (self-imposed or otherwise) hoped to reestablish age-old privileges, an objectionable sight to many French men and women.

Exiled intellectuals returned as well, and their ways of seeing and thinking about France had also been reshaped by their time abroad. The Swiss-French philosopher and politician Benjamin Constant returned to Paris for the first time in more than a decade, after being expelled by Napoleon for expressing overly liberal views. Constant's former mistress, the brilliant Madame de Staël, was back as well, still thinking of herself as "a stranger in her native land." She wrote that her own absence from France was more painful than the exiled Napoleon would ever be able to understand, because she

> was born on the banks of the Seine, where his only claim to citizenship is tyranny. He saw the light of day on the island of Corsica, practically within Africa's savage sway. . . . The air of this beautiful country is not his native air; how can he understand the pain of being exiled from it, he who considers this fertile land only as the instrument of his victories. Where is his *patrie*? It is any country that accepts his domination. His fellow-citizens? They are whatever slaves obey his orders.

Louis XVIII and his ministers wanted to foster unity within the growing bureaucracy and so tried to find places not only for the returned émigrés and intellectuals, but also for people who had served under Napoleon. The official tasked with processing all the incoming requests for jobs and titles complained that he was working "like a wild beast," keeping ungodly hours hunched over his desk in a tiny chamber above the king's study at the Tuileries as he dealt with twice as many petitioners as there were available positions. "There is not one self-styled gentleman but thinks the King of France returned for his own particular benefit," wrote one prefect. "They must have all their positions, pensions, and decorations."

Under pressure from his ministers, Louis "granted" the French people a Constitutional Charter, helping to usher in a period of relatively unprecedented freedom in the circulation of ideas, money, and people, though these gains were still largely circumscribed. The right to vote, for instance, applied to only one in 360 men. But while the charter had only officially been given to the French people by the grace of Louis XVIII, called back to France by "Divine Providence" after so long an absence, and in whose person all judicial, executive, and legislative authority nominally resided, it was still the most liberal European constitution of the era. The result was that the Bourbon restoration was the only major regime change in the nineteenth century not to require massive purges.

People who supported the Bourbons did so for many reasons. There had been pockets of royalist resistance long before 1814, from the plotters who tried to assassinate Napoleon in 1800 to the hard-core Knights of the Faith, whose members had been trying to bring about a restoration for years and who had referred to their exiled sovereign as Louis *le Désiré*, Louis the Longed-For. Some royalists combined their monarchism with deep religiosity, while others had only wanted to see Napoleon replaced by anyone with a significant dynastic claim.

Many people opposed the restoration outright, with their own complicated motives. Some were as opposed to a Bourbon monarchy as they had been to Napoleon's empire and wanted to return to the revolutionary struggle. Others hoped to forge a middle way toward a new kind of liberalism within a monarchical framework. Others still pined for Napoleon. A few idealists saw this as the time to finally acknowledge the danger in following any ruler so slavishly as people had Napoleon. Benjamin Constant had voiced this sentiment in a pamphlet passed around Paris in the months preceding the abdication:

> While patriotism exists only by a vivid attachment to the interests, the ways of life, the customs of some locality, our so-called patriots have declared war on all of these. They have dried up this natural source of patriotism and have sought to replace it by a factitious passion for an abstract being, a general idea stripped of all that can engage the imagination and speak to the memory.

Above all, French men and women wanted some kind of return to normalcy as they sought to make meaning out of the past years of carnage. Was Napoleon's fall the end of the republican experiment? Proof that people weren't ready to be trusted with democracy? Had the fall of Paris come as some kind of cosmic punishment for the excesses of the Revolution? The historian and statesman François Guizot, a young man at the time of the restoration, recalled that he'd never seen "such public inertia in the midst of so much national anxiety." People without power grumbled even though they abstained from taking action, he wrote, while officials were eager to disavow

Louis XVIII even while they served him without complaint. France was full "of exhausted spectators who had lost the ability to intervene in their own destiny, and who didn't know which final act they should wish for or fear in this terrible drama in which they themselves were the stake being wagered."

What was clear was how much the French had learned over the past quarter century about political authority and the forms it could take. The republican experiment, though derailed, had shown that power didn't have to emanate from a single man claiming divine right and could instead be created and enacted daily by the people themselves through their choice of dress, through the specific words they used, through the festivals they celebrated, through the songs they sang and the stories they told. The genie of revolution, that "Death-Birth of a World!," as Thomas Carlyle called it, couldn't be returned to its bottle. People had seen too much to become uniformly, unthinkingly, or permanently attached to any one person or single way of governance. "Nowadays," wrote Chateaubriand, "a straggler in this life has witnessed the death, not only of men, but also of ideas: principles, customs, tastes, pleasures, sorrows, opinions, none of these resembles what he used to know."

From then on any French ruler would only be able to hold on to power by negotiating with the people in apparent good faith about how that power was to be deployed. And yet, as evidenced by Louis XVIII's late brother, who sped his own demise just by publicly acknowledging that his subjects had minds and voices of their own, monarchy and compromise do not easily go hand in hand. As one historian has written, when the Bourbons returned, they faced "nothing less than the task of reclaiming their exclusive right to rule France, in a world where such a right no longer existed."

IN LATE AUGUST, Louis XVIII made his first public appearance since his coronation three months earlier, for the Feast of Saint-Louis, his name day. After a coach ride through some of the main boulevards he stood alongside his relatives on one of the Tuileries terraces to wave to the massive crowds. Just as they understood the political value in keeping the Bourbon court in Paris, among the people, rather than returning it to the traditional seat at

Versailles, his advisers also understood that any display of royal grandeur must also include his brother the comte d'Artois as well as the comte's sons, the duc d'Angoulême and the duc de Berry, and Marie-Thérèse, Madame Royale, last surviving child of Louis XVI and Marie Antoinette.

The future of the Bourbon reign rested on the power of history, for without the authority of "the eternal yesterday," as Max Weber worded it, no monarch could claim the right to govern. One of the stated goals of Louis's charter, in renewing the peerage, was to "bind all memories with all hopes, in bringing together former and present times." But while the Bourbons traded on a legitimacy gained through lineage, they simultaneously espoused the idea of *oubli*, obliviousness or disregard for the past. As the charter read, "All investigations of opinions and votes expressed before the Restoration are forbidden. The same disregard is demanded of both the courts and the citizenry." A complicated kind of forgetting was required of the French people, who were encouraged to erase from their memories any horrors experienced prior to Louis XVIII even while the king himself reached back to before the Revolution to which he owed his current status (since only his brother's execution had put him in line for the throne) to revive and capitalize on the symbology and rituals of the Old Regime.

SOMETHING THAT PROVED EASY to disregard from the safety of the Tuileries was the payment promised to Napoleon on Elba. With the budget overly taxed, Louis XVIII and his ministers thought it contrary to the public interest to honor the terms of a treaty that would fund the livelihood of their enemy, at least for the time being.

Meanwhile, a man who had not only survived but prospered through several regime changes over the past decades in France surveyed the current political scene with caution. He was Joseph Fouché, Napoleon's former minister of police, and he thought that Napoleon on Elba was like "Vesuvius next to Naples." In a letter to Beugnot, the current head of police, he predicted the following spring would "bring Bonaparte back to us, with the swallows and the violets."

FALL

25

HE IS TOLERABLY HAPPY

CAMPBELL RETURNED TO Portoferraio in early October. He wrote in his journal that he "had been assured from good authority that [Napoleon's] funds are nearly exhausted," which prompted "a great diminution in the expenses, but not in the extent, of his household and establishment." The island's salt marshes had failed and iron sales were slack due to an influx of old British guns into Genoa since the lifting of the wartime blockades. By Campbell's rough calculations, Napoleon was likely to spend about twice as much as he would bring in as revenue from Elba's natural resources. He learned that Bertrand was switching out the Mulini's collection of imported wines for the rougher and cheaper local vintage.

French agents also heard about Napoleon's apparent economic woes. "So many people have been dismissed from his entourage," read one report, "that he does almost everything for himself except go to market." But many saw this as a positive, reasoning that dwindling funds would keep Napoleon from ever being able to raise a proper army.

Napoleon, for his part, later claimed that money had never been a great concern for him on Elba. He calculated that the island should have brought him around half a million francs a year between the iron mines, the fisheries, other properties, taxes, and customs, and he figured his personal and administrative expenses at one hundred thousand francs. The annual surplus would have been more than enough for him, he said, especially if paired with the pension owed to him by the French government and the existing kitty that Peyrusse amassed before the exile.

A true accounting of the financial situation on Elba likely lies somewhere between Campbell's fretful predictions and Napoleon's boastful claims made in hindsight. Napoleon had always paid careful attention to balancing his empire's finances, but on Elba he spent relatively wildly and unsystematically, switching money from one account to another, recording purchases when he felt like it, and using vague headings without marking whether he was spending state income or his own capital. He economized where he could, but was far from miserly. When Drouot presented his military budget, for instance, Napoleon asked why he hadn't included himself on the payroll, to which Drouot answered that room, board, a secretary, a servant, and a horse were enough for him. In the final budget Napoleon allotted an extra six thousand francs for Drouot nonetheless.

THERE WERE A FEW DEVELOPMENTS to keep Campbell on alert that October. Elba was still at a standoff regarding back taxes, and many people, including the entire population of Capoliveri, had yet to pay anything at all. For now Napoleon refused to have his troops do much more than walk around menacingly. To Campbell it seemed that the Elbans, who had long before given up on loving Napoleon, now no longer even feared him. "Napoleon is never now saluted with cries of *Vive l'Empereur!*," he wrote. He also heard that morale among the troops had taken a hit after a bout of venereal disease raged through the barracks. Napoleon imposed a fine for anyone who sought relief at the hospital for their ailments, which had insulted the soldiers, who thought the price of treatment should be covered by the treasury. Streetlights were installed at every ten meters in Portoferraio with the aim of curbing prostitution, and each member of the Guard was guaranteed an ounce of rice per day to "help ward off sickness."

Late in the month Campbell discovered that a Tunisian corsair had anchored off the coast and that its commander had barged into the customs house demanding a private audience with the "Great Lord of the Earth." Cambronne denied his request and the man returned to his ship, which then saluted the *Inconstant* with five guns. Napoleon's ship returned the salute and the two crews later exchanged gifts. Campbell wondered if Napoleon had planned this spectacle in advance. While the dey of Algiers had publicly threatened Elba, the Tunisians hadn't declared themselves one way or the other, and Campbell thought Napoleon might have arranged some kind of pact with them. He later recorded his amazement at seeing this same Tunisian corsair giving chase to some ships near Piombino, writing, "It appears certain that Napoleon has established himself on an amicable footing with this Power or that he has bribed the captain of this ship with the advantage of taking shelter in his ports, to be able perhaps to communicate with France."

He meanwhile discovered that Napoleon had taken a trip "with some ladies and several others belonging to his household" to Pianosa, ostensibly for a luncheon. Campbell thought the neighboring island might be serving as a rendezvous point for "receiving persons from the Continent, and particularly Naples and Corsica, without any possible means of detecting it." He wrote to Castlereagh about his theory, though his journal doesn't mention any response from the foreign secretary on the matter.

He'd also noticed how Bertrand was trying "by little hints" to deduce when he next planned to leave and for how long. Bertrand had remarked casually on how frequently Campbell seemed to be traveling lately. "I can't say whether this was in order to ascertain the footing upon which my stay was prolonged," wrote Campbell, "or merely in the way of accidental observation from my making frequent excursions to the mainland, without any other meaning." He figured that since Bertrand and Napoleon had always received him so kindly, if less frequently than they once had, there was no danger in telling Bertrand plainly that Castlereagh had directed him to remain in residence on Elba at least until the closing of the Congress of Vienna and that after that date, whenever it came, he "presumed that His Majesty's Government would enable me to exhibit the powers of a permanent and ostensible employment."

Napoleon summoned Campbell for an interview. Their talk turned to France, where according to Napoleon there was now "universal disgust" with the Bourbons. Louis XVIII had made a bad tactical error by recognizing the Duke of Wellington as ambassador a few weeks earlier, he said. It was an insult to grant an ambassadorship to the same man who had devoted so much energy to destroying France. Campbell wrote that Napoleon predicted "a violent reaction of the whole nation before five years were over." The French, he said, were "martial beyond any other nation, by nature as well as in consequence of the Revolution and their ideas of glory," and that the French spirit, "once roused, cannot be opposed. It's like a torrent." He next spoke favorably about the Italians, "quick and proud," and good fighters. He told Campbell that "all the young men were attached to the French, from having served with them in the army, and their minds were bent upon the formation of Italy into a kingdom."

After making these fiery statements Napoleon again tried to reassure Campbell that he was only speaking hypothetically and without any "personal motives or expectations." He repeated his refrain about being retired from the world of politics and war, saying:

> I am a dead man. I was born a soldier. I have mounted the throne and I have descended. I am ready for everything. They can send me away. They can assassinate me. I'll stick out my chest to receive the dagger. As General Bonaparte I gained much, but they have taken it all away.

Despite these troubling signs, Campbell described Napoleon as seemingly at peace with his current situation and far less active than he'd been only a few months earlier:

> He has four places of residence in different parts of the island, and the improvements and changes of these form his sole occupation. But as they lose their interest to his unsettled mind, and the novelty wears off, he occasionally falls into a state of inactivity never known

before, and has of late retired to his bedroom for repose during several hours of the day. If he takes exercise, it is in a carriage, and not on horseback as before. His health, however, is excellent, and his spirits appear not at all depressed. I begin to think he is quite resigned to his retreat, and that he is tolerably happy, excepting when the recollections of his former power are freshened by sentiments of vanity or revenge, or his passions become influenced by want of money, and his wife and child being kept from him.

Meanwhile, Henri Bertrand, who did have his wife and children with him, also seemed tolerably happy with life on Elba, though he and Fanny struggled to care for their sickly son, born just a few days after Fanny had reached Portoferraio. An inexperienced local pharmacist had mishandled the birth and the Bertrands had kept mostly to themselves since then, although Fanny never turned away any callers.

The ascetic Drouot was apparently happiest of all. He wrote to a colleague in France:

> We've made it through the hot season, which the locals say is the hottest one they've had in many years. I haven't been inconvenienced by the weather in the least. In fact it's been a long time since I've passed such an agreeable summer. I continue to lead the life of an anchorite, but for me this life holds the greatest of charms. It's impossible to be happier. I wake at five or six and take care of my governor's duties until nine, and then I breakfast. From ten to three I study the sciences, and then I dine. From six to eight I walk, and then I read. At nine I get into bed and read some more. I'm enjoying the best health, am well-liked by all those around me, and you of course know about my situation here.

26

The Vulgar Details
of Married Lives

Napoleon had in many ways tried to distance himself from his Corsican past during his rise to the head of France, but now after a few months in exile he began surrounding himself with a new inner circle of Corsicans, some with long-standing family connections to the Bonapartes. They knew the region and local customs, but were still outsiders without the deep ties to Elba that might lead them to confuse their loyalties. Napoleon had Corsicans running the secret police, manning the palace gates and the ports, and handling the mail. The Corsican Santini, who after several months had finally found work at the Mulini as a kind of guard for the palace papers, seems to have played some role within this new entourage, and may have traveled to the neighboring island as a secret agent. Years later, Santini would number among the seventy-six individual beneficiaries named in Napoleon's will, nineteen of whom had joined him on Elba for the exile.

Another reminder of Napoleon's past arrived in the form of Pauline, who reached Portoferraio on October 31 after a stay at their sister Caroline's villa near Vesuvius. She passed out candies as she disembarked. At her welcome ball the following evening musicians greeted her entrance with a popular tune from a sentimental opera, "Où peut-on être mieux qu'au sein de sa famille?" (Where can one be better than in the bosom of one's family?) Pons wandered over to have the band play the "Marseillaise," sparking a good-natured chuckle from Napoleon, who had once officially disowned the republican anthem.

Pons found Pauline a bit overdramatic, something of a hypochondriac, and not necessarily as bright as the rest of her siblings, but she was so "full of gaiety" and so clearly kindhearted that he came to think of her as "a consoling angel . . . the most precious treasure of the palace." She was installed in what would have been Marie Louise's rooms and her arrival brought a final end to the renovations, since the palace would be devoted primarily to entertaining from then on. Pons wrote that Portoferraio "lit up" with her presence. There were more masked balls, more dances, and more plays, usually performed by local youths who made audiences laugh with their ineptitude. None of the Elban families felt compelled to host a soirée, since the calendar was so full of events hosted by Napoleon or his sister.

With Pauline's arrival the atmosphere at the Mulini instantly felt less "martial," as the valet Marchand recalled. She enjoyed fine displays and grand entrances. She "always dressed most carefully," recalled another valet, "Ali" (Louis-Étienne Saint-Denis), "in the style of a young girl of eighteen," though she'd just turned thirty-four, and she "had all the beautiful proportions of the Venus di Medici." Citing her fragile health, exacerbated by the unruly climate, Pauline liked to have the valets carry her up or down stairs while she was seated atop a velvet pillow, and she preferred to take in the sights by sedan chair rather than by carriage.

Ali admired how she "always found some way to escape being at divine service." Yet she respected the Mulini's strict court etiquette, performing a deep curtsy like everyone else if she passed her brother in one of the narrow halls or staircases. Once, when her black velvet dress displeased Napoleon, she went immediately to change, and the same thing happened a few days later when she wore a ghostly white dress, because something about it reminded Napoleon too much of the 1790s craze for dressing à la victime, when French fashionistas had playfully imitated the looks of people executed at the hands of the Revolution with scarlet chokers around their necks, or hair cut short where a guillotine blade would have hit.

Some of Napoleon's contemporaries, including one French minister in a letter to Talleyrand, suggested that the charged relationship between brother and sister turned incestuous on Elba. While the evidence supporting such claims is tenuous, it does seem that Pauline acted as a kind of procurer, arranging for paid companions to visit Napoleon, the system apparently organized through little notes. A Spanish woman, married to one of Napoleon's Polish lancers and renowned for the way she danced the fandango, was among those who reportedly participated in this arrangement on Elba.

Pauline seemed to be more at ease when she was away from her brother at the Saint-Cloud property, where, as Pons wrote, she "seized any chance to multiply her pleasures," and was often seen in the company of an amorous officer named Loubers. She liked to dance with Cambronne, who couldn't keep up with her, and to flirt with the devout Drouot. As Peyrusse recalled, her "presence was a source of pleasure and enjoyment for the Emperor's court, for the women of the town, and for the garrison." In short, life was not altogether unpleasant for her or for the members of her retinue. "I would be happy to live at Portoferraio, the town seems to me a little Paris," wrote one of Pauline's attendants. "There are fine grenadiers and handsome Poles on horseback. One would think one hadn't left France." But Pauline recognized that the idyll couldn't last forever and to her the situation felt as unsettled as the mercurial climate. "There are great winds here," she wrote from Elba, "the weather is very changeable. I enjoy being with my brother, but I am anxious for the future."

Having his sister and mother nearby would have been a great comfort for Napoleon, who had been raised by an extended family of women, which included an aunt, two grandmothers, and a nursemaid, all overseen by the young widow Letizia. "Elsewhere they see you rich, noble, or learned," he once said, "but in Corsica you brag about your relatives. They are what make a man praiseworthy or feared." Their presence at Portoferraio elicited memories of their old Ajaccio home on Saint Charles Street. One night at the Mulini, Napoleon remembered the time Madame Mère had caught him and his sister imitating one of their wizened grandmothers, who was "bent . . . like an old fairy." Letizia had only punished Pauline, since it was "easier to pull up skirts than undo breeches," as Napoleon put it, though he was the older sibling by eleven years.

Pauline's arrival would have helped Napoleon financially as well. She'd started selling off her properties out of a presentiment that the Bourbons would sequester them without compensation, since she hadn't seen any sign of her own state pension, promised, as with Napoleon's, by the Treaty of Fontainebleau. She sold her place on the rue du Faubourg Saint-Honoré to the British government and it was turned over to the Duke of Wellington to use as ambassador to Louis XVIII's court.

DOMESTIC LIFE AT PORTOFERRAIO was not all joyful that autumn. The Bertrands' infant son died just a few weeks after Pauline's arrival. Napoleon encouraged the grieving Fanny to walk the grounds at San Martino. She'd been a regular guest at the original Saint-Cloud, where she often rode for pleasure, and he thought she might find some comfort in this ersatz Elban version. Eventually he was able to visit with her and became a frequent guest at the Bertrand home at the Biscotteria. Afternoons Napoleon and Fanny went off in his carriage or out on his rowboat, sometimes accompanied by young Napoleon Bertrand, the couple's eldest child, who enjoyed playing at wooden swords with his namesake. French agents learning of this closeness assumed the relationship between Napoleon and Fanny was strictly platonic. Though she often dined at the Mulini without her husband, she was always seen returning home directly after the meal's end. She sometimes brought her children along to the meals and Napoleon made sure they left with sweetmeats and candies.

During the final exile Henri would allude in his diary to Napoleon's making advances on Fanny, which sometimes left her in tears. "Give her another child," Napoleon told him, at a point when Fanny was so desperate to leave Saint Helena that she bordered on the edge of madness. "That will postpone your departure for a year, and will also give her something to interest her." He seems to have been fascinated by Henri's devotion to the elegant Fanny. "What love!" he said of the couple. "I've never seen anything like it!" Perhaps with her aristocratic Martinique upbringing and blood ties to Joséphine, Fanny reminded him too much of his former wife. In the last feverish days of his life Napoleon told Bertrand that he "held it against" Fanny for not having become his mistress.

After the death of his son, Henri would do most of his work from home and went to the Mulini only when summoned, which Napoleon took as an insult. On Saint Helena he claimed that Henri had been of little use to him on Elba, since "he was always with his wife and children." But in fact he was vital to Elba's government. Each new idea Napoleon wanted to put into action first passed through him, and Henri reworked his off-the-cuff dictation into readable prose, sometimes annotating for clarity or making suggestions. The valets got used to hearing the shouted insults that such advice could prompt. More than once, while Napoleon was mid-rant, they would see Bertrand walking out of the room, his face as red as wine.

Pons thought that these bouts were merely the natural result of putting two men of such vastly different temperaments in close quarters, bound together by circumstance rather than true friendship. He was sure that Bertrand couldn't have been too pleased by the types of mundane assignments he was given on Elba. The grand marshal struck him as a decent and hardworking man, compromised in Napoleon's eyes because of his sentimental attachment to Fanny, a coupling that apparently thrilled him as much as it disturbed him. But then Napoleon, wrote Pons, had always shown "too great a liking for finding out the vulgar details of married lives."

27

Don Giovanni, Cinderella, and Undine

Marie Louise's time at the spa came to an end after Talleyrand advised Metternich that "it would suit us both if her stay at Aix was not prolonged." When she crossed the French border on September 7, leaving her adopted country for the last time, her traveling companions saw no great display of emotion.

She reached Lausanne, where the Princess of Wales happened to be passing through, and Marie Louise invited her to dine. There was a post-meal duet from *Don Giovanni* with Neipperg on piano. Marie Louise timidly sang soprano as Zerlina, fighting off seduction by the titular libertine, while the Princess of Wales belted out Don Giovanni's plaintive baritone. The latter, wrote Méneval, "sang with a voice of which I will say nothing except that it really showed this princess's courage."

A few days later, Marie Louise reached the town of Küssnacht abutting the shore of Lake Zug. They headed up a narrow mountain path that led to a chapel devoted to William Tell and passed the spot where Tell's arrow pierced and killed the hated Austrian overlord Gessler. Waylaid by a huge mountain storm, Marie Louise, Neipperg, and the rest of the party had to spend the night at the Golden Sun inn nearby. Just before bed, Marie Louise dismissed the footman who normally stood watch at the door of her bedroom. Méneval occupied the neighboring room. A short while later, Méneval wrote to his wife, "I can no longer fool myself that she is the pure and spotless angel whom I held above reproach."

She reached Vienna on October 7, having just missed the Feast of Saint Francis of Assisi, her father's name day, perhaps on purpose. The Bonaparte coat of arms was removed from the panels of her carriages as soon as she was out of sight. She was to be addressed as Archduchess, never as Empress, and her son, whose full name was Napoléon François Charles Joseph Bonaparte, was to be referred to as Franz. Courtiers were instructed to spare her any mention of her husband's name. Metternich allowed a few of Napoleon's messages to reach her, but only after they had been properly vetted. Neipperg was formally named as her chamberlain.

When duty required, she would receive dignitaries who were in Vienna for the congress, among them Tsar Alexander, but she avoided the nightly feasts and dances, so full of malicious talk. People called her Madame Neipperg behind her back. One night she watched from behind glass as a carnival party unfolded with tumblers, musicians, torchbearers, cavalrymen, and diplomats arriving in golden sleighs, filing into the palace to be treated to an enormous feast and a performance of *Cinderella*. People talked about her as if she were a nun, she told a friend. The police inspector tasked with monitoring her movements in Vienna requested a change of assignment.

She saw little benefit in continuing to play the public role of royalty. She practiced her guitar and read her books. She took her son to the palace Tiergarten, the oldest zoo in the world, to see the bears and buffalo and kangaroos from New Holland. She played at billiards and called on Neipperg when it pleased her. She worked at translating from French to German the fairytale novella *Undine*, which tells the story of a water nymph who marries a dashing knight to gain a soul. Tossed aside by her spouse for a less mysterious human woman, she returns to kill him with a poison kiss as he sleeps beside his new love.

. . .

ALTHOUGH POLITICAL IN its origin and focus, the Vienna conference was also one of the greatest social events of the nineteenth century. Giddy at the prospect of creating a new era of lasting peace, the delegates and their hangers-on transformed the Austrian capital into the site of a nonstop bacchanal (although Castlereagh complained about the lack of decent wine). They went through six hundred rations of coffee a day, kept in enormous kettles, and made use of the fourteen hundred horses and three hundred carriages, many built specially for the event, that Francis had put at their disposal. Noting the prodigious spending on all things gastronomic, an Austrian agent remarked that Francis had discovered "a new way to wage war: eat your enemy."

The treasury was already overstretched; the Austrians had fought France more often and at greater expense over the past twenty years than any other power except Britain. But Francis recognized the value in being seen as Europe's most magnanimous host and, hopefully, its prime peacemaker. And all the socializing served a larger aim. People of different nations and dynastic houses were forced to spend a lot of time together, often sleeping under the same roof, and political matters were discussed in informal settings, on hunts and over meals, which lessened the chance of some kind of blowup that might result in a duel, or diplomatic incident.

Entitled by the treaties of Fontainebleau and Paris to take up her position as Duchess of Parma, Piacenza, and Guastalla, Marie Louise had yet to be allowed to claim these Italian territories. The Spanish and French contingents at Vienna were working to have the lands given to the Spanish infanta, Maria Luisa, queen of Etruria, whose claim stemmed from a complicated set of territorial exchanges involving Spain and France during Napoleon's rule. Francis was meanwhile secretly trying to have his daughter's claim deferred for as long as possible. He wanted to keep her from taking power in lands so close to Elba, where her presence might stir up Italian nationalists looking to drive the Austrians out of Tuscany and turn their disparate lands from "a mere geographic expression" (as Metternich described Italy) into a sovereign nation, perhaps with Marie Louise as queen and an escaped Napoleon and Murat as military commanders. Metternich, who had helped secure these lands for Marie Louise in the first place, now counseled her to be satisfied with the rights and pensions afforded to her as an Austrian archduchess and ask for nothing more. "Each day there was a fresh story," wrote Méneval. "Today Parma was assured to her, on the morrow it had been given to somebody else."

Her husband's exile was another among the many contentious issues under discussion. Talleyrand suggested to some of the other diplomats that an island somewhere farther away like the Azores would be a better place to send Napoleon. Castlereagh thought it possible for the allies to secure an island from the Portuguese, though he added that they would have to offer Napoleon compensation for the loss of Elba as a way to persuade him to change locations. Talleyrand wrote to Louis XVIII with this idea, mentioning his unease at the potential cost. The king replied that he would find a way to free up whatever money was necessary to see "the excellent idea of the Azores be carried out." Talleyrand meanwhile made inquiries into the suitability of Trinidad, Saint Lucia, and Botany Bay as alternatives. Talleyrand was especially keen on Saint Helena, given its isolation in the South Atlantic. A Swiss diplomat wrote in his journal that the king of Bavaria had sworn to him that Napoleon's move to Saint Helena was imminent.

The Parisian papers began hinting that a fateful decision had been reached concerning Napoleon's exile. Matters were made more complicated by the arrival in Vienna of Luigi Boncompagni, the ancestral Prince of Piombino, who brought a valise full of documents outlining in detail why he was the legitimate sovereign of Elba, which, as he argued, should have been handed to him when Napoleon abdicated. Meanwhile, whether motivated by cunning, malice, or economic pragmatism, Louis XVIII stood his ground on denying Napoleon his pension, even though this alienated him from the allied leaders in Vienna, who thought his decision not only rash but ignoble. Talleyrand told him that Alexander, Castlereagh, and Metternich were harassing him with questions about "the silence of the budget on this matter." Alexander had complained that "the treaty isn't being carried out, and we cannot depart from its stipulations in any way." Alexander had asked Talleyrand how they could expect Napoleon to keep his word with them, "when we did not do so with him?"

There had likely never been so many people talking politics in such a relatively confined space for so long as there were in Vienna that fall and winter. That much of this talk turned to the subject of Napoleon only reinforced how conspicuous he was by his absence. Many of the states represented at the congress had at some time or another been aligned with Napoleon, and the memories of those times were not all terrible. Like awkward strangers at a party abandoned by their host who seek comfort by discussing the foibles of their mutual friend, the delegates swapped endless stories about the emperor. One night's salon might find the Duke of Rocca Romana, Murat's handsome representative, spinning tales of his adventures in 1812, removing a glove to reveal the loss of four fingers to the Russian cold, while another would be commandeered by the naval hero Sidney Smith detailing how he'd handed "Boney" one of his rare defeats at the siege of Acre, the "key to Palestine."

Every battle he waged, every law he passed, every crime he committed could be dissected and debated. Some delegates even ventured to say that with his boundless energies Napoleon would have pushed the congress to resolve its issues at a pace far faster than the one set by the victorious but ineffective sovereigns, muddling through with so much talk and so little action. By the letter of the law, the Emperor of Elba should have been allowed to send his own emissary to Vienna, since his island was recognized as a sovereign principality. Europe's rulers, however, were interpreting the technicalities of the Treaty of Fontainebleau as they saw fit, and it would have been bizarre to invite him to participate. Napoleon did send one of the Mulini's chefs to Vienna to find employment as a courier so he could send back reports, but even with a loose network of supporters and informants, there was no way for him to keep up with the daily workings of the congress or of how the conversations in Vienna might somehow come to upend his life on Elba.

28

I THINK HE IS CAPABLE
OF CROSSING OVER

IN NOVEMBER, NAPOLEON SAW a copy of an edition of the London *Courier*, sent to him by a British Bonapartist, the Baroness Holland, which reported that the diplomats in Vienna were working to "finally determine the future residence of Napoleon Buonaparte" and that it was "believed to be quite certain" he would be transported from Elba as soon as the congress closed. The article mentioned the Caribbean island of Saint Lucia as the likely destination. (In his will, Napoleon would remember Lady Holland—who also sent him rare seeds and other items during his final exile—with the gift of a golden snuffbox.)

Campbell had been the one to relay the baroness's correspondence to Elba, either because he wasn't worried about whatever effect the story in the *Courier* would have on Napoleon or because he was consciously trying to antagonize him, for whatever private reason. Napoleon asked Campbell how long he thought the congress would last, saying he didn't think it was possible for so many rulers to be gathered for any decent stretch of time without some kind of rupture, but Campbell had no information that would allow him to predict the conference's length any better than Napoleon could.

After this conversation he wrote his most urgent letter yet to Castlereagh:

> If pecuniary difficulties press upon him much longer, so as to prevent his vanity from being satisfied by the ridiculous establishment of a court which he has hitherto supported in Elba, and if his doubts are not removed, I think he is capable of crossing over to Piombino with his troops, or of any other eccentricity. But if his residence in Elba and his income are secured to him, I think he will pass the rest of his life there in tranquility.

With no clear sense of how the congress was unfolding, Napoleon assumed the worst. The threat of being sent to somewhere such as Saint Lucia or Saint Helena likely helped solidify whatever abstract thoughts of escape he might have had until that point. His decision to finally end the monthslong tax standoff in Capoliveri may have been prompted by the reports out of Vienna. If he was actively planning to leave he would have wanted to gather as much ready cash as possible. On November 16, Drouot sent twenty gendarmes, ten cavalry, and another 180 troops to Capoliveri, marching in time so they would arrive at the hilltop village as a fearsome whole. A priest suspected of leading the tax uprising was arrested along with two conspirators. The soldiers fired warning shots into the air, but the villagers still refused to pay, so Napoleon had quartered troops among the fifty families who owed the most taxes, with each soldier entitled to collect a heavy portion of meat and wine, a burden that finally made Capoliveri yield. All outstanding taxes were paid in the next few weeks and the troops were removed, though the priest remained imprisoned at Portoferraio.

Campbell chose this tumultuous time to leave again for Florence. When he arrived there in late November he was likely shown a notice in the *London Gazette* announcing that he was to be knighted by the prince regent for "highly distinguished services" performed in Martinique, Guadalupe, Ciudad Rodrigo, and Salamanca, and for "the great zeal and ability manifested by him while attached to the Russian army." The announcement made no mention of his current assignment.

None of Campbell's Tuscan contacts seemed concerned by his reports on the Tunisian corsair that had made contact with Portoferraio a few days earlier, nor did anyone have much to tell him about the recent interrogation of a Bonapartist agent arrested at Livorno while traveling back from Elba. In the meantime, Ricci had written to tell him that Elban troops were loading guns and shot onto the *Inconstant*, which was being prepared to sail, apparently for a trade run.

Frustrated by the indifference of the Tuscan officials and irked by Ricci's letter, Campbell decided his worries about Napoleon trumped any desire for secrecy. He sought out the French agent Hyde de Neuville and spoke openly with him about his role on Elba:

> I showed him Lord Castlereagh's instructions, and gave him every information connected with my own duties, Napoleon's situation, and his dispositions, desiring to call his attention to the unlimited freedom of person and communication with the Continent which Napoleon possessed. I then distinctly pronounced to him my opinion that Napoleon was not sufficiently watched; that I had no means of preventing him from escaping; that he was still of a most restless disposition; that discontented persons of an adventurous spirit from France and Italy frequented Elba; that it was a very suspicious circumstance, the communication held with the Tunisian ship; that I had traced her coming to Elba. I even supposed it possible to him, that a conspiracy might be formed in Napoleon's favour at Toulon [where the Tunisian corsair had reportedly docked]; he could be conveyed in that ship.

Hyde de Neuville transcribed everything Campbell told him and rushed to Paris to advise officials to send another patrol squadron from Toulon to enforce a closer watch on Elba and that troops garrisoned in southern France should be switched out to ensure that only loyal men who hadn't made arrangements with anyone from Elba would be stationed there. Hyde de Neuville told Beugnot they should weed out any officials in Corsica of dubious character and should look more closely at any French representatives along the Italian peninsula, while doubling efforts to intercept letters from Elba to France. He also wrote directly to Louis XVIII, warning that

> the English will do little or nothing to keep him on his island. If he leaves, he can again overturn Italy or start a civil war in France. . . . I continue to believe that one must put the seas between him and Europe.

29

THE OIL MERCHANT
AND OTHER VISITORS

ON THE LAST DAY of November a dapper Italian disembarked at Portoferraio and presented a passport in the name of Alessandro Forli to Cambronne, who was charged with overseeing the lazaretto. He appeared to be a prosperous Italian merchant and said he'd come to sell olive oil. He arrived alongside a well-known Italian nationalist who claimed to want to organize a Bonapartist insurrection on the peninsula, and this man's company was enough to vouch for the merchant's character. He installed himself in Portoferraio and spent a good part of each day lounging at the Buon Gusto on the main square. He had a good ear for accents and could usually guess people's origins with great accuracy, which he used as a way to strike up conversations with strangers.

Alessandro Forli was almost certainly an alias; to French officials he was known only by his code name: the Oil Merchant. He was likely a career spy, fond of veiled meanings and invisible inks, and always dubious about any information acquired, striving in his reports to filter out as much café talk as possible. He was astute to pose as a seller of fine oils, likely assuming that the members of the exiled entourage could be enticed by the promise of good eating in any season and despite reportedly dwindling funds. He never breached the Mulini palace directly but managed to sell oil to Madame Mère's household and to others close to Napoleon's inner circle. In one report he complained that so much of his day was spent actually conducting his oil business that there was little time left for spying. But there were enough people at the Buon Gusto with lips loosened by the earthy aleatico to keep him alerted to any major developments.

Women provided him with much of his information and were evidently drawn to him; among his unknowing informants were the mistress of a commandant of the Guard and the wife of an officer employed at the Mulini. From the commandant's mistress he learned of a conversation in which Napoleon asked Drouot, "What do you think? Would it be too soon to leave the island at Carnival time?" He approached this hearsay cautiously, just as he did when some drunken soldiers boasted that they would return Napoleon to the throne as soon as their friends on the continent were ready. Nor did he panic when he overheard some Italian travelers saying that as soon as Napoleon appeared on the peninsula, fifty thousand men would rally to his side. He knew that there were many frustrated men on Elba and beyond who claimed to be ready to follow Napoleon, but he remained convinced, at least for the time being, that this was all just daydreaming and grumbling.

The Oil Merchant's reports flowed to Talleyrand via a diplomat named François Antoine Mariotti, the French consul at Livorno, who numbered among the network of agents, informants, and officials that Talleyrand had assembled to gather information about Napoleon, his court, and anyone suspected of harboring sympathy for his cause. Born in Corsica, Mariotti had helped Napoleon to secure Elba more than a decade earlier as a battalion chief in the army. He'd also served as the longtime personal guard to Elisa Bonaparte, who, perhaps for romantic reasons, tried to secure him a promotion until Napoleon rejected the request. After Mariotti rallied to the Bourbon cause, Talleyrand had posted him to Livorno, naming him a baron as soon as he took up the post. Mariotti made gathering intelligence about Napoleon his only real job, ensuring that no letter made it through Livorno without his first seeing it, including Campbell's private correspondence. He referred to himself as a "machine" built specifically to fight Napoleon.

Through the Oil Merchant and other informants, Mariotti came to know the most intimate details about Napoleon's life on Elba: whom he dined with and when, how much he paid for his properties, and how often he exercised. When Napoleon's carriage crushed a chicken just outside Porto Longone and the bird's owner, failing to get compensation for her loss, cursed the emperor and the foul winds that had brought him to Elba, Mariotti knew about it, and when a few days later an ordinance was posted forbidding Elbans to let their chickens roam free in the streets, he knew about that as well. He knew that Napoleon had only left his tent twice during the whole time of Marie Walewska's visit to the mountain hermitage.

Talleyrand shared pertinent information gleaned from Mariotti's reports with Louis XVIII, Tsar Alexander, and Metternich. One item that caught his attention in November claimed that some Elban troops had been in contact with Murat, and told of the *Inconstant*'s recent friendly exchanges with the Tunisians who had docked at Portoferraio. This led Talleyrand to think, as Campbell had, that Napoleon was crafting some kind of southern alliance. "The conclusion which I draw from all this," he wrote to Louis XVIII, "is that it would be well to get rid without delay of the man of the island of Elba, and of Murat."

THE OIL MERCHANT WASN'T the only stranger to show up in Portoferraio in the last weeks of fall. Drifting soldiers on half-pay came to haunt the doors of the Mulini in sporadic bursts, eager to flatter their hero. Among them was an old *grognard* who recounted a long journey filled with nights spent on sweat-stained cots and thin mattresses. He said that in cafés and billiard rooms all the way from Lyon to Genoa people said again and again how much they hoped for the glorious return of their emperor. The Bourbons wouldn't last another six months, he predicted, and any fool who had once believed that with the restoration "the larks would tumble into their mouths ready roasted" was by now sorely disappointed. He claimed that only a few nobles and members of clergy remained loyal to Louis XVIII and that they were "cow-ards who wouldn't dare to show themselves" if Napoleon returned to take his throne.

British travelers were also often granted audiences with Napoleon. A Welsh copper-master named Vivian claimed that when he showed up unan-nounced at the Bertrand house asking to see the Emperor of Elba, Henri in-vited him to dine, lent him some books, pressed tickets into his hands for an upcoming ball, and later took him to meet all three Bonapartes on the island. Pauline complained to him about how badly her brother was being misrepre-sented in the papers, while Fanny Bertrand explained to him how the Bour-bons had managed to rob Napoleon of nearly all his wealth. There is little reason to doubt Vivian's account, or that of the Whig politician Lord Ebring-ton, who wrote that when he visited Elba, Napoleon asked him if he would be stoned by an angry mob if he were to walk down the streets of London, to which he answered that he would be safe, "since the violent feelings which had been excited against him were daily subsiding now that we are no longer at war." By flattering British visitors with his presence, Napoleon was able to gather information about developments on the mainland while also setting them up to return home with sympathetic reports about his supposedly shabby treatment at the hands of the Bourbons.

All of these visits put spies and their superiors on alert, though no one was sure exactly how to react to this information. The wealthy diplomat John Fane, Lord Burghersh, who had recently accepted a post in Florence making him the senior British official in the region, wrote to Castlereagh about some British travelers who had been "received with attention," and added that all sorts of "foreigners" had been given audiences with Napoleon, who always spoke "without reserve upon the many transactions of his life. From the gen-eral manner of his reception, it is difficult to decide the degree of importance which should be attached to the visits of persons of intriguing characters."

Tuscan officials meanwhile questioned a Frenchwoman named Berluc who returned from Elba after reportedly enjoying a romantic liaison with a captain of the Guard, which had allowed her access to Pauline's inner circle. She told her interrogators that Napoleon was actively recruiting and training a small army with the aim of returning to the continent. She said he would land either in southern France or on the Ligurian coast. Police Chief Beugnot did nothing with this information except to write to Louis XVIII that while Napoleon undoubtedly had ambitions to return "to trouble the world," there was no feasible way he could pull it off. "They speak of his *army*," he wrote. "As if he would land in France with seven or eight hundred men, of which the most part would desert as soon as they could!"

{ 30 }

HE HAD BEEN CALLED COWARD!

CAMPBELL RETURNED TO ELBA on December 3 and confirmed Ricci's report that soldiers had loaded the *Inconstant* with guns and shells removed from the Porto Longone citadel. Campbell figured that Napoleon had realized there was little reward in maintaining fortifications relatively far from his capital and wanted to sell off whatever materiel he could spare. He'd just sold a building in Porto Longone that had been used as a barracks, for a mere fifteen hundred francs, and had discharged some of his servants, which Campbell interpreted as more evidence that he'd put himself on a tighter budget, like a retiree who finally accepts that he can no longer live in the same manner as during his most productive years.

During another talk at the Mulini, Napoleon asked if Campbell had seen the newspapers calling for him to be divorced from Marie Louise, to which he said that he'd read something along those lines but only in some "foreign papers," which were always full of lies. He tried to cheer up Napoleon by saying that he'd heard during his recent travels that when the Princess of Wales complemented Marie Louise on her skill at music, she said she'd studied especially to please her husband. The story only seemed to sadden Napoleon, who complained to Campbell about how his capricious wife had broken her promise to write him every day after her time at the spa, and about his father-in-law, who had taken the King of Rome from him "like the children taken by conquerors in ancient times to grace their triumphs." He told Campbell he would have done better to have married one of the Romanov girls.

As always, he tried to get some sense of how Louis XVIII was faring in France, adding that "the French knew what he had done for them" and then listing how much money he'd brought into the country and all the public works projects he'd started, which he said "were now ascribed to his predecessors. Before him there wasn't a sewer in all the streets of Paris. . . . Posterity would do him justice." He told Campbell he was tired of being abused in the papers and of having the words of Nero and Brutus applied to him; he ranted about Talleyrand, that "villain, a defrocked priest," who he said would prove to be no more loyal to his king than he'd been to his emperor.

Campbell suggested that Napoleon might plead his case in the court of public opinion by following up on the promise he'd heard him make at Fontainebleau to write his memoirs in exile. He even offered to act as a kind of literary agent, saying that he "had received many letters from booksellers in London, totally unknown to me, expressing great anxiety on the subject. One in particular, who had published his brother Lucien's poem of 'Charlemagne,' wished to propose terms." Campbell wrote that Napoleon answered, "Yes, I shall publish my 'Memoirs,' but they won't be very long."

But literary dreams offered only momentary distraction. Napoleon was soon back to railing against his enemies. He rehashed the fall of Paris, saying that his men at Fontainebleau had been only a day's march away from the capital and that if he'd seized the moment and attacked they would have taken it back easily. He could, he said, have carried on the war for years and his people would have continued to follow him. The worst of it, according to Campbell, parroting Napoleon, was that "he had been called coward! 'I say nothing of my life as a soldier. Is it no proof of my courage to live here, shut up in this shack of a house, separated from the world, with no interesting occupation, no men of learning with me.'" And yet he said he harbored no regrets about abdicating and would do the same again, all in the name of protecting France. The rest of the night's talk was dedicated to retracing his biography, "at great length . . . from the beginning of the Revolution, and with more fire and precision than usual."

Afterward, Campbell wrote to Castlereagh that

> if the means of subsistence which he was led to expect on coming to Elba are given to him, he will remain here in perfect tranquility, unless some great opening should present itself in Italy or France. He does not dissemble his opinion as to the latter, in regard to the present temper of the people, and what may be expected hereafter.

In the meantime, Campbell promised to "keep a lookout upon all vessels belonging to this island," and produced a detailed list of all the ships under Napoleon's command. He next wrote to Burghersh to assure him that any recent reports about Napoleon's planning to return to the mainland had been overblown, because aside from worrying about Marie Louise he seemed very satisfied with life on Elba. "The more I see of him the more I am convinced of this. He is in good health and spirits!"

WINTER

A Last Goodbye

A FEW WEEKS AFTER her twenty-third birthday, Marie Louise addressed a letter "To His Majesty the Emperor Napoleon at Portoferraio" and dated it January 3, 1815. It was the first time she'd written to her husband since leaving Aix-les-Bains in the summer. She gave the letter to her father to send on to Elba:

> My Darling, it seems a hundred years since I was last able to write to you, or received any letters from you, then suddenly my father produced your dear letter from November 20. I felt a great weight lifted from my heart when I heard that you were well and did not doubt all my love for you. I can imagine how troubled you must have been at not getting news of your son or of me for such a long time. I know just what it feels like, from the anxiety which fills my own heart when I'm left for months at a time without a single scrap of news from you and without knowing whether you are well. I hope this year will be a happier one for you. At least you'll be at peace in your island, and will live there happily for many, many years, to the joy of all who love you and who are, as I am, deeply devoted to you.
>
> Your son sends you a kiss and begs me to wish you a happy

New Year and to tell you he loves you with all his heart. He often talks about you, and is growing taller and stronger in the most astonishing fashion. He had been rather out of sorts this winter. I at once consulted Frank, who completely reassured me by saying they were only passing bouts of fever, indeed he recovered almost immediately. He's beginning to know Italian fairly well and is learning German too. My father is treating him with the greatest kindness and affection, he appears to love him devotedly and spends a great deal of time playing with him. He is heaping kindnesses upon me too, in fact all my family are treating me with the utmost affection and going out of their way to make me forget all our misfortunes.

Hardly a day passes without my going to see my father, who often asks whether I have heard from you. It is he who had undertaken to send this letter to Portoferraio with the help of the Grand Duke of Tuscany. If it reaches you safely, I do most earnestly beg you always to use this channel of communication. I'll take advantage of it too, then at least I'll know how you are.

My health is completely restored. The waters, the Swiss climate and the mountain air have had a really wonderful effect on it. I've put on a lot of weight and feel none the worse for the bitterly cold weather we've been having for some time now. I'm living an extremely secluded life at Schönbrunn, befitting my personal inclinations and my position so long as the allied sovereigns remain here. I hardly ever see more than 3 or 4 people in the evenings. We have a little music, or I chat by my fireside. Please remember me to Madame and to Princess Pauline. Write to me soon. Once again I wish you a happy New Year and send you a loving kiss.

Louise

Napoleon never saw the letter. Marie Louise never wrote to him again.

{ 32 }

THE SADNESS OF MY RETIREMENT

CAMPBELL RETURNED TO ELBA in late December after another brief trip to Florence, where he'd learned that the Austrian commissioner Koller was heading from Vienna toward Elba for some unknown reason. At the Mulini, Napoleon asked Campbell what he thought of Koller's impending visit. Did it mean his wife and child would finally be allowed to join him? Or could it mean the allies had finally arranged to ship him off somewhere else? Campbell had no idea what to make of it.

Campbell could sense that a distance was growing between Napoleon and himself. "He has gradually estranged himself from me, and various means are taken to show me that my presence is disagreeable. Of this, however, I could not be certain for a long time, as it was done by hints which could not well be noticed." When Lord Ebrington had come to Elba a few weeks earlier he was invited to dine at the Mulini, but Campbell, who had always been asked to join in meals with British visitors, received no invitation:

> [This] was intended as a marked slight, for the purpose of inducing
> me to quit Elba entirely. But, always expecting the Congress to be
> brought to an end, I have resolved to make the sacrifice of my own

feelings until that event, occasionally going to Livorno, Florence, and the baths at Lucca for my health and amusement, as well as to compare my observations here with the information of authorities on the Continent and the French Consul at Livorno. My return always gives me an opportunity of asking for an interview with Napoleon, to pay my respects. Of late he has evidently wished to surround himself with great forms of court, as well to preserve his own consequence in the eyes of the Italians as to keep me at distance; for I could not transgress on these without the probability of an insult, or the proffer of servile adulation inconsistent with my sentiments.

Over the next weeks Campbell began devoting less and less space in his journal to the details of his assignment. He recorded little by way of direct observation, relying mostly on secondhand chatter, and his letters to colleagues and superiors shrank to a few sentences each. In one, in which he thanked Mariotti for sending some newspapers, he wrote that the distraction had helped "diminish the sadness of my *retirement*."

He received word from the Foreign Office refusing his request to be stationed somewhere on the continent close to Elba. Yet he would manage to spend about as much time that winter away from the island as he did at his post.

33

THE (NEAR) WRECK OF
THE *INCONSTANT*

IT SNOWED ON PORTOFERRAIO in the first week of the new year. Just as no one had been able to recall a hotter summer, nor could anyone remember ever having seen a bigger snowfall. Some of the more superstitious Elbans attributed the odd weather patterns to Napoleon's presence among them.

The squall hit just as Captain Taillade had been piloting the *Inconstant* back from Civitavecchia, returning empty-handed from a trade run because the port's merchants had orders from the pope not to deal with Napoleon's representatives. Before sailing, Taillade had lost his valise during a dockside donnybrook orchestrated by Civitavecchia's portmaster, who sought evidence of what he believed to be Napoleon's forthcoming attack on the Holy See. The valise held a letter from Bertrand advising an unnamed confederate to prepare for a message that would be transmitted verbally by a Corsican tax official at some later date, which inflamed the portmaster's fears of impending intrigue. After riffling through a shipment of books bound for Portoferraio, he also discovered an unsigned letter addressed to Bertrand advising him to read volume 127, and tucked into the volume in question he found letters from Murat to Napoleon and Pauline Bonaparte. They were brief and divulged nothing scandalous—Murat stressed to Pauline that she should say nothing about Napoleon in her reply, and his standoffish message to his brother-in-law said only that his family sent good tidings and that he heard Napoleon's wife and son were in good health—but they were the first real signs of direct communication between Napoleon and the king of Naples, despite their public feud. The portmaster would have arrested Captain Taillade on the spot if he'd thought he could have done so without causing an international incident.

The *Inconstant* and its crew were left undisturbed by the Tuscan authorities only to be assailed by a powerful easterly gale that blew the ship so far off its intended course that it wound up past the northern tip of Corsica. Taillade finally secured a firm anchorage just off Saint-Florent, though this put him within firing range of Corsican guns.

Taillade elected to stay anchored in this unlikely position for more than a week, later claiming that he'd wanted to wait out the foul weather while repairing some rigging and that he'd judged that particular anchorage the safest place to do so. Taillade would never adequately address the later accusations that several Corsicans made contact with the *Inconstant* while it was moored off the coast, or that he spoke in clipped English (he had once been a British prisoner of war) with some of these visitors to keep their conversations from being understood by his second in command, an officer named Jean François Chautard. It's unclear how seriously, if at all, Taillade flirted with switching allegiances during this time. On January 10 he abruptly decided to leave Corsica and guided the *Inconstant* back toward Elba despite fierce winds blowing sleet and snow.

It took two backbreaking days of sailing to get the ship close to Portoferraio. On the night of January 12, in choppy water, Taillade navigated the narrows between the lighthouse atop Fort Stella and the skerry a few hundred meters to its north, Lo Scoglietto (the Little Rock), sailing dangerously by the lee in the darkness. The *Inconstant* got caught in irons, stalled by oncoming winds, and was eventually blown westward at speed across the harbor toward a jagged beach. Taillade dropped two anchors, but they failed to hold. He fired a cannon shot in distress. The *Inconstant* ran aground.

Napoleon woke to alarm bells and reached the beach just as the first rays of sunlight came through the dark clouds. He saw the abandoned *Inconstant* pounded by waves and tangled in its rigging. The storm lifted just long enough for the crew to rush back on board and toss some guns and heavy cargo to save the ship from sinking. After a cursory investigation, Drouot officially blamed Taillade for "incapacity and peculation" and demoted him, though he would remain in Napoleon's service. Command of the *Inconstant* passed to the inexperienced Chautard.

Writing a few days later, Campbell reported that "some persons say that Napoleon suspects [Taillade] of a secret understanding with the existing Government of France, and of a wish to destroy the brig." And yet according to Peyrusse's memoirs, Napoleon himself had planned the grounding of the *Inconstant,* as a way to provide cover for it to be outfitted for his escape while appearing to be under repair. But this seems doubtful. Even a master sailor couldn't have been certain the *Inconstant* would survive a mock shipwreck, and Taillade was no master. To risk destroying the surest means of connecting Elba to the continent would have been foolishly bold. The near sinking of the *Inconstant* was more likely an accident, and if so, might have provided the final push that Napoleon needed to decide on quitting Elba for good. The narrowly avoided loss of the key ship in his meager fleet would have served as a blatant reminder of how vulnerable he remained so long as he stayed on the island.

CAMPBELL MISSED the drama of the *Inconstant* by a day, having gone to Genoa to offer a naval escort to Baron Koller, figuring that the Austrian diplomat would be arriving there shortly on his way to Elba and that it would be good for them to have a chance to discuss Napoleon's situation privately before reaching the island. But he left Genoa after a few days of waiting, without any sign of Koller or news from Vienna concerning his whereabouts.

As soon as he reached Portoferraio, Campbell was subjected to the usual onslaught of questions. Napoleon had read another news item predicting his "removal" to Saint Helena or Saint Lucia, and swore to Campbell he would rather die defending Elba than be taken away. He then asked "with a kind of suspicious curiosity" whether Campbell had communicated with any of the French warships that had lately been seen cruising the channel between

Corsica and Elba, but Campbell avoided answering. Growing more frantic as the conversation went on, Napoleon told him that he was certain the governor of Corsica had sent someone to kill him and that the assassin had already landed on Elba with the help of one of those French ships, but that the gendarmes would find him soon enough. "He appeared much agitated," wrote Campbell, "and impressed with a belief in the truth of what he stated."

Napoleon by that point would likely have learned that on Christmas Eve, British and American representatives at Ghent signed a treaty ending the War of 1812 that had tested the strength of the young republic across the ocean, whose capital had been burned to the ground a few months earlier. Now battle-hardened men would be returning to Europe, meaning more ships and crews would soon be available to be dispatched to patrol the waters of the Mediterranean. Peyrusse noticed that Napoleon's temper seemed to be growing worse with the revelation of each new bit of news from abroad; his words that winter "were few, his evenings were short, and his ill humor was plain to see."

34

BOURBON DIFFICULTIES

DISTURBING REPORTS CONTINUED TO pile up on the bureaus of French officials that January. The governor of Corsica, Louis Guerin de Bruslart, wrote to the French minister of war, General Dupont, to say that Napoleon was so spooked by rumors he would be transported that his troops were marching at Portoferraio day and night, and that there were fifteen hundred men ready to sail with him at a moment's notice. Members of the Mulini staff seemed less talkative than usual, "as though they had some secret to guard," wrote Bruslart. One agent reported that the date of escape had been fixed for January 15, though the day came and went without incident.

The *Cabinet noir,* France's postal censors, intercepted an unsigned letter from Portoferraio to Jean-Baptiste Dumoulin, the son of a wealthy glovemaker in Grenoble, thanking him for the information he'd provided. Later, another anonymous letter was discovered, which spoke of an impending escape and also mentioned the help of a confederate in Grenoble. Talleyrand read a report about a secret ceremony in which the members of an army regiment had burned the eagle standard they had once proudly waved under Napoleon's command and swept the ashes into goblets of wine so they could toast to their emperor in exile.

French officials did little to investigate these leads. There had been so much noise over the past months, so many conflicting reports and unsubstantiated chatter, that it was as though every fresh piece of intelligence canceled out some other piece. Information from Elba flowed from different sources at different times, to many different points: to Mariotti, to Talleyrand, to Beugnot and then to Beugnot's successor as head of police, Antoine d'André, to Dupont, and sometimes directly to Louis XVIII himself. No single overarching system guided the French operation, leading to the siloing of information that hindered any single official from getting a proper sense of what was really happening on Elba. Beugnot, for instance, received reports directly from a young clerk of Swiss origin known as Agent no. 50 who had infiltrated the Mulini, where his brother served as a footman, but Mariotti never learned about this agent, who in any case reported that he was too closely watched to learn anything significant and whose suspicious arrival soon led to his brother's dismissal.

Besides which, it seemed too unlikely and illogical that Napoleon would actually want to leave Elba, let alone convince hundreds of others that he was capable of landing on the mainland without getting them all killed. And even if anyone in France had felt a true sense of urgency, they would have struggled to properly mobilize because the various parts of the sprawling Bourbon bureaucracy had yet to coalesce into a coherent whole. Louis XVIII did, however, authorize a naval patrol of the Tuscan archipelago, detaching two ships, the *Fleur de Lys* and the *Melpomène,* which were on course to begin sailing near Elba by early February.

French officials were in some ways correct in refusing to put much stock into the various reports they fielded. There were indeed plenty of isolated pledges by soldiers gathered in cafés and inns, and a great deal of bold talk, often fueled by alcohol, in favor of Napoleon, or at least in disfavor of the Bourbons. And some Bonapartist supporters did meet secretly to hypothesize his return. The young Dumoulin of Grenoble did reportedly visit Elba and helped disseminate Bonapartist propaganda, and may have sent Napoleon information about the kind of reception he would get in Grenoble if he ever returned to France. But there was never really any large-scale or organized plan in France to actively bring Napoleon back to power, no widespread conspiracy to discover, regardless of what people claimed after the fact.

THE BOURBON REGIME was meanwhile stumbling. There was simply too much to accomplish, too short a time span in which to do it before people lost patience, and not enough talent necessary to pull off such a gargantuan feat. As a historian of the restoration summarized:

> To bind up the wounds of war; to rebuild the house of France from the ruins of the great European Empire; to fit the old monarchical, patriarchal, theocratic, and feudal institution into the new Napoleonic, national, secular, administrative state; to balance the new society emerging from the Revolution with the old privileged classes who intended to reoccupy their places along with the king—all of this was a superhuman and infinitely delicate task, which would have required for lack of a brilliant monarch, a council of exceptional ministers. The misfortune of the Restoration was that it had to undertake this work with mediocre princes and a weak and heterogeneous government team.

Writers in the French press grew more hostile toward the government, though they waged their attacks in a roundabout way since the regime had tightened censorship laws that summer. Most often this meant poking fun at the pretensions of the nobility as a whole, as in the popular caricatures chronicling the misadventures of the courtiers Lord Gullible, Lord Bluster, and Lord City-Snob. A more pointed critique came from Lazare Carnot, famed revolutionary and Napoleon's former minister of war, who sold more than sixty thousand copies of his *Petition to the King in July 1814*, which advised anyone wanting to be received at court:

> Be careful not to say you are one of the twenty-five million citizens who defended their country with considerable courage against

enemy invasions, because they will answer that these twenty-five million so-called citizens are twenty-five million rebels, and these so-called enemies are and always were our friends.

The government antagonized many people on January 21 by marking the anniversary of the execution of Louis XVI on that day in 1793, the first time the event was officially commemorated. Louis XVIII ordered that the remains of his brother and sister-in-law be exhumed from the common grave they occupied on the rue d'Anjou and returned to the Basilica of Saint-Denis, traditional necropolis of French kings, where their bodies had briefly lain following their executions, until the basilica was ransacked. The funeral procession, involving several Bourbon family members, took ten hours. Businesses were closed for the day. In the pages of the *Gazette de France* and the *Moniteur* the dead king Louis XVI was made to speak, telling his brother that "God has willed that the error of the French people be forgotten," and asking his subjects to "stifle the memory of your disastrous dissensions."

Traveling through France in 1815, the writer Walter Scott heard people speaking of their sovereign as though he were some kind of placeholder; "Louis the Inevitable," they called him. In roadside inns, workmen and soldiers on half-pay were heard loudly toasting "Long Live the King!" and then muttering "of Rome, and his Papa" under their breaths. Prompted by a false story that when leaving Fontainebleau, Napoleon had promised to return in a year's time along with the blooming violets, some of his supporters took to wearing that flower neatly tucked in alongside their Bourbon cockades. "Do you believe in Jesus Christ?" someone would ask a potential ally to sound them out, and the proper response was "yes, and his resurrection." People spoke of Napoleon lying in wait, an ember burning low, about to burst into flame. "I no longer take snuff," says a pipe-wielding Napoleon in one French caricature. "I smoke."

A French memoirist and politician, Antoine Thibaudeau, cut to the heart of why the Bourbons struggled during the time of Napoleon's exile. "There were many eloquent attacks on the emperor," he wrote. "He was called usurper, despot, tyrant, Nero, and Attila. But the man in question had pulled himself up alone by his genius, he came from our ranks, we gave him our votes. If he oppressed our liberties, that was between him and us. He wasn't imposed on us by the foreigner, he was eminently national. The Bourbons weren't." In other words, Napoleon, dangerous though he may be, was still their Napoleon, and whatever new story "Louis the Inevitable" and his ministers were trying to tell about France could never be as exciting as the one Napoleon and the French people had authored together.

35

NIGHTS AT THE THEATER

A BRITISH POLITICIAN NAMED John Macnamara arrived at Elba, having come down from Paris for no other reason than curiosity. He arranged to be standing at the edge of the main road out of Portoferraio as the emperor's carriage passed. Napoleon spotted the well-dressed stranger, interrogated him, and, after learning that he'd just been in Paris, invited him to the Mulini for a long talk that touched on everything from Napoleon's supposed suicide attempt (which he denied), to his marital difficulties, to his plans for a hypothetical surprise attack on Britain.

Napoleon was thrilled to hear Macnamara's slyly worded answer to one of his usual attempts to take the temperature of French public opinion. "We had a storm last night," said Macnamara. "Now there is no wind, but the sea is agitated." Macnamara asked him for his impressions of Campbell, to which he answered, "I know him very little, this *Monsieur*." Napoleon in turn asked why he thought Campbell was so often at Elba, to which Macnamara answered plainly, "To watch [you]."

The diarist John Cam Hobhouse, who recorded Macnamara's recollection of his conversation with Napoleon verbatim, wrote that halfway through their interview Napoleon "told Macnamara to wait for him whilst he went into another room, which he did. Macnamara went near the door, half-tempted to look, which did not please Napoleon. He had been to make water. . . . During this conversation Macnamara once or twice rubbed his eyes, and Napoleon asking him for what, said, 'I can scarcely believe my eyes, that I am alone talking with you.'" When Macnamara said he feared he was taking up too much of his time, Napoleon said, "I assure you, I am as glad to talk to you as you are to me—a stranger is a great entertainment for me." He left the talk so impressed by Napoleon's friendliness that he told Bertrand, "I think it is impossible he should ever be in a passion or other than in the best humour," to which Bertrand smiled and said, "I know him a little better than you."

MACNAMARA DIDN'T STAY on Elba long enough to witness Napoleon presiding over the opening night of Portoferraio's Teatro dei Vigilanti on the night of January 22. The theater was housed in a former Carmelite chapel that had been used for storing military supplies. Napoleon funded its renovation, which had been ongoing since at least November, when the Oil Merchant reported that laborers were at work on the project. Napoleon appointed Pauline as "Organizer of Theatrical Performances on the Island of Elba," and she sold boxes in advance to the wealthier Elbans. Subscriptions to its sixty-five seats went quickly. All subscribers were also enrolled in the newly created Elban Academy of Arts, whose motto was "*A noi la sorte!*" (We are the lucky ones!). A troupe of players was brought in from Livorno for the opening run. A smoke-screen, monument, and parting gift to the Elbans, all in one little building.

Bertrand sent an invitation to the opening night gala to the British officer John Adye, who as captain of the *Partridge* was still making regular patrols between Livorno and Elba. Adye declined. "I'll explain that I'm indisposed," he wrote to his wife. "In fact, I have no desire to go and be insulted by some French officer, as is their habit." The opening gala was one of more than half a dozen celebrations hosted by Pauline between late January and the first weeks of February. Her parties took place in a makeshift gazebo on the Mulini's terrace. Pauline's ladies-in-waiting and Napoleon's officers made up the bulk of the guest list.

But while nights at the theater offered a little bit of levity, members of Napoleon's entourage noticed that he seemed preoccupied by other matters. Pons recalled that Napoleon "adopted a dreamier look than was his custom" and that Pauline and Drouot had also made comments to him about his change in mood and preference for solitude. Bertrand also noticed a change. In the first months in exile Napoleon had written as many as five directives a day, but he issued only ten for all of January and February, most having to do with petty financial matters.

As news of the little theater and its related frivolities reached London, Paris, and Vienna, along with reports of Napoleon's increased isolation, the stories morphed into tales of senility, or in some versions, outright madness. Campbell made a passing reference to Napoleon's increasing "decrepitude" in a letter to Castlereagh around this time, which might have helped to fuel such talk.

THE FINAL REPAIRS to the *Inconstant* were completed, after Drouot had put out a call for every skilled laborer on Elba to come contribute to the work so that it would be done as quickly as possible. With the *Inconstant* back in commission, Napoleon sent Pons a message asking him to produce a report on the feasibility of "organizing an expeditionary flotilla." It was the first inkling Pons had that Napoleon was considering an escape. They talked privately at the Mulini a short while later. Napoleon asked Pons, "Shall I listen to the wishes of the army and the nation, who hate and mistrust the Bourbons?" Pons answered that Napoleon's return to France would be a cause for joy so long as it didn't lead to war.

Napoleon later explained that he'd chosen Pons as the first person to hear his plan "because his cooperation was essential to the preparation of the necessary ships." He controlled the transport vessels that worked the Rio mines: a brig, the *Saint-Joseph*, and two old feluccas, the *Abeille* and the *Mouche*. Without these ships Napoleon wouldn't have had enough space to carry the men and materiel necessary for his landing. It may be possible that he knew

Pons would be a good person to negotiate, as he later did, with Marshal Mas-séna, who was then in command of the French regiment in Toulon.

Shortly after speaking with Pons, Napoleon asked Peyrusse to amass five hundred thousand francs in cash and to stuff another cashbox and hide it at Fort Stella. "I knew enough to guess at the reason for this removal," wrote Peyrusse. "So, in great secrecy, I put by some flour, some wine, some pota-toes and some salt beef, and I waited to see what would happen." When Pey-russe saw some Neapolitan ships sail by Portoferraio and exchange salutes with the forts early in February, he suspected that Napoleon was planning something with Murat.

{ 36 }

PIETRO ST. ERNEST, OTHERWISE
KNOWN AS FLEURY DU CHABOULON

CAMPBELL NOTICED THAT NAPOLEON traveled around the island less frequently than before and adopted a strangely formal demeanor during his rare public appearances. He seemed not to have any new projects on the horizon and all roadwork and renovation projects had been brought to a halt. "This is, I think, on account of the expense," Campbell wrote in his journal. He learned that the Council of State had met to discuss whether Napoleon could sell Portoferraio's town hall to a private buyer, though opinions were divided and the sale was delayed indefinitely.

But along with these warning signs, Campbell had also seen Napoleon's troops planting gardens all around the palace and the barracks as though they were settling in for a long stay. And during his brief talk with Napoleon on February 2, the emperor seemed smug and aloof, which Campbell attributed to some secret information he must have received that had relieved him of any worry about being transported to another island. Sending a cursory summary of the interview to colleagues on the mainland, he reported little other than that Napoleon had appeared "unusually grave and dull." It was the last time he would ever speak to Napoleon.

A few days later, some of Napoleon's troops went over to the tiny islet of Palmaiola, in the Piombino Channel about two miles from Elba's northeastern tip. The French had once used Palmaiola to fire on passing British ships, and two abandoned cannons and a howitzer still remained. Campbell guessed that Napoleon had sent soldiers there either to spot and capture deserters or to hold meetings with confederates coming over from the Italian coast. He tried to broach the subject in conversation with Bertrand by mentioning that he'd heard the maneuvers on Palmaiola had attracted attention in Italy and that it might be wise to tread carefully, but Bertrand made no effort to explain the matter and treated the whole thing "quite lightly."

This pushed Campbell to formally request a personal inspection of Palmaiola. Bertrand replied that while Napoleon was indebted to him for the role he performed as the British commissioner, he couldn't grant the request, and he tried to convince Campbell that whatever he might have heard about Palmaiola was surely overblown, and besides which, "there could be no treason or injury to the British Government in a few small vessels arriving there from Genoa or Naples. . . . The Emperor lived quietly in his retreat and therefore considered all of this as meddling."

During the ensuing conversation, which grew "loud and warm," Campbell told Bertrand that it was his "duty to notify him that neither Pianosa nor Palmaiola had been given over to the possession of Napoleon, and that I should report to the British Government what had passed in regard to the points now under discussion." In reality, as he noted in his journal, he had no official "right to interfere in these matters, holding no ostensible situation excepting that of Commissioner, which had been prolonged there originally for their advantage and at their request."

Napoleon had also sent soldiers to be quartered in some villages on the western side of the island. Campbell wasn't sure if this was meant to stop Napoleon's Corsican troops on Elba from deserting, or if it was "a blind" meant to draw people's attention away from Portoferraio. He was also hearing the first rumors that Taillade had grounded the *Inconstant* on purpose as part of some covert Bourbon mission. Fanny Bertrand told him she thought Taillade was about to quit the island for good, with his Elban wife in tow.

To add to his confusion he spotted the two French cruisers that had started patrolling the coast with more frequency, and all sorts of visitors were showing up daily at Portoferraio aboard smaller private ships. "Mysterious adventurers and disaffected characters continually arrive here from France and Italy and then proceed to Naples," he wrote. He was bothered by the unexpected appearance of a Greek named Theologue, who "was much attached to Napoleon and had been greatly employed by him in the affairs of Turkey and Persia," who arrived from Paris and left soon afterward for Naples, and by a Norwegian named Kundztow who met with Napoleon and left dazzled by his knowledge of the population of Norway, which Campbell guessed was the result of research in his library in advance of the man's visit.

There were too many arrivals and departures in the first two weeks of February for him to track them all properly:

> It is scarcely possible to convey an idea of Portoferraio, which is like the area of a great barrack, being occupied by military, gendarmes, police officers of all description, dependents of the court, servants and adventurers—all connected with Napoleon, holding some place of honour or emolument in subservience to him. The harbor is constantly filled with vessels from all parts of Italy, bringing over almost hourly supplies of provisions for this great increase of population, as the island itself furnishes nothing but wine. Vessels, too, of all nations frequently anchor here, from motives of curiosity and speculation, or detained by contrary winds.

At midmonth a young man calling himself Pietro St. Ernest arrived at Portoferraio, claiming to be a sailor from Lerici. Campbell doubted that story, after learning that Cambronne and a few other officers had gone to meet with St. Ernest at the nondescript inn to which he'd retired after clearing customs, and then "ordered him not to be disturbed."

Pietro St. Ernest was in reality an out-of-work French official named Fleury du Chaboulon, who had served as subprefect of Reims until Napoleon's abdication. He'd been sent to Elba by Napoleon's former private secretary and minister, Hugues-Bernard Maret, duc de Bassano. Though French travelers to Elba were closely watched by authorities and sometimes denied passports if they were thought to be sympathetic to Napoleon, Maret trusted that the wily Fleury would get through if he was properly disguised. He told Fleury that he was in no position to explicitly advise Napoleon about whether or not he should return to France. His only mission was to deliver what turned out to be the most detailed firsthand account of how things stood in France that Napoleon had heard since sailing from Fréjus. Maret told Fleury that the emperor would know best what to do with the information he presented.

In his memoir Fleury claimed to have crossed from Lerici with the help of a roguish gang of smugglers. After Cambronne became aware of his presence in Portoferraio, Fleury was quietly taken to meet Bertrand, who after grilling him about his background sent him back to his inn, telling him to hide his army decorations and reveal nothing about himself to anyone. Under the empire, Fleury had done little to distinguish himself from the pack of minor officials and there was no one on Elba to vouch for him, but he managed to gain Bertrand's trust and a half hour later a messenger came to tell him to stroll up to the edge of Napoleon's garden, as if he were a sightseer.

Napoleon met him at the garden gate, made a bit of small talk, and then motioned for Fleury to join him inside. They talked privately, with Drouot and Bertrand in another room nearby trying to listen in as best they could. Fleury said that people in France were growing increasingly restless, especially the soldiers, who felt humiliated by defeat. Foreign competition was hurting certain industries and many people were underemployed or had no work at all. Housing markets had cooled because speculators were unsure if lands purchased during wartime would remain in French hands or be reconstituted to former enemies. People protested against the exporting of grain to England and there were food riots at several ports. In the countryside, he said, lingering resentments between royalists and Bonapartists had bubbled over into bloody feuds and vendettas. Former revolutionaries were feeling reinvigorated, while liberals who had hoped to advance their platform within the new regime had become disillusioned, and each side lacked for leadership or bold direction. Fleury said that people complained about the Bourbons and regretted having abandoned their emperor, and that they stood at the precipice of "a general insurrection." Napoleon asked if the soldiers "still loved" him, to which Fleury answered, "Yes, Sire, and may I even venture to say, more than ever."

After the interview Fleury dined with the Bertrands at the Biscotteria, where Henri offered the "misery" of their bare quarters as proof that Napoleon had not taken any huge amount from the French treasury before going into exile, as he assumed was being said of him in France. Fleury sailed back to the mainland that same evening. A few months later he would become Napoleon's personal secretary in Paris.

CAMPBELL FOUND HIS LIFE becoming increasingly "disagreeable . . . remaining at Elba as an obnoxious person, upon a kind of sufferance, and gradually slighted by inattentions." He cheered himself with the thought that he wouldn't be required to stay for too much longer, since the congress was sure to end any day now, which he assumed would result in either Napoleon's transportation to another remote island, or a more permanent and official codification of his status on Elba. Either way, Campbell's assignment would come to an end. In the meantime he would give himself a break with "a short excursion to the continent for my health," to see a "medical man at Florence on account of the increasing deafness, supposed to arise from my wounds." He may also have planned to see the Contessa Miniaci.

On February 16, Adye took Campbell toward Livorno aboard the *Partridge*, with the arrangement being that they would meet back in Livorno ten days later to return together to Elba. In the meantime he wanted Adye to continue patrolling around the island and to "visit Palmaiola for my information." Though Bertrand had blocked his own request to investigate, there was nothing stopping Adye from passing by Palmaiola on his regular route and asking to land so he could take a look around.

The *Partridge* was escorted out of the harbor by Napoleon's schooner, the *Étoile*, which Campbell assumed was heading on to Porto Longone for a standard supply pickup. In reality Napoleon had sent out the *Étoile* to sail just far enough to make sure that Campbell and Adye were indeed heading for Livorno as they had claimed.

{ 37 }

The Eagle Prepares for Flight

Preparations for Napoleon's departure started as soon as the *Étoile* returned to report that Campbell and the *Partridge* had sailed out of sight. Napoleon ordered Drouot to have the *Inconstant* brought into dry dock so it could be repainted like a British merchant brig and outfitted with salted beef, rice, cheese, biscuits, eau-de-vie, and wine, much of which was drawn from the last of his personal supply of Chambertin and Constantia. He specified that the supplies should last 120 men for three months at sea, which, calculated another way, would also supply 1,000 men for ten days, and he wanted the ship ready to sail by February 24 or 25. He told Drouot to prepare his map case and campaign riding bags and he repeated a version of Fleury's report, telling him that the whole of France regretted having deposed him and wanted him back.

Drouot later claimed that he and Napoleon had never spoken about returning to France before that point, and that when Napoleon finally did reveal his plan, he tried everything "humanly possible" to make him see that the results would be disastrous. He said that he also voiced his opposition to Pauline, Madame Mère, and to one of the commanding officers, Lacour, telling him that he was "convinced we're making a huge mistake in quitting Elba, and if it were up to him we would be staying." When asked on Saint Helena if Drouot had opposed his decision to leave Elba, Napoleon denied it, saying, "I do not allow myself to be governed by advice."

A year after the escape, under interrogation in a trial that could have ended with the order of his execution, Drouot explained his state of mind during those last days at Portoferraio:

> Abandoning the sovereign, to whom I had promised fidelity, seemed to me to be an act of cowardice. . . . I was dogged on one side by the desire to withdraw and on the other by the shame of abandoning, in a moment of danger, the sovereign with whose fate my own had until then been entwined. I chose the side of honor and fidelity.

While confiding in Drouot and Pons, Napoleon wanted to keep Bertrand from discovering the upcoming mission until the last possible moment, for unknown reasons. On February 19, he wrote a long letter to Bertrand detailing the work that would need to be done for a retreat to the Madonna hermitage that upcoming summer, for himself, Madame Mère, Pauline, Bertrand, Drouot, and fifty members of the Guard. He told Bertrand to organize a barge to bring across supplies and to arrange for additional housing near the hermitage. Then he called an inaugural session for the newly formed court of appeal, setting the meeting for March 6, and he approved Bertrand's budget for bringing a small opera troupe to the island, booked for twenty-two performances.

Soldiers were meanwhile given new allotments of land and told to devote their energies to the spring sowing. Gardeners planted a line of mulberry trees on the road to the San Martino property, while painters started whitewashing the interior of the Mulini, whose exterior was being outfitted with a wooden balustrade. The gunners were drilled at an exhausting pace and soldiers put on round-the-clock patrols.

38

THE OIL MERCHANT RETURNS

THE OIL MERCHANT RETURNED to Portoferraio on February 21 after a few weeks on the mainland. Right off, he felt a change in the atmosphere. The soldiers were jumpy. They were dutifully working on their gardens "more as if they were settling in than as if they were getting ready to leave," which only made him want to watch them more closely. The customs officials at Portoferraio were inspecting passports and personal papers more intensely than they ever had and every arriving ship was boarded and searched with special scrutiny. He heard that Napoleon now rarely attended any public functions, which he attributed to another round of reports of a would-be assassin on Elba. Contacts at the Mulini told him Napoleon lurked about the palace like a jungle cat ready to spring.

He saw supplies coming into Portoferraio from other parts of the island. Sixty crates of cartridges were loaded onto the *Inconstant* in a single night. Three companies of the Guard had just been kitted out with fresh topcoats and boots. The horses of the Polish lancers were brought back from pasturage on Pianosa. He learned of the arrival and quick departure of the mysterious Pietro St. Ernest. Someone told him that two British aristocrats had also arrived at Portoferraio, were granted an audience with Napoleon, gave him two packages, and left soon afterward. He heard from one of Napoleon's officers that the British were fed up with Louis XVIII and secretly arranging for Napoleon to sail to France on the condition that he accept harsh new terms imposed by the British. He grew increasingly suspicious of Campbell, who just before leaving Portoferraio had participated in "several interviews with Napoleon." All of the isolated signs the Oil Merchant had seen over the past weeks were coalescing into a frightening whole.

39

CAMPBELL IN FLORENCE

IN FLORENCE, CAMPBELL RECEIVED a dressing-down from Lord Burghersh, who chastised him for the lax way he'd been carrying out his duties in the past months, during which he had been so often away from Elba. Burghersh had already written to Castlereagh to suggest that the Foreign Office should make the most out of his colleague's apparent wanderlust, advising him to send Campbell to Naples to get the lay of the land there. Castlereagh, in his usual enigmatic way, had answered, "I should be glad to know what is going on everywhere, but I do not wish Colonel Campbell to engage in the proposed mission. When I have anything more precise to say to you, you may rely on hearing from me."

At dinner with Burghersh and Edward Cooke, the undersecretary of state, who had come down from Vienna, Campbell tried to explain what it would be like for him when he returned to Elba. Napoleon, he said, would harangue him with a thousand questions about the congress, his unpaid annuity, and the whereabouts of his wife and child. He asked the other officials to give him even the slightest bit of information he could pass on to Napoleon, which would help to calm him and keep him from doing anything rash. Cooke answered that such "uneasiness" about Napoleon's state of mind was unwarranted and that when he got back to Elba he should tell him "that everything is amicably settled at Vienna; that he has no chance; that the sovereigns will not quarrel. Nobody thinks of him at all. He is quite forgotten—as much as if he never existed!" Campbell underlined this final sentence in his journal.

Cooke was a seasoned diplomat, more experienced than Campbell in clandestine affairs, and for a moment Campbell believed he'd overreacted to what he'd recently seen at Portoferraio and heard about troops on Palmaiola. Perhaps, he thought, he was too close to the situation to see things clearly:

> I did feel very uneasy at the position of Napoleon and the seeming inconsistencies of his conduct; but, after Mr. Cooke's remarks I began to fancy that my near view of him and of the state of Elba had induced me to exaggerated circumstances.

But Campbell abandoned that line of thinking as soon as he arrived in Livorno on February 25, when he received several "very absurd, contradictory, and confused reports" from Elba. The most alarming one came from Ricci, who said that the *Inconstant* was being loaded with salts and meats and military stores and that all the horses had been recalled from Pianosa, while saddlers were seen working steadily. "The troops," wrote Ricci, "are full of expectation of some great event." Ricci reported that he'd heard Napoleon spent a whole night out on his boat, and that he and Madame Mère had held a long and heated conversation, after which she was seen leaving for her own apartments, full of emotion, and giving orders to have her luggage packed.

Campbell had always been skeptical of Ricci's abilities, and so the next morning he compared Ricci's letter with Mariotti's own intelligence and with reports gathered by the governor of Livorno. Between them they learned that chests full of Pauline's expensive plate had been sent to be sold at Livorno and that this transaction's timing coincided neatly with an order Campbell had already traced to an unknown person on Elba requesting a British merchant vessel to be hired in the same town; that all horses belonging to Napoleon's

Polish lancers had been recalled from Pianosa and that gendarmes were seen frequently at the harbor giving all sorts of instructions to the portmaster and the health inspectors; that an unusual amount of grain had been sent from Porto Longone to Portoferraio to be stored; and that two of the transport ships used for the Rio mines had sailed to Portoferraio, but carrying no cargo.

The three men agreed that Napoleon was "prepared to quit the island immediately with his troops." While Campbell waited for Adye to arrive at Livorno to ferry him back to Elba, he tried to make sense of his recent actions in his journal, writing, as if for posterity:

> My access to Napoleon has for some time past been so much less than at first, as to afford me very little opportunity of personal observation; and besides, the etiquette of a sovereign and court were studiously adhered to. So that during the last few months our intercourse has been continued under different feelings upon both sides, although no expression to that effect was ever pronounced by either of us; and when he did grant me an interview he always received me with the same apparent courtesy as formerly. Sometimes I could only ascribe his reserve to a dislike of his appearing in the eyes of the world as a prisoner, and to my stay being prolonged beyond the period which he perhaps expected, owing to the duration of the Congress. Or possibly he had projects and communications of an improper nature, which he was afraid might be discovered by me, in case of my associating with his mother and sister. The latter, I know, desired such intimacy, and had taken several steps for that purpose, in which she was counteracted.
>
> I nevertheless considered it my bounden duty not to break off the ties which still existed, in hopes of being useful to my sovereign and his ministers, who had been pleased to honour me with this confidential appointment. So that I have looked forward for a long time, with impatience and daily anxiety, to the conclusion of the Congress of Vienna, as the period which would produce

an order to that effect from Lord Castlereagh and close my mission. By absenting myself occasionally from the island, I had a pretext for requesting an interview both before my departure and again upon my return, and this became latterly my only opportunity of conversing with Napoleon.

40

MARDI GRAS

NAPOLEON POPPED HIS HEAD into Peyrusse's room, interrupting a conversation between the paymaster and an Elban official. He seemed distracted and kept staring out the window toward the barracks where some grenadiers were marching. He left without saying much, no doubt because he'd expected Peyrusse to be alone. Peyrusse ended his meeting with the Elban official as quickly as he could and rushed over to the Mulini, where Napoleon asked him what they had been talking about; he admitted that they had been speculating about his escape and had come to the conclusion that he was about to leave for Naples.

Napoleon touched Peyrusse on the cheek and told him he was silly to think such things. But then he asked how much ready money he could get his hands on and what he thought the precise weight of such a stash might be. He told Peyrusse to arrange for the gold reserves to be stowed away in some traveling cases filled with books from the palace library and instructed him to "pay . . . but don't pay," which Peyrusse took to mean he should settle up as many outstanding accounts as he thought fair, but do so as cheaply as possible. As Peyrusse was leaving, Napoleon added that he should start preparing for a journey and to pack lightly.

Peyrusse wrote that Napoleon had spoken to him as though they were planning a holiday jaunt, which led him to seek out his next-door neighbor, Drouot, hoping he would reveal the details of the plan. Drouot, however, was in a foul mood and unwilling to talk, aside from saying that the time had come for them to leave, although he'd done all he could to convince Napoleon otherwise. Peyrusse left Drouot's apartments more anxious than ever. He turned his attention to settling accounts across the island, though he was sure that people would notice he was paying them mostly in silver rather than the customary gold.

THE NIGHT OF FEBRUARY 22 was Pauline Bonaparte's Elban triumph. She organized a Mardi Gras procession that wound through Portoferraio's lanes and ended with a lavish masked ball at the palace. One of Napoleon's officers headed up the cortege dressed as a sultan, riding a white charger draped in Pauline's cashmere shawls. A skinny Polish lancer rode alongside him on the most run-down horse that could be found, as a kind of mock Don Quixote. Pauline arrived sporting the latest Neapolitan fashions. The night reached its peak when some members of the Guard carried Pauline around the Mulini in a mock funeral to mourn the end of her long career of lovemaking, at least momentarily, as she had to give up on fun for the holy season. Pons thought she'd carried off the festivities with "exquisite taste, and a seductive grace, looking even more beautiful than ever."

The next morning Napoleon went down to the docks as though for a routine inspection of the *Inconstant* and some other ships. He boarded the two-hundred-ton *Saint-Esprit*, which Pons had chartered from a local merchant. The *Caroline* and the two feluccas were on their way from Rio. The flotilla would eventually comprise seven ships in all (*Inconstant, Caroline, Saint-Esprit, Abeille, Étoile, Mouche,* and *Saint-Joseph*), none of them especially fast or powerful.

The escape plans were nearly undone that night when the *Partridge* was spotted coming toward Portoferraio. Captain Adye had returned earlier than expected from his regular patrol route and Bertrand rushed to wake

Napoleon, who ordered that the *Inconstant* be made ready to sail right away. But just before midnight Adye anchored about a nautical mile away from the *Inconstant*. Napoleon guessed that Adye wouldn't have passed so near to Portoferraio's guns if he suspected anything was amiss and so he canceled the order to sail and brought all work at the docks to a halt. He briefly considered trying to sink the *Partridge*, but opted for a more measured strategy, and at dawn Captain Chautard took the *Inconstant* out to sea to see if it would raise any alarms from the watchmen aboard the *Partridge*. Amazingly, no one on board the British ship seemed to pay much notice to the *Inconstant*, despite the fact that it had been repainted in the colors of one of their own merchant brigs.

The oblivious Adye disembarked at Portoferraio that morning, Friday, February 24, and dropped off a few British tourists who had asked to be taken to the island aboard the *Partridge*. He went to the Bertrand home for a chat. Adye told Henri that he'd heard some talk at Livorno that Napoleon was set to escape any day now. Henri joked that there were all sorts of "absurd reports" going round and "only fools" would believe them. Adye asked where Napoleon was at the moment and Henri told him he was somewhere nearby but momentarily indisposed. Fanny added that she'd walked with him the day before and she thought he'd caught a cold. They invited Adye to dinner but he said he wanted to make sail that night. Right before he left, Henri made sure to mention that Napoleon had just sent the *Inconstant* off to Livorno for repairs and told Adye about its grounding a few weeks earlier.

Adye walked around the town for a while and saw soldiers turning the soil and planting shrubs in their barracks gardens. At two that afternoon, he put out toward Palmaiola, which he'd yet to inspect, but not before Filidoro, the portmaster, had repeated the story that the *Inconstant* was headed off for repairs.

The Oil Merchant had seen Adye walking in Portoferraio, but left him alone because he was by that time convinced that the British were behind Napoleon's impending escape. "One can't take a step without being noticed," he wrote in his report to Mariotti. "Today everyone is speaking quite plainly about a departure. I begin to be convinced that it is probable." Rather than trying any bold move, he walked down to the customs house and requested permission to sail the following day in his fishing boat. Filidoro denied his request and took his passport without explaining why he did so. "I begged, I offered bribes, I made promises," wrote the Oil Merchant, "but to no effect." All fishermen had been barred from sailing out to open waters, and no ships were allowed to dock. Campbell's Elban contact Ricci had meanwhile been trying to get Adye a message detailing all the recent and suspicious activity, but failed to reach him in time.

41

TOWER OF BABEL

EVERYWHERE ONE LOOKED, people were packing up their goods or saying tearful goodbyes or squeezing in some last bit of revelry. The cafés overflowed. Soldiers were patrolling all across the island, everyone on edge. "I seem to have been transported this morning into a Tower of Babel," wrote the Oil Merchant. "Here, someone laments the loss of the soldiers; there someone cries about the loss of some cherished possession; someone else is busy building castles in Spain." He couldn't persuade any of the local fishermen to try ferrying him quietly to Piombino, regardless of what price he offered.

Napoleon had made no official declaration and stayed shut away at the Mulini, writing the proclamations he intended to distribute on landing in France while a printer's devil waited on hand to rush them into production. He summoned Peyrusse and told him to set aside some money for the few soldiers who would be left behind under the leadership of Dr. Lapi, the commandant of the Elban Guard, who would act as governor after Napoleon was gone.

At midday on February 25 the *Partridge* was spotted yet again. Adye hadn't returned to Livorno the night before as he'd told Bertrand he would, likely because the winds hadn't been in his favor. While it remained anchored some distance from Portoferraio, Napoleon had the guns at the fort trained on the ship with the order to fire if Adye tried to enter the harbor. But that evening Adye made sail again for Livorno, trying to take advantage of some strong northwesterly winds.

Napoleon for the first time told Bertrand, Drouot, and Cambronne in full detail the plan for escape. They would sail to Antibes and land at the small beach there, Golfe-Juan. Landing at Marseille would have offered a straight shot to Paris through relatively easy terrain, but Napoleon wanted to avoid the port and surrounding area, which was staunchly royalist. From Antibes they would march through the Dauphiné province (encompassing the present-day departments of Isère, Drôme, and Haute-Alps), which would mean hard treks through winding mountain passes, but would allow them to bypass Provence, where they had received such a violent welcome on the way to Fréjus the previous spring.

Napoleon liked to say that France needed him more than he needed France, but his plan to sail there rather than for the much closer target Italy suggests the opposite. He was betting that the French people would rally to his side at the sight of him and that any deserters from the Bourbon forces could come more quickly and directly over to him than if he landed on the Italian peninsula. An Italian landing was the relatively safer option, but what would be the symbolic reward of risking everything only to land among Italians, and not much closer to the Tuileries than he'd been on Elba?

Napoleon knew that as soon as Captain Adye reached Livorno he would tell Campbell what he'd seen and between them they would figure things out and raise the alarm. The flotilla would have to leave as soon as possible and sail quickly. Each ship needed to be as light as could be, meaning no materiel should be on board unless absolutely vital. The same went for men.

Under Napoleon's rule the French had never rivaled the British as a sea power, and he was no great naval strategist. But he'd enjoyed a few thrilling feats at sea, for instance, when trading on lightness and the element of surprise to slip past the British fleet undetected on the return from Egypt, a small personal victory after the tremendous French naval losses at the battle of the Nile. Now the entire success of his operation would depend on skill and luck on the open ocean. If the flotilla encountered resistance at sea, it wouldn't have the option of turning back to a safe port, since as soon as the escape became known, French and British ships were sure to rush to be the first to seize the poorly defended island.

If reaching France proved impossible, the plan was for the flotilla to make for Corsica, where Napoleon and his troops could hide out in the mountains. He anticipated that between his soldiers and the population of Corsica, which would surely come over to his side, they could hold the island indefinitely. To make provision for this option Napoleon arranged for three feluccas—each holding fifteen or sixteen influential Corsicans recruited specially for the mission, and carrying plenty of powder, food, and water—to leave shortly after the main flotilla. They were to sow disorder, capture Governor Bruslart, fly the tricolor, and establish a junta government. They would then raise troops from among the Corsicans and send them to Golfe-Juan, where they would form a rear guard for the landing party, which would by then be marching for Paris.

A few months earlier some Corsican soldiers who had snuck off to serve Napoleon on Elba had returned home, complaining that they had been mistreated by the emperor and that they had seen the error of their ways. In reality they had served as a kind of sleeper cell, loyal to Napoleon and ready to be activated if and when the time for escape presented itself. In February they had sent word to Napoleon that Corsica teetered on the edge of a general uprising and that the coup he envisioned could be carried off easily. Unknown to anyone in Napoleon's camp was that a few days earlier Bruslart had written from Bastia to warn General Dupont that rebels camped out in the mountains threatened his control over Corsica and that there were reports from around the island of attacks on gendarmes and other officials. "I have reason to believe that Elban insurgents are behind this uprising," he wrote.

. . .

THE FINAL EVENING AT THE MULINI was a quiet one. Napoleon played cards with his mother and sister. Pauline, in tears, went into one of the other rooms, where the valet Marchand had been listening in on the family's conversation. She pressed a diamond necklace into Marchand's hands, telling him to sell it to raise money for the coming campaign. When she said adieu to Marchand he said he hoped it would instead be au revoir, implying that they would all be reunited soon enough, she answered, "That's not how I see it."

Napoleon took a moonlit stroll on the terrace with his mother, who would later recall telling him that "if Heaven intends that you shall die, my son, and has spared you in this time of ignominious exile, I hope you will not perish by poison but with your sword in your hand!" On Saint Helena, Napoleon said that despite her lifelong reluctance to part with even the smallest amount of money, his mother would have "doomed herself to live on brown bread" to help him. Before retiring for the night Napoleon distracted himself with a book, a life of Emperor Charles V of Austria, which he left open on his desk, alongside a few bits of scribbled paper torn into shreds.

It was a difficult night for Henri Bertrand. He was worried the landing would throw France into civil war, though Napoleon had tried to calm him by promising not to seek harsh revenge against his former enemies once he returned to power. Fanny and the children would be staying at Portoferraio so that they could later travel with Madame Mère to Rome and then on to Paris, once they received word that it was safe to do so. Henri wrote to his father to explain his reasons for continuing to serve alongside Napoleon rather than staying behind with his family. On Elba, he wrote elliptically, "there was, on my part, only sacrifices; no future. I couldn't do it any longer."

Just before the sailing Henri hid a letter among Fanny's things so that she would only discover it after he was gone. It said that if the landing in France wasn't "crowned with success" she should stay with her father's family in England for as long as was needed, but should return to France as soon as she could. "Our children cannot and must never cease to be French," he wrote.

"Consult my father on their education, their fortune. . . . Be brave, you owe it to your children. Until the final moment of my life you will be the object of my sweetest and most tender affection." The letter, discovered years later, had the creases to show that someone had crumpled it up into a tight ball.

Henri later recalled how worried he'd been that his headstrong wife would ignore his instructions to stay at Portoferraio until she heard from him again and that she would instead make her own way to France to rejoin him more quickly. He'd pictured her and the children on some tiny boat sailing for Marseille where they would all be arrested.

{ 42 }

EVERYTHING WAS QUIET AT ELBA

ON THE MORNING OF FEBRUARY 26, Campbell sighted the *Partridge* just beyond Livorno's harbor, where it was becalmed for several hours because of slack wind. He wrote to Castlereagh to say he thought that Napoleon would escape at any moment and then turned to his journal to plan out a course of action. Approaching the situation methodically, he reasoned that Napoleon would likely land at Piombino, the closest Italian port, and that he'd already arranged a pact with Murat, who must have learned that the delegates in Vienna were set to denounce his rule in Naples and so had teamed with his brother-in-law to "throw down the gauntlet in defiance of the sovereigns of Europe."

Next he resolved that if the *Partridge* encountered Napoleon's ships (he was certain that even Napoleon wasn't bold enough to try escaping in a single ship) and if these carried troops, military stores, and provisions, then he and Captain Adye would be compelled "to intercept, and in case of their offering the slightest resistance, to destroy them." With eighteen guns and a crew of ninety, the ship was a decent match for the similarly sized *Inconstant*. Perhaps anticipating that his journal might be seized by the enemy, or even serve as evidence for his own court-martial, he wrote that he and Adye would

be justified by our sovereign, our country, and the world, in pro-
ceeding to any extremity upon our own responsibility in a case of so
extraordinary a nature. I shall feel that in the execution of my duty,
and with the military means which I can procure, the lives of this
restless man and his misguided associates and followers are not to be
put in competition with the fate of thousands and the tranquility of
the world.

At noon, the *Partridge* finally docked at Livorno. It had taken Adye eighteen hours to tack up from Elba. In response to Campbell's flurry of questions, he said that he hadn't seen or heard anything on Elba to give them cause
for concern. He'd been chatting breezily with the Bertrands at their home just
two days earlier, he said, and he'd seen soldiers carrying earth to their barracks and planting shrubs. While he hadn't seen Napoleon, Fanny Bertrand
had mentioned walking with him. (Campbell, in recording Adye's comments,
revealed how close he'd grown to the half-British Fanny Bertrand, noting that
her statement must have been true, since she "would neither be made the tool
of covering his departure, nor is she capable of dissembling her uneasiness, if
such circumstance had taken place.")

Adye told Campbell everything he'd done after leaving Portoferraio: Bertrand had told him there would be no issue with his landing at Palmaiola and
so he'd headed there to investigate, but variable weather kept him from getting near enough before dark, so he lay to for the night of February 24. The
next morning he was refused a berth by the portmaster, who said he'd just
received an order from Napoleon not to allow any person to land, though he
gave no reason why. Adye elected to keep sailing north, less bothered by the
incident at Palmaiola than he was by the light winds that threatened to keep
him from reaching Campbell in time for their appointment. Making his way
from Palmaiola to Livorno brought the *Partridge* back in sight of Portoferraio,
he said, which gave him a chance to see again that "everything was quiet at
Elba." At last evening's sunset he'd seen the "topmasts of the *Inconstant* within
the harbor."

Campbell brought Adye up to speed with all the distressing intelligence he'd gathered while he was away and then asked if *now* he thought there might be anything more worth mentioning, even if "it might not at the time have attracted his notice."

Adye absorbed this information. Yes, come to think of it, General Bertrand had been very persistent in asking him about his exact movements and probable return, and he'd told him his schedule in detail. And it was confusing, he admitted, that while Bertrand and the portmaster told him the *Inconstant* was heading to Livorno, some other officers said the ship was going to Genoa, while the movements of the *Inconstant* itself were unusual because on Friday morning he'd seen it heading northward, but later in the day he saw it sailing southward, hugging the Italian coast, and then a few hours later, after he'd left Portoferraio and turned into the channel of Piombino, he passed the *Inconstant* again, but this time heading back toward Portoferraio alongside two smaller ships that appeared hastily manned. He admitted to Campbell that he couldn't see any logical reason why that trio of ships should have been out sailing. Campbell figured that Napoleon had sent the smaller boats out precisely so they could spot the *Partridge* and relay that news back to the *Inconstant* so the escape could be delayed.

Campbell and Adye prepared to head back to Portoferraio but were kept in port by the calm weather. The superstitious Adye whistled to bring wind but without any luck.

Campbell returned to his journal:

> I think he will leave General Bertrand to defend Portoferraio, as he has a wife and several children with him to whom he is extremely attached, and probably Napoleon will not communicate his intention to him until the last moment. But he will certainly take with him General Cambronne (a desperate, uneducated ruffian, who was a drummer with him in Egypt) and those of his Guards upon whom he can most depend, embarking them on board the *Inconstant*, the *Étoile*, and two other vessels, while he himself probably, with General Drouot, will precede them in the *Caroline*. The place of disembarkation will be Gaeta, on the coast of Naples, or Civita Vecchia, if Murat

has previously advanced to Rome. For I cannot persuade myself that Napoleon will commit himself openly, until the former has moved forward with his troops; but it is very likely that they will endeavour to have an interview immediately at Pianosa or Montecristo.

As with Mariotti, Talleyrand, and other officials, Campbell remained fixated on Italy because he thought Murat to be Napoleon's last potential ally and that Napoleon believed he could bring over Italian insurrectionists to his cause by landing in Tuscany and promising them that together they would drive out the Austrians. Campbell had likely also been misled by Napoleon's feigned interest in Italian liberation during their talks together.

Campbell wrote to Captain Thomson, the senior officer at Genoa, where a line-of-battle ship, a frigate, and a brig were in port, advising him to detach the ships to take immediate possession of Pianosa and Palmaiola. That way if British ships caught Napoleon in open waters, he couldn't claim that he'd only gone to visit Pianosa or Palmaiola and been blown off course on the way back toward Elba.

Campbell and Adye were kept at Livorno through the night. They discussed what they do would once they finally reached Portoferraio. Campbell wanted to dock and request a formal interview with Bertrand, after which he would remain on board the *Partridge* to survey all ships going in and out, waiting to see how his request would be answered, while hopefully being able to communicate with some of the French men-of-war patrolling the waters. Adye predicted they would be seized as soon as the *Partridge* was anchored.

{ 43 }

INCONSTANT

NAPOLEON WOKE EARLY on Sunday, February 26, a bright blue morning. He would have heard the shouts of "Long Live the Emperor!" from the crowd that had gathered outside the Mulini. A soft breeze carried the scent of freshly turned loam and citrus.

As on any Sunday at the palace, courtiers pressed in to watch Napoleon being dressed during the levee, the traditional waking ceremony. He took special care selecting each item of clothing and accessory, opting for a dark blue coat with scarlet cuffs and white lapels, adorned with the Legion of Honor and the Iron Crown of Italy, complemented by a black silk stock collar, white waistcoat, white knee breeches of fine wool, and white silk stockings. The Elban emblem on his black beaver hat had been replaced with the tricolor cockade.

During the levee Napoleon made the first public statement that he would be leaving Elba, though he wouldn't reveal where he was going. "I leave you peace," he said. "I leave you prosperity. I leave you a clean, fair city. I leave you my roads and trees, for which your children at least will thank me." Pons thought he looked tired, as though he'd aged a decade overnight.

At nine Napoleon attended mass at the little church near the harbor and then performed the customary review of the Elban National Guard in the town square. After the drills a few of the Elbans were posted to the Mulini to replace the regular palace guards. At noon the drums sounded to call an assembly, during which Drouot told the soldiers to continue their work as normal, including tending their gardens, and to return to barracks at three for final preparations. They were to dress themselves as if for battle.

This was the first time any of the soldiers heard from a trusted source that they would in fact be leaving Elba. None of them had any idea what the coming campaign would require of them or where it would take place. There had been no additional training to prime the troops for battle. An officer rushed to find Drouot to ask if he could bring his wife along on the journey. Drouot told him to follow his orders as he received them.

Napoleon had by then sent a message to Murat, requesting that he send out a squadron to cruise around Elba in case his flotilla needed to retreat toward Naples. He stopped short of asking his brother-in-law to escort his ships to their destination, probably because he was counting on the dramatic visual effect of landing with his own small fleet flying the tricolor. (Murat would wait until early March to send off his naval squadron, by which point Napoleon had already landed.)

ON SEEING THAT SHIPS were preparing to sail, the Oil Merchant figured the time had come for him to leave, with or without his passport. He bribed a fisherman to get him across to the mainland, but they were stopped by the crew of the *Inconstant* as soon as they tried to leave the harbor and were threatened with arrest. After returning to shore the Oil Merchant rode toward Rio hoping to find someone else to get him off the island but found his path blocked by patrolling soldiers. He went back to Portoferraio to wait things out, taking a difficult and twisting route to avoid meeting any more soldiers. But back near the harbor he was spotted by Cambronne, who remembered him from his landing and a few encounters in town. Recalling that the man had spoken of his military connections, Cambronne thought that he now numbered among the people leaving with Napoleon and barked at him to go find his place on the appropriate ship. Luckily a nearby French officer with whom he'd become friendly intervened on the Oil Merchant's behalf after the latter explained that he would trail the flotilla in his own boat as soon as he had settled all his outstanding accounts on the island, a story that satisfied the distracted Cambronne.

At around two, a sailor returning from patrol passed beneath the Mulini in his rowboat to give the all clear. Guards had already shut the town gates. Pauline joked to an officer that "tonight's ball has been cancelled by history." Pons was summoned to the palace, thinking he was going to be named governor to replace Drouot. Instead Napoleon told him to prepare to sail in a few hours at his side aboard the *Inconstant*. He wasn't allowed to bring his family. Dr. Lapi was named as de facto governor, with the order "to cede to no one, and fight until death."

Napoleon burned some of his personal papers. A few crumpled scraps of writing in his hand were found on the floor of the Mulini's study, which later sparked speculation that he had tried at some point during the exile to draft his memoirs.

At seven that evening, in his gray traveling coat, Napoleon took his last ride down from the Mulini and through the Water Gate to the harbor. He had borrowed his sister's carriage, which would be loaded onto the *Inconstant*, and traveled at the slow pace of the soldiers who marched alongside, without any music or fanfare until they reached the marina. Drouot, Peyrusse, and Pons numbered among those on foot. Bertrand rode on horseback.

In a repeat of the welcome they had given him the previous May, the people of Portoferraio placed candles in their windows to illuminate the harbor. Mayor Traditi, struggling for eloquence as badly as he had on Napoleon's landing, broke down in tears and abandoned his efforts.

The prevailing sound at the harbor that night, wrote Pons, "was sobbing all around." Officials distributed a proclamation, signed in the name of the new governor, Dr. Lapi:

> Elbans! Our august sovereign, recalled by Providence in the pursuit
> of glory, shall quit our island. . . . "I am leaving," he said, "I have

been extremely pleased by the people's conduct; I trust them with the defense of this land to which I attached the highest value; I cannot give them any greater proof of my trust in them than to leave my mother and sister under their watch."

The soldiers boarded the *Inconstant* and the six smaller boats. Peyrusse was on the *Saint-Esprit*, completing some final business with its captain and owner, who had offered his services but had yet to name his rate. Peyrusse had barely slept, having spent the night "in violent agitation" struggling to make enough room in his suitcase for anything besides his accounting registers. He was looking over the ship's books to help him negotiate a fair price, while some of the Polish lancers tossed everything deemed nonessential into the bay, eliciting curses from the captain. Peyrusse looked up from the ledgers to see Napoleon, who had been rowed out to the ship to see about the delay. Napoleon grabbed the papers, threw them in the air, and yelled at Peyrusse to pay the captain whatever he wanted and be done with it. Peyrusse handed the captain twenty-five thousand francs.

As the sun was setting around eight o'clock, Napoleon was rowed to the *Inconstant* and boarded, which was marked by a single cannon shot. The plan was to wait for darkness before sailing, both to avoid being spotted by enemy patrols and so that no one on Elba would later be able to report whether the flotilla had headed south or north from Portoferraio. The ships couldn't have left just then in any case, since they needed a strong southeasterly wind to get out of the roadstead and pull clear of the island. Nor'easters were far more common that time of year, and this had been a particularly calm week.

The seven ships sat unmoving for two more hours. Despite all the effort to streamline, they were still dangerously heavy. They carried four guns, ammunition, and a million francs in bullion. Six hundred members of Napoleon's Old Guard were on the *Inconstant*, which was so jammed that there was hardly place for everyone to stand on the decks. Just under five hundred more soldiers and eighty civilians, mostly servants, were split among the other ships. Even with all the materiel they carried, Napoleon's ships would likely be outmatched by any British or French warships encountered, which would have more guns but still be faster because their crews would be several times smaller.

The seven boats were still bobbing in the water as the first stars appeared. The troops bolstered themselves by singing the "Marseillaise," the song of liberty, again and again, lit by a slim crescent moon. They still hadn't been told where they were heading.

By midnight, it seemed suicidal to stay in the harbor any longer. The boats were rowed out to open waters at an agonizing clip so that the captains could try their luck with the winds out in the roadstead. Finally a breeze started to carry them northwest. Whatever minuscule lead Napoleon had calculated on having against the *Partridge* was diminishing by the hour.

{ 44 }

At Sea

Napoleon's flotilla was only five leagues from Elba when the sun came up over Portoferraio. It took until noon before the crowds gathered at points along the coast saw the last of the sails disappear over the horizon.

The ships would head straight north from Portoferraio, keeping clear of Livorno and the Tuscan coast to avoid arousing suspicion during the first leg of the journey, since so many trading fleets regularly crossed the waters between Corsica and Livorno in all directions. To look less conspicuous they sailed single file, each separated by a few kilometers of blue; the *Inconstant* led the way, gaining some speed after one of its rowboats was jettisoned.

Just as the *Inconstant* rounded the northwest coast of the island of Capraia by backing and filling, a midshipman on watch called out. What was soon identified as the French battleship *Melpomène* (named for the muse of tragedy) was sailing off the port side, navigating the narrow channel separating Capraia from Corsica. The crew of the *Inconstant* had yet to discover that another French patrol ship, the forty-four-gun *Fleur de Lys*, was meanwhile sailing just to the north near the small island of Gorgona. Captained by a die-hard royalist, it carried more than two hundred sailors. A third French ship, the brig *Zéphir,* was also nearby to the northeast, heading for Livorno on its usual patrol, but still yet to be spotted.

The flotilla muddled along in light wind under a cloudless sky. At midday the topsails of another ship came into sight, rocking in the distance some fifteen miles to the east. Napoleon and his officers rightly guessed that this was the *Partridge,* carrying Adye and Campbell. The British sloop traveled at a much faster clip than their own.

By early afternoon Napoleon was convinced that Adye and Campbell had sighted his flotilla and he opted to press on northward to try his luck against the *Melpomène* rather than ease off and risk facing the *Partridge.* There was a chance the *Melpomène*'s captain might let them pass without a fight. The *Inconstant* was often seen traveling those waters to trade or ferry people to and from Elba, though the accompanying flotilla, however meager, was sure to raise concern. Napoleon might also have been wagering that the *Melpomène* would let him pass out of support for his cause, or even better, that its crew could be persuaded to accompany the flotilla to safe landing and would join in against the *Partridge* if necessary.

ADYE AND CAMPBELL had managed to get out of Livorno at four on the morning of February 27, and were steadily making their way west toward Napoleon's ships, but early that afternoon the *Partridge* veered off sharply, headed toward Portoferraio. If the crew of the *Inconstant* had recognized the *Partridge* on this bell-clear day, why was the reverse not also true? By its recorded coordinates, the *Partridge* at one point in the day came within twelve nautical miles of the *Inconstant.* The log from the *Partridge* shows an entry at 11 a.m. noting that its lookout had spotted "three sail." But this doesn't necessarily mean that anyone on board realized they were seeing the escaped *Inconstant* or any other ships that would have put them on alert. Merchant vessels sailed the waters fairly regularly, and Adye knew that some English and Swedish ships had left Livorno at roughly the same time as had the *Partridge.*

Campbell's journal from this time is troublingly sparse. His entry reads only:

At 9 p.m. [on the twenty-sixth] I went down below, and thought the brig was getting up her anchor. But as it turned out, on account of there being no wind, she did not leave the harbor until early this morning [the twenty-seventh]. In the course of the day we saw the French brig *Zéphir*.

This could have been a case of mistaken identity, since the *Zéphir* and the *Inconstant* were produced in the same shipyard, both to plans from the master shipbuilder Jacques-Noel Sané, and were launched within a year of each other. Mariotti had informed Campbell that the *Zéphir* would be patrolling the region, so its sighting wouldn't have caused him or Adye any great surprise. They were apparently so convinced Napoleon was either heading toward Italy to join Murat or still on Elba, where they might catch him if they hurried, that any ship sailing north toward France would have failed to pique their interest enough for them to pursue and lose time reaching Portoferraio.

At a later and unspecified date, Campbell added a footnote to his original entry, writing that "we must have been nearly in sight of Napoleon's flotilla, as the *Zéphir*, it is since known, spoke [*sic*] the *Inconstant* [meaning maneuvering close enough for an exchange of communications]."

THAT THE *PARTRIDGE* MISSED Napoleon's flotilla is easier to explain than that all seven of Napoleon's ships passed the French *Melpomène* without any issue in the early afternoon of February 27. The ship's captain, Collet, took no action against the flotilla as it sailed by within plain view. Napoleon spoke on Saint Helena of having been totally confident that the *Melpomène* would never fire on them. "We knew enough about the feeling of the officers of these vessels, let alone the crews, to be sure they would hoist the tricolor and defend the Emperor against the English corvette," he told Bertrand.

Under interrogation by Lord Burghersh in early March, Campbell's Elban agent Ricci swore that the "three sail" spotted by Adye and Campbell must have been the *Inconstant*, the *Melpomène*, and the *Fleur de Lys*, parting after a preordained ocean rendezvous somewhere north of Elba. Warned by Burghersh "against deceiving himself and the world upon a matter of so much consequence," Ricci stuck to his claim, adding that he'd seen the three ships himself from the high ridge of Portoferraio. The captains of the three French ships never properly accounted for their exact whereabouts and actions during the course of February 27, though through their vagueness they could just as easily have been trying to protect themselves against charges of carelessness or cowardice as they were against charges of collusion.

THE DAY'S MOST BAFFLING episode of all came when the *Inconstant* passed in close range of the *Zéphir*, which was sailing toward Livorno, where its captain, Andrieux, was to get confidential instructions from Mariotti concerning its "cruise of observation" in Elban waters. When the *Zéphir* was first spotted, Napoleon had ordered his crew to battle stations, but then called off the order when he recognized the warship as a French one. He later claimed that his officers had wanted to board the *Zéphir* to give Andrieux the chance to peacefully come over to their side, but he'd calculated that the reward of an extra ship on their side wasn't worth the risk of a failed boarding mission.

North of Capraia, the two ships passed close enough for their respective crews to communicate through loud-hailers and by shouting. The uniformed troops lay down on the decks so as not to be spotted. Napoleon said that he hid behind the wheelhouse and that his grenadiers had quickly taken off their bearskin hats and replaced them with the tied scarves of seasoned sailors. On Saint Helena, Napoleon claimed that Andrieux had hailed the *Inconstant* and then, presuming it was on a standard trade run, had asked only for news out of Elba, but in another recounting of the escape he said that Andrieux had known who he was dealing with and had simply decided not to involve his crew in stopping the flotilla. Andrieux, for his part, later said that he'd recognized the *Inconstant* and that while he never saw Napoleon, the unusual number of men on board made him suspect it carried the emperor; he explained that he thought the ship was bound for Naples and that if he'd known France was the destination, he would have immediately taken down the Bourbon white and sailed alongside Napoleon.

In his memoir, Peyrusse described what appears to be the most plausible alternative to the versions produced by Napoleon and Andrieux, writing that the French captain had recognized his colleague Taillade aboard the *Inconstant* and so maneuvered his ship so they could talk, and that they had a casual conversation, mostly about nautical matters, during which Taillade said they were headed for Genoa and asked Andrieux if he had any message he wanted to get to Elba when it returned. Peyrusse claimed that Andrieux, apologizing for being impolite, asked after Napoleon's health, and that was that. Later, the Polish officer Colonel Jerzmanowski, who joined in the landing, recalled the encounter in a way that corroborated Peyrusse's account, though he added a bit of embroidery, saying that when Andrieux had asked after Napoleon's health, the hidden Napoleon himself had shouted across that the emperor was "wonderfully well." Whatever the truth of this episode, Andrieux did receive a promotion during Napoleon's brief return to power.

AT DINNER THAT NIGHT, by which time they were a few miles north of Gorgona in open waters, Napoleon comforted the troops aboard the *Inconstant* with stories of past victories and defeats. While many of the soldiers were shaken by the day's adventures, Napoleon seemed energized by having so narrowly escaped British as well as French ships. He said to Peyrusse that it had been "a day to match Austerlitz." He was by then a master at this kind of act. Years earlier, in the worst times of the Egyptian campaign, he'd gone out of his way to lay hands on soldiers who were victims of the plague at Jaffa, showing himself to be immune from fear and evidently disease as well.

On the *Inconstant* the men gathered around him in a circle, while Bertrand sat by his side. Napoleon told them that the taste for danger was part of "their Gallic heritage"; for French soldiers, he said, "the love of glory and courage is instinctive, a sixth sense. How many times in the heat of battle have I seen our young conscripts jump into the fray: honor and courage came out of their very pores." It was a variation on a theme he had played in many previous speeches: follow me and count for something bigger than yourself.

Drouot sat silently, alone and outside this circle. "I know that if I had listened to our sage I wouldn't have left," Napoleon told the soldiers, motioning over to Drouot. "But there was even greater danger in staying at Portoferraio."

By nightfall the exhausted troops were bedding down wherever they could. Few of them had slept since the night before leaving Elba. Aboard the *Inconstant* they were piled on top of each other, many of them crowded into the hold. The valet Marchand slept out on the deck, where "the moon was full; the sea, beautiful." Napoleon retired to his camp bed, which had been set up in the captain's cabin. Bertrand lay nearby on a thin mattress on the floor. They played a few games of chess before nodding off.

{ 45 }

CAMPBELL LANDS AT ELBA

BY THE MORNING OF Tuesday, February 28, the *Partridge* was becalmed about four miles north of Portoferraio, safely out of range of Elban guns. Adye and Campbell had no way of knowing if the *Inconstant* still lay anchored in the harbor on the other side of the high ridge of Portoferraio that would have blocked its sails from sight. Campbell set off for shore in a rowboat while Adye stayed aboard the sloop with instructions to send off an emergency dispatch to Burghersh in Florence if he wasn't back in two hours.

He rounded into the sheltered waters and saw that the *Inconstant* had sailed. Expecting to be captured as soon as he reached the quay, he planned to surrender without a struggle, hoping he would eventually be allowed to talk with Bertrand. But no one came to arrest him. The port was quiet and the few people he did see at the harbor paid him no interest. He walked to the health office, apparently in such a daze that he could think of nothing better to do than repeat the customary first stop of anyone landing at Elba. The Elban who had been left in charge of the lazaretto told him that everyone had left, including Henri Bertrand, and that they had gone to Palmaiola.

Campbell headed toward the town hall to see if Fanny Bertrand was still on the island. He encountered a British gentleman named Henry Grattan, one of the tourists Adye had mentioned ferrying into Portoferraio a few days earlier. Grattan described the events of the previous days and said he had it on good authority that the ships were bound for Naples, though he'd also heard Milan and Antibes mentioned. He told Campbell that he'd hired a boat to take him out to the harbor to watch the flotilla preparing to leave until one of Napoleon's men discovered that an "Englishman" had come close to their ships (Grattan didn't explain how the soldier was able to discern his nationality), interrogated him, and then sent him back to shore. He said he was surprised not to have been "fired at or seized."

Campbell and Grattan reached the Biscotteria, where Campbell found Fanny Bertrand "alternately smiling and expressing her anxiety." She told him that Napoleon had kept her husband in the dark about the escape until the last possible moment and that he'd only been given fifteen minutes to say his goodbyes and prepare his portmanteau for a sea journey of unknown length. She said she had no idea where they were headed but added that she'd heard people talking about Pianosa.

Campbell thought that "by moving her feelings" he might get her to divulge whatever secrets she was keeping, and so he told her that Napoleon had lured her husband into taking "a most desperate step," since the British had known about the escape plans well ahead of time and had already captured the flotilla. He wrote that she asked him "with great earnestness, where was her husband, and what was become of him? Were they really taken? If so, she, as an Englishwoman, claimed my protection, as well as that of Lord Burghersh." Campbell answered that he couldn't say for certain that they had been captured just yet, "but that they were so situated they could not escape, for there were British as well as French men-of-war all round them." He said he knew they were heading to Naples and a squadron from Sicily was already waiting for them. "On this she became more relieved and quite collected," he wrote. "From which I concluded that her opinion of their destination was north, and not south, as I thought at first."

She explained that Dr. Lapi had been left in charge as governor, so Campbell headed for the fortress complex next to the Mulini. He assumed he would find Lapi there and would finally have to surrender himself to whatever guards he had under his command. But when he walked through some open doors into the fortress he was received cordially by a few men lounging in the main room, Dr. Lapi among them. No one seemed to be doing that much.

Campbell tried to give his entrance some kind of official gravitas, declaring that he came "as one of the Commissioners of the Allied Powers, who had accompanied Napoleon to Elba, in which character I had prolonged my stay there," which entitled him to know in what position he was to consider Dr. Lapi. The latter answered, as governor of Elba, on behalf of Napoleon. Maintaining his official tone, Campbell asked whether as governor he would relinquish possession of Elba to the British, or to the grand duke of Tuscany, or to the allied sovereigns. Lapi said he had no intention of handing it over to anyone and that he controlled forces sufficient to defend Portoferraio. If pressed he would fight any attacker, he said, until hearing any further orders from his emperor. Campbell answered that they should all now consider themselves under a state of blockade.

Though bluffing, Campbell had by saying this effectively declared war against Elba on behalf of Great Britain, despite not knowing Napoleon's present location, destination, or intention, a huge overstepping of his rank. He bowed as if to leave, but then walked toward the governor and in a booming voice said that if he wished "to prevent misery to the inhabitants" he should immediately announce that they were under blockade and bar any contact with the mainland. As he wrote in his journal, the grandiose language and loud voice had been for the benefit of the few officers at the fort, who might have been uncertain about who was in charge of what and could be cowed into not arresting him if it looked like he exercised some form of authority. They had, after all, often seen him talking and dining with Napoleon. He also hoped that his warnings would keep the Elbans from colluding any further with agents of Napoleon or Murat, and that some people would be frightened enough to pass along some intelligence or otherwise try to help the British take the island.

He left the fortress without any attempt made to detain him and went to Madame Mère's house, where Pauline Bonaparte was also staying, and where some members of the Elban Guard stood sentry. Rather than try to get past them, Campbell said, as if in passing, that he was about to sail for Livorno if the Bonaparte women wanted to give him any letters or ask him to perform any task for them on the continent. He kept walking for the docks until one of the guards ran after him to say that Pauline wanted to see him.

He was kept waiting in her antechamber long enough to make him stand up and pretend to leave again, saying that his ship would sail without him. At that moment Pauline came out and asked him to sit down beside her, "drawing her chair gradually still closer," wrote Campbell, "as if she waited for me to make some *private* communication." He repeated his line about having only stopped in to offer his services as a messenger. As he recalled:

> She asked me, with every appearance of anxiety, if I had nothing to say to her, and what I would advise her to do; said she had already written to her husband, Prince Borghese, who was now at Livorno, and requested me to tell him that she wished to go to Rome immediately.

Campbell told her he thought it wisest for her to stay on Elba for now. He wrote that she kept protesting that she knew nothing about Napoleon's intentions until the last moment, had no idea where he was heading, and "laid hold of my hand and pressed it to her heart, that I might feel how much she was agitated." But to Campbell she looked remarkably calm, "and there was rather a smile on her countenance." She asked if he thought her brother had been captured, to which he answered that this was the most likely conclusion. She then hinted that he was heading for France. Campbell thought she did this to throw him off course, which reinforced his original suspicion that Naples was the landing point. He wrote, mysteriously, that he stayed with Pauline for "two or three minutes" more before taking his leave. He went to his boat without meeting any opposition. He made no mention of seeing Madame Mère.

Mr. Grattan met Campbell at the harbor. Ricci was also there, finally able to tell Campbell everything he'd wanted to report to Adye a few days earlier. He said that Napoleon was almost certainly headed for France. Campbell commandeered two local fishing boats, the first of which would speed

Grattan to Livorno with dispatches for Castlereagh describing all that they had learned so far, and the second to take Ricci to Piombino, from where he would ride to Florence with duplicates of these messages for any allied and French officials he could find.

He rowed back to the *Partridge* to decide on next steps. Neither he nor Adye put much stock in Pauline's or Ricci's talk of France. No matter how brave or loyal they might be, Napoleon's troops surely wouldn't follow on a mission that began with such an obvious tactical error. They didn't doubt that Paris was the end goal; but Italy was the place to start. An Italian landing would be "more reconcilable to the national feelings of his officers and men," wrote Campbell in the day's journal entry, "and they will think it probably less hazardous than raising the standard of rebellion in France, where they would be considered traitors."

Adye wanted to sail south to what he thought was the likeliest destination of Naples. Campbell wanted to sail north toward the Ligurian coast. He was now convinced that Napoleon would set up a beachhead there to proclaim an independent state and so draw disaffected Italians to his side, while Murat would try something similar in the south. He based this guess on reports that the *Inconstant* had been loaded with several horses and guns and a significant number of civilians alongside the troops. To slow his sailing speed with so much bulk was an unnecessary encumbrance if he was planning to land in Naples, where he could draw on Murat's horses and guns. He allowed that Napoleon might have brought this materiel along precisely to throw him off course and then dump the horses and guns, but Campbell thought he was unlikely to want to waste a day on a wild-goose chase while risking being slowed by calm wind, left bobbing under the hot sun while ships circled in from all directions.

Maybe self-interest was what really drove Campbell to push to sail north, rather than to Naples, because if he was right, and both he and his target were heading north, then there remained a chance for the *Partridge* to overtake the *Inconstant* despite its head start, and Campbell could have a chance for a glorious standoff at sea. On the other hand, if Napoleon had headed for Naples he was very likely to reach his destination well before the *Partridge* even got close to him, so a bet on the south, even if correct, offered little chance for distinction. Worse still, it could have led to their capture or sinking by a joint force led by Napoleon and Murat.

In his journal Campbell showed no sense of guilt over the escape:

> No part of Napoleon's plan for quitting Elba could have increased my *general* suspicions of his possibly taking that step at some time or another, even had I been there from the 16th to the 26th, nor could have authorised me to report to the British Government any fact which could be considered as a certain proof of that intention. There would have been no positive criminality in any act previous to his embarkation of the troops and his actual departure, a period of six hours, during which time the gates of Portoferraio were shut.

He decided that his being away was actually the best thing that could have happened, since if the *Partridge* had been in harbor it would have been captured and put into service as part of the flotilla, while he and Captain Adye would have been arrested, "and thus made more subservient to the easier execution of his plan." As though penning his mea culpa, he wrote that while he'd often thought that this "restless and unprincipled person" might one day try to wage war on the continent, especially if his funds ran low or if he was subjected to some special form of humiliation by his enemies, Napoleon had given him no real reason to believe he had the necessary support to try retaking France, a country whose "apparent tranquility" had led Campbell to think he had "no chance of success there, and that he himself has despaired of every hope in that quarter."

He hashed out his final defense:

> With the free sovereignty of Elba, four armed vessels of his own, and seventeen belonging to the mines, which sailed in every direction, I knew well that Napoleon had it in his power to avail himself

any day of these means of escape, without any chance of my preventing him, dependent as I was on the occasional calls of a
man-of-war, which cruised between Civita Vecchia and Genoa [the
Partridge] and the frequency of whose visits was subject entirely to
the captain.

{ 46 }

OUR BEAUTIFUL FRANCE

TAILLADE SAW THE FIRST faint signs of land in the distance at eight in the morning of Tuesday, February 28. "We're either in Spain or Africa!" he shouted. Napoleon heard about Taillade's assessment, wandered over to the former captain, and asked him to repeat it. Then he laughed, saying, "Not quite," and revealed that they were headed for France. Peyrusse described how this revelation

> revived our spirits and relieved our anxieties. After four days of con-
> stant agitation, thrown into an adventure without knowing how it
> was to end, terrified by the boldness of the enterprise, confronted
> with danger at each step of the way, it was with the greatest of joy
> that we raised the veil that had covered His Majesty's plans.

Suffering from seasickness just as badly as he had on the crossing ten months earlier, Peyrusse tried his best to share in the sense of joy while running to the rail to empty his stomach. Napoleon teased him, saying that only good Seine water could cure him and promising that he would be in Paris to drink it in time to celebrate the birthday of the King of Rome, which fell on

March 20. He advised Peyrusse to head down to the cabin to "join the other pen-pushers."

Napoleon carried with him the proclamations he had printed up at Elba, each one written with the same mix of bombast and self-assuredness. In the first he claimed to have never been defeated by the armies of the allied coalition but rather betrayed by a small number of his marshals. He framed the Bourbon rule as one imposed on France by "foreigners" who had only been "momentarily" victorious. The Bourbons, he said, "had learned nothing and forgotten nothing," and wanted to return France to the ways of the ancien régime. Only he could bring peace and order to Europe. He sounded a republican tone, saying:

> Frenchmen, your complaints and your desires have reached me in
> my exile. You have asked for the government of your choice, which
> is the only legitimate government. I have crossed the sea, and I am
> here to resume my rights, which are also your own.

A second proclamation he directly addressed to veterans of his campaigns:

> Soldiers! Rally around the standard of your chief. He lives only for
> you, his rights are only those of the people and your own. Our vic-
> tory advances like a charging line of battle! The eagle shall carry the
> tricolor from steeple to steeple until it reaches the spires of Notre-
> Dame!

The third, Napoleon addressed to all who had joined him in exile and were now risking their lives for his cause. He brought out the draft copy of the document, as if he'd composed it spontaneously on board, and instructed the men to make copies from his dictation. "Friends and comrades in arms, return to your duty," he said. "Trample the white cockade, the badge of shame!"

Napoleon later said he regretted not bringing a portable printing press with him from Elba so that more copies of these proclamations could have been distributed on the landing. Only a hundred copies "were made by hand," he recalled to Gourgaud, "but such written documents do not produce so much effect upon the public as those that are printed. Printing seems to act as the seal of authority." Drouot signed his name to all of these proclamations, which would later become a key issue in his trial for treason. Napoleon later claimed that Drouot himself had drafted one of the documents.

Napoleon announced that everyone who had followed him from Fontaine-bleau would be awarded the Legion of Honor, and he presented a makeshift strip of red ribbon to Captain Chautard for so skillfully navigating them out of Elba. Taillade received one as well. That afternoon, Napoleon told the crew:

> There is no precedent in history for what I am about to do, but I've counted on the element of surprise, the state of public opinion, the resentment against the allies, and the love of my soldiers, in short all of the attachments to the Empire that still linger in our beautiful France.

Marchand wrote that he'd never seen Napoleon looking more handsome than he did then, speaking of France, while the sun reflecting off the Mediter-ranean had helped to restore some color to his pallid complexion.

By sunset they could just make out some of the peaks of the range to the north of Antibes now known as the Préalpes d'Azur, their first sight of French territory. Napoleon, who had been at his desk, came out to the deck and said, "Look at our beautiful France, our beloved country!" The final evening on board felt like a wedding feast, recalled Pons, full of wine, sausages, pâtés, songs, laughter, and dances in the moonlight. No one slept. Napoleon spent most of the night in his cabin, writing.

THE *PARTRIDGE* IN PURSUIT

THE *PARTRIDGE* HAD PUSHED off from Portoferraio at two in the afternoon on February 28, which put Campbell and Adye about forty hours behind Napoleon. But they had the help of strong wind behind them and passed the northern tip of Corsica at a decent eight-knot clip by two the next morning. A light in the distance turned out to be the French frigate *Fleur de Lys*, whose crew didn't yet know about Napoleon's escape.

The captain, de Garat, told Campbell that they had already been at sea in horrible weather for more than a month and that only a wild stroke of luck would have allowed him to stop, let alone sight, Napoleon's flotilla. Adye, Campbell, and de Garat agreed that the two ships should head in tandem toward the Ligurian coast, and for a time they were—unknown to them—gaining steadily on Napoleon's fleet, which at that point would have been near Monaco, about ninety miles to the north.

This was when Adye and Campbell made a fateful error. They couldn't shake the feeling that Napoleon was heading for southern Italy. Seeing little point in having two ships heading toward the same hypothetical target, they decided that while the *Fleur de Lys* continued its course, the *Partridge* should turn back to investigate Capraia and Gorgona. Napoleon might have left a false trail pointing north before doubling back to one of these islands to wait until his pursuers had gone far enough down the wrong path to let him slip away to Livorno or Naples.

So the *Partridge* turned around and sailed into the wind. It would only reach Capraia two days later, where the local commander told Campbell he knew nothing about Napoleon's escape, though he'd seen some brigs passing by in tandem a few days earlier, bound northwest, which was enough to change Campbell's mind about where the landing would take place. Again, the *Partridge* reversed course and sailed north.

{ 48 }

GOLFE-JUAN

AT SUNRISE ON MARCH 1, Napoleon gave the order for all Elban flags to be lowered and replaced by the tricolor. His soldiers followed by taking ribbons of red, white, and blue from their travel kits and pinning them to their hats. Marchand handed Napoleon his hat through the hatchway and when he donned it the troops cheered and stamped their feet, a noise that sounded to Marchand as loud as all the batteries being fired in unison.

By noon, with the peninsula of Antibes tantalizingly near, Napoleon delivered one last speech:

> I have long weighed and most maturely considered the project; the glory, the advantages we shall gain if we succeed I need not enlarge upon. If we fail—to military men, who have from their infancy faced death in so many shapes, the fate which awaits us is not terrific: we know, and we despise, for we have a thousand times faced the worst which a reverse can bring.

The ships anchored off the beachside of Golfe-Juan roughly between Antibes and Cannes. Napoleon ordered the senior captain of the Guard,

Lamouret, to row to the beach with two dozen men to scout the coast and if possible take the Gabelle fort across the harbor. There was a bit of miscommunication when Lamouret began rowing straight for the citadel until Napoleon had a gun fired to recall him, saying, "Where are you off to Captain?" and pointing him west toward Golfe-Juan.

People in those parts would have been accustomed to seeing men sailing to and from Elba, and Lamouret and his troops were to tell anyone they encountered that they were a section of the Elban Guard on leave. They landed a bit farther west than intended, at a little stony beach near Cannes. A while later while securing the coastal road they happened to pass the commander of the Cannes National Guard, who was returning home along with his wife after having purchased some olive groves nearby. They were arrested and their donkey, borrowed from a neighbor and loaded down with olives, was requisitioned. The commander and his wife were freed a few hours later; the donkey was not.

At four o'clock, after a hundred grenadiers led by Cambronne landed to form an advance guard at the beachhead, Napoleon was rowed to shore alongside Bertrand, Drouot, and Pons. He walked into an olive grove where Cambronne and the soldiers had bivouacked. They set up Napoleon's campaign chair, lit a fire, and tied his horse nearby.

There were only four fishermen's huts by the beach and a small settlement at Vallauris, in the hills a few miles north. At first the local fishing families stayed in their homes, terrified that pirates had landed. Then they recognized the members of the Old Guard by their uniforms and thought that these men had deserted and were returning home. By evening the soldiers dropped all attempts at secrecy and the locals soon learned that Napoleon was among them. The scene took on the feel of a carnival. Villagers came to join in the fireside meal of a hearty soup, the trees bedecked with tricolor flags.

Napoleon would describe to Gourgaud on Saint Helena how on that night in the olive grove

> a great crowd of people came around us, surprised by our appearance and astonished by our small force. Among them was a mayor,

who, seeing how few we were, said to me: "We were just beginning
to be quiet and happy; now you are going to stir us all up again."

Gourgaud, who had apparently tired of this old battle tale, made a note at
the bottom of the section of his memoir that records the landing at Golfe-
Juan: "Napoleon several times related this narrative."

That evening the squadron commander Jerzmanowski took some grenadiers to secure the eastern road to Antibes. Peyrusse, who for some reason
was brought along on this mission, wrote that he lagged behind the troops and
wore a large coat to disguise his decorations. Cambronne was off securing the
western road to Cannes. Napoleon had told him he wouldn't have to fire a
single shot, since he would "find only friends," and reminded him that he
wanted to retake his crown without bloodshed. He was to spread a false report
that Murat was at that same moment entering France with troops landed at
Toulon.

It would take until the following morning to ferry all the troops, horses,
cannon, and supplies to shore, along with Pauline's carriage and Peyrusse's
treasure boxes. The military band entertained the sappers as they unloaded
the heavy gear, playing the same melodramatic tune, "Où peut-on être mieux
qu'au sein de sa famille?," that had heralded Pauline's arrival on Elba four
months earlier.

Captain Lamouret and his men had by then captured the Gabelle fort without difficulty. Whether by luck or by some prior arrangement, the French
soldiers of the 106th Regiment that normally guarded the area were off on
maneuvers in the hills. But when Lamouret's soldiers pressed deeper into Antibes to demand the surrender of the garrison, they discovered they were
badly outnumbered and were soon caught and arrested.

A rider sent to investigate the delay returned with news of the capture.
Napoleon decided against trying to rescue Lamouret's men. "I heard mur-
murs in my very presence because I was not marching on Antibes," he said
later on Saint Helena. "A few bombs, they declared, would have been enough."
But he calculated "that it would have been the loss of half a day. If I succeeded
it would be a matter of small importance; if I failed, which was very possible,

such a check at the outset would give confidence to my enemies, and afford them time to organize themselves." He wanted to quickly reach Grenoble, the center of the province, where there was an arsenal with multiple cannons and a substantial garrison of troops to be turned to his cause.

The imprisoned men at Antibes would be well treated by the French soldiers who held them. Prisoners and guards played together at pétanque. A few nights after their capture they would attempt a daring but unsuccessful escape, which left one officer with a broken back after he leapt from the ramparts. The prisoners were transferred to Toulon, where they were kept only a short while longer.

NAPOLEON AND HIS TROOPS left at moonrise, marching in silence. Cambronne led an advanced guard of a hundred men. Not even Bertrand knew which route they would take until the point where the road led either to Avignon or Grasse and Napoleon shouted, "To the right!" There were so few horses that some troops had to drag the wagon carts carrying hundreds of muskets by hand along the poorly paved road. They reached a hillside near Grasse by midnight.

The seven ships had by then sailed back out to sea. Filidoro, the Elban portmaster, had been named as the senior officer and put in command of the *Inconstant*, which would sail for Naples to be put into Murat's service while the other ships in the flotilla would head for Portoferraio so they could ferry relatives to the mainland. Napoleon was uninterested in leaving his landing party any form of ocean escape.

49

Most Reluctantly I Have Felt Called Upon to Mention It

The Oil Merchant finally left Portoferraio on March 1 after regaining his passport. He arrived at Livorno the following day, and though unable to circumvent the standard three-day quarantine, he sent reports on the escape to Mariotti, mentioning that he'd heard Napoleon was heading for Fréjus and that thousands of soldiers were waiting to join his cause. He highlighted Campbell's absence from Elba.

In Florence, Mariotti debriefed Burghersh and then fled to Genoa, asking for protection from the English and Austrians, as Murat was set to go on the offensive in the south. Burghersh then wrote to Castlereagh:

> It is with feelings of very great regret I think myself called upon to mention the subject of Colonel Sir N. Campbell. From an unwillingness to act unkindly towards an officer of Sir Neil Campbell's merit, I have abstained from bringing under your lordship's consideration the improper manner in which, I felt, he did the duties of the situation in which he was placed. His absences from the Elba were constant, and at times of considerable duration. I

represented my feelings to him at various times, and begged—at least till the Congress was over and the world placed at rest—he would remain steadily at his post.

Sir Neil felt that his situation about Bonaparte was unpleasant, and that the duty was better done by occasional visits. This opinion was at variance with mine. I begged Mr. Cooke, of the Foreign Office, who happed to be here, to speak in recommendation of a more continued residence. Mr. Cooke spoke to him in that sense, but Bonaparte was gone before Sir Neil Campbell had returned. I do not mean that any residence of a British officer could have prevented the event which has taken place; information, however, with regard to the intention might have been obtained. Sir Neil Campbell is one of the most zealous officers I know in the service; I differed with him on the subject I have stated. Most reluctantly I have felt called upon to mention it.

Years later, Burghersh added a more damning note to his copy of this letter, claiming that if only Campbell had listened to his previous advice to stay more regularly on Elba, or if he'd only returned from Florence as soon as Burghersh had told him to, he could have single-handedly prevented Napoleon's escape, since the well-armed *Partridge* would have overpowered his flotilla, and "the misfortune of the war of 1815, for that time at least, would certainly have been avoided."

50

IN AN IRON CAGE

WORD OF NAPOLEON'S LANDING reached Paris on the afternoon of Sunday, March 5. A line of aerial telegraphs connected the capital to as far south as Lyons, but beyond that news traveled mainly by courier, giving Napoleon and his soldiers four days on French soil before the Bourbon government could properly begin to mobilize. No one was sure how many men he'd landed with, although some thought the number to be as low as fifty.

At the Tuileries, Louis XVIII and his ministers joked about the "rogue" Bonaparte and his delusions of grandeur. "It is just as well that the man from Elba has attempted his crazy undertaking," wrote Marshal Ney on March 10, "for this will be the last act of his tragedy, the final curtain of the Napoléonade." French troops were dispatched from the main southern garrison in Marseille, trailing behind their quarry as he marched north. Ney promised his king that he would bring Napoleon back to Paris "in an iron cage." Marshal Macdonald headed to Lyons to take command of the troops there.

The first French engravings that imagined the scene at Golfe-Juan began to circulate. In one, *The Imperial Stride,* a dashing Napoleon in full regalia steps easily across the waters separating France and Elba with Paris already in his sights. Frightened members of the Bourbon family watch his crossing through telescopes, two of them wearing candle snuffers as hats, a reference to the so-called Order of Extinguishers, said to comprise ultraroyalists who wanted to snuff out all the lights of progress and modernity. "Let's pack it up!" says one of them, while Napoleon waves a tricolor capped by a golden eagle and emblazoned with *"Honneur et Patrie,"* his aquiline nose pointing him like Don Quixote to tilt at the windmills of Montmartre.

As French soldiers went to hunt their former emperor, his former subjects remained remarkably calm. In opera boxes and corridors and cafés, all it took was to say that *he* was back and people understood. The novelist Fanny Burney, who was then in Paris, recalled that while the general feeling in the city was wonder at Napoleon's "temerity," it was "wonder unmixed with apprehension." In her memoir she described how

> a torpor indescribable, a species of stupor utterly indefinable, seemed to have enveloped the capital with a mist that was impervious. Everybody went about their affairs, made or received visits, met and parted, without speaking, or, I suppose, thinking of this event as a matter of any importance.

Burney admitted that she'd been as guilty as anyone else of such magical thinking. She'd lived for a decade under Napoleon and knew his intimates, who spoke freely around her because of "her spotless husband," who served in the king's guard. She knew his character, which meant, as she wrote in hindsight, that she should have known what he was capable of achieving.

When Mary Berry, another English writer, learned that Napoleon had landed on French soil, she wrote to a friend that it wasn't worth worrying about because no nation could be "so degraded and so stupid as to wish again for a military despotism, after having gone through so dreadful an experience of it."

Louis XVIII would flee Paris less than two weeks later.

51

URGENT

A COURIER DASHED UP the marble stairs of the Austrian chancellery early in the morning of March 7, carrying a message marked URGENT. He entered Metternich's chambers, despite strict orders not to bother the foreign minister, who had only gotten to bed two hours earlier after another long committee meeting. Metternich glanced at the letter, assumed it was just more congress work, and left it unopened on his nightstand. But he couldn't get back to sleep. He reached for the letter and saw that it had been sent from the royal consulate general in Livorno:

> The English Commissary, Campbell, has just appeared in the harbor to inquire whether Napoleon has been seen at [Livorno], as he has disappeared from the island of Elba. This question being answered in the negative, the English ship has again put out to sea.

He dressed quickly and went to tell Emperor Francis, who, as Metternich remembered, "said to me quietly and calmly, as he always did on great occasions: 'Napoleon seems to wish to play the adventurer. That is his concern;

ours is to secure to the world that peace which he has disturbed for years.'"
Francis told him to inform Tsar Alexander and the king of Prussia, and to say
that he was ready "to order my army to march back to France. I do not doubt
but that both monarchs will agree with me."

Metternich went to the Hofburg palace next to the chancellery, going first
to the Amalienburg residence to tell Alexander, then rushing back across the
inner courtyard to find the king of Prussia, and finally returning to the chancellery to discuss strategy with the Austrian field marshal Prince Schwarzenberg. By ten o'clock the ministers of Austria, Prussia, Russia, and Britain had
sent couriers to order their respective armies to halt where they were. "The
war," wrote Metternich, "was decided on in less than an hour." He was speaking figuratively, but having representatives of the major powers gathered
within a few hundred feet of one another in Vienna allowed them to organize a
response to the landing far more quickly than would otherwise be possible, as
Napoleon must have anticipated when calculating the risks of his escape.

When Metternich told Talleyrand the news, the latter feigned nonchalance
and said he was certain Napoleon would land somewhere on the coast of Italy
and then go into Switzerland. This aligned with the prevailing logic in Vienna, where, for instance, Napoleon's Corsican rival Pozzo di Borgo, who
was serving as adviser to Tsar Alexander, said that if Napoleon dared to set
foot in France he would "be seized the moment he lands, and hanged from the
nearest tree."

Talleyrand wrote to Louis XVIII, repeating his prediction that Napoleon
would land somewhere in the north of Italy, and adding that Metternich and
Schwarzenberg had told him they would be "greatly embarrassed" if Napoleon had indeed landed in Tuscany, since they didn't yet have soldiers in place
to properly counter him if he managed to rally the people in the region to his
cause. While Talleyrand refused to "believe that he would dare to make any
attempt upon our southern provinces," because he couldn't "venture to do this
unless he had confederates there, which we can hardly suppose possible," he
advised that they should send some carefully selected troops into Provence,
just as a precaution. As evenhanded as ever, he added that while "the

consequences of this event cannot yet be foreseen . . . they may be fortunate if we know how to turn them to account," implying that they might now have the chance to lawfully kill Napoleon and his assumed confederate Murat.

First, Napoleon had to be stripped of the protection that came with his title as a legitimate European sovereign. "I will do all in my power to keep people here from going to sleep," Talleyrand promised Louis, "and to induce the Congress to depose Bonaparte from a rank which, by an inconceivable weakness, he has been suffered to preserve, and to render him at length incapable of preparing fresh disasters in Europe." If Napoleon did try any action in France, it would be "the act of a brigand, and it is thus that he ought to be treated, and every measure lawful against brigands ought to be employed against him."

NEIPPERG TOLD MARIE LOUISE about the escape that same afternoon while they were out riding. Back at Schönbrunn she discovered some of the members of her largely French retinue clapping their hands in excitement. She tried to act as if nothing had happened. "There was dinner, billiards, and music as usual," wrote Méneval. Marie Louise told Neipperg she worried about how Napoleon's actions would influence her claims to Parma as well as her son's inheritance. She wanted to make it clear she had nothing to do with the escape. Later that evening people heard her crying in her room.

With Neipperg's help she drafted a formal letter to her father, writing in French, the language of diplomacy, so that the message could be circulated to the congress delegates:

> At this moment when . . . further misfortunes menace me I cannot
> hope for a surer asylum . . . than the one I claim for myself and my
> son from your paternal affection. In your arms, my very dear father,
> I take refuge with the person who is most dear to me in this world. . . .
> We will not seek any other instruction than yours. With your ha-
> bitual gentleness, you may order all our comings and goings.

That night in one of the Hofburg's ballrooms an amateur production of a Kotzebue play was performed by a cast that included Metternich's daughter, Marie, Talleyrand's niece, Dorothée, and Alexander's current mistress, Princess Auersperg. The major figures of the congress, all in the audience, kept their opera glasses trained at the stage as though it was the only thing on their minds, wanting to avoid a panic but also out of respect for their friends and relations onstage. But speculation about Napoleon's landing soon spread among the audience and then to the performers backstage and the show was ruined. "Though there was every attempt to conceal apprehension under the mask of unconcern," wrote one of the British delegates in attendance, "it was not difficult to perceive that fear was predominant in all the Imperial and Royal personages there assembled." Reality had become far more interesting than anything that could be put up onstage. "The events are so extraordinary, so unexpected, so magical," wrote Geneva's ambassador to the congress in his journal. "When one sees all that is happening, it is as though the *One Thousand and One Nights* is coming true, and everything happens by the waves of a wand of some invisible magician."

The conference delegates were already blaming the British for Napoleon's escape, and some accused them of outright collusion. At dinner one night in Vienna, Castlereagh's hard-drinking half brother, Charles Stewart, burst out, "Are we Napoleon's keepers? We're not at war with him." People were carrying on "as if they had put a dangerous man in prison, refused him bread and then left the door open," and then complained when he escaped, wrote one of the Danish delegates. Nowhere in the Treaty of Fontainebleau was Napoleon actually forbidden from leaving Elba.

WHEN THE DELEGATES in Vienna finally learned that Napoleon had landed not in Italy but at Golfe-Juan, "the news spread with the speed of an electric spark," as one French diplomat remembered. "The waltz was interrupted, and while the orchestra continued in vain with the melody it had started, we looked at each other in shock and started with our interrogations. . . . *He's in France!*"

The Viennese papers stopped printing their daily updates on the city's social life and diplomatic developments. "All festivities ceased in Vienna from this time and gave way to silent activity," wrote Méneval. "The sitting of the Congress was involved in impenetrable mystery." Communications with France were prohibited. The infant King of Rome, or Prince Franz, as he was then being called, was separated from his French handlers. His governess, Madame de Montesquiou, who had watched over him since birth, was dismissed on suspicion of a Bonapartist plot to kidnap the boy, now potentially heir to the French throne, and replaced by a Polish woman recommended by Neipperg.

The signatories of the Treaty of Paris would release a declaration drafted by Talleyrand, which branded their common adversary an outlaw, "beyond the pale of civil society," who had hijacked his country to serve his own goals. To rhetorically place Napoleon "beyond the pale" sent the message that anyone could kill him on their own initiative without fear of reprisal. The sovereigns of Europe's main powers felt justified in pursuing this course, reasoning that by landing in France with armed men Napoleon had openly declared himself as the enemy of peace and had reneged on all the terms of his surrender, meaning that he forfeited any claim to an imperial title and was no longer entitled to be under the protection of any treaty or law. From then on, in their view, he was no longer Napoleon, Emperor of Elba, but a common outlaw named Bonaparte.

52

LAFFREY

NAPOLEON AND HIS SOLDIERS continued their brutal march along the Alpine route toward Grenoble, where thousands of French soldiers were garrisoned, with plans to capture the arsenal there. By capitalizing on the element of surprise and moving so quickly through the countryside, Napoleon had opened the campaign with the same daring and speed that had marked his greatest military victories. His troops had covered more than two hundred miles in the six days since their campfire on the beach at Golfe-Juan. Despite some halfhearted protests by local officials, they were for the most part welcomed by villagers as they passed.

On March 7 the column reached the edge of the village of Laffrey, on a high plateau about seventy-five miles south of Grenoble, where they would have their first encounter with a potentially hostile force. Here were eight hundred infantrymen of the 5th Regiment, all of whom had sworn oaths that they would be willing to give their lives protecting the Bourbon reign.

Napoleon ordered his musicians to play the "Marseillaise," and then walked, unarmed, toward the opposing troops. Cambronne, Drouot, and Bertrand trailed closely behind. A cold wind whipped off the Grand lac de Laffrey.

A soldier tried to halt Napoleon's progress. "If you don't withdraw," he shouted across the field, "you'll be arrested." The members of the royalist battalion put their muskets at aim and the Elban corps did the same.

Napoleon told his troops to lower their weapons and continued walking. He stopped about twenty feet from the first row of infantrymen, whose muskets were still pointed at his head and chest. In his heavy Corsican lilt he shouted, "Soldiers! I am your emperor. Do you not recognize me?"

Silence.

He moved forward again, now a dozen feet from the battalion, and opened his greatcoat to expose his stocky trunk, offering it as a target.

"If there is any one among you who wants to kill his emperor, here I am!"

No one moved.

A voice cried out from the royalist battalion: "Fire!" But no one shot and again there was silence.

Then came a single shout from one of the soldiers of the 5th, which quickly grew to a roar: "Long Live the Emperor! Long Live the Emperor! Long Live the Emperor!"

Men from both sides of the field threw down their guns and surrounded Napoleon. Some of them cried; some of them laughed. They embraced one another. They shouted their vivas, again and again.

53

TO CONTEMPLATE ALL OBJECTS
AT A CERTAIN ANGLE

A FEW HOURS AFTER Napoleon's encounter at Laffrey, the *Partridge* anchored at Antibes, not far from the *Fleur de Lys*. In his journal, Campbell blamed the time spent communicating with the French ship for denying him and Adye "the glorious chance, which was so nearly at our command, of destroying [Napoleon]."

The town's commanding officer presented Campbell with the dubious story that he'd been away at Île Sainte-Marguerite when Napoleon landed, enjoying a picnic with some guests near the island's recently dismantled fort, when he saw a tall ship flying the tricolor, an outlawed symbol, as he knew well, along with some smaller craft landing at Golfe-Juan, but had taken them for Algerian corsairs who must have captured some smaller fishing boats and were flying the tricolor as a ruse. Only after two dispatches reached him did he understand what was going on, causing him to scramble up some rocks and through heavy bushes—he showed Campbell the marks on his arms—to avoid being seen by Napoleon's troops, but had only reached Antibes after they had left.

Campbell found it "most extraordinary" that Napoleon's landing and a full day of encampment had failed to attract more notice or any action from the authorities at Antibes. He stayed in the area to try to learn as much as he could about the past few days and in speaking to witnesses fixated on the smallest details while trying to recreate the scene, noting that "during the afternoon the band continued to play," that Napoleon "wore a gray great coat," that "at night he lay down on a mattress with a coverlet turned over his head," and that Bertrand "always kept off his hat when he approached him, as did all others."

For the next weeks Campbell buzzed between Nice, Genoa, and Livorno trying to figure out where Napoleon was headed. In a strange bookend to the theft of his belongings during his battlefield convalescence almost exactly a year earlier, some highwaymen robbed him along the Ligurian coast early on March 20, just as Napoleon was entering Paris. He abandoned his pursuit the next day and headed for London to face Castlereagh and the prince regent. His ensuing journal entries record little other than places and dates as he pushed through Milan, Luxembourg, Brussels, and Ostend.

He reached London on All Fools' Day and was summoned the next morning for separate interviews with Castlereagh and with the prince regent. His journal leaves no record of what was said at the meetings.

People were already beginning to learn the details of his strange assignment. His younger brother, Patrick Campbell, a major general, told anyone who would listen that Neil had been frantically warning the government of Napoleon's scheme for months. A damning piece in the *Times* quoted "a private letter from Livorno," whose writer remarked that it was

> inconceivable why so dangerous a man was not better watched. Colonel Campbell, who was to watch over him, was almost always here or at Florence. He contented himself with sending a corvette once a week to reconnoiter the harbor of Portoferraio.

A few weeks later, the future parliamentarian John Cam Hobhouse attended a posh dinner in Paris whose star guest was Colonel Jerzmanowski, a commander of the Polish lancers during the exile. While regaling his dining companions with tales of Elba and the landing at Golfe-Juan, Jerzmanowski described Campbell as "too much of a politician and too little of a soldier." But

Hobhouse knew Campbell and thought the opposite: that he was a decent sol-dier who had been forced into a political role to which he was badly suited. "What a change a little place of court can make in a man," wrote Hobhouse. "No one was less diplomatic than Campbell when I knew him in Germany."

Though Campbell's full journal wouldn't be published for another five de-cades, Hobhouse somehow managed, shortly after Napoleon's landing, to get hold of a "half official memoir" drawn from Campbell's papers. After reading it, Hobhouse wrote that he pitied Campbell, just a few years older than he was, for having experienced what must have been a life-changing disillusionment. By regarding the Emperor of Elba from as close a distance as he had, Camp-bell must have discovered a sad truth about Napoleon. He was neither histo-ry's greatest genius, nor its most terrifying monster, but simply human, "a very commonplace-minded man."

As Hobhouse put it:

> Campbell, when I knew him, was a most worthy, sensible man, but it is just possible that being accustomed to . . . the dignities of this world, he was astounded perhaps at first, and then disgusted, at finding so much of human frailty, of the weaknesses of common life, in a general and a sovereign. The colonel might have been but little surprised to have seen him shoot a grenadier a day. There would besides have been more of dignity in guarding such a Nero. But to find that his prisoner had none of the trappings of legitimate tyr-anny, that he could not discover one trait in his manner or conversa-tion which affected him or gave him a superiority over himself; that he talked freely and playfully on the passages of his former life and sometimes of his future destination and even projects; that he took no pains to conceal any weakness or error; that he was, in short, al-together such a being as himself; this was intolerable, and would be so to any eye accustomed to contemplate all objects at a certain an-gle, and to mistake elevation of position for height of stature.

EPILOGUE

NAPOLEON, MARIE LOUISE, CAMPBELL, AND ELBA

· ——————— ·

Here was an experiment, under the most favorable conditions, of the powers of intellect without conscience. Never was such a leader so endowed and so weaponed; never leader found such aids and followers. And what was the result of this vast talent and power, of these immense armies, burned cities, squandered treasures, immolated millions of men, of this demoralized Europe? It came to no result. All passed away like the smoke of his artillery, and left no trace. He left France smaller, poorer, feebler, than he found it; and the whole contest for freedom was to be begun again. The attempt was in principle suicidal. France served him with life and limb and estate, as long as it could identify its interest with him; but when men saw that after victory was another war; after the destruction of armies, new conscriptions; and they who had toiled so desperately were never nearer to the reward,— they could not spend what they had earned, nor repose on their down-beds, nor strut in their chateaux,— they deserted him. Men found that his absorbing egotism was deadly to all other men.

—RALPH WALDO EMERSON, "Napoleon: The Man of the World" (1850)

To be rooted is perhaps the most important and least
recognized need of the human soul.

—SIMONE WEIL, *The Need for Roots* (1949)

NAPOLEON WAS PRAGMATIC about the relative ease with which he retook
the Tuileries on March 20—his son's fourth birthday—recognizing it mainly
as the result of his dexterity and its stupefying effects, just as he intended.
When a French financier came to congratulate him on his first night at the
palace, he answered, "They let me come, just like they let them go," referring
to the Bourbons. Though people were dazzled by the temerity of his lightning
march on Paris they were never rationally persuaded that his return would be
for the greater good, and Napoleon never gained widespread support during
his brief return to power, now known as the Hundred Days. The shock factor,
lingering support from veterans of his wars, and a great deal of bluster were
enough to keep him propped up, but only for a short while.

He wrote to Marie Louise several times during his march. He wanted her
and the King of Rome with him in the capital, perhaps out of affection, or
perhaps because if there was to be a restored empire he needed to show people
his dynasty was intact. He planned a coronation ceremony that would include
his wife and child. His letters to Marie Louise were intercepted and never
reached her directly, but she did learn of their contents. She said she would
rather enter a convent than be reunited with Napoleon, and indeed she never
saw him again. Caulaincourt returned the red portfolio of her letters that Napoleon had asked be set aside for his son ten months earlier. One morning in
May, one of Napoleon's ministers found him at the Tuileries crying, looking at
a portrait of his son.

After Waterloo, Napoleon again tried abdicating in favor of his son, without success. He dreamed of escaping to America, but the British naval

blockade made that impossible. Louis XVIII returned to retake the throne on July 8, and a week later Napoleon surrendered to the British aboard the *Bellerophon*. Again he became Britain's problem, again he thought he might be exiled to England, and again the British were hamstrung, not feeling justified in executing him and fearful of the repercussions if they did.

A letter from the British prime minister, Lord Liverpool, to Castlereagh showed that they had learned something from their first mistake:

> We are all decidedly of the opinion that it would not answer to confine him in this country. . . . You know enough of the feelings of people in this country not to doubt he would become an object of curiosity immediately, and possibly of compassion in the course of a few months: and the circumstances of his being here, or indeed anywhere in Europe, would contribute to keep up a certain degree of ferment in France.

They would send him to Saint Helena instead, where there was "a fine citadel," as Liverpool wrote, and "only one place in the circuit of the island where ships can anchor, and we have the power of excluding neutral vessels altogether, if we should think it necessary. At such a distance and in such a place, all intrigue would be impossible, and being so far from the European world he would very soon be forgotten."

Liverpool was only half right. Few events captured nineteenth-century imaginations as did the Hundred Days. Though the results of Napoleon's return were disastrous, its sheer boldness likely did more to shape his popular legend than any other aspect of his career. Until his return from Elba, Napoleon "had portrayed himself as primarily a strong charismatic ruler and as a military conqueror," writes the historian Sudhir Hazareesingh. "The events of the Hundred Days would initiate the process through which Napoleon's image would be reinvented. Very soon the creator of a new Empire would come to be seen as an upholder of the Revolutionary principle of equality; the expansive ruler of the world as a patriotic defender of his country; the martialist conqueror as a law-giver; and, perhaps most extraordinarily of all, the autocratic and despotic ruler as the potent symbol of liberty. The manner in which Napoleon's rule ended, in short, proved decisive in the launching of his legend."

People in France and beyond were clearly fascinated by tales of Napoleon's exile and escape from Elba, especially the first stretch of his march from Antibes to Grenoble, known as the "Flight of the Eagle." In 1836, Joseph Beaume painted a massive (nearly ten feet by six feet) rendering of the scene at Portoferraio on Napoleon's last day on Elba, with all the supporting characters behind him and crowds hailing his departure, though sad to see him go. Two years later, Stendhal went to question villagers at Laffrey about their memories of that fateful day on the fields. A few months after Stendhal's trip, Chateaubriand—certainly no admirer of Napoleon's—made a kind of pilgrimage to Golfe-Juan to see where "Bonaparte, in debarking, changed the face of the world and our destinies." The following year found Victor Hugo, who as a one-year-old army brat lived in Portoferraio for a few months in 1803, at the same beach fueling his romantic imagination by "walking on the same sand where this man walked twenty-four years ago." A few years later, with *The Count of Monte Cristo*, came Dumas's description of "a return which was unprecedented in the past, and will probably remain without a counterpart in the future," when, "at a sign from the emperor the incongruous structure of ancient prejudices and new ideas fell to the ground." Today, plaques, busts, and massive columns topped by gilded eagles guide hikers and bikers along the officially designated Route Napoléon, the two-hundred-mile path marking the Flight of the Eagle, and at Laffrey an oversized equestrian statue of Napoleon looms over the lake.

Looking back from Saint Helena, Napoleon remembered the march from Golfe-Juan to Paris as the happiest time of his life. After complaining that his life would have had a more glorious end if only he'd died at Moscow, Las Cases ventured that if he'd died then he wouldn't have had the chance to live "the extraordinary episode of the return from Elba," to which Napoleon answered, "Well, maybe there's something to that. All right then, let's say I should have died at Waterloo."

Instead, the man born on an island died on one as well, most likely of stomach cancer, in 1821. Henri and Fanny Bertrand were at his bedside at

Longwood House in the last moments of his life. "The Emperor is what he is," Henri had written during the final exile, "and we cannot change his character. It is because of that character that he has no friends, that he has so many enemies, and indeed that we are at Saint Helena." In 1840, Bertrand returned to Saint Helena to bring Napoleon's remains back to Paris, a round trip of several months. "The return of the ashes," as the event came to be known, marked another milestone in building the modern Napoleonic myth, thanks in part to poetic descriptions of the funeral cortege through Paris from Hugo and others. Four years later, Bertrand was buried at the Invalides, not far from Napoleon.

IN THE CLOSING MONTHS of the Vienna congress, delegates debated whether Marie Louise's claims to her Italian duchies should be nullified since her husband had broken the terms of the Treaty of Fontainebleau on which she based her claims to these lands. She finally attained sovereignty over her Italian duchies in June 1815. A few weeks later, after learning her husband would be sent to Saint Helena, she wrote to her father:

> I hope that we shall have a lasting peace now that the Emperor Napoleon will no longer be able to disturb it. I hope he will be treated with kindness and clemency and I beg you, dearest Papa, to make certain that is so. It is the only request I feel I can make, and it is the last time I shall busy myself with his fate. I owe him a debt of gratitude for the calm unconcern in which he let me pass my days instead of making me unhappy.

Neipperg had gone to southern Italy to fight Murat, who in a desperate bid to keep control of Naples had declared war on Austria. Spurred by Napoleon's return, Murat had promised his subjects an alliance between his kingdom and France. Neipperg's corps played a decisive role in forcing Murat into the battle of Tolentino that led to his fall in late May 1815. Murat escaped into southern

France and then Corsica. A few months later he attempted his own Golfe-Juan, landing at the Calabrian seaport of Pizzo with a few dozen men, to reclaim his kingdom. He was beaten close to death by an angry mob. Facing a firing squad made up of his own soldiers, Murat told his executioners to aim for his heart and spare his face.

Neipperg's wife died of a chest infection while he was on campaign, and by the start of 1816 he was living openly as Marie Louise's companion in Vienna. They moved to Parma so Marie Louise could assume her place as August Sovereign. She also took possession of the horses that Napoleon had sent there two years earlier, when he was still expecting her to pass through Tuscany on her way to join him on Elba. In 1817 she gave birth to a daughter; a son was born two years later. She married Neipperg in the summer of 1821, a few weeks after learning of Napoleon's death, and gave birth to a daughter that same summer, but the child did not survive infancy; Neipperg died in 1829.

Her son with Napoleon hadn't been allowed to travel with her to Parma because Francis thought it too dangerous. When the boy's tutor wrote to her to ask what he should tell the boy about Napoleon, she advised him to "speak truthfully . . . while never saying that he was a bad man and mentioning only his brilliant qualities, persuade him that it was inordinate ambition which led him from the finest throne in the world to the prison where he is today, so that his son never conceives the idea of imitating him."

In the end, the boy who had been born the King of Rome and was then demoted to Prince of Parma died as the Duke of Reichstadt. The title had been invented by his grandfather, who set aside some Habsburg land for him to inherit in what is now Zákupy, in the Czech Republic, hoping this would be enough to keep him from being tempted to claim any kind of rule in Italy or France. He was forbidden from having any communication with his father for the same reason.

Napoleon, in the valediction of his will at the end of his life, his final public utterance, had made a declaration that ended with him saying, "The love of glory is like the bridge that Satan built across Chaos to pass from Hell to Paradise: glory links the past with the future across a bottomless abyss. Nothing to my son, except my name!" The inheritor of this name never had a chance to consider any bold move one way or the other. His cloistered, unhappy life ended at twenty-one at the Schönbrunn palace, after a bout with tuberculosis.

Marie Louise wrote to the eighty-two-year-old Madame Mère in Rome to inform her of her grandson's death, the last contact she ever had with the Bonaparte family. She married for a third time, to a pleasant widower, and lived a quiet life in Parma. Unlike so many who were close to Napoleon, she didn't write a memoir. She died in 1847 at fifty-six, having lived to see an older age than her first two husbands.

In the late fall of 1940, a few months after seeing Paris for the first time in his life—a three-hour victory tour alongside the Nazi architect Albert Speer that culminated at Napoleon's tomb—Hitler arranged for the Duke of Reichstadt's remains to be transferred from Vienna to Paris to be placed alongside his father's at Les Invalides.

CAMPBELL WASN'T ASSIGNED as an attaché to any headquarters of the allied armies to join in the fight against Napoleon because, as he wrote in his journal, it "was feared that my presence might excite irritating discussions with me upon this subject." He was still a member of the 54th Regiment, part of the armed force under the command of the Duke of Wellington gathering in Belgium. He rejoined the regiment in Brussels on June 15, carrying a letter from Castlereagh that excused him from any wrongdoing when it came to Napoleon. He missed connecting with Wellington, who was already marching to Charleroi in response to Napoleon's surprise attack there.

Brussels was in such upheaval that Campbell was delayed in getting equipped for battle, and he only caught up with headquarters on June 18, when he witnessed, but didn't participate in, the battle of Waterloo. He was later given command of the light companies of the 35th, 54th, and 91st regiments, which stormed Cambrai on June 24, for which Campbell received the Waterloo Medal. He returned to Britain and was invalided by his own request, still struggling from his pierced lung, the first time he'd been on half-pay since starting his service in 1797.

He continued to be skewered in pamphlets and newspapers. One caricature showed him dozing while Napoleon tiptoes over him. His reputation wasn't helped by Marshal Ney's trial that autumn, in which Ney swore that when he met the first of Napoleon's emissaries after the landing they showed him a letter from Bertrand saying that "England had favored his escape."

During public debates in the House of Commons, Castlereagh made excuses while trying to distance himself from the mission that he'd helped to conceive. He said that if he and his colleagues were guilty of anything, it was only "an excess of deference to the feeling of the French people, and a great desire for reconciliation." He suggested that rather than attack the drafters of the Treaty of Fontainebleau people should focus their anger on "the man who had a thorough contempt for all treaties and engagements." It wasn't as if Bonaparte had been locked away in some tower under allied guard, he said, and besides which, trying to blockade Elba to prevent an escape "would have been beyond the power of the whole navy of Britain."

Castlereagh specifically avoided condemning Campbell and thereby condemning himself for choosing him. Instead, he said that

> as to diplomatic agents, we had none resident in the isle of Elba. Colonel Campbell only accompanied Bonaparte to the island, but he afterwards had been permitted to reside there or at Livorno. He never, however, supposed that he could have exercised any sort of daily inspection over Bonaparte, or that such an attempt would have been tolerated. The fact was, that he resided but for a short time on the island. If he had been, however, there when Bonaparte mediated his expedition, he could have by no means prevented it.

Campbell bounced around for the next few years, traveling through Spain and France. Along with his brother and two sisters he settled in Normandy in 1817. He seems to have felt most at ease in Paris, where he became something of a roué during the decade after Waterloo, often dining with the marquis de Canisy in the Faubourg Saint-Germain, and counting Bernard François de Balzac, father of the novelist, as a friend. He never married.

As with many nineteenth-century Europeans dissatisfied with life at the nominal center of things, Campbell evidently sought some other answer at the outskirts of empire. In 1826, restless for a permanent assignment, he found one when the governor of Sierra Leone died of yellow fever. That man's predecessor had also died early, shot in battle by an Ashanti soldier. Campbell petitioned for the governorship and was granted the post as well as the rank of major general. He ruled ruthlessly and died of yellow fever in the summer of 1827 after nine days of intense suffering. He was buried at the Circular Road Cemetery in Freetown, though his tombstone no longer exists. None of the three Campbell sons produced heirs, and the family lands in Scotland eventually fell into other hands.

THREE HUNDRED FRENCH SOLDIERS and eighty Corsicans had been left to defend Elba under Lapi's governorship. After pushing off Campbell, Lapi next resisted a ruse by Bruslart, whose aide-de-camp arrived at Portoferraio in a French ship on March 9 to announce that Napoleon had been captured and that Lapi was to cede the island to the Corsicans. Lapi had the officer detained. A few days later a Neapolitan ship arrived, and its captain announced that he would unload three hundred men to help hold Elba. Lapi refused him as well.

From the Tuileries, Napoleon ordered Bertrand to have anything valuable left behind on Elba to be sent to Paris. "I attach great importance to my Corsican horse, if he be not sick," he wrote. "The yellow travelling carriage, the big carriage, and the gala carriages are worth bringing back, as well as the body linen. I make a present of my library to the town, also my house, which can serve as a casino."

Elba became a kind of colony of the empire, with the three-bee flag replaced by the tricolor. Napoleon coaxed the original governor, Dalesme, out of retirement to replace Lapi. In early June 1815 the delegates at the Congress of Vienna decreed that with Napoleon's imminent defeat, Elba would fall under the control of the Grand Duchy of Tuscany and by June 20 British ships had enforced a blockade around the island, cutting the Elbans off from the continent. News of Waterloo only reached Dalesme in late July. He ceded the island to Tuscan troops under orders from the restored Louis XVIII. The last of the soldiers to have followed Napoleon into exile left Elba in September. His Elban residences became property of the ducal government. Elba became part of the Kingdom of Italy in 1861.

Napoleon left a few paved roads where there had once been dirt ones. Properties had been refurbished and the fortifications were better armed. Some new trees had been planted and water and drainage systems implemented. The silkworm had been introduced and potatoes became a more regular crop. There was a small and handsome theater. Unresolved legal issues no longer had to be taken to Florence but could be handled locally at the new court of appeal. The mining industry was left little better than it had been before Napoleon's arrival, and he'd taken its effective administrator along with him on his misadventure.

THE LEGACY OF HIS BRIEF STAY may be minimal, but I have found no other place in Italy where they seem so genuinely fond of Napoleon as they do on Elba. Though its economy is far from booming, Elba is better off than other places in the region, especially in terms of infrastructure. And there is profit to be made from Napoleonic nostalgia. Collectively, the island's imperial residences compose the second most visited museum site in Tuscany after the Uffizi. Wandering Portoferraio, you see Napoleon beer to be bought, Napoleon honey soap, Napoleon eau de cologne. My own guilty purchase was a solar-powered Napoleon, with a hand that goes hypnotically in and out of his greatcoat. But Elba is quite sleepy outside of the summer season and even on the busiest July weekend Portoferraio can hardly match the glitz of Capri or Palermo. There must be something here that goes deeper than gratitude for tourist dollars.

For a lot of people the point of going to an island is to leave it, returning to one's mainland refreshed by the experience. But islanders don't want to think of their home as a kind of purgatory. Only natural, then, for them to yearn for some sense of permanence. Perhaps Elbans value the association with Napoleon, for all his tremendous faults, because it makes them feel something people in Beijing, New York, Paris, and elsewhere take for granted every day: the sense that at one point in history, outsiders were truly concerned about the place where they live, and that what happened there once changed the world.

POSTSCRIPT

· ——————— ·

My great talent, what characterizes me the most, is that in
everything I see clearly. . . . I can see, under all its aspects, the
heart of the matter.

—NAPOLEON, on Saint Helena

What a pity to see a mind as great as Napoleon's devoted to
trivial things such as empires, historic events, the thundering
of cannons and of men; he believed in glory, in posterity, in
Caesar; nations in turmoil and other trifles absorbed all his
attention. . . . How could he fail to see that what really
mattered was something else entirely?

—PAUL VALÉRY, *Mauvaises pensées et autres*

AT SOME POINT IN his decades of reading, Napoleon likely encountered the
following meditation offered by another emperor, Marcus Aurelius:

> In man's life his time is a mere instant, his existence a flux, his per-
> ception fogged, his whole bodily composition rotting, his mind a
> whirligig, his fortune unpredictable, his fame unclear. To put it

shortly: All things of the body stream away like a river, all things of the mind are dreams and delusion; life is warfare, and a visit to a strange land; the only lasting fame is oblivion.

Napoleon would have found such ideas terrifying. His version of existence was a constant battle against flux, fogginess, and oblivion. He lived as though constantly feeling the need to show himself to be alive, to make his life story heroic, monumental.

Why did he leave the comforts of Elba to make war? Because he thought it was what Napoleon ought to be seen to do.

As editor of an exhaustive collection of Napoleon's written and spoken words, *The Mind of Napoleon,* the scholar J. Christopher Herold likely spent as much time as anyone pondering what exactly drove Napoleon to do the things he did. In a brief introduction to his book, Herold offered as cogent a summary of Napoleon's career as has anyone in the half century since he wrote it: "In his 'romantic and epic dream'—the words are his—he created a hero to suit the needs of his imagination, a humanity to suit the needs of this hero, and a background to suit the magnitude of the action."

Elba, then, was a stage of insufficient magnitude on which to perform his romantic epic. Napoleon the happy retiree, puttering around an island idyll, simply didn't look right, which to so visually attuned a man living in so visually attuned an age meant it didn't feel right either. One hears the stifled emperor reborn as Norma Desmond, around the time Herold was compiling his volume: "I *am* big. It's the pictures that got small." As with the chatelaine of Sunset Boulevard, Napoleon was an actor. Feeling compelled to act, he also felt compelled to return to the stage that best suited him, which waited in Paris. He felt these compulsions so strongly that he was willing to risk starting another massive war to sate himself.

But who, really, was to blame for those compulsions? Napoleon lived in a martial age. He and his collaborators had worked skillfully to craft their generation's image of the great man, perfectly suited to the culture in which they lived: as brilliant a conqueror as he was a statesman, a warrior gripped by a fiery genius and wrestling with an unyielding life force that urged him to forge ahead through all the world's snowy mountain passes while weaker men fell all around him, the tamer of wild chargers that were in reality mules.

From his first military triumphs, which were simultaneously triumphs in media manipulation, Napoleon promised those who followed him that they would be forever bathed in glory and forever on the right side of power, that they too could achieve greatness by supporting him. "I walk with the God of war and the God of victory!" he intoned during the 1799 coup that brought him to power as First Consul, after which he declared the Republic's need to be "respected abroad and feared by its enemies." To walk with gods required him to be forever fighting and forever unbeatable, even while perpetually claiming that he made war only to one day yield a permanent peace.

Napoleon didn't force this image of himself onto a bunch of unthinking dupes. To have any meaning, an image must be created and recreated in an ongoing conversation between producer and viewer. Napoleon and his supporters gave many people—not all people, but many people—exactly what they craved, and they responded with devotion. It isn't accurate, however comforting it might be, to assume that this devotion was solely the blind kind.

By returning from Elba in the role of undaunted adventurer, was Napoleon not demonstrating his great ability to see, as he put it, "the heart of the matter"? Did he not give people what they and the era itself wanted most from him? Herold again offers insight: "It may be a costly process for humanity to produce Napoleons, but if humanity should ever cease to produce them it would be a sign that its energies are exhausted. In order to turn its Napoleons to better enterprises than conquest and war, humanity first would have to turn away from war. To prove Napoleon wrong humanity must change."

Perhaps. But Napoleon, too, must be held to account. On Saint Helena, explaining why he left Elba, despite being "so well off," he said, "I was insulted in all their newspapers! Well! I'm a man, and being a man, I felt that I should show them I was alive."

But his show had only ever been meant for an audience of one. Though he presented the landing at Golfe-Juan as the start of a daring bid to lead the world toward something new, it was never anything more than a desperate retreat into the only version of himself he ever understood or inhabited with any comfort, his last flailing attempt to make sense of Napoleon. Tens of thousands died at Waterloo because of one restless, middle-aged man's crisis of identity, which was, above all, a crisis of vision. A failure to see what really mattered.

ACKNOWLEDGMENTS

·———·

Many thanks to the staffs of the Biblioteca Foresiana, Bibliothèque Nationale de France, Museo Nazionale della Villa dei Mulini, Stanford University Libraries, Teatro dei Vigilanti, University of British Columbia Library, Vancouver Public Library, and Villa de San Martino.

The people of Porto Azzurro were wonderful hosts. Thanks to Dianora, Elena, and especially Paola, who arranged for me to tour the former Spanish citadel at Forte Longone, now a high-security prison.

Thank you to Giovanna Ceserani for sharing her memories of Elba and for offering sage advice concerning research in Italian sources, as did Deb Harkness, Paula Findlen, and Hannah Marcus.

Talking about this project with Ann Godoff and Will Heyward has been one of the highlights of my career, and I'm delighted to have found a home at Penguin Press. Will edited the book with great skill and understanding. I picture a world in which everyone would turn to Will for guidance before saying anything out loud, and it's a world filled with elegant people, saying smart things, and understanding one another perfectly. Thanks also to Matt Boyd, Colleen Boyle, Bruce Giffords, Sarah Hutson, and Roland Ottewell. Christopher King and Darren Haggar produced the gorgeous jacket.

Becky Sweren is a force of nature and an all-around wonderful person. I'm honored to call her my agent. I thank her also for pulling me out of traffic on Hudson Street while I was in a joyful daze following our initial meeting at Penguin. David Kuhn was the first person to really get excited about all things Elba, several years ago, before I'd written the proposal for my first book. His enthusiasm for the idea has given me a great deal of confidence and comfort since then. At Aevitas, thanks also to Chelsey Heller, William LoTurco, Kate Mack, Laura Nolan, and Allison Warren.

Very special thank-yous to David Bell, J. P. Daughton, Dan Edelstein, Matthew Fox-Amato, Chris Friedrichs, Stéphane Gerson, Karen Halttunen, Pico Iyer, Colin Jones, Ross King, Ed Lake, Zack Silverman, Tobias Wolff, and the students in my seminars on celebrity culture and on travel writing. Vanessa Schwartz has shaped my understanding of—and love for—history and visual culture more than anyone.

Love and gratitude to the Averills, Braudes, Cowens, Dixons, Fine-Poquets, Irene Jarman, the Leysers, Myers, Pokroys, Rittles, Smiths, Taubs, Tulks, Ayelet, Chris, Daylan, Giorgio, Graham, Josh, Jon, Marc, Mike, Reuben, and Poppy.

As always, none of this would have been possible, or any fun, without Laura Braude: enemy of clichés, clunky words, and unnecessary dad jokes; lover of Italian beaches, Italian food, and Italian wine.

A NOTE ON SOURCES

Any text within quotation marks comes from a primary or secondary document. I've tried to limit my use of words such as "reportedly," "allegedly," and "it was said"—too many of which would be tedious. Unless I had sufficient archival material to do so, I tried to avoid making definitive statements about any historical actor's mental state or psychological motivations, difficult enough to do among the living, let alone the long dead with only the archival record as guide. I've used "perhaps," "likely," "might," and "it may be" when it felt necessary to do so. I trust that readers can deduce my degree of certainty about any given claim made within this text by its supporting footnote.

Place names are referred to as they would have been in 1814–15, with spellings that reflect how they would have been spelled by the local population, hence Portoferraio and Livorno, rather than Porto Ferrajo and Leghorn, as they appeared in the British correspondence I consulted. I've modernized the spelling and punctuation of quoted sources wherever it seemed helpful to the reader to do so. On very rare occasions, I've changed certain words of French sources that I read in translated English and from whose context I felt confident in divining the original French word being translated. I did this only if I couldn't track down the original French source myself, and if I felt that making the change would diminish the jarring effect of translations that draw more attention to the time and place of their translation than to the language of the original source itself.

Several secondary sources served as valuable guides during my research, not only for the information and arguments they contained but because their footnotes often pointed to additional materials that I could track down and explore on my own. Some especially useful and recently published books include David Bell, *The First Total War: Napoleon's Europe and the Birth of Warfare as We Know It* and *Napoleon: A Concise Biography;* Tim Blanning, *The Romantic Revolution: A History;* Pierre Branda, *La Guerre Secrète de Napoléon;* Gregor Dallas, *The Final Act: The Roads to Waterloo;* Steven Englund, *Napoleon: A Political Life;* Peter Fritzsche, *Stranded in the Present: Modern Time and the Melancholy of History;* Patrice Gueniffey, *Bonaparte: 1769–1802,* translated by Steven Rendall (the publication of Gueniffey's second volume of his biographical project will no doubt shed new light on the period covered in this book); Jean-Paul Kauffmann, *The Black Room at Longwood: Napoleon's Exile on Saint Helena;* Sheryl Kroen, *Politics and Theater: The Crisis of Legitimacy in Restoration France, 1815–1830;* Thierry Lentz, *Nouvelle Histoire du Premier Empire, IV, Les Cent-Jours: 1815;* Philip Mansel, *Paris Between Empires: Monarchy and Revolution, 1814–1852;* Alan Palmer, *Napoleon and Marie Louise: The Second Empress;* Munro Price, *Napoleon: The End of Glory;* Andrew Roberts, *Napoleon the Great;* Emmanuel de Waresquiel and Benoît Yvert, *Histoire de la Restauration: 1814–1830;* Jenny Uglow, *In These Times: Living in Britain Through Napoleon's Wars, 1793–1815;* and Adam Zamoyski, *Rites of Peace: The Fall of Napoleon and the Congress of Vienna.*

NOTES

· ——— ·

INTRODUCTION

xvii **From the towers:** Chateaubriand, *Memoirs*, 259; Horne, *Age of Napoleon*, 173; Mansel, *Paris*, 7. For a detailed firsthand account of the fall of Paris, see Boigne, *Memoirs*, 290–95; for descriptions of Paris on March 31, 1814, in secondary sources, see Bew, *Castlereagh*, 349; Englund, *Napoleon*, 416; Hussey, *Paris*, 221; Jones, *Paris*, 262; Lieven, *Russia*, 519; Mansel, *Paris*, 8–14.

xvii **Cossacks crouched round:** Underwood, *A Narrative*, 73.

xvii **Though the result:** Houssaye, *1814*, 427; Mansel, *Paris*, 6–8; Price, *Napoleon*, 218; Zamoyski, *Rites*, 176-178. The Paris National Guard was a bourgeois militia whose task since its formation in 1789 had been to protect the propertied classes of Paris from the threat of the "vile populace" as much as from any outside invader. By 1814, fear of a popular uprising had prompted the local prefect to allow men with known royalist sympathies into the ranks. In reference to "beyond the gates," note that the Parisian Wall of the *Ferme générale* had been built for the purposes of taxation and offered little in the way of military defense. On the lack of a defensive wall, see Jones, *Paris*, 262.

xvii **"fashionable loungers of both sexes":** Underwood, *A Narrative*, 90.

xviii **Each side suffered:** Houssaye, *1814*, 519.

xviii **After a year and a half:** Collectively these forces were known as "the Sixth Coalition," which also comprised armies from Portugal, Sweden, and Spain. I use "allies" in the rest of this text to refer to these four major powers.

xviii **Joseph Bonaparte warned:** Sauvigny, *Bourbon Restoration*, 17. In similar fashion to Joseph Bonaparte, Napoleon's aide-de-camp Hugues-Bernard Maret, duc de Bassano, had tried, unsuccessfully, to suggest by way of an elegant metaphor that Napoleon was misguided in thinking that the failure to secure a crushing victory automatically meant an embarrassing defeat; pointing to some desperate soldiers who adopted the old revolutionary battle cry of "Victory or Death!," he argued that the binary was far too simple to be applied to an entire country. Nations never died, he told Napoleon, but they did "tire of the need for constant victory." The various representatives of the principal allied powers struggled to agree among themselves about how or even if they should negotiate with their common enemy. "You scarcely have an idea of how *insane* people in this country are on the subject of any peace with Buonaparte," the British prime minister, Lord Liverpool, had written to Castlereagh before Napoleon's defeat. Napoleon had meanwhile tried to tear apart the coalition by making vague overtures to the Austrians about separate terms. Maret as quoted in Price, *Napoleon*, 250; Liverpool as quoted in Zamoyski, *Rites*, 157.

xviii Having risen from: Several biographers have made this point; see, for instance, Price, *Napoleon*, 3.

xviii But by the time: Marchand, *Mémoires*, II (Marchand consulted in e-book format without page numbers; chapter numbers will be referenced by numerals); Price, *Napoleon*, 225; Thompson, "Napoleon's Journey," 2; Zamoyski, *Rites*, 177. Napoleon had scrambled to attack the rear of the force descending on Paris, but it was too far gone by that time.

xviii They brought down: Note that the displays described didn't necessarily reflect an overwhelming or uniform support for the Bourbons, though the allies were quick to think so, and that many Parisians adopted white symbols to show peaceful intentions, just as some allied troops had pinned white cockades to their uniforms to demonstrate that they likewise wanted to avoid a bloodbath. On Napoleon's promise to make Paris the most beautiful city that had ever existed, see Rowell, *Paris*, 14.

xix At Fontainebleau, surrounded: Caulaincourt, *Mémoires*, 231–53; Éloi-Vial, "4, 6 et 11 avril," 3–24; Houssaye, *1814*, 604; Lentz, *Nouvelle histoire*, I (Lentz consulted in e-book format without page numbers; chapter numbers will be referenced by numerals); Macdonald, *Souvenirs*, 265–67; Price, *Napoleon*, 223.

xix Every village and town: Hobsbawm, *Revolution*, 92–93; Schom, *One Hundred Days*, 5. Hobsbawm, stressing that any estimate of the number of war deaths from 1792 to 1815 would be mere guesswork, puts the number somewhere between one and two million, while other estimates range between four and six million. The path of destruction stretched well beyond Europe, from the West Indies to Egypt.

xix Most of these deaths: Hobsbawm, *Revolution*, 73–74. "Between 1800 and 1815 Napoleon lost 40 per cent of his forces (though about one third of this through desertion)," writes Hobsbawm. "But between 90 and 98 per cent of these losses were men who died not in battle but of wounds, sickness, exhaustion and cold. In brief, it was an army which conquered all Europe in sharp bursts not only because it could, but because it had to."

xix It was common: Mansel, *Paris*, 2.

xix "Nothing but abdication . . . to act out": Houssaye, *1814*, 604; Price, *Napoleon*, 233.

xix "What a novel my life has been!": As quoted in Gueniffey, *Bonaparte*, 1. This statement originates with Emmanuel de Las Cases's *Memorial de Sainte Helene*, but the recent discovery of an original manuscript of Las Cases's book has brought into question whether Napoleon actually said this to Las Cases of if the latter added Napoleon's supposed remark a few years after their time together on Saint Helena.

1: THE MORNING OF THE POISON LUMP

3 Through the thin wall: "Ali" (Louis-Étienne Saint-Denis), *Napoleon*, 69; Caulaincourt, *Mémoires*, 262–65, 361–63; Fain, *Manuscrit*, 395–97; Marchand, *Mémoires*, II; Roncière, *Napoleon's Letters*, 261–62; Roberts, *Napoleon*, 715. Some accounts have the valet on duty that night at Fontainebleau as Hubert, not Pelard, and describe the valet seeing the drink being made rather than hearing it. Caulaincourt claims that he sat with Napoleon through the night, while Napoleon's secretary, Baron Fain, who was at Fontainebleau that morning but not actually present in the bedroom, makes no mention of Caulaincourt's presence in his own memoirs.

Fain claimed to be describing the event exactly as it was relayed to him by witnesses who were in the room, while remaining self-conscious about dealing in hearsay. The construction of this sentence nods in homage to the opening of Gabriel García Márquez's *The General in His Labyrinth*. While writing the history I often thought about Márquez's stories of strongmen and solitude.

3 **It was three:** I have calculated two days' hard ride based on a distance of sixty kilometers between Fontainebleau and central Paris and a single rider going at a fair clip.

3 **Napoleon was forty-four:** Regarding Napoleon's children: Some biographers suggest that Napoleon may have fathered more than one illegitimate child. Françoise-Marie LeRoy in 1805 gave birth to Émilie Pellapra; Eléonore Denuelle gave birth to Charles Léon in 1806; and Albine de Montholon gave birth to Hélène de Montholon on Saint Helena in 1816—Napoleon has been named as the biological father of each of these children at different times by different writers, but these claims are based only on speculation, which is why I do not add them to my tally. The claim that Alexandre Colonna-Walewski, to whom I refer when saying that Napoleon had two young sons, is descended from Napoleon is, on the other hand, supported by deeper research in several sources, as well as a recent sequencing of DNA materials.

3 **Yvan ordered hot drinks:** Branda, *La guerre secrète*, 38–39, 419; Caulaincourt, *Mémoires*, 364; Fain, *Manuscrit*, 394–96; Marchand, *Mémoires*, II; Roncière, *Napoleon's Letters*, 262; Roberts, *Napoleon*, 715. There is some disagreement on Yvan's precise remedy. Roncière, for instance, says "compresses and hot beverages," while Roberts writes that Yvan "induced vomiting, possibly by forcing him to swallow ashes from the fireplace." Other accounts have Napoleon demanding that Yvan give him something to put him out of his misery for good, with Yvan refusing, and that no real remedy was applied besides waiting. On Saint Helena, when pressed about the lump he swallowed at Fontainebleau, Napoleon said to Charles Tristan, marquis de Montholon, that "time had taken away its strength." Branda is skeptical about that statement and wonders if Napoleon was trying to reshape his legacy by claiming that he knew all along that he would survive, or if perhaps Montholon had already been influenced by so many other accounts of the night that were in circulation by the time he published his own book. I agree with Branda that Caulaincourt's account seems the most accurate of all, given its relatively evenhanded language and the closeness of Napoleon and his grand equerry. One question remains, unanswered: Why was Yvan, whom Napoleon had named to the Legion of Honor and provided with a healthy salary, so riled by the night's work that he would suffer a minor breakdown and quit Napoleon's staff forever? He would have known his services were largely unnecessary, given that he was dealing with just a small bit of nearly two-year-old poison. It may be that in the course of his task the doctor worked himself into an anxious state by anticipating that whatever change of events might have driven Napoleon to such a desperate act would surely lead to some horrible future for France and for himself. It may also simply be that Yvan had by the morning reached his limit as to how much of Napoleon's dramatics he could stomach.

4 **"The allied Powers":** Fain, *Manuscrit*, 389.

4 **"respect the integrity":** Guizot, *History of France*, VIII, 109.

4 **Talleyrand—brilliant, elegant:** Talleyrand-Périgord, *Mémoires*, II, 122. "Fittingly for a statesman longer on talk than performance," writes Colin Jones, "the street-names with which [Napoleon] supplied the city—usually commemorating his military victories (Castiglione, Pyramides, Rivoli, Ulm, Iéna, Austerlitz, Montebello and so on)—are one of his most enduring legacies." Jones, *Paris*, 259.

4 **"shit in a silk stocking":** Lacour-Gayet, *Talleyrand*, II, 272. Robin Harris dispels the notion that Napoleon actually said this directly to Talleyrand in a moment of fury, though he allows

that it may have been "just possible that Napoleon said it and that all concerned were too ashamed to reproduce it." Harris, *Talleyrand*, 204–6, 385. The original source for this remark may be Sainte-Beuve, "Essai," 30.

5 **Though he was compensated:** Lentz, *Nouvelle histoire*, I. My key sources on Talleyrand throughout include Cooper, *Talleyrand;* Dwyer, *Talleyrand;* Harris, *Talleyrand;* Lacour-Gayet, *Talleyrand;* Lawday, *Napoleon's Master;* Orieux, *Talleyrand;* and Waresquiel, *Talleyrand*. Talleyrand's memoirs are also an important, if occasionally problematic, source. Roberto Calasso's quirky treatment of Talleyrand in *The Ruin of Kasch* was also of use. Talleyrand's secret work with Alexander evinced the strategy that governed his entire career: to establish as moderate a rule over one's own people as possible while maintaining equilibrium among rival powers, promoting general prosperity, and to do so subtly and softly, while suspending moral judgments about any single action done in the name of this larger goal. "He rarely gives advice, but can make others talk," Napoleon once said about him; "I never knew anyone so entirely different to right and wrong." Talleyrand had also been working with the Austrian foreign minister Count Klemens von Metternich, who had risen to become top consigliere to the Austrian emperor Francis despite being a social outsider, not setting foot in Vienna until the age of twenty-one. Metternich was adept at anticipating who was strongest among his enemies and allies and then brokering and shifting alliances accordingly. "He rarely gives": Roberts, *Napoleon*, 145. On Metternich: King, *Vienna*, 15–18; Sebag Montefiore, *The Romanovs*, 309. Note that Metternich at this point in time was not yet a prince, hence Count Metternich.

5 **"only a matter of dates":** During an 1808 peace conference, Talleyrand told Alexander that "the French people are civilized, their sovereign is not. The sovereign of Russia is civilized, but his people are not," a conversation he later repeated verbatim for Metternich. After his successful overtures to the Russians and Austrians, he'd waited patiently for the opportune moment to make good on these alliances. He boasted that in his life he "had never hurried, but was always on time." Metternich, *Memoirs*, II, 298.

5 **Talleyrand gently helped:** Talleyrand had briefly considered a regency, as Napoleon had first proposed in an early draft of his abdication. He would have been the natural candidate for prime minister under such a setup, and it offered a potentially easier solution than a Bourbon restoration, which entailed a symbolic step back into the pre-Revolutionary past. For a moment Tsar Alexander had been in favor of calling on one of Napoleon's marshals, Jean-Baptiste Bernadotte, to become the new French monarch. Four years earlier, and quite improbably, Bernadotte had been elected crown prince and de facto ruler of Sweden and so had enough of the whiff of monarchy about him to please the tsar. Alexander also considered Napoleon's stepson, Prince Eugène de Beauharnais, for the task, but soon dropped these far-fetched plans, which would have been too hard to sell to the other allies, let alone to the French people. Castlereagh, especially, recognized early on that if they declared their support for any would-be monarch with too much force, it would only help Napoleon's hand, and that he could rally his soldiers around the perceived threat of a future puppet regime that would be secretly run by a foreign power. It seemed illogical to Castlereagh to insist on one particular "usurper" as the replacement for the existing one. For a time leading up to the abdication, Castlereagh had privately thought that the Duke of Orléans might be a worthier candidate than Louis, whom he deemed "personally incapable." Things would have been easier if Napoleon were dead, as Talleyrand wrote to a confidant: "If the Emperor were killed his death would guarantee the rights of his son" and a "regency would satisfy everyone." A British official put it more simply: "The misfortune to us at this moment is that Bonaparte remains in existence." But to pass the throne to the infant King of Rome while his father was still alive was far too risky. So long as a Bonaparte remained nominal ruler of France the door remained open for Napoleon's return. Fearing for themselves as much as for the fate of the Bonaparte dynasty, the members of the Regency

Council in Paris, including Talleyrand, had arranged for Marie Louise and the King of Rome to escape the city on March 29, following Napoleon's instructions that they should be removed from the capital at any sign it might fall. They relocated to a chateau in the hillside village of Blois, accompanied by Joseph Bonaparte and other members of the Council, who were to continue governing France from this new headquarters. Talleyrand was supposed to join as well, and while guns were firing on the city from the north and east, he made as if to leave for Blois, packing several chests full of clothes and taking his carriage out to the city's western gate. There the officer of the National Guard on duty, enlisted earlier to help him play out the charade, barred him from leaving by citing obscure technicalities so that Talleyrand could say he'd tried to follow his empress and remained loyal to the house of Bonaparte. See Castlereagh, *Correspondence*, IX, 451; Price, *Napoleon*, 221–23; Zamoyski, *Rites*, 153, 175–77.

5 **"having always had"**: Price, *Napoleon*, 224.

5 **People knew little**: "The young generation knew nothing of our princes," wrote the comtesse de Boigne, who recalled that her younger cousins could never get the Bourbon family tree quite right, and the only person they could identify with certainty was the duchesse d'Angoulême, orphaned by the scaffold. Boigne, *Memoirs*, 349.

5 **The allied leaders had never**: Lentz, *Nouvelle histoire*, I; Zamoyski, *Rites*, 152–53.

5 **A Bourbon restoration**: Lieven, *Russia*, 519. Napoleon had first come to power in a similar fashion, as one of several options from which to choose in the wake of the Terror and its aftermath. As the historian Isser Woloch has argued, the Terror "unleashed a cycle of recrimination, hatred, and endemic local conflict that made future prospects of democratic polity in France very dim. General Bonaparte represented one possible outcome of that dilemma, or a cure worse than the malady, depending on one's point of view." Woloch, *The New Regime*, 431–32.

5 **To stave off**: Regarding the negotiations of the terms of Napoleon's abdication, see Talleyrand-Périgord, *Memoirs*, II, 125; Caulaincourt, *Mémoires*, 316–34.

5 **He still inspired**: No tour of Paris in that era was complete without seeing the site of Louis XVI's execution, the current Place de la Concorde, where, according to legend, horses and cattle were too spooked by the smell of blood to cross. The name changes of this famous square do much to show the tumult of Parisian politics between the late eighteenth and early nineteenth centuries. Built between 1755 and 1772, as an octagon with moats on all sides and providing some much-needed public space between the Champs-Elysées and the Louvre, it was originally known as Place Louis XV and its main feature was a statue of that Bourbon king. Revolutionaries tore the statue down and a guillotine was put up in its place. As with so many other places in the city, it was renamed, a symbolic disavowal of the monarchic past, and Place Louis XV became Place de la Révolution. Here huge crowds witnessed the executions of Louis XVI, Marie Antoinette, and Charlotte Corday, the young woman who murdered the ferocious journalist Marat. Robespierre, who had made such frequent use of the guillotine, ascended the scaffold in this same square. In 1795, it was renamed as Place de la Concorde, the name reflecting the concord that people hoped to achieve in the wake of such a divisive and violent few years. The Place de la Concorde kept its name for several years, though Paris and France did not find absolute reconciliation. With the Bourbon restoration it briefly returned to its name as Place Louis XV, and finally went back again to Place de la Concorde. See Hussey, *Paris*, 169.

6 **"not simply been"**: Englund, *Napoleon*, 420.

6 **When Caulaincourt proposed**: Caulaincourt, *Mémoires*, 342. Barry O'Meara, the Irish doctor who attended to Napoleon on Saint Helena, made the dubious claim that Bonaparte once told him that Castlereagh had actually begged him to live in London, "where he would be received with the greatest of pleasure," and that *he* had been the one to turn down the British offer. See O'Meara, *Napoleon*, II, 50. Castlereagh did write to Liverpool on May 5, 1814, asking, "If [Napoleon's] taste for an asylum in England should continue, would you allow him to

reside in some distant province? It would obviate much alarm on the Continent." See Webster, *Foreign Policy,* 250.

6 **"a very strong letter":** "Napoleon to Marie Louise, April 3, 1814," Palmstierna, *My Dearest Louise,* 153.

6 **The marriage forged:** Palmer, *Napoleon and Marie Louise,* xi; Judson, *The Habsburg Empire,* was also a useful source.

6 **"The principal thing":** Metternich, *Memoirs,* II, 552.

6 **"I am more his friend":** Caulaincourt, *Mémoires,* 156–58.

7 **"Angel" who had finally:** Dallas, *The Final Act,* 23.

7 **"If he were a woman":** Englund, *Napoleon,* 293. Though each man could sympathize with the pressures the other faced as sovereign, they differed greatly in their paths to power. Napoleon's ambition was legendary, while Alexander feared the crown handed to him at twenty-three after his father's murder and fantasized about sneaking off to live in obscurity on a little farm on the banks of the Rhine. See Sebag Montefiore, *The Romanovs,* xxiii.

7 **After ten days:** Branda, *La guerre secrète,* 20.

7 **He and Caulaincourt fixed:** Caulaincourt, *Mémoires,* 224–26; Branda, *La guerre secrète,* 19. Price, working from some of Caulaincourt's unpublished papers, argues that it was Caulaincourt who suggested Elba and that Alexander accepted, but Price doesn't offer much detail about how exactly they came to choose this particular location. Corsica had been good enough, eighteen centuries earlier, for Seneca, banished following an alleged affair with Caligula's youngest sister, Julia Livilla. Napoleon made the dubious claim to Las Cases on Saint Helena that he had decided on the site of his exile, and that he might have had Corsica, but "the humor of the moment led me to decide in favor of Elba." See Price, *Napoleon,* 238; Las Cases, *Memorial,* 348.

7 **He might also:** For theories about the tsar's motivations, see Lieven, *Russia,* 518–19, and Branda, *La guerre secrète,* 30. Lieven writes that Alexander's "blunder" in allowing Napoleon sovereignty of Elba stemmed in part from his "desire to be, and to be seen to be, generous to a defeated foe."

7 **He simply announced:** Kraehe, *Metternich's German Policy,* 10. "The marshals must deliver the act to Napoleon this very night," Alexander said as soon as he'd decided on Elba.

8 **The British contingent:** Castlereagh's half brother, Sir Charles Stewart, wrote to Lord Bathurst that "it might be well to consider, before the act is irretrievable, whether a far less dangerous retreat might not be found, and whether Napoleon may not bring the powder to the iron mines which the island of Elba is so famed for." Castlereagh, *Correspondence,* IX, 451.

8 **Castlereagh thought this:** Sebag Montefiore, *The Romanovs,* 313. "The most dangerous for us is the *chevaleresque* tone of Emperor Alexander," he had written to his prime minister that January. "He has a *personal* feeling about Paris, distinct from political-military considerations." Indeed, Alexander told one of his ministers that during a break in the peace negotiations he fell to his knees "and there before the Lord made an effusion of my heart," to which he was answered with "a hard resolution of will and a kind of blazing clarity of purpose: take Paris!" As quoted in Montefiore.

8 **But Castlereagh recognized:** A year later, pressed to explain how they had bungled Napoleon's first exile so badly, the prime minister, Lord Liverpool, would blame the need for a quick resolution, which "afforded the only means of avoiding a civil war in France, and of bringing the marshals over [to the Allied cause]." MacKenzie, *The Escape from Elba,* 25.

8 **"The whole nation":** Castlereagh, *Correspondence,* IX, 480.

8 **He saw no advantage:** Lieven, *Russia,* 519. Castlereagh did attach an "act of accession" to the formal notes concerning the April meeting in Paris that witnessed the discussion of the treaty's terms. This act confirmed Great Britain's acceptance of everything having to do with

territories and borders but nothing else. The document sought to position Great Britain as an observer to this arrangement, brokered by the other three main allied powers and the French Provisional Government. Castlereagh codified this arrangement in an official declaration on April 27, 1814. See d'Angeberg, *Le Congrès*, I, 147–48, 155–56; Branda, *La guerre secrète*, 29; Dallas, *The Final Act*, 258.

8 **"They give to others":** Metternich, *Memoirs*, II, 552. Francis added that "at any rate it must be arranged that Elba, if this matter cannot be prevented, shall come to Tuscany after Napoleon's death."

8 **"the biggest baby":** Kraehe, *Metternich's German Policy*, 10; Zamoyski, *Rites*, 184.

8 **Privately, he feared:** Harris, *Talleyrand*, 224.

8 **But Talleyrand sensed:** Schama, *Citizens*, 12.

9 **"I see Talleyrand":** Castlereagh, *Correspondence*, IX, 454.

9 **The French held it:** In 1809, Elba and the rest of the Tuscan archipelago had been formally attached to the territory overseen by Napoleon's sister Elisa, who was named Grand Duchess of Tuscany.

9 **Across the Atlantic:** Chernow, *Alexander Hamilton*, 7. See also Dubois, *Avengers;* James, *Black Jacobins*.

9 **Such mysteriousness was what:** "King John II of Portugal was only too happy to feed the fantasies of landless nobles by doling out fiefs on yet undiscovered islands," writes the historian John Gillis. "Don Quixote offered the Island of Baratania to Sancho Panza in return for loyalty." Gillis, *Islands of the Mind*, 41.

9 **There is no evidence:** Elba's population in 1814 stood at 11,380. Tardieu and Denesle, *Notice sur l'île d'Elbe*.

9 **Napoleon would retain:** A transcription of the treaty can be found in d'Angeberg, *Le Congrès*, I, 148–51.

9 **The Russians had almost:** For a detailed analysis of the treaty, see Hicks, "Napoleon on Elba," 53–67. Regarding the British contributions: Edward Cooke, undersecretary of state, in an April 9, 1814, letter to Castlereagh, wrote, "I hope the Allies will not forget that we deserve something for the £700,000,000 we have spent in the contest, and that we cannot pay a soldier, a clerk, or a magistrate, before we have spent £40,000,000 for interest and redemption of debt." See Castlereagh, *Correspondence*, IX, 454. The treaty was backdated to April 11. On signing, it was known as the Treaty of Abdication. Talleyrand as representative of the French Provisional Government agreed to the terms in a separate document. Dalberg also signed on behalf of the French Provisional Government. Louis XVIII would also officially agree to the terms, later, on May 30, 1814. He hadn't been consulted on the terms during the negotiations leading to the treaty. In 1988, two American scholars stole one of the ten original copies of the treaty from the French national archives; one of the thieves was a retired history professor who had taught at Marquette and the second was an aspiring writer of historical novels. They were arrested in 2001 at the Tennessee home they shared, after a five-year investigation prompted by their trying to sell it and other pilfered documents to Sotheby's. It seems the older of the two men had acquired the documents simply by calling them up from the archives and then leaving with them hidden. See McFadden, "Long After Napoleon's Conquests."

10 **"Napoleon in the Isle":** MacKenzie, *The Escape from Elba*, 110.

10 **For centuries, Europeans:** The key works here are Braudel, *The Mediterranean;* Corbin, *The Lure of the Sea;* and Cohen, *The Novel and the Sea*.

10 **For the same reasons:** It was the symbolism and not the perceived security of island exile that had made the practice so common during the reigns of Augustus and Tiberius, for instance, at a time when coastal settlements were far easier to sack than hilltop fortresses. See Wilson, *The*

Greatest Empire, 82. Wilson suggests that a Roman emperor "could modulate the expression of his rage by his choice of geographical location for the exile. Relegation or exile to an island sounded worse than being sent to a mainland area. He might choose a far-distant island, for the worst kind of crime, or a nearby one, for a less outrageous infraction. By these standards, Seneca's punishment [exile to Corsica] was relatively mild." The same can be said about Napoleon's banishment to an island a few miles off the coast of Italy, as opposed to, say, Saint Helena. A notable exception to the practice of island exile is the case of Ovid, among the best-known exiles of all, punished for what he called "a poem and a mistake," who was sent not to an island but to the coastal town of Tomis, present-day Constanta, in Romania.

10 **Napoleon would be following:** On islands and exile, see Gillis, *Islands of the Mind;* Schalansky, *Atlas of Remote Islands;* Edmond and Smith, *Islands in History;* Gaertner, *Writing Exile;* Grove, *Green Imperialism;* Mansel and Riotte, *Monarchy and Exile;* Seidel, *Exile and the Narrative Imagination;* and Stabler, *The Artistry of Exile.* "A precarious, restricted, and threatened life, such was the lot of the islands, their domestic life, at any rate. But their external life, the role they have played in the forefront of history far exceeds what might be expected from such poor territories," wrote Braudel. Braudel, *The Mediterranean*, 154. "The events of history often lead to the islands. Perhaps it would be more accurate to say that they make use of them." (A bit of Napoleonic intrigue on Elba is what eventually lands poor Edmond Dantès on desolate Montecristo in Dumas's other great island tale.)

2: A LODGER IN HIS OWN LIFE

11 **His face was a mess:** Campbell, *Napoleon*, 96–102; Campbell's wounds are also detailed in the *London Gazette*, April 9, 1814.

11 **"I cried out lustily":** Campbell, *Napoleon*, 96.

12 **The worse news:** Before traveling to Elba, Campbell would need to secure a medical certificate from Dr. Crichton, who cleared him to go but wrote, "It is but my duty to add that this journey, undertaken before the complete cure of his wounds, and while laboring under the symptoms just mentioned, is accompanied with very considerable danger, and that nothing but the idea that Colonel Campbell is going to a warmer climate, and his extreme anxiety to obey the orders he had received, could have justified his setting out before the complete cicatrisation of his wounds." Campbell, *Napoleon*, 102.

12 **"Being still unable . . . to accompany":** Campbell, *Napoleon*, 153.

12 **"to attend . . . directed to reside":** Campbell, *Napoleon*, 153–55.

13 **"discretion as to the mode":** Campbell, *Napoleon*, 155. That this choice of words told him it was to be a clandestine assignment, see Gruyer, *Napoleon*, 99.

13 **Castlereagh would have wanted:** We don't know how precisely he came to choose Campbell, but I base my claim on the fact that Castlereagh had plenty of bright, decorated, and loyal officers to choose from, many with more seniority than Campbell, and that he knew each man's credentials inside and out, having personally appointed nearly the entirety of the British Diplomatic Service. It appears he may have first offered the job to a more seasoned, though younger diplomat, the stately John Fane, Lord Burghersh, who along with his adventurous young wife, Priscilla, had traveled closely alongside Castlereagh during the last campaign, during which Lady Burghersh read Byron by the battlefields. It was said that his great wealth had robbed Burghersh of much ambition. Burghersh claimed to his father that he declined the Elban assignment because he didn't fancy leaving Paris just then, and besides, as he wrote, "I don't think I should have gained credit. On the contrary, I should have honored the beast Napoleon too much in dancing attendance upon him." When Jacques-Claude Beugnot, minister of the interior and future director of the police, returned to his Parisian apartment that

month he found Burghersh comfortably quartered there and in no rush to leave, telling
Beugnot that he'd grown particularly fond of his library. Burghersh may have been persuaded
to turn down the assignment by his wife, who knew she wouldn't be allowed to be a camp fol-
lower this time around and who found the whole thing unpleasant. "I am in the greatest rage
that ever was tonight!" she wrote to a friend from Paris on April 13. "Just as I was beginning
to enjoy myself and be quite happy here, thinking all my lonely hours are at an end for ever,
Burghersh is named to attend Napoleon to the Isle of Elba. . . . I would go with him with all my
heart, but that they won't allow and I suppose, indeed, I could not do so, as they will travel
with him, dine with him &c. It will be just like guarding a wild beast." Perhaps burned by the
Burghershes, Castlereagh decided to find someone less senior, less wealthy, and unattached:
Campbell. On Castlereagh's achievements with the British Foreign Office, see Webster, *Foreign Policy*, 44–48. See also Weigall, *Correspondence of Lord Burghersh*, 60; Weigall, *The Letters
of Lady Burghersh*, 224; and Beugnot, *Mémoires*, II, 87.

13 **Born just a few weeks:** Dallas, *The Final Act*, 39. Castlereagh, writes Dallas, "came from an
offshore island, off an offshore island, yet he yearned to be part of the main; he was an Irish-
man, who became an Englishman, who wanted to be a European."

13 **He'd once cheered:** Zamoyski, *Rites*, 42.

14 **"in most melancholy terms":** Campbell, *Napoleon*, 156.

14 **"on whom":** Campbell, *Napoleon*, 2.

14 **"strange feeling that":** Campbell, *Napoleon*, 157.

14 **He had seen Napoleon:** Gray, "An Audience of One," 604.

14 **"I saw before me":** Campbell, *Napoleon*, 157. We don't know what Campbell smelled like to
Napoleon, who had a very keen sense of smell. "I have seen him move away from more than
one servant, who was far from suspecting the aversion he had inspired," wrote his secretary
Baron Fain in 1813. See Kauffmann, *The Black Room at Longwood*, xvi.

15 **Long and lanky:** Scott, *An Englishman*, 90, described Campbell as tall and thin.

15 **Learning that Campbell:** The work of Ossian, supposedly an ancient Scottish poet, caused a
craze after its "discovery" in the late eighteenth century, though these purportedly lost poems
were in fact forged by the man claiming to have collected and translated them, James Macpher-
son. Napoleon was such a fan of Ossian that when his sister Pauline and her first husband,
Charles Leclerc, had asked him as godfather to their firstborn son to choose his name, Napoleon had decided on the uncommon Dermide, a hero of many of these poems. Fraser, *Pauline
Bonaparte*, 28. "very warlike": Campbell, *Napoleon*, 158.

15 **"Yours is the greatest":** Campbell, *Napoleon*, 159.

15 **"expressed satisfaction at hearing":** Campbell, *Napoleon*, 159–60.

15 **"I have been your greatest enemy":** Campbell, *Napoleon*, 159–60. Here we should pause to
question the dependability of Campbell's journal, which only came into the public view in
1869, when his nephew, a vicar named Archibald Neil Campbell MacLachlan, decided to
transcribe the worm-eaten and faded journal that had been under lock and key in his drawer
for several years. The younger Campbell added a brief biography of his uncle. I have tried to
approach the source with the necessary skepticism. It does seem odd, for instance, that Napoleon said such flattering things about the British as recorded above, given that the same man
in 1798 had said, "If my voice has any influence, England will never have an hour's rest from
us. Yes! Yes! War to the death with England! Always!—until she is destroyed!" We have no
other witnesses to this conversation to corroborate or dispute Campbell's account. And yet I
think his recollections are likely quite accurate. In the coming months many others would
observe Napoleon making sure that British visitors of all ranks heard him giving far headier
praise to their country. And indeed Napoleon had been taught a healthy respect for Great
Britain in school, even while learning to think of it chiefly as an enemy from a young age.

Further, we can also reason that there was little for Campbell to gain by lying in his own unpublished journal. While he may, like so many other diarists, have secretly hoped his writing would be published after his death, which might have led him to puff up Great Britain as well as his own position by attributing false statements to Napoleon, even the most ardent patriot or self-aggrandizer hopefully recognizes that the posthumous gains of deceitful propaganda are minimal, and that a fair and true reckoning of events holds much more value, both literary and political, and Campbell strikes the reader of his journal as rational, above all. His memoirs, which span well beyond his time with Napoleon, offer an evenhanded recounting of events large and small, as he either witnessed them or heard of them firsthand from those involved. "If my voice has influence": Bell, *Total War*, 233. Bell reminds us that "Napoleon, like most of the French at the time, routinely conflated England and Britain." See Bell, 349. On Napoleon learning to respect but be antagonistic toward Britain, see Roberts, *Napoleon*, 13.

15 **"or at any rate"**: Hobsbawm, *Revolution*, 189. Hobsbawm reminds us that this openness wasn't meant to extend to all careers, "and not to the top rungs of the ladder." Napoleon and his equally precocious generals had captivated French men and women by their youthful ascension to power. As Hobsbawm notes, "In 1806, out of 142 generals in the mighty Prussian army, seventy-nine were over 60 years of age. . . . But in 1806, Napoleon (who had been a general at the age of twenty-four), Murat (who had commanded a brigade at twenty-six), Ney (who did so at twenty-seven) and Davout, were all between twenty-six and thirty-seven years old." Hobsbawm, *Revolution*, 86.

16 **Earlier in his life:** By David Bell's count, Napoleon encountered at least four serious assassination attempts during his life. Bell, *Total War*, 186.

16 **He gave away cherished:** Campbell, *Napoleon*, 171.

16 **"the subject of punishment by impaling":** Campbell, *Napoleon*, 173. See also, MacKenzie, *The Escape from Elba*, 164.

16 **He would have to pay:** See Treaty of Fontainebleau, Article V.

17 **Later, he wrote:** Branda, *La guerre secrète*, 184; Englund, *Napoleon*, 418.

17 **"This means 400,000":** Palmstierna, *My Dearest Louise*, 166–67. With the Treaty of Fontainebleau the French government also pledged to provide a healthy alimony for Joséphine, to whom Napoleon had promised three million francs a year when they divorced. See Treaty of Fontainebleau, Articles II, III, and IV.

17 **He failed to mention:** Metternich, *Memoirs*, II, 549.

17 **But she was already:** King, *Vienna*, 101.

17 **Emperor Francis wrote:** Branda, *La guerre secrète*, 43–44.

17 **"he'll be a good, kind father":** Palmstierna, *My Dearest Louise*, 176.

17 **She never got the letter:** Palmstierna, *My Dearest Louise*, editorial commentary, 176.

17 **Metternich's band of spies:** Zamoyski, *Rites*, 84.

18 **Indicating the hallway:** Campbell, *Napoleon*, 176–77.

18 **Roustam later claimed:** Branda, *La guerre secrète*, 42; Roustam, *Souvenirs*, section IV (consulted online, without page numbers given).

19 **"Do not lament":** For details of the Fontainebleau farewell, see Napoleon, *Correspondance*, XXVII, 362, and XXXI, 2; Chateaubriand, *Memoirs*, 268. The Cour du Cheval Blanc came to be known as the Cour des Adieux.

19 **Napoleon later said:** Gourgaud, *Talks*, 167.

19 **Working together in:** In the early 1940s, having escaped the Nazis by fleeing to America, thanks to help from James Joyce, the Austrian Jewish novelist Hermann Broch finished his dreamy *Death of Virgil*, in which he imagined Virgil wandering Brundisium in the last hours

of his existence. In describing Napoleon on his last at Fontainebleau, I couldn't help but think of the words Broch used to describe the Roman poet in the summer of 19 BC, which could also apply to the French emperor in the spring of 1814, and provide this chapter's title: "He had become a rover, fleeing death, seeking death, seeking work, fleeing work, a lover and yet at the same time a harassed one, an errant through the passions of the inner life and the passions of the world, a lodger in his own life." Hermann Broch, *The Death of Virgil* (Pantheon, 1945).

3: NAPOLEON IN RAGS

20 **A dozen cavalrymen:** Accounts of the journey south can be found in "Ali," *Napoleon*, 72; Branda, *La guerre secrète*, 47; Campbell, *Napoleon*, 36–41; Gruyer, *Napoleon*, vii; Monier, *A Year of the Life;* Napoleon, *Correspondance*, XXXI, 2–10; Roncière, *Napoleon's Letters*, 273–74; Schuermans, *Souverain*, 415–18; Waldbourg-Truchsess, *Nouvelle relation*, 14–48.

20 **The young paymaster:** Peyrusse, *Mémorial*, 220; Pons, *Souvenirs*, 75.

20 **Those joining the exile:** Treaty of Fontainebleau, Article XVIII.

20 **Most of these followers:** Branda, *La guerre secrète*, 118.

21 **The devoted Caulaincourt:** Branda, *La guerre secrète*, 42.

21 **If Napoleon remained:** Some might also have joined the exile simply for the chance to live in unprecedented proximity to Napoleon. Antoine Lilti makes a similar point about Las Cases's motivations for joining the final exile on Saint Helena. Lilti, *Celebrity*, 207.

21 **Santini scrounged up:** Chautard, *Santini*, 24–25.

21 **Napoleon had offered:** Nollet-Fabert, *Drouot*, 115–17. See also Serieyx, *Drouot*.

22 **Drouot had thought:** Branda, *La guerre secrète*, 96.

22 **Campbell suspected that:** Campbell, *Napoleon*, 29.

22 **To be insulted:** Dallas, *The Final Act*, 259.

22 **Royalist and Catholic:** Branda, *La guerre secrète*, 49; Price, *Napoleon*, 244.

22 **"The countryside":** Sauvigny, *Bourbon Restoration*, 50. For a thoughtful discussion on the difficulties that Napoleonic scholars face in navigating the "fragmentary" archival records left by prefects and other bureaucrats, who may have downplayed or exaggerated reports of Napoleon's popularity depending on their relative positions of power within the state at any given moment, see Hazareesingh's introduction to *The Legend of Napoleon*.

23 **The Prussian commissioner:** Waldbourg-Truchsess, *Nouvelle relation*, 25–30.

23 **He changed costume:** "Henri Bertrand to Caulaincourt, April 28, 1814," Bertrand, *Lettres à Fanny*, 432; Waldbourg-Truchsess, *Nouvelle relation*, 32. Talk of Napoleon's disguise had already made it to London via French newspapers by that May: see "French Papers," *Times* (London), May 11, 1814.

23 **"Paulette," as he preferred:** Fraser, *Pauline Bonaparte*, 205; Branda, *La guerre secrète*, 53.

24 **With the close of the war:** Aside from Ussher's letters in *Napoleon Banished*, much useful information on Ussher and the *Undaunted* can be found in Byrne's massive *Naval Biographical Dictionary*. See also MacKenzie, *The Escape from Elba*, 61–62. Ussher had come in to port a few days earlier, just as bulletins detailing Napoleon's fall reached Marseille. From the deck of the *Undaunted* he had seen the white flag of surrender raised in port and pushed in to anchor. This spooked some French battery gunners into firing on the ship, leading Ussher to open his broadside. After ten minutes of fire, the battery was silenced and people gathered on the ramparts to wave white handkerchiefs. On his disembarking, men carried Ussher on their shoulders to the town hall to be hailed with eloquent speeches and toasts; at least this was how he reported the event in a letter to a young woman, a certain Mrs. M., back in England, adding that various ladies begged to shake his hand and he was "almost suffocated with kisses." He

told his Mrs. M. that he saw "thousands of women with their hands clasped and extended to Heaven, bewailing the loss of husbands, brothers, sons, but partaking in the general joy of deliverance from a tyranny that cannot be conceived much less described." According to Napoleon's later recollections, couriers from Marseille reached him a short while later with reports that corroborated those of Ussher, saying that the British had entered the city in triumph and people had trampled the tricolor and shattered a statue of the emperor. Ussher, *Napoleon Banished*, 7–9; Napoleon, *Correspondance*, XXXI, 6.

24 **"It has fallen"**: Ussher, *Napoleon Banished*, 7.

24 **The arrangement satisfied**: An Austrian aide-de-camp, Count Heinrich Karl von Clam-Martinic, described the dinner in a letter to Prince Schwarzenberg the next day. "It would be difficult to imagine two more opposite and contradictory facets in one person, as Napoleon showed in the performances he gave us on the 25th and yesterday," he wrote. "In the first he hid in a lonely inn, pale and trembling, anxiously asking everyone's advice . . . begging them to give the landlady no suspicion by their behavior that he was the Emperor, jumping at every footfall. To see him there, in the ruins of his lost empire, was enough to make one take him, without exaggeration, for a wretched cowardly usurper. But yesterday we saw him again as if he was weaving spells around us, inviting us to his table, expanding on the plans that would have made him master of Europe within two years . . . proving to the Russians that he had not been defeated by them but only by his own mistakes, and assuring us all that he had made France the first Power in the world." We owe the discovery of this letter to the research of Munro Price and to Carl Philip Clam-Martinic, who shared unpublished family papers with Price. It is valuable not only in the information it provides but also for being a private correspondence that corroborates Waldbourg-Truchsess's description of Napoleon's fearfulness in his published memoir, which otherwise might have been dismissed as having been exaggerated for political purposes. Price, *Napoleon*, 248; Waldbourg-Truchsess, *Nouvelle relation*, 43–44.

25 **"My health is good"**: "Napoleon to Marie Louise, April 28, 1814," Palmstierna, *My Dearest Louise*, 198–99.

25 **"happy travels . . . insults"**: "Henri to Fanny, April 28, 1814," Bertrand, *Lettres à Fanny*, 431–32.

25 **Under his command**: Cole, *Napoleon's Egypt;* Mitchell, *Colonising Egypt;* Reiss, *The Black Count*, 218–27.

26 **Absence had been his ally**: Napoleon, *Correspondance*, XXXI, 9. As Englund has written about Napoleon's return from Egypt, "Bonaparte had left home famous; he returned more famous." Englund, *Napoleon*, 152.

26 **"His sword was . . . 'Allons'"**: Ussher *Napoleon Banished*, 10–11.

26 **"his conscience . . . in Egypt"**: Ussher, *Napoleon Banished*, 12.

26 **Twenty-one guns saluted**: "G. Peyrusse à son père (en mer et à l'île d'Elbe, 28 avril–2 mai 1814)," Peyrusse, *Lettres*, 201.

26 **"bugles sounding, drums beating"**: Ussher, *Napoleon Banished*, 11.

4: This New Country

27 **From his leaking cabin**: "G. Peyrusse à son père (en mer et à l'île d'Elbe, 28 avril–2 mai 1814)," Peyrusse, *Lettres*, 201–2; Peyrusse, *Mémorial*, 229.

27 **Ussher had given**: Ussher, *Napoleon Banished*, 12.

27 **Out on the bridge**: Campbell, *Napoleon*, 199; Ussher, *Napoleon Banished*, 12.

27 **The ailments from which**: I base my claim concerning Napoleon's apparent happiness—with "apparent" being the key word—primarily on the firsthand accounts of Campbell, Peyrusse, and Ussher. There is, however, record of one dissenting British officer who refused to

believe in the genuineness of Napoleon's light mood, writing home to say that his fellow passenger "assumed an affability which certainly did not appear to be natural to him." On Napoleon's health: Baron Gourgaud on Saint Helena reported that Napoleon's followers first noticed the signs of his failing health at Moscow in 1812, when his legs swelled. "My mind resists, but my body gives in," he was heard muttering a few months earlier at Leipzig, the so-called "Battle of the Nations" that anticipated his final defeat and abdication. Price also notes the scholarship that suggests Napoleon may by then have been suffering from some kind of disorder of the pituitary gland, which might have affected his mental state as well. In 1815, John Cam Hobhouse wrote in his diary that he had heard directly from Neil Campbell that Napoleon had "a clap," meaning gonorrhea, at the time of his trip to Elba and that Campbell seemed to indicate that he had seen Napoleon "inject," assumedly as treatment for this purported malady. Regarding Napoleon's list of complaints being relatively ordinary, see Bell, who writes that "few people reached their forties in the early nineteenth century without accumulating a colorful collection of chronic ailments and parasites." Concerning Napoleon being a poor sailor, see Bell, *Napoleon*, 80–81; Cochran, *Byron, Napoleon*, 78; Gourgaud, *Talks*, 158; MacKenzie, *The Escape from Elba*, 62; Price, *Napoleon*, 9; Roberts, *Napoleon*, 166.

28 **Campbell overheard some:** Campbell, *Napoleon*, 199.

28 **When Santini started:** Chautard, *Santini*, 12–13.

28 **Accustomed to commandeering:** Ussher, *Napoleon Banished*, 12. Ussher said he told Napoleon "that I was astonished His Majesty should give such an order, as it was contrary to his system to denationalize. He turned round and gave me a pretty hard rap, saying 'Ah, Capitaine!'"

28 **"leaned on my arm":** Ussher, *Napoleon Banished*, 12. Peyrusse was also proud of being so physically near to Napoleon aboard the ship. He boasted to his father how each day brought the two men into closer contact, and that he even had the chance to help Napoleon locate some maps.

28 **The Royal Navy:** MacKenzie, *The Escape from Elba*, 61.

29 **His face would:** For contemporary renderings of Napoleon, including the variations I've described, see Ashton, *English Caricature*. Concerning Napoleonic visual culture, I have also consulted Hanley, *Napoleonic Propaganda*, and Jourdan, *Napoléon: Héros, imperator, mécène*. "With reference to caricatures," wrote Campbell during the crossing, "I told Napoleon that no one in England was exempt from them, neither our Sovereign nor the ministers. Napoleon remarked that there were plenty of him, at any rate in England, and that no doubt his present voyage would form a fertile subject for them. Captain Ussher said it would immortalize the *Undaunted*." We can add "pulverized dead King" to the list of materials used to create depictions of Napoleon. Luc Sante notes that the poet Blaise Cendrars spoke of "a black tint sold to painters under the brand name Égalité, alleged to have been derived from a royal cadaver, perhaps that of Louis XV, exhumed from the crypt at Saint-Denis during the Revolution. David may have employed it in his *Coronation of Napoleon* (1806) and Ingres in his *Portrait of Monsieur Bertin* (1832)." Campbell, *Napoleon*, 211–12; Sante, *The Other Paris*, 56.

29 **"He laughed at":** Ussher, *Napoleon Banished*, 19.

29 **"The portrait . . . a great compliment":** Ussher, *Napoleon Banished*, 12–20.

29 **He hadn't visited:** Palmer, *Napoleon and Marie Louise*, 17. Englund describes a state dinner in which Napoleon was pulled aside by the king of the northern Italian territory of Etruria, who "said to him in Italian, 'But honestly, you're one of us.'" Napoleon had answered, "Je suis français." Englund, *Napoleon*, 203.

30 **Instead, Campbell had:** MacKenzie, *The Escape from Elba*, 63.

30 **Napoleon walked away:** Campbell, *Napoleon*, 213.

30 **Among them was a travelogue:** Branda, *La guerre secrète*, 61; MacKenzie, *The Escape from Elba*, 65.

30 **"roads rugged . . . of sorrow":** Berneaud, *A Voyage*, 94.

30 **"endowed . . . with ribbons"**: Berneaud, *A Voyage*, 11–12.

31 **Seafaring people had**: Gillis, *Islands of the Mind*, 2. "There have been times when it was continents that were remote and isolated, the outposts of islands," writes Gillis. "Up to the end of the eighteenth century insularity was associated with mainlands, not islands."

31 **He'd once controlled**: Houssaye, *Retour*, 4.

32 **The French commander**: Dallas, *The Final Act*, 262; MacKenzie, *The Escape from Elba*, 68; Marchand, *Mémoires*, II; Rebuffat, "Portolongone," 294–95.

32 **On the first**: MacKenzie, *The Escape from Elba*, 71.

32 **It was replaced**: MacKenzie, *The Escape from Elba*, 68–71; Marchand, *Mémoires*, II.

33 **"Each of us"**: "G. Peyrusse à son père (en mer et à l'île d'Elbe, 28 avril–2 mai 1814)," Peyrusse, *Lettres*, 204.

33 **Dalesme ordered them**: MacKenzie, *The Escape from Elba*, 69.

33 **"The inhabitants"**: Campbell, *Napoleon*, 214.

33 **"whose integrity"**: MacKenzie, *The Escape from Elba*, 69.

34 **"It would have been"**: Pons, *Souvenirs*, 9.

34 **"republican before there was"**: Pons, *Souvenirs*, 11.

34 **"Now I was . . . a frightful dream"**: Pons, *Souvenirs*, 13.

35 **"carefully dressed . . . a soldier"**: Pons, *Souvenirs*, 14. "This wasn't Themistocles banished from Athens," wrote Pons. "This wasn't Marius at Minturnae. His physiognomy could belong to no one else but him." On people immediately noticing Napoleon as he entered a room, even in the early days of his career when he was still relatively obscure, see Englund, *Napoleon*, 89.

35 **"the perfection of"**: Pons, *Souvenirs*, 10.

35 **"a violent intriguing"**: Campbell, *Napoleon*, 382.

35 **Pons recalled that**: Pons, *Souvenirs*, 14.

36 **He would have seen**: Pons, *Souvenirs*, 10.

5: GILDED KEYS

37 **Napoleon had "chosen"**: Marchand, *Mémoires*, II.

37 **Following Bertrand's request**: Pons, *Souvenirs*, 28.

37 **Some of the more prosperous**: Pons, *Souvenirs*, 28.

38 **The white with red**: MacKenzie, *The Escape from Elba*, 73.

38 **"What a childish"**: Ussher, *Napoleon Banished*, 15.

38 **"Evidently he is greatly"**: Campbell, *Napoleon*, 215. Napoleon may have found comfort in the following bit from Berneaud's Elban travelogue, if he had spotted it: "The practice of carrying stilettoes, and of employing them on the most trivial quarrels, a practice so common among the Genoese and Romans, does not exist in the island of Elba. . . . There has not occurred a single assassination of this sort within the memory of man." Berneaud, *A Voyage*, 16.

38 **"The peasants, considering"**: Ussher, *Napoleon Banished*, 13.

38 **Napoleon heard people**: While waiting on board, Campbell told Bertrand that Elba reminded him of the colonies. Colonel Vincent, who had spent sixteen years in Saint-Domingue, was inclined to agree. "Henri Bertrand to Fanny, May 4, 1814," Bertrand, *Lettres à Fanny*, 432.

39 **"good health and better luck"**: MacKenzie, *The Escape from Elba*, 62. On Napoleon's rewarding loyalty with food and other supplies, see Bell, *Total War*, 197.

39 **This was an old trick**: MacKenzie, *The Escape from Elba*, 76. Some historians have suggested that Napoleon may have had an eidetic memory. See, for instance, Chandler, *The Campaigns*, xxxvi.

39 **"pretty little faces"**: "G. Peyrusse à son père (en mer et à l'île d'Elbe, 28 avril–2 mai 1814)," Peyrusse, *Lettres*, 206.

39 **Napoleon had a crowd:** Pons, *Souvenirs*, 43, makes a similar point.

39 **There they heard:** For insight on the Te Deum in France, see Chartier, *Cultural Origins*, 128; Jones, *Great Nation*, 4; Kroen, *Politics and Theater*, 28.

39 **There were N's:** Chateaubriand, *Memoirs*, 276; Peyrusse, *Mémorial*, 234; Pons, *Souvenirs*, 40–41.

40 **"What is a throne?":** Herold, *The Mind of Napoleon*, 83.

40 **The fortifications, the church:** Christophe, *Napoleon on Elba*, 91. Piazza d'Armi is now known as the Piazza della Repubblica.

40 **"Anyone who thought":** Pons, *Souvenirs*, 42.

40 **On a thin mattress:** Campbell, *Napoleon*, 218.

41 **"I've arrived in":** "Napoleon to Marie Louise, May 4, 1814," Palmstierna, *My Dearest Louise*, 203.

6: ROUGH MUSIC

42 **Before marrying him:** Her full name before marriage was Maria Ludovica Leopoldina Franziska Therese Josepha Lucia von Habsburg-Lothringen.

42 **"was with much joy":** Palmer, *Napoleon and Marie Louise*, 79.

42 **The Habsburg empire:** King, *Vienna*, 19. While negotiating the Austrian surrender, Napoleon survived yet another assassination attempt, botched by a teenaged German patriot named Friedrich Saps.

42 **"for the welfare of the nation":** Palmer, *Napoleon and Marie Louise*, 88; Hibbert, *Napoleon*, 173–76. "The secret of nobility," Karl Marx would later write, "is zoology." Palmer is among those writers who suggest that Napoleon, with the help of his sister Caroline, also conducted an earlier experiment with one of Caroline's ladies-in-waiting, Eléonore Denuelle, who gave birth to a son, though no one could be sure the father was Napoleon. There were also rumors that the father was Caroline's husband, Joachim Murat. As Palmer writes, the only thing that was certain was that the baby was not Eléonore's husband's, as he was in jail for forgery at the time of her pregnancy. Palmer, 76; Marx quoted in Wilson, *Victoria*, 19.

43 **The split with Joséphine:** Englund, *Napoleon*, 203.

43 **Napoleon sent her:** Hibbert, *Napoleon*, 176.

43 **Napoleon wanted to combine:** Sebag Montefiore, *The Romanovs*, 295.

43 **"that to see this creature":** Palmer, *Napoleon and Marie Louise*, 86.

43 **"I'm only sorry for":** Roncière, *Napoleon's Letters*, 4.

43 **"I'm certain . . . dearest Papa":** Palmer, *Napoleon and Marie Louise*, 90.

43 **Francis was unmoved:** Palmer, *Napoleon and Marie Louise*, 91. Palmer points out that there appears to be no prior or future mention of a romance with the archduke.

43 **He had Metternich:** Metternich had in turn written to Schwarzenberg prepping him on how to handle Marie Louise if she went to him for advice on the matter, telling him, "You will assert as a private remark coming from yourself, my Prince, that though no secondary consideration, no prejudice will ever influence the decisions of the Emperor, there are laws to which he will always submit. His Majesty will never force a beloved daughter to a marriage which she abhors, and he will never consent to a marriage which would not be in conformity with the principles of our religion." "Metternich to Schwarzenberg, December 25, 1809," Metternich, *Memoirs*, II, 371.

44 **"I desire only":** Marie Louise, *The Private Diaries*, 26.

44 **"brilliant qualities . . . your regard":** "Napoleon to Marie Louise, February 23, 1810," Roncière, *Napoleon's Letters*, 5.

44 **He'd never met:** Hibbert, *Napoleon*, 178–79; Roncière, *Napoleon's Letters*, 5.

44 **"When I heard"**: Gourgaud, *Talks*, 134.

44 **"Madame my Sister"**: "Napoleon to Marie Louise, February 25, 1810," Roncière, *Napoleon's Letters*, 7.

45 **Maria Luisa asked**: Hibbert, *Napoleon*, 180.

45 **A proxy wedding**: Palmer, *Napoleon and Marie Louise*, 95. At this point she received her trousseau of twelve dozen embroidered chemises, three dozen petticoats, two dozen jackets, more than sixty dresses from the famed Parisian couturier Leroy, various nightcaps, stockings, dressing gowns, cashmere wraps, fichus and handkerchiefs, and a diamond parure said to be worth more than three million francs. Hibbert, *Napoleon*, 179–80.

45 **"meant to excel"**: Palmer, *Napoleon and Marie Louise*, 97.

45 **For many observers**: Michelet described the marriage as "a human sacrifice. Marie-Louise, for all her rosy luster and the freshness of a girl of twenty, was like a dead woman. She was handed over to the Minotaur, to the great enemy of her family. . . . Would he not devour her?" Barthes, *Michelet*, 112.

45 **At court in Vienna**: King, *Vienna*, 17.

45 **Marie Louise painted**: Palmer, *Napoleon and Marie Louise*, 105.

45 **"she liked it so much"**: I have used Palmer's translation. In his footnotes Palmer cites Gourgaud, while Kauffman writes that Napoleon actually said this to Bertrand and translates it as, "The first night she asked for more." Palmer, *Napoleon and Marie Louise*, 99; Kauffmann, *The Black Room at Longwood*, 141.

45 **Napoleon sent some**: Hibbert, *Napoleon*, 171.

46 **"save the mother"**: Palmer, *Napoleon and Marie Louise*, 111.

46 **The commandant of**: Fayot, *Précis*, 1.

46 **"Never would I believe"**: Palmer, *Napoleon and Marie Louise*, 113.

46 **He promised that**: Napoleon tried, through the family physician Corvisart, to persuade Francis to let Marie Louise skip Vienna and instead allow her to take the waters in the French spa town of Aix-les-Bains, but he denied this request. Roncière, *Napoleon's Letters*, 262–63.

46 **"Would you ever"**: "Marie Louise to Napoleon, April 16, 1814," Palmstierna, *My Dearest Louise*, 181–82.

46 **"I'm hoping . . . deeply unhappy"**: "Marie Louise to Napoleon, April 16, 1814," Palmstierna, *My Dearest Louise*, 181–82.

47 **In notes omitted**: Caulaincourt's private notes are quoted in Price, *Napoleon*, 242–43. Other secondary sources, likely not privy to these private notes, remark more vaguely that Joseph made "amorous advances" (as in Zamoyski, *Rites*, 186) to Marie Louise at Rambouillet.

47 **"that she was willing"**: Price, *Napoleon*, 242–43. For Caulaincourt's published version, see Caulaincourt, *Mémoires*, 385–88.

7: The Robinson Crusoe of Elba

48 **"He liked every"**: MacKenzie, *The Escape from Elba*, 136.

48 **Decades earlier, the governor's**: MacKenzie, *The Escape from Elba*, 77–78.

49 **Along with a hexagonal**: Branda, *La guerre secrète*, 67.

49 **"made a better bargain"**: MacKenzie, *The Escape from Elba*, 77.

49 **"about two leagues"**: Ussher, *Napoleon Banished*, 16.

50 **When Ussher commented**: Ussher, *Napoleon Banished*, 16.

50 **Years later, Napoleon**: Napoleon, *Correspondance*, XXXI, 12.

50 **On approaching Napoleon's**: Concerning Napoleon's visit to the mines, see Pons, *Souvenirs*, 45–54.

50 **He caught a**: Pons, *Souvenirs*, 46.

51 **"have never agreed"**: Bartlett, *Elba*, 38.

51 **"Babbo! [Father!]"**: Pons, *Souvenirs*, 48.

51 **Napoleon bristled at**: Regarding Corsica and Paoli, see Englund, *Napoleon*, 6. Englund renders the word in Corsican as "Babbu."

52 **"He asked . . . you going?"**: Pons, *Souvenirs*, 50.

52 **Pons had been**: Branda, *La guerre secrète*, 126–33; Napoleon, *Correspondance*, XXXI, 13; Pons, *Napoléon* (Bourachot edition), 11.

52 **"it was easier"**: Bartlett, *Elba*, 27.

52 **Napoleon laughed off**: Concerning honorifics, see Bell, *Napoleon*, 30–31, and *Total War*, 197.

53 **"But you've written"**: Pons, *Souvenirs*, 52.

53 **Remembering their exchange**: Pons, *Souvenirs*, 52.

53 **"He was right"**: Pons, *Souvenirs*, 53–54.

53 **A few months later**: "Napoleon to Peyrusse, undated (but written in response to news from August 27, 1814)," Napoleon, *Le registre*, 93.

8: MY ISLAND IS VERY LITTLE

54 **"isle of rest"**: "Napoleon to Marie Louise, April 19, 1814," Palmstierna, *My Dearest Louise*, 187; Houssaye, *1814*, 5.

54 **"I have never"**: Campbell, *Napoleon*, 243.

54 **"What a pity"**: Roberts, *Napoleon*, 285. As the historian H. A. L. Fisher put it in one of his series of lectures on Bonapartism in 1906, Napoleon was "one of those rare men who assume that everything they come across, from a government to a saucepan, is probably constructed on wrong principles and capable of amendment." Fisher, *Bonapartism*, 75.

55 **"common devotion . . . very little!"**: Campbell, *Napoleon*, 225.

55 **"with great ease"**: Campbell, *Napoleon*, 219.

55 **"Italian music, which"**: Campbell, *Napoleon*, 219.

55 **"enumerate his greatest"**: Campbell, *Napoleon*, 219.

56 **Even the most casual**: There had long been fierce competition among the island's respective villages and towns. Describing the people of Marciana, for instance, Pons said that they considered themselves "at least the equals of the Portoferrese," which meant that "when Portoferraio says white, Marciana says black, even when black is against its interests." Bartlett, *Elba*, 38.

56 **"firing of musketry . . . devout"**: Campbell, *Napoleon*, 233.

56 **"education at the hands"**: Campbell, *Napoleon*, 219. For a sense of Porto Longone during this time, see Rebuffat, "Portolongone."

56 **On such surveys**: Descriptions of Elba based on my own observations, as well as various primary and secondary sources too numerous to list, but especially Bartlett, *Elba*; Branda, *La guerre secrète*; Christophe, *Napoleon on Elba*; Campbell, *Napoleon*; Gruyer, *Napoleon*; King, *Vienna*; MacKenzie, *The Escape from Elba* (especially 65–66); Marchand, *Mémoires*; and Pons, *Souvenirs*; as well as Napoleon's recollections in *Correspondance*, XXXI.

57 **"isle renown'd for steel"**: *Aeneid*, Dryden translation.

57 **"deserters and robbers"**: Laflandre-Linden, *Napoléon et l'île d'Elbe*, 82. Prior to the French taking possession its territory had been split among three dynastic powers: the Grand Duchy of Tuscany had controlled Portoferraio, Sicily controlled Porto Longone, and the prince of Piombino had controlled the rest.

57 **Portoferraio was populated mainly**: Bartlett, *Elba*, 30–31, 38–39; Branda, *La guerre secrète*, 64; Dallas, *The Final Act*, 261. Napoleon later said that when he arrived on Elba it seemed made of three separate "islets" that had been forced together. The first of these imagined

islets, at the west end of Elba, housed the granite vault of Monte Capanne and the main communes of Marciana and Campo; the second, separated from the first by the plains of Campo, stretched from Portoferraio to the hilltop settlement of Capoliveri; the third, to the northeast, featured Monte Grosso and the mines of Rio. Napoleon, *Correspondance,* XXXI, 12.

57 Soil tended to run: Dallas, *The Final Act,* 261.

58 With so many men: Branda, *La guerre secrète,* 64.

58 It was a landscape: Napoleon claimed that he introduced potatoes to Elba, a crop that no one had tried to cultivate before his arrival. Napoleon, *Correspondance,* XXXI, 13.

58 "passion for monuments": Englund, *Napoleon,* 304.

58 "knew his island": Pons, *Souvenirs,* 142.

9: LOUIS THE GOUTY AND THE WEATHERVANE MAN

59 "Sire, you are": Sauvigny, *Bourbon Restoration,* 51. Concerning Louis's exile, see Mansel, *Louis XVIII and Paris,* 3. Nagel, *Marie-Thérèse,* was also helpful.

60 "At this present": "Lord Byron to Thomas Moore, April 20, 1814," Moore, *Letters and Journals.*

60 London had just: Dallas, *The Final Act,* 31. The Russian grand duchess Catherine, freshly arrived in London, wrote to her brother that the joy there bordered on madness. Wherever she went, she told him, they begged to see "the sister of Emperor Alexander, the deliverer of the world." "Catherine to Alexander, London April 4, 1814," and "Catherine to Alexander, London April 11, 1814," *Alexander I and Grand Duchess Catherine, Scenes,* 220, 225.

60 People rushed out: I draw heavily on Uglow's excellent research to understand British reactions to the events of 1814–15, and am grateful for her archival finds. See Uglow, *In These Times.* I have also consulted Alger, *Napoleon's British Visitors,* and Semmel, *Napoleon and the British.* Though I focus here on anti-Napoleon sentiment, nuanced studies such as Semmel's remind us that British feelings toward Napoleon and the French were varied and that minds could be changed as the facts did.

60 Over a roast beef: Semmel, *Napoleon and the British,* 149.

60 "Nap the Mighty": Uglow, *In These Times,* 600.

60 At a time: Uglow, *In These Times,* 598. To give some sense of London readership in that era, we can draw on Peter Ackroyd, who counts the total number of newspapers sold in London in 1801 at sixteen million copies. The city's journalists and their readers gained a reputation for being extremely fickle, and such was the case with the coverage of Napoleon in the 1810s and 1820s. Ackroyd, *London,* 400.

60 Caricaturists competed to: I have consulted caricatures from the period at the Bibliothèque nationale de France (BNF) too numerous to list here. See, for example, "Départ pour l'île d'Elbe," undated, not credited, BNF, De Vinck, 8993. My other main sources on Napoleonic caricatures are Ashton, *English Caricature* (especially 195–200), and Broadley, *Napoleon in Caricature.*

60 "He is deserted": Graham, *Byron's Bulldog,* 122. Around the same time, the wealthy Irishwoman Frances Calvert wrote to a friend that she'd learned Napoleon was "to retire to Elba. I own I would rather there was an end to him. I dread his starting up again. Everybody seems to despise Bony for his submission." Calvert, *An Irish Beauty,* 220.

61 At one time: Clubbe, "Between Emperor and Exile."

61 "ought to have died": Gourgaud, *Talks,* 158.

61 Talleyrand also hoped: Castlereagh, *Correspondence,* IX, 487–88; Mansel, *Paris,* 24; Sauvigny, *Bourbon Restoration,* 54; Underwood, *A Narrative,* 189; Uglow, *In These Times,* 602. As Duff Cooper put it, the French in 1814 were "loth to pretend that during the days when the eagles and the tricolor swept invincibly over Europe the fat old gentleman at Hartwell had really been the King of France." The king and his most influential minister jostled for position from the start. When they were first reunited, at Compiègne, Louis kept Talleyrand waiting for hours and then gave him an elaborate greeting cut with irony, saying, "I am very happy to see you. Our houses date from the same period. My ancestors were cleverer. If yours had been more, you would say to me today: Take a chair, come forward, let us speak of our affairs. Today it is I who say: Sit down and let us talk." Cooper, *Talleyrand*, 238; Harris, *Talleyrand*, 390.

61 **"a cloudless sky"** ... **"was most horrible":** Underwood, *A Narrative*, 190. For another description see Sauvigny, *Bourbon Restoration*, 55. The literary scholar Margaret Cohen has remarked on the heavy symbolic charge of the Porte Saint-Denis, quoting André Breton on his feeling strangely drawn to this "very beautiful and very useless" gate, a deep and unconscious connection, perhaps, with "the political and often explicitly revolutionary resonance of this monument." Cohen quotes from a guidebook: "In 1830, during the days of 27, 28, and 29 July which cost Charles X the throne, cobblestones were thrown from the top of the monument onto the cuirassiers of Maréchal Marmont." Cohen, *Profane Illumination*, 90.

62 **"There was but little":** Underwood, *A Narrative*, 191. Additional details from Houssaye, *1815*, 1; Mansel, *Paris*, 25; "I must own that as far as I was concerned the morning had been painful in every way," wrote the royalist comtesse de Boigne. "The people in the open carriage didn't respond to the hopes I had formulated." Boigne, *Memoirs*, 348.

62 **There were still:** Sauvigny, *Bourbon Restoration*, 46.

62 **"brought their great":** Chateaubriand, *Memoirs*, 271.

63 **Parisians were soon:** Mansel, *Paris*, 26.

63 **Another caricature showed:** Sauvigny, *Bourbon Restoration*, 71.

63 **He could play:** Louis XVIII was "able to make a majestic trait out of his idol-like immobility." Sauvigny, *Bourbon Restoration*, 57.

63 **Shouts of "Long":** Mansel, *Paris*, 25.

63 **A few hundred meters:** Horne, *Seven Ages of Paris*, 204.; Sauvigny, *Bourbon Restoration*, 56. A bronze version of the statue was completed in 1818.

63 **The new king slept:** Alger, *Napoleon's British Visitors*, 288; Jones, *Paris*, 266; Sauvigny, *Bourbon Restoration*, 46.

63 **"To be at":** Baring-Gould, *The Life*, 253.

63 **He'd watched over:** Schama, *Citizens*, 14.

64 **An 1815 bestseller:** Mansel, *Paris*, 20. Regarding the *Dictionary* as Michelin Guide, see Dutourd, "'Le Dictionnaire des girouettes.'"

64 **"by invoking . . . by glory":** Price, *Napoleon*, 228.

10: PRETTY VALLEYS, TREES, FOREST, AND WATER

65 **In his first week:** Napoleon once opined, "Work is my element. I am both born and built for work. I have known the limitation of my legs, I have known the limitations of my eyes; I have never been able to know the limitations of my working capacity." When asked after his final surrender how he would pass the time on Saint Helena, Napoleon answered, "We must work. Work is also the scythe of time." MacKenzie makes a similar point about Napoleon taking pleasures in the picayune while on Elba, perhaps inspired by Walter Scott, who not long after the events in question described Napoleon on Elba as "like a thorough-bred gamester who, deprived of the means of depositing large stakes, will rather play at small game than leave the table." Mackenzie, *The Escape from Elba*, 82; Scott, *The Life of Napoleon Buonaparte*, 167; Herold, *The Mind of Napoleon*, xx–xxi; Kauffmann, *The Black Room at Longwood*, 25.

65 **"dictated letters about":** MacKenzie, *The Escape from Elba*, 122.

65 "On Sunday hoist": Napoleon, *Correspondance*, XXVII, 366–67.

66 Next, in a three-page: "Napoleon to Drouot, May 28 and 29, 1814," Napoleon, *Le registre*, 1–9. See also Branda, *La guerre secrète*, 78–81; Marchand, *Mémoires*, III; MacKenzie, *The Escape from Elba*, 88.

66 "I defy you": Englund, *Napoleon*, 191.

66 "gotten by . . . Emperor's door": Pons, *Souvenirs*, 77–78.

66 Napoleon did manage: Campbell, *Napoleon*, 232; MacKenzie, *The Escape from Elba*, 89; Gruyer, *Napoleon*, 102.

67 "A hat of": Berneaud, *A Voyage*, 11.

67 "the most beautiful": Bartlett, *Elba*, 39.

67 "went round the": Campbell, *Napoleon*, 231.

67 Drouot settled into: Descriptions of Drouot's furnishings can be found in Chevallier et al., *Le Mobilier*, 64–65.

67 "to wish . . . for her": "Drouot to Dupont, April 18, 1814," Nollet-Fabert, *Drouot*, 116. The transcript of Drouot's trial, in Saint-Edmé, *Repertoire*, has also been helpful.

68 "I've been ordered": "Drouot to Evain, May 5, 1814," Nollet-Fabert, *Drouot*, 118.

68 "I'm still . . . inexpressible pleasure": Nollet-Fabert, *Drouot*, 118–19.

68 He was set to propose: Macdonald, *Souvenirs*, 446; MacKenzie, *The Escape from Elba*, 137. Branda speculates that Napoleon enjoyed Henriette Vantini's favors at some point during the exile. Branda, *La guerre secrète*, 169, 183.

68 "You should get married": Houssaye, *Le retour*, 1.

68 "I would love": Branda, *La guerre secrète*, 83.

68 "a young queen": Rosebery, *Napoleon*, 137–38. Concerning the education of her children: Rosebery makes a similar point about Fanny's worries about the quality of education for her children, in this case during the exile on Saint Helena. Rosebery, 139.

69 In the end, Henri: A family relation remembered Bertrand as "a man of limited ideas," though "said to possess much capacity in his own profession . . . but I think that his true merit was blind and unlimited devotion." Boigne, *Memoirs*, 242.

69 He closed the letter: Vasson, *Bertrand*, 130.

69 "pretty valleys . . . passable": "Henri to Fanny, May 4, 1814," Bertrand, *Lettres à Fanny*, 432–33.

69 "playing the adventurer": Branda, *La guerre secrète*, 83.

69 They assumed: "Henri to Fanny, April 11, 1814," Bertrand, *Lettres à Fanny*, 425.

69 "We'll go see Naples": "Henri to Fanny, May 4, 1814," Bertrand, *Lettres à Fanny*, 432–33.

70 Campbell asked Koller: Campbell, *Napoleon*, 218.

70 "I'm having fairly": "Napoleon to Marie Louise, May 9, 1814," Palmstierna, *My Dearest Louise*, 203.

70 Napoleon gave Koller: Campbell, *Napoleon*, 226.

70 "obtain information of": As quoted in MacKenzie, *The Escape from Elba*, 84.

70 Campbell's presence was: MacKenzie, *The Escape from Elba*, 83, 96.

71 "His best information": Campbell, *Napoleon*, 219–26.

71 "by leading our fleet": Campbell, *Napoleon*, 228–29.

71 "movements upon a coast": Campbell, *Napoleon*, 338–39.

71 "so openly . . . of war": Campbell, *Napoleon*, 242, 244.

11: THE EMPEROR IS DEAD

72 By the time Napoleon: MacKenzie, *The Escape from Elba*, 85.

72 "All of Europe": Campbell, *Napoleon*, 217.

72 **They would plant:** Campbell, *Napoleon*, 217, 233.

73 **"after getting up half-way":** Campbell, *Napoleon*, 234.

73 **On another occasion:** Gruyer, *Napoleon*, 119.

73 **Back at Portoferraio:** We can date the first night at the Mulini thanks to the itinerary provided by Schuermans, *Souverain*, 419.

73 **"The Emperor is":** Méneval, *Memoirs of Napoleon*, 1070.

74 **They would eventually:** Campbell, *Napoleon*, 241; Gruyer, *Napoleon*, 89–92; Marchand, *Mémoires*, II; MacKenzie, *The Escape from Elba*, 91.

74 **"how little Napoleon":** Campbell, *Napoleon*, 218.

74 **"The *éclat* given":** Campbell, *Napoleon*, 230.

74 **Campbell also figured:** Campbell, *Napoleon*, 230.

75 **"who is more your":** Marchand, *Memoirs*, II.

75 **"Smiling, with an air":** Campbell, *Napoleon*, 232–33.

75 **The British navy:** I've deduced the rough number of ships in the Royal Navy by drawing from the 1813 count of 899 and patterns of previous years that put the number in the nine hundreds. There are no figures for 1814. Morriss, *The Royal Dockyards*, 12.

75 **The allies had honored:** MacKenzie, *The Escape from Elba*, 93.

76 **"interrupted from attending":** Campbell, *Napoleon*, 237.

76 **"had seduced him . . . Englishman?":** Campbell, *Napoleon*, 239. Campbell's report about Ussher's claims about these rumors is corroborated by Calvert's memoirs: "Bonaparte has arrived at Elba, in spite of many ridiculous reports which have been circulated to the contrary. It was said that he would not be received at Elba, that he was gone to Gibraltar, about to come to England etc., etc." Calvert, *An Irish Beauty*, 222.

76 **"Oh! the Emperor":** Campbell, *Napoleon*, 239. Exile as death dated back to the time of Seneca, at least. Germaine de Staël once wrote, "One is dead when one is exiled. It is merely a tomb where the post arrives." Boigne, *Memoirs*, 231.

76 **They took turns:** MacKenzie, *The Escape from Elba*, 93. King et al., *A Sea of Words*, helped me to understand how night-glasses were constructed, and that whatever one saw through a night-glass would have appeared upside down.

12: AND EVERY TUNA BOWS TO HIM

77 **Technically this was:** Campbell, *Napoleon*, 240; MacKenzie, *The Escape from Elba*, 94.

77 **Montcabrié wasn't actually:** Campbell, *Napoleon*, 240. More details about the arrival of the Guard can be found in Pons, *Souvenirs*, 132–35.

78 **He heard how:** Concerning Portoferraio's being like an amphitheater: along with direct observation, I consulted the contemporary account of Vivian, *Minutes*, 6.

78 **"try the disposition":** Campbell, *Napoleon*, 240.

78 **"more unsteady, more vague":** Las Cases, *Memorial*, 183 (I have slightly reworked this translation after consulting the original French).

78 **"Napoleon speaks most gratefully":** Campbell, *Napoleon*, 241.

79 **He ended by seeing:** Gruyer, *Napoleon*, 89–92; Marchand, *Mémoires*, II. The horses Coco and Tauris were collectively known as "the white charger."

79 **His face was:** Napoleon, *Correspondance*, XXXI, 2.

79 **In the last days:** Branda, *La guerre secrète*, 139–40.

79 **"also had French hearts":** MacKenzie, *The Escape from Elba*, 94.

79 **While they were crossing:** MacKenzie, *The Escape from Elba*, 94.

79 **Cambronne told of:** Gruyer, *Napoleon*, 79.

79 **"to tire myself out":** Campbell, *Napoleon*, 244.

79 **By evening he was:** For details on lodging for Napoleon's entourage, see Chevallier et al., *Le Mobilier*. See also Branda, *La guerre secrète*, 100; MacKenzie, *The Escape from Elba*, 94.

80 **Drouot tried to bolster:** Gruyer, *Napoleon*, 81; Chevallier et al., *Le Mobilier;* Houssaye, *Retour*, 3–4; MacKenzie, *The Escape from Elba*, 97–98. Napoleon had the idea of dividing this local militia into four companies of roughly a hundred men (each one consisted of three officers, ten noncommissioned officers, eighty-seven men, and a drummer), with each company putting only twenty-five men on duty for a week out of the month in rotation, meaning he would have four hundred Elbans on active reserve but paid the wages of a fraction of that number. Drouot also hired some miners from Rio to come to Portoferraio and put their laboring skills to use as sappers.

80 **Pons claimed that:** Pons, *Souvenirs*, 133.

80 **The ships were:** In regular service the *Inconstant* required a crew more than a hundred strong, while at Portoferraio it was never manned by more than sixty men at any one time.

80 **Campbell was nonplussed:** Campbell, *Napoleon*, 252; MacKenzie, *The Escape from Elba*, 97.

81 **There was no chance:** On the importance of a sense of collective purpose, see Adam Gopnik's sharp comments in a review essay on Napoleonic biographies: "Napoleon's crucial insight was that it was not, in the long run, the romance of the nation, or of the cause, or of the Republic, that would keep a democratized army in battle. It was the army's romance of itself, of its own existence." Gopnik, "The Good Soldier."

81 **Of the six hundred thousand:** Price, *Napoleon*, 15.

81 **"New tuna soldiers":** The image, as well as the translation of the caption, comes from the University of Warwick's "100 Days in 100 Objects" project. The source is listed as "Coloured etching, 160 x 200 mm/copper below centre: caption in Italian; below right: Milano 1814," contributed by Alberto Milano from a "Private Collection." www.100days.eu/items/show/4. The print carried a Milan address to mislead authorities. Another caricature from the period shows Napoleon firing a cannon at four straw men (the cannon is also built of straw) while a fisherman nearby worries that the "Madman's Amusement" will scare away all the fish.

82 **"that in case":** Campbell, *Napoleon*, 241.

82 **"indispensable for his":** Campbell, *Napoleon*, 241.

82 **"I can only reiterate":** Campbell, *Napoleon*, 242.

13: A DEATH, A TREATY, AND A CELEBRATION

83 **"as if he had ruled":** Mansel, *Paris*, 19. His sentiment was echoed by a British magistrate who wrote to Mary Berry in London, "Paris is certainly at this moment the most wonderful showbox in the world. It has within its walls as many live emperors, kings, generals, and eminent persons of all kinds, as the ingenious Mrs. Salmon ever exhibited in wax. Of the five great sovereigns of the Christian world, four are here actually present. . . . This is very curious, at least to those that, like me, partake largely in the gratification the vulgar feel in staring at famous people. But what is a matter of greater interest and greater surprise is to see France—to see the great nation that only a few months ago seemed so near realizing its old plan of universal dominion—not only beaten, but delivered over bound hand and foot to foreign masters." Berry, *Extracts*, 11.

83 **Allied diplomats and soldiers:** Lieven, *Russia*, 519–20; Horne, *Seven Ages of Paris*, 204. During this heady time the Prussian field marshal Blücher reportedly lost more than a million francs in a single night's play at the Palais-Royal. Elite members of the Russian guard received a special allowance to partake in the city's delights. "Never has so much gold flowed through Paris," wrote a French officer to a friend in Vienna. "Millions of ducats change hands each day

in this immense *******; the sellers are running out of goods; 60,000 c***s, without counting the honest wives, civilian and military, are in constant service." Montet, *Souvenirs*, 122.

83 **"This capital is"**: MacKenzie, *The Escape from Elba*, 101.

84 **"It is only"**: Wolff, *The Island Empire*, 185. "Desolated at" in Wolff's translation sounds clunky to my ear, which I have guessed is likely due to a too-literal translation of "désolée," and I have changed it to "saddened by," though some might prefer "sorry for."

84 **"permit my accompanying"**: d'Abrantès, *Memoirs*, 454.

84 **"Goodbye, my friend"**: Napoleon, *Lettres de Napoléon à Joséphine*, II, 194–95.

85 **With the redrawing**: Dallas, *The Final Act*, 48; Harris, *Talleyrand*, 226; King, *Vienna*, 6; Lentz, *Nouvelle histoire*, I; Sauvigny, *Bourbon Restoration*, 64; Uglow, *In These Times*, 602. The French had to relinquish claims in the Low Countries and Holland and withdraw from Germany, Italy, and Switzerland, but were allowed to keep some recently acquired lands and recover many of their Caribbean colonies (but not Saint-Domingue, which had declared a hard-won independence), the onetime papal headquarters of Avignon, and lands in the northeast and in Savoy. The British even returned a few territories that they had taken from the French over the years. Regarding reparations: this was aside from the costs incurred by evacuating allied troops from certain territories. The allies would eventually change course on the issue of looted artworks. Note that the French government, by the terms of the treaty, still had to make good on any debts to private individuals as a result of contracts or loans enacted during wartime.

85 **"No sooner than"**: Lentz, *Nouvelle histoire*, I.

85 **Their word for "quickly"**: Dallas, *The Final Act*, 70; Harris, *Talleyrand*, 226; Hussey, *Paris*, 222; Mansel, *Paris*, 27. The allies would for the moment leave seventy thousand troops stationed nearby at various points beyond Paris, at Talleyrand's behest, to help enforce the authority of the Bourbon government.

85 **Castlereagh also left:** "You never saw such a beauty as Lord Castlereagh has become," wrote Priscilla Burghersh to her mother. "He is brown as a berry, with a fine bronzed colour, and wears a fur cap with gold and is really quite charming." Weigall, *Letters of Lady Burghersh*, 205–6.

85 **Guns were fired:** Zamoyski, *Rites*, 192.

86 **"England is never"**: Bew, *Castlereagh*, 358. As Edward Cooke had written to Castlereagh when Napoleon's surrender was being negotiated, "It will be hard if France is to pay nothing for the destruction of Europe, and we are to pay all for saving it." Metternich had predicted the treaty's terms would be "found too harsh in France and too soft beyond the frontiers." Even though he and the other allied representatives had shown mercy, given that complete destruction of France was their right after "the evils she has brought Europe for twenty years," people would still manage to fault their good intentions; such was the fate "of all human things." Indeed this was no less true in France than it was in Britain or Austria. French police reports noted that "the armistice conditions have seemed harsh, they satisfy no one." Castlereagh, *Correspondance*, IX, 454; Dallas, *The Final Act*, 42, 70, 258; Mansel, *Paris*, 27; Sauvigny, *Bourbon Restoration*, 50; Zamoyski, *Rites*, 200.

86 **On the Strand:** Bew, *Castlereagh*, 361; Dallas, *The Final Act*, 4, 32; Uglow, *In These Times*, 603; Zamoyski, *Rites*, 215.

86 **The allied sovereigns:** The idea of a congress in Vienna had already been raised by Tsar Alexander at the battle of Leipzig in 1813 but was originally only meant to include sovereigns and representatives from the victorious nations. Dallas, *The Final Act*, 48; King, *Vienna*, 7.

86 **That the conference:** King, *Vienna*, 30; Mansel, *Paris*, 38.

87 **"This quarter century"**: Bell, *Total War*, 17.

87 **Though some royalists:** "Like a biblical scapegoat," writes Isser Woloch, "Napoleon alone would bear the official royalist animus against twenty-five years of revolution and usurpation. While the pariah was banished to the toy principality of Elba, his close collaborators would be left in peace to enjoy pensions, titles, and memories at home." Woloch, *Collaborators*, 221.

87 **The Lycée Napoléon:** Mansel, *Paris*, 18–19. More specifically, the newspaper had been titled *Journal des débats et des décrets* before Napoleon changed the name and became *Journal des débats politiques et littéraires* during the restoration.

14: A RIDICULOUS NOISE

88 **Townspeople gathered at:** A detailed description of the San Cristino mass and festival can be found in Charrier-Moissard, "Journal," Savant, *Toute l'histoire*, 37–67, as cited in Hicks, "Napoleon on Elba," FN 28–30. See also Pons, *Souvenirs*, 228–35; MacKenzie, *The Escape from Elba*, 112.

88 **There is no record:** On another occasion, Pons left a copy of Fenélon's *Les Aventures de Télémaque*, a popular pedagogic text about the travels and education of Ulysses's son (widely interpreted, if not necessarily intended, as a critique of autocratic rule), open in his study for Napoleon to see, having underlined a few passages, such as "The King ought to be more free from ostentation and pride than any other man" and "Minos loved his people more than his own family." Pons, *Souvenirs*, 122; Gruyer, *Napoleon*, 118.

89 **Conducting a postmortem:** Pons, *Souvenirs*, 228.

89 **"walking in the streets":** Englund, *Napoleon*, 300.

89 **"big noise":** Herold, *The Mind of Napoleon*, 39.

89 **Pons worried that:** Pons, *Souvenirs*, 230–31; Dallas, *The Final Act*, 264.

90 **"Ah! Madame":** Pons, *Souvenirs*, 136.

90 **She gave him:** Branda, *La guerre secrète*, 180; Fraser, *Pauline Bonaparte*, 208–9; MacKenzie, *The Escape from Elba*, 112.

90 **When Napoleon hid:** Hibbert, *Napoleon*, 173; Palmer, *Napoleon and Marie Louise*, 89.

90 **"He seems to want":** Masson, *Napoleon et sa famille*, 328.

90 **The Bonapartes had:** Treaty of Fontainebleau, Article XIV. Englund writes of the Bonaparte brothers that during the period of exile, "all but Louis might have visited their brother in the fullness of time." Englund, *Napoleon*, 420.

91 **She complained of:** Masson, *Napoleon et sa famille*, 328.

91 **But Campbell recognized:** I infer Campbell's doubt from his diary entry, which gives a sense that he thinks the lady doth protest too much. He wrote, "They were at pains to state that the Neapolitan frigate had been sent by the Queen of Naples of her own accord for her sister." Campbell, *Napoleon*, 245.

92 **He chatted with:** Pons, *Souvenirs*, 233–38.

92 **Pons wrote that:** Pons, *Souvenirs*, 235–38.

93 **"be killed a":** Pons, *Souvenirs*, 134. Dalesme was named a Chevalier of Saint Louis on his return to France, and put on nonactivity.

93 **He told Pons:** Pons, *Souvenirs*, 134.

93 **"suffering through his smile":** Pons, *Souvenirs*, 135.

15: THE MORE UNFAVORABLY DOES HE APPEAR

98 **Campbell failed to:** Campbell, *Napoleon*, 246.

98 **But there's no evidence:** Concerning the "lazaretto war," see Campbell, *Napoleon*, 246–47, as well as Branda, *La guerre secrète*, 98, 141, and MacKenzie, *The Escape from Elba*, 113.

MacKenzie suggests that Campbell wondered if Napoleon had orchestrated the lazaretto dispute as a possible test run, but I've found nothing in Campbell's journal to back MacKenzie's claim, which leads me to think that MacKenzie inferred this suspicion on Campbell's behalf.

98 **Morale was already:** Branda, *La guerre secrète*, 129.

99 **Napoleon liked the idea:** Pons, *Souvenirs*, 95–98; Campbell, *Napoleon*, 250.

99 **The island's contributions:** Branda, *La guerre secrète*, 94. Branda calculates Elba's typical annual tax yield at roughly 120,000 francs.

99 **"occasioned unusual outcry":** Campbell, *Napoleon*, 248.

99 **"all the devotion":** Pons, *Souvenirs*, 202–3.

99 **Napoleon had quietly:** Pons, *Souvenirs*, 203.

100 **"the dregs of":** Pons, *Souvenirs*, 201.

100 **Pons thought that:** Pons, *Souvenirs*, 201. For the tax standoff see also Branda, *La guerre secrète*, 167; Marchand, *Mémoires*, IV.

100 **"Napoleon appears . . . among them":** Campbell, *Napoleon*, 248–49.

100 **"to give . . . he appear":** Campbell, *Napoleon*, 248–51.

101 **"Even the attachment":** Campbell, *Napoleon*, 249.

101 **He'd heard a soldier:** Campbell, *Napoleon*, 249.

101 **And some of his men:** Branda, *La guerre secrète*, 141, 161. From Elba, Cambronne wrote to a friend who had managed to switch allegiances from Napoleon to the Bourbons without losing his high rank that he, too, would be pleased to serve the king "should the death of Napoleon leave me free to return to France and reestablish my standing and rights as a French citizen."

101 **"Those he made":** Roberts, *Napoleon*, 714.

16: *Ubicumque Felix Napoleon*

102 **Many summer nights:** Marchand, *Mémoires*, III; Chateaubriand, *Memoirs*, 276; Wolff, *The Island Empire*, 8. To Chateaubriand, the Napoleonic persona was perfectly encapsulated by this time among "his bricklayers" on Elba: "His strength was derived from the masses, his rank from his genius; this is why he passed effortlessly from the market-place to the throne, from the kings and queens who crowded round him at Erfurt to the bakers and grocers who danced in his barn at Portoferraio. He had something of the people among princes, and of a prince among the people." Chateaubriand, *Memoirs*, 276.

102 **He grew a large garden:** Gopnik has the following to say about Voltaire, exile, and gardening: "[Voltaire] quickly turned his exile into a desirable condition—a version of the ancient Horatian ideal of escape from the corrupting city into a small enclosed country house. Pope had done the same thing when he built his grotto at his little house in Twickenham, and wrote about it as enthusiastically. Yet Pope's grotto is playful, an obvious mock hermitage. Voltaire's ideas were far more bourgeois; he wanted to play host to as many people as he could, and to build the sweetest garden he could, and, after renting the villa, he started shopping like Martha Stewart newly freed from prison." Gopnik, "Voltaire's Garden."

102 *Bada di sotto!:* Branda, *La guerre secrète*, 96–97.

103 **He instructed his officers:** Napoleon, *Correspondance*, XXVII, 370; Gruyer, *Napoleon*, 88–89.

103 **"in the family":** Pons, *Souvenirs*, 140.

103 **"so little stuffing":** "Ali," *Napoleon*, 74. My key source for describing the Mulini as it looked at the time is Chevallier et al., *Le Mobilier*, which includes a reprint of the original inventory for the Mulini and other residences on Elba produced in October 1814. My descriptions of the environment and sight lines are also based on visits to the current site of the Palazzo dei Mulini, which is now a museum. For other descriptions of the Mulini in 1814–15, see Gruyer, *Napoleon*, 103; Pons, *Souvenirs*, 140; Vivian, *Minutes*, 6–7.

103 **Aside from the:** "Ali," *Napoleon*, 75.

103 **The approved books:** Concerning the Mulini library and its contents, see "Bibliothèque de l'Empereur: inventaire, undated," Archives nationales, Fonds Betrand, 390 AP 22; "Orders to Drouot, October 3, 1815," Napoleon, *Le registre*, 113.

103 **Napoleon's way of:** Englund, *Napoleon*, 13, 307.

103 **He fed on books:** He had brought a custom-built traveling library with him on the Egyptian campaign, which included Captain Cook's *Voyages*, Goethe's *Sorrows of Young Werther*, Montesquieu's *The Spirit of the Laws*, and works by Julius Caesar, Herodotus, Thucydides, Plutarch, Tacitus, Homer, Virgil, Racine, and Molière. So too in his heyday did people far from France follow the reports of his dazzling campaigns as though they were reading installments in some sweeping serial. Roberts, *Napoleon*, 163.

104 **Among his collection:** MacKenzie, *The Escape from Elba*, 87.

104 **There were books:** Wolff, *The Island Empire*, 9. One wonders if in his Elban reading nook, Napoleon, with his passion for Roman lives, read any Seneca. He might have found wisdom in the Stoic's *Consolation to Helvia*, written during his eight-year exile on Corsica and addressed to his mother, as though Seneca were comforting the grieving woman on his own death. He wrote that an exile had no reason to "regret his former dress and house" because "it is the mind which makes men rich: this it is that accompanies them into exile, and in the most savage wildernesses, after having found sufficient sustenance for the body, enjoys its own overflowing resources." If a banished man "sighs for a purple robe steeped in floods of dye, interwoven with threads of gold and with many coloured artistic embroideries, then his poverty is his own fault, not that of Fortune: even though you restored to him all that he has lost, you would do him no good; for he would have more unsatisfied ambitions, if restored, than he had unsatisfied wants when he was an exile." In another work, quoting and then commenting on the banished Publius Rutilius Rufus, Seneca wrote, "My wish is that my country should blush at my being banished, rather than that she should mourn at my having returned. An exile, of which every one is more ashamed than the sufferer, is not exile at all." Seneca, *Of Consolation: To Helvia*, XI, and *On Benefits*, VI, XXXVII. I have also consulted Wilson's insightful analysis of Seneca's life and works, Wilson, *The Greatest Empire*, especially 84–85.

104 **He amused himself:** Las Cases, *Memorial*, 230.

104 **"He has not made":** Campbell, *Napoleon*, 244.

104 **The laborers stopped:** Pons, *Souvenirs*, 117; Branda, *La guerre secrète*, 84.

104 **He'd been charmed:** Gruyer, *Napoleon*, 108. I wrote some of this book in a small room overlooking this hillside estate.

104 **But he dropped:** Pons, *Souvenirs*, 138.

105 **"I'm not rich":** Pons, *Souvenirs*, 139; Gruyer, *Napoleon*, 107.

105 **It was the finest:** Pons, *Souvenirs*, 139–40.

105 **Pons thought he overpaid:** Pons, *Souvenirs*, 138–39. Pons thought Napoleon overpaid not because the seller was dishonorable, but because Napoleon failed to realize how costly it would be to bring the property up to his standards. I have deduced that Pauline helped to pay for the residence based on Napoleon's letter to Drouot about being undecided as to whether he would have the deed put in his name or hers and later correspondence from Betrand to Peyrusse concerning Pauline's claim to the property. Napoleon, *Correspondance*, XXVII, 368; Marchand, *Mémoires*, IV; Peyrusse, *Mémorial*, 251–52.

106 **"paved with marble":** Gruyer, *Napoleon*, 113–14. See also MacKenzie, *The Escape from Elba*, 124.

106 **The Egyptian campaign:** Napoleon may also have enjoyed recalling his time in Egypt while on Elba because it had been there, on the ascendant, that he had felt the very opposite of the weakened, circumscribed man he was in exile. Each day in Egypt saw him confronting

danger. And while warding off his own death, Napoleon brought it to so many others in brutal fashion. "Citizen general," he had told his chief of staff in response to a rebellion in Cairo, "give the order to the commander in the square to cut the throats of all prisoners who were taken bearing arms. They will be brought tonight to the banks of the Nile . . . and their headless corpses thrown in the river." Bell, *Total War*, 212–13.

106 **Ever since that campaign:** Bell, *Total War*, 212–13; Reiss, *The Black Count*, 218–27. Cole, *Napoleon's Egypt*, and Mitchell, *Colonising Egypt*, were also helpful.
106 **"I found myself":** Bell, *Total War*, 212.
106 **To the veterans:** Pons, *Souvenirs*, 139.
106 **As a valet:** "Ali," *Napoleon*, 83.
106 **The work resumed:** Branda, *La guerre secrète*, 145–46; Napoleon, *Le registre*, 77–78.
107 **He showed the same:** Branda, *La guerre secrète*, 100. Branda posits that Napoleon traveled between residences so frequently as a security measure.
107 **"I've seen no chateau":** Englund, *Napoleon*, 203.
107 *Ubicumque felix Napoleon*: Campbell, *Napoleon*, 310; Gruyer, *Napoleon*, 113; MacKenzie, *The Escape from Elba*, 125.

17: SIROCCO

108 **"keeping my journal . . . their tone":** Campbell, *Napoleon*, 257.
108 **That summer was the hottest:** Nollet-Fabert, *Drouot*, 120.
109 **"Bertrand showed . . . that effect":** Campbell, *Napoleon*, 252–53.
109 **There was no mention:** *London Gazette*, June 7, 1814. Campbell was also mentioned in the *London Gazette* the following week, when it was announced that the prince regent had officially granted him "license and permission" to accept and wear the decorations he had already received from Russia for his services in the field. Again there was no mention of his Elban assignment.
109 **"I have reason":** Campbell, *Napoleon*, 234.
109 **Campbell dealt mostly:** Gruyer, *Napoleon*, 102.
109 **"Napoleon continues":** Campbell, *Napoleon*, 248.
109 **He didn't seem:** Concerning various pet projects, see Branda, *La guerre secrète*, 97, 167; Campbell, *Napoleon*, 248.
110 **The goal was to:** Branda, *La guerre secrète*, 124; MacKenzie, *The Escape from Elba*, 123.
110 **"cleaned out . . . my approval":** Gruyer, *Napoleon*, 110.
110 **Napoleon declared that:** Napoleon, *Correspondance*, XXVII, 368.
110 **He subjected the:** Gruyer, *Napoleon*, 109; Napoleon, *Le registre*, 81–82.
111 **Fists were raised:** Pons, *Souvenirs*, 338.
111 **When the weather:** Napoleon, *Le registre*, 61–62.
111 **"what all the complaints":** Napoleon, *Correspondance*, XXVII, 387.
111 **Another storm:** Napoleon, *Le registre*, 3; Schuermans, *Souverain*, 419–20.
111 **Pons thought that:** Gruyer, *Napoleon*, 117; Pons, *Souvenirs*, 114.
111 **On Elba, denied:** Zadie Smith's "Two Paths for the Novel" was helpful in thinking about "filling" space with time. See also Harvey, *The Condition of Postmodernity*.

18: SULTRY CONFINEMENT

112 **He made no other:** MacKenzie, *The Escape from Elba*, 114.
112 **"relieve my mind":** Campbell, *Napoleon*, 256–57.
113 **After docking at Livorno:** Campbell, *Napoleon*, 257.
113 **"convinced they were sent":** Campbell, *Napoleon*, 259.

113 "the suppression of": Hyde de Neuville, *Mémoires*, 18.

113 "Don't you think": Hyde de Neuville, *Mémoires*, 14.

113 "Each time he": Hyde de Neuville, *Mémoires*, 35.

114 She could have been: MacKenzie, *The Escape from Elba*, 167.

114 "schemes begin to": Campbell, *Napoleon*, 266.

114 "some questions of": Campbell, *Napoleon*, 306.

114 "mixed up in": Hyde de Neuville, *Mémoires*, 35.

114 They had even stopped: Campbell, *Napoleon*, 261–62; O'Dwyer, *Papacy*, 135; Zamoyski, *Rites*, 237.

115 "the public spirit": Campbell, *Napoleon*, 260, 268–69.

115 "until sufficient proofs": Campbell, *Napoleon*, 274.

115 "very pleasant and": Campbell, *Napoleon*, 272.

116 "must have been": "Ali," *Napoleon*, 80.

116 She hadn't helped: Branda, *La guerre secrète*, 177; Campbell, *Napoleon*, 277.

116 "continue to consider": Campbell, *Napoleon*, 273.

116 "Louis [the fifth oldest]": Campbell, *Napoleon*, 278.

116 "many sighs and": Campbell, *Napoleon*, 272.

19: THE ONE-EYED COUNT

117 At one point: Palmer, *Napoleon and Marie Louise*, 176–79.

117 "What a heartrending fate": Palmstierna, *My Dearest Louise*, editorial note, 204.

117 "I only wish": "Marie Louise to Napoleon, June 5, 1814," Palmstierna, *My Dearest Louise*, 208–9.

118 "If I were": Houssaye, *Retour*, 14.

118 Francis secured permission: Palmer, *Napoleon and Marie Louise*, 181.

118 "Do please . . . to me": "Marie Louise to Napoleon, June 22, 1814," Palmstierna, *My Dearest Louise*, 209–11.

119 "It's papa's necktie": "Image 11.58, 1814," Broadley, *Napoleon in Caricature*, II, 57.

119 On the first: Méneval, *Memoirs of Napoleon*, 1074.

119 "Receptions weary me": "Marie Louise to Napoleon, June 22, 1814," Palmstierna, *My Dearest Louise*, 209–11.

120 And at the Château: See Caulaincourt's unpublished notes regarding Rambouillet, *Mémoires*. This was the same castle where Voltaire passed some of his exile from France.

120 When she reached: Palmer, *Napoleon and Marie Louise*, 183.

120 "With all necessary": MacKenzie, *The Escape from Elba*, 131.

120 "rather suited the": Méneval, *Memoirs of Napoleon*, 1075.

120 Before leaving for: Marchand, *Mémoires*, FN 176; Palmer, *Napoleon and Marie Louise*, 183.

121 "I just can't": MacKenzie, *The Escape from Elba*, 132.

121 "capable of . . . of you": "Marie Louise to Napoleon, July 21, 1814," in Palmstierna, *My Dearest Louise*, 213–14.

20: A PERFECTLY BOURGEOIS SIMPLICITY

122 "She seemed greatly": Campbell, *Napoleon*, 278–79.

122 Meanwhile, a messenger: Marchand, *Mémoires*, IV; Masson, *Napoleon et sa famille*, 360.

122 "a handsome house": Méneval, *Memoirs of Napoleon*, 1072. For details on the Vantini house, see Marchand, *Memoirs*, IV.

123 "the emperor has": Masson, *Napoleon et sa famille*, 361.

123 **"It pains ... be done"**: "Napoleon to Bertrand, September 6, 1814," Napoleon, *Le registre*, 100.

123 **"I've seen eminent"**: MacKenzie, *The Escape from Elba*, 119.

123 **Though Napoleon sometimes**: Englund, *Napoleon*, 13; MacKenzie, *The Escape from Elba*, 119–20.

123 **Napoleon typically rose**: Branda, *La guerre secrète*, 190.

123 **As he left**: "Ali" added that "as the broth was very good and the quantity they sent from the kitchen was much more than the Emperor needed, the *valets de chambre* would take it when the Emperor had gone to his study, and, like their master, they would each drink a drop of Constance. They thought that what the Emperor liked they also ought not to dislike. It prepared their stomachs for breakfast." We know that Napoleon ordered Groot Constantia during his Saint Helena exile; whether he ordered wine from this same estate while on Elba is unclear. "Ali," *Napoleon*, 79. Detailed descriptions of life at the Mulini can also be found in Marchand, *Mémoires*, III.

124 **"We ate, we drank"**: Pons, *Souvenirs*, 250.

124 **During these trips**: Pons, *Souvenirs*, 250–51.

124 **Pons recalled that**: Gruyer, *Napoleon*, 105–6.

124 **After the initial**: Branda, *La guerre secrète*, 191.

124 **During one of these**: Marchand, *Mémoires*, III.

125 **In the early evenings**: "Ali," *Napoleon*, 79.

125 **"in continual movement"**: Napoleon, *Correspondance*, XXXI, 11.

125 **Occasionally he and**: Nollet-Fabert, *Drouot*, 119.

125 **A valet recalled**: Marchand, *Mémoires*, IV.

125 **"a perfectly bourgeois"**: Pons, *Souverain*, 149.

125 **"Napoleon, you're cheating ... mother"**: Roberts, *Napoleon*, 724; Peyrusse, *Mémorial*, 239. Michelet and Barthes were both fascinated by Napoleon's "lucky" name: Bonaparte, the good part, or the lucky share. "Grace, which is at the origin of all Micheletist evil, wears many masks," wrote Barthes in his study of Michelet. "Consider the magnificent theme of gambling: in the eighteenth century, politics is a gamble, a throw of the dice. . . . Napoleon? Doomed to Chance (Buona-parte), his reign is one of farce and lottery." Barthes, *Michelet*, 56.

126 **This was the signal**: MacKenzie, *The Escape from Elba*, 137.

126 **He sang to himself**: "Ali," *Napoleon*, 76; Marchand, *Mémoires*, III.

21: TALL FANNY AND THE TWO EMPRESSES BONAPARTE

127 **They had even**: Concerning the couple's various plans for the exile, see Henri's letters to Fanny from April–May 1814, *Lettres à Fanny*, 423–36.

127 **Most of the family's**: Paulin, *Notice biographique*, 28.

127 **He pressured her**: "Henri to Fanny, April 11, 1814," and "Henri to Fanny, April 22, 1814," Bertrand, *Lettres à Fanny*, 426, 429–30.

128 **Word got round**: Branda, *La guerre secrète*, 211; Caulaincourt, *Mémoires*, 415; Christophe, *Napoleon on Elba*, 100; Marchand, *Mémoires*, IV; Welvert, *Napoléon et la police*, 62–63.

128 **Later, on Saint Helena**: Gourgaud, *Talks*, 138. Napoleon may have first learned of Joséphine's death from a letter from Caulaincourt that evaded the censors, in which he assured Napoleon that even in her last feverish moments Joséphine had been thinking of him. If he did learn the news this way, perhaps Fanny was remembering a particularly emotional discussion with Napoleon about the subject, or less likely, Napoleon out of politeness didn't tell her that he already knew about the death. Napoleon also received two letters from Eugène de Beauharnais about the death, but long after the fact. Eugène told his stepfather, "Everything she said to us about you in the last moments of her life showed us clearly how sincerely she was devoted

to you. . . . My sister and I hope that when Your Majesty learns of the irreparable loss we have just suffered, and of the deep sorrow which overwhelms us, you will feel you are sharing it with us." See "Eugène de Beauharnais to Napoleon, May 31, 1814," and "Eugène de Beauharnais to Napoleon, June 11, 1814," Palmstierna, *My Dearest Louise*, 235–36; Branda, *La guerre secrète*, 188; Caulaincourt, *Mémoires*, 413.

128 "What, Sire! Bertrand!": Boigne, *Memoirs*, 241.

128 "his face did not": Gourgaud, *Talks*, 138.

128 "humane instincts and": Gourgaud, *Talks*, 138.

128 "The Devil shit": Kauffmann, *The Black Room at Longwood*, 9.

128 "I think, although": Gourgaud, *Talks*, 136.

129 As with Napoleon: Roberts, *Napoleon*, 70.

129 "the wife who": Gourgaud, *Talks*, 56.

129 "France . . . the head": Roberts, *Napoleon*, 800. Roberts includes an alternate version of Napoleon's final words that is also sometimes cited: "France . . . Army . . . head of the Army."

129 He admonished Marie Louise: Palmer, *Napoleon and Marie Louise*, 184.

129 "in September . . . is despicable": "Napoleon to Marie Louis, August 18, 1814," Palmstierna, *My Dearest Louise*, 219–20.

22: TAKING THE CURE

130 "I'll never . . . to die": Méneval, *Memoirs of Napoleon*, 1078–79.

130 "Her complexion . . . cruel absence": "Marie Louise to Napoleon, July 31, 1814," and "Marie Louise to Napoleon, August 3, 1814," Palmstierna, *My Dearest Louise*, 215–17.

131 "surrounded by . . . devoted Louise": "Marie Louise to Napoleon, August 18, 1814," Palmstierna, *My Dearest Louise*, 221–22.

131 "he may be extremely useful": Palmstierna, *My Dearest Louise*, 222.

132 He found Marie Louise: MacKenzie, *The Escape from Elba*, 133; Palmer, *Napoleon and Marie Louise*, 186.

132 "the idea of the journey": MacKenzie, *The Escape from Elba*, 134.

132 "Be assured that": MacKenzie, *The Escape from Elba*, 134.

132 "thoughtless . . . to do so": Méneval, *Memoirs of Napoleon*, 1073; Palmer, *Napoleon and Marie Louise*, 186; Palmstierna, *My Dearest Louise*, 223.

23: TOURIST SEASON

133 "came up tripping": Campbell, *Napoleon*, 281.

133 As he readied: Campbell, *Napoleon*, 284.

134 "He told me . . . a spy!": Campbell, *Napoleon*, 287–88.

134 "require immediate dispatch": MacKenzie, *The Escape from Elba*, 121.

134 "did not wish": Campbell, *Napoleon*, 290.

135 Pons won a prize: MacKenzie, *The Escape from Elba*, 122; Marchand, *Mémoires*, IV.

135 The night could: Bell, *Napoleon*, 82.

135 "I am here": "Napoleon to Marie Louise, August 28, 1814," Palmstierna, *My Dearest Louise*, 222–23.

137 "considers his exile": MacKenzie, *The Escape from Elba*, 129. Branda, *La guerre secrète*, XXI, FN 732, cites the correspondence between Napoleon and Murat concerning Napoleon's son with Walewska. For details on Walewska's visit, see Marchand, *Mémoires*, IV; Pons, *Souvenirs*, 212–14; Campbell, *Napoleon*, 135–37, 303–4; MacKenzie, *The Escape from Elba*, 126–30; Branda, *La guerre secrète*, 184–86. Branda (Annexe I) includes a lengthy report on Walewska's

visit from Mariotti to Talleyrand. Marie Walewska was briefly reunited with Napoleon during his return and then went to Naples. She married Napoleon's cousin General d'Ornano in 1816 and died the following year. Her son Alexandre Walewski, said to look like Napoleon though he was much taller, gained some renown as a French diplomat.

137 **"the person of"**: Campbell, *Napoleon*, 293; MacKenzie, *The Escape from Elba*, 164.

137 **The mayor of**: Branda, *La guerre secrète*, 224; Campbell, *Napoleon*, 299; MacKenzie, *The Escape from Elba*, 128; Marchand, *Mémoires*, IV.

138 **"the Algerines . . . of Moscow"**: Campbell, *Napoleon*, 297.

138 **"so weak as to"**: Campbell, *Napoleon*, 299.

138 **"nothing beyond my"**: Campbell, *Napoleon*, 299.

138 **"with warmth . . . to Elba"**: Campbell, *Napoleon*, 297.

138 **"I bowed and told"**: Campbell, *Napoleon*, 298.

139 **"Enlarging for some time"**: Campbell, *Napoleon*, 302–3.

139 **"It strikes me"**: Campbell, *Napoleon*, 303.

139 **"with the hope"**: Maxwell, *My Adventures*, 145.

139 **"I'm an object"**: Alger, *Napoleon's British Visitors*, 297.

140 **"A more hot unwholesome"**: Maxwell, *My Adventures*, 157.

140 **"whiff their cigars"**: Maxwell, *My Adventures*, 157.

140 **"now took a nap"**: Maxwell, *My Adventures*, 163.

140 **"pointing and giving"**: Maxwell, *My Adventures*, 170–71.

140 **"his majesty had"**: Maxwell, *My Adventures*, 172–73.

140 **"the film seemed"**: Maxwell, *My Adventures*, 175–76.

141 **"I now . . . human heart"**: Maxwell, *My Adventures*, 176.

141 **"asked if the Genoese"**: Maxwell, *My Adventures*, 181.

141 **"We're neighbors!"**: Maxwell, *My Adventures*, 183.

141 **"Campbell," he wrote**: Scott, *An Englishman*, 80–94. See also Young, *Napoleon in Exile*, 250–51.

141 **He landed at**: Campbell, *Napoleon*, 306.

24: The Politics of Forgetting

142 **Louis XVIII spent**: Dallas, *The Final Act*, 86.

142 **"It seems that his"**: MacKenzie, *The Escape from Elba*, 158.

142 **"tavern war against"**: Sauvigny, *Bourbon Restoration*, 81.

143 **Some even spoke**: Horne, *Age of Napoleon*, 175; Englund, *Napoleon*, 424. The king's top general, Dupont, who in April had gone from imprisonment in the Jura mountains to minister of war, had demobbed more than three hundred thousand men and the shakeup left about half of the armed forces on inactive duty at half-pay. Paris experienced a spike in petty crime along with their return.

143 **French public opinion**: Hussey, *Paris*, 224; Sauvigny, *Bourbon Restoration*, 74–81.

143 **"multitude of English"**: Alger, *Napoleon's British Visitors*, 282. Despite the police chatter, foreigners were on the whole welcomed openly, especially by shopkeepers and innkeepers.

143 **While financial markets**: Lentz, *Nouvelle histoire*, I; Horne, *Age of Napoleon*, 175.

143 **So many British**: Alger, *Napoleon's British Visitors*, 280.

143 **"watch, judge . . . discontented"**: Horne, *Age of Napoleon*, 175. Concerning émigrés feeling out of time and place, see Fritzsche, *Stranded*, 56; Mansel, *Paris*, 29.

143 **Exiled intellectuals returned**: Fritzsche, *Stranded*, 66. Though concerning a later period, Kramer, *Threshold of a New World*, was also helpful.

143 **"a stranger in"**: Fritzsche, *Stranded*, 75.

144 "was born on the": De Staël, *Ten Years Exile*, 188–89. De Staël was soon petitioning Louis XVIII for two million francs that she felt was owed to her father. "The first article of the rights of man in France is the right of every Frenchman to a government job," she'd once quipped. She could have pointed to Chateaubriand, whom the grateful king had recently named a colonel and ambassador to Sweden though he performed no real diplomatic duties.

144 The official tasked: Mansel, *Paris*, 32; Sauvigny, *Bourbon Restoration*, 73. It would take several years to sort all the claims for lost privileges and lands.

144 "There is not one": Sauvigny, *Bourbon Restoration*, 77.

144 Under pressure from: Kroen, *Politics and Theater*, 161. "Suffrage was limited to one in 360 men," writes Kroen. "The right to hold office was even more restricted. . . . Freedom of expression, freedom to meet in public, and to express one's views were all officially restricted during the Restoration." Article VIII of the charter reads, "The French people have the right to make public and to print their opinions, while conforming to the laws that must repress abuses of this freedom." Todorov, in Hollier, *A New History*, 618.

144 The result was: Mansel, *Paris*, 28; Sauvigny, *Bourbon Restoration*, 74.

145 Some royalists combined: Chateaubriand, *Memoirs*, 273; Englund, *Napoleon*, 424; Harris, *Talleyrand*, 222; Plongeron, *Des résistances religieuses*. The Knights of the Faith wanted a clean break from everything that had happened in France since the Revolution, including the ascendancy of Talleyrand, who had to outmaneuver the Knights during the regime change to retain his powers.

145 "While patriotism exists": Constant, *Political Writings*, 161–63. Constant's critique of the Napoleonic cult of personality reads in retrospect as a "prophetic statement about the true nature of twentieth-century totalitarianism," as the historian Andrew Hussey has suggested. Hussey, *Paris*, 224–25.

145 Had the fall: Hussey, *Paris*, 222.

145 "such public . . . being wagered": Guizot, *Mémoires*, I, 24–25. See also Lefebvre, *Napoléon*, 580.

146 The republican experiment: On French political culture, see Hunt, *Politics, Culture, and Class*, and Ozouf, *Festivals*.

146 "Death-Birth of a World!": Carlyle, *French Revolution*, 213.

146 "Nowadays," wrote Chateaubriand: Fritzsche, *Stranded*, 55.

146 "nothing less than": Kroen, *Politics and Theater*, 6–7.

146 Just as they: Dallas, *The Final Act*, 87; Jones, *Paris*, 266; Mansel, *Court of France*, 98, 102–5. Antoine Lilti has described how "the revolutionary era profoundly changed the autonomous nature of political power because of the phenomenon of public opinion. . . . Even the status of royal family members had profoundly changed, with the nature of celebrity progressively contaminating the traditional concept of monarchical representation." Lilti, *Celebrity*, 161.

147 "bind all memories": A full English translation of the charter can be found in Maloy, *The Constitutions*.

147 A complicated kind: Kroen, *Politics and Theater*, 40–41. As Kroen points out, *oubli* can be translated as "oblivion, disregard, or forgetting." See also Carpenter, *Aesthetics*, 73–84; Englund, *Napoleon*, 424.

147 With the budget: Branda, *La guerre secrète*, 201–2.

147 "Vesuvius . . . the violets": Thibaudeau, *Mémoires*, 417; Horne, *Seven Ages of Paris*, 204. The violet became a Napoleonic symbol during the Hundred Days and was sometimes called "the Emperor's flower." An unfounded rumor held that before leaving Fontainebleau, Napoleon had said he would return within a year, just like the violets in the palace gardens.

25: HE IS TOLERABLY HAPPY

151 **"had been assured"**: Campbell, *Napoleon*, 307–8.

151 **By Campbell's rough calculations**: Campbell, *Napoleon*, 253–56; Mackenzie, *The Escape from Elba*, 100.

151 **He learned that Bertrand**: MacKenzie, *The Escape from Elba*, 174.

151 **"So many people"**: MacKenzie, *The Escape from Elba*, 174.

151 **But many saw**: Branda, *La guerre secrète*, 216.

152 **The annual surplus**: Napoleon, *Correspondance*, XXXI, 14. He did complain that for the whole of his time on Elba "Josephine's bills came pouring in upon me from all parts of Italy.... She possessed in an eminent degree the taste for luxury, gaiety, and extravagance, natural to Créoles. It was impossible to regulate her expenditure; she was constantly in debt." Las Cases, *Memorial*, 299.

152 **Napoleon had always**: MacKenzie, *The Escape from Elba*, 99. See some of Peyrusse's Elban accounting and calculations in Peyrusse, *Mémorial*, 264–68. Herold has written that "the best clue to Napoleon's aim in life lies in his curious way of making budgets. If, for instance, he ordered the construction of some public work or edifice, he would make sure that it was built in stages and that at the end of each stage it could be put to some use, no matter how many years might elapse before the whole was completed. If the wing of a palace, or a stretch of road or canal, could be put to use after the first year, then its cost could be amortized in the following year and could be charged off the budget. By the time the whole was completed, it had paid for itself. By this sleight of hand, Napoleon combined long-term objectives with his passion for immediate usefulness. He did not expect the present generation to sacrifice itself for an indefinite future, nor did he wish future generations to pay the debts of the present. Such husbanding does not bespeak an unprincipled mind. In precisely the same manner, he seems to have looked upon his destiny as something that was revealed to him in installments, as the occasion arose. Each installment had to pay for itself, regardless of what the future might bring. To look too far beyond the present installment was futile. When the last installment came and he sat dying for six years on his rock, he still regarded it as a positive stage in his destiny. 'My downfall raises me to infinite heights,' he said. It was amortization of immortality." Following Herold's logic, one could point to Napoleon's relatively unsystematic spending on Elba as evidence of his struggle to make sense of his life's meaning in this intermittent stage when he was still dealing with loss of true power and had yet, as on Saint Helena, to fully resign himself to defeat so that he might concentrate on posterity. Herold, *The Mind of Napoleon*, xxx.

152 **When Drouot presented**: Nollet-Fabert, *Drouot*, 121.

152 **"Napoleon is never"**: Campbell, *Napoleon*, 304.

152 **Streetlights were installed**: Branda, *La guerre secrète*, 98, 118.

153 **"Great Lord of"**: MacKenzie, *The Escape from Elba*, 165.

153 **"It appears certain"**: Campbell, *Napoleon*, 318. It doesn't appear that Napoleon had any direct involvement with Tunisia while on Elba. A few years later, during the final exile, Bertrand remembered the time he had asked some Tunisian sailors docked at Portoferraio if they had come to do ill, to which they replied, "Against the Great Napoleon! ... Oh! Never.... We do not wage war on God!," and Napoleon added that the flag of Elba was held sacred by all Barbary ships and that even "the Algerines" worshipped him like a deity. Las Cases, *Memorial*, February 20, 1816.

153 **"with some ladies"**: Campbell, *Napoleon*, 305.

153 **"receiving persons from"**: Campbell, *Napoleon*, 305–6.

153 **"I can't say"**: Campbell, *Napoleon*, 312.

153 **"presumed that His Majesty's"**: Campbell, *Napoleon*, 312.

154 **Louis XVIII had made:** Indeed Parisians decried the ambassadorship of "Monsieur le duc de Vilainton," though they had greeted him with cheers at the opera only a few months before. Mansel, *Paris*, 59.

154 **"a violent . . . a torrent":** Campbell, *Napoleon*, 313–16.

154 **He told Campbell:** Campbell, *Napoleon*, 313.

154 **"personal motives or":** Campbell, *Napoleon*, 317.

154 **"I am a dead man":** Campbell, *Napoleon*, 317.

154 **"He has four places":** Campbell, *Napoleon*, 304–5.

155 **"We've made it through":** Nollet-Fabert, *Drouot*, 120. By using the word "agreeable" I risk a too-literal translation of Drouot's *agréable*, which would be more commonly translated as "pleasant" or "nice," but I like that "agreeable" implies a kind of joint decision by Drouot and factors beyond his control to make this a happy summer.

26: THE VULGAR DETAILS OF MARRIED LIVES

156 **Napoleon had Corsicans:** Pons, *Souvenirs*, 340.

156 **The Corsican Santini:** Chautard, *Santini*, 17; Branda, *La guerre secrète*, IX, XX.

156 **Years later, Santini:** Branda, *La guerre secrète*, 149–50.

156 **She passed out candies:** Campbell, *Napoleon*, 317.

156 **At her welcome ball:** Pons, *Souvenirs*, 239–40. For more details on the song, see Weckerlin, *Chansons populaires*, 283.

157 **Pons wandered over:** Pons, *Souvenirs*, 239–40.

157 **Pons found Pauline:** Pons, *Souvenirs*, 238. In Pauline's defense, though she did often complain about ill health, she had good reason to, suffering from anemia, jaundice, and some lingering effects of yellow fever from her time in Saint-Domingue, and likely gonorrhea as well. Fraser, *Pauline Bonaparte*, 213–14.

157 **Pons wrote that:** Pons, *Souvenirs*, 238.

157 **With Pauline's arrival:** Marchand, *Mémoires*, IV.

157 **"always dressed . . . di Medici":** "Ali," *Napoleon*, 76–81.

157 **Citing her fragile health:** Fraser, *Pauline Bonaparte*, 213; Branda, *La guerre secrète*, 180–81; Pons, *Souvenirs*, 242.

157 **"always found some way":** "Ali," *Napoleon*, 78.

157 **Once, when her:** Fraser, *Pauline Bonaparte*, 213.

158 **A Spanish woman:** Branda, *La guerre secrète*, 182–83; Fraser, *Pauline Bonaparte*, 213; Las Cases, *Memorial*, 165. Branda, *La guerre secrète*, XI, has done the most diligent archival work here and I base my respective claims concerning incest and procurement on his research and arguments.

158 **"seized any chance":** Pons, *Souvenirs*, 240, 242.

158 **"presence was a source":** MacKenzie, *The Escape from Elba*, 176.

158 **"I would . . . left France":** Fraser, *Pauline Bonaparte*, 212.

158 **"There are great winds":** Fraser, *Pauline Bonaparte*, 215; Branda, *La guerre secrète*, 181.

158 **Having his sister and mother nearby:** Englund, *Napoleon*, 13.

158 **"Elsewhere they see you":** Englund, *Napoleon*, 34.

159 **"bent . . . undo breeches":** Fraser, *Pauline Bonaparte*, 4.

159 **She sold her place:** Fraser, *Pauline Bonaparte*, 211. It still houses the British embassy in Paris today.

159 **She'd been a regular:** Christophe, *Napoleon on Elba*, 101; Boigne, *Memoirs*, 74; Marchand, *Mémoires*, IV; Pons, *Souvenirs*, 214.

159 **Afternoons Napoleon and Fanny:** Branda, *La guerre secrète*, 87, 242; Pons, *Souvenirs*, 216.

159 She sometimes brought: Broughton (Hobhouse), *The Substance of Some Letters*, 268.

159 During the final exile: Kauffmann, *The Black Room at Longwood*, 44.

159 "Give her . . . interest her": Kauffmann, *The Black Room at Longwood*, 258.

160 "What love!": Kauffmann, *The Black Room at Longwood*, 217.

160 "held it against": Kauffmann, *The Black Room at Longwood*, 275.

160 "he was always": Branda, *La guerre secrète*, 84.

160 The grand marshal: Pons, *Souvenirs*, 75.

160 "too great a liking": Pons, *Souvenirs*, 189.

27: DON GIOVANNI, CINDERELLA, AND UNDINE

161 "it would suit us": MacKenzie, *The Escape from Elba*, 133.

161 When she crossed: Méneval, *Memoirs of Napoleon*, 1086–92; MacKenzie, *The Escape from Elba*, 133; Palmer, *Napoleon and Marie Louise*, 187.

161 "sang with a voice": Méneval, *Memoirs of Napoleon*, 1091. For details on this duet, see Palmer, *Napoleon and Marie Louise*, 188.

162 "I can no longer": MacKenzie, *The Escape from Elba*, 134; Palmer, *Napoleon and Marie Louise*, 188.

162 She reached Vienna: Several sources, including Palmer, list her arrival as October 4, but King, drawing on contemporary Viennese sources, makes a much stronger case for October 7. See King, *Vienna*, 359. Concerning Marie Louise's life in Vienna in the fall and winter of 1814, I have drawn on Bright, *Travels*, 45; King, *Vienna*, 44, 102; Méneval, *Memoirs of Napoleon*, 1092–1100; MacKenzie, *The Escape from Elba*, 134, 179–81; Palmer, *Napoleon and Marie Louise*, 189–90; Palmstierna, *My Dearest Louise*, 189, 223–24; Zamoyski, *Rites*, 256.

163 Although political in its: My main sources concerning the Congress of Vienna are: King, *Vienna;* Kissinger, *A World Restored;* Nicolson, *Congress;* Lentz, *Nouvelle histoire*, III; Webster, *Congress;* Gabriëls, "Cutting the Cake"; Zamoyski, *Rites*. The conference had been originally slated for the summer but was pushed back until October at the request of Tsar Alexander, who explained that he needed to return to Petersburg after so many months away, though orchestrating the delay also served to remind everyone of his top rank among sovereigns.

163 Giddy at the prospect: Zamoyski, *Rites*, 254.

163 They went through: On the Vienna congress as social event (including the detail about coffee kettles), see King, *Vienna*, 12–15, and Palmer, *Napoleon and Marie Louise*, 190.

163 "a new way to wage": King, *Vienna*, 157.

163 The treasury was: King, *Vienna*, 19.

163 But Francis recognized: Palmer, *Napoleon and Marie Louise*, 189.

163 And all the socializing: Palmer, *Napoleon and Marie Louise*, 190–91. As Lefebvre wrote, "The congress never really came together. Everything took place in committee, and the important questions were decided by the four [main allied powers]." Lefebvre, *Napoléon*, 576.

164 "Each day there was": King, *Vienna*, 141; MacKenzie, *The Escape from Elba*, 180–81.

164 Her husband's exile was: Branda, *La guerre secrète*, 201; King, *Vienna*, 105; MacKenzie, *The Escape from Elba*, 156–57, 182.

164 Talleyrand wrote to: "Talleyrand to Louis, October 13, 1814," Talleyrand-Périgord, *The Correspondence of Prince Talleyrand and King Louis XVIII*, 24–29.

164 "the excellent idea": "Louis to Talleyrand, October 21, 1814," Talleyrand-Périgord, *The Correspondence of Prince Talleyrand and King Louis XVIII*, 42–43.

164 "the silence of the budget": "Talleyrand to Louis, October 13, 1814," Talleyrand-Périgord, *The Correspondence of Prince Talleyrand and King Louis XVIII*, 24–29; MacKenzie, *The Escape from Elba*, 171.

164 "the treaty . . . with him?": MacKenzie, *The Escape from Elba*, 181; Roberts, *Napoleon*, 729.

165 That much of this: Lentz, *Nouvelle histoire*, Avant-Propos.

165 One night's salon: King, *Vienna*, 115, 183; Pocock, *Thirst for Glory*, 130.

165 Some delegates even: King, *Vienna*, 115.

165 Europe's rulers, however: Zamoyski, *Rites*, 449.

165 Napoleon did send: Branda, *La guerre secrète*, 153.

28: I Think He Is Capable of Crossing Over

166 "finally determine the": Lean, *The Napoleonists*, 145; MacKenzie, *The Escape from Elba*, 157.

166 In his will: See records of Bonhams auction 22277, lot 66, "Napoleonic French Gold, Enameled and Cameo-set Snuff Box."

167 "If pecuniary difficulties": Campbell, *Napoleon*, 318–19.

167 On November 16: "Orders to Drouot, November 16, 1814," Napoleon, *Le registre*, 198.

167 All outstanding taxes: Campbell, *Napoleon*, 316–19, 344.

167 "highly distinguished . . . Russian army": *London Gazette*, October 15, 1814.

168 None of Campbell's: Campbell, *Napoleon*, 320.

168 In the meantime: Campbell, *Napoleon*, 320.

168 "I showed him": Campbell, *Napoleon*, 323.

169 "the English will": Concerning Hyde de Neuville's advice and this quotation, see MacKenzie, *The Escape from Elba*, 168–70.

29: The Oil Merchant and Other Visitors

170 He was likely: Pellet, *Napoléon à l'île d'Elbe*, is the main source on the Oil Merchant. Pellet had reproduced much of this agent's correspondence with the Chevalier Mariotti, the French consulate at Livorno, based on his work in the archives of said consulate. Additional information about the Oil Merchant can be gleaned from Mariotti's reports to Talleyrand, cited below, some of which relay intelligence originally reported by the Oil Merchant. MacKenzie posits that the Oil Merchant had likely served in the Italian army somewhere in the region, meaning that there were several people on Elba who could vouch for his good standing. MacKenzie, *The Escape from Elba*, 150–51. See also Branda, *La guerre secrète*, 245.

171 He never breached: Pellet, *Napoléon à l'île d'Elbe*, 118.

171 In one report: Pellet, *Napoléon à l'île d'Elbe*, 127.

171 But there were enough: Pellet, *Napoléon à l'île d'Elbe*, 56.

171 Women provided him: Pellet, *Napoléon à l'île d'Elbe*, 120.

171 "What do you think?": Pellet, *Napoléon à l'île d'Elbe*, 129.

171 Nor did he panic: "Mariotti to Talleyrand, November 15, 1814," Talleyrand-Périgord, *The Correspondence of Prince Talleyrand and King Louis XVIII*, 104–5.

171 The Oil Merchant's reports: Concerning Mariotti, see the correspondence housed in the French Diplomatic Archives: Mémoires et Documents (France), 1800: "Mémoires, lettres et documents divers relatifs au traité du 11 avril 1814 et au séjour de Napoléon à l'île d'Elbe"; as well as MacKenzie, *The Escape from Elba*, 163; Hyde de Neuville, *Mémoires*, 28–29. Branda, *La guerre secrète*, 237–43, has also been very useful.

172 When Napoleon's carriage: Branda, *La guerre secrète*, 239–42.

172 "The conclusion which I": "Talleyrand to Louis XVIII, December 7, 1814," Talleyrand-Périgord, *The Correspondence of Prince Talleyrand and King Louis XVIII*, 100–103.

172 Drifting soldiers on: Houssaye, *Retour*, 10.

172 "the larks . . . show themselves": MacKenzie, *The Escape from Elba*, 154.

173 **A Welsh copper-master:** Vivian, *Minutes*, especially 31–37.

173 **"since the violent feeling":** Ebrington, *Memorandum*, 15; MacKenzie, *The Escape from Elba*, 141.

173 **By flattering British visitors:** Roberts, *Napoleon*, 725–26.

173 **"received with . . . intriguing characters":** "Burghersh to Castlereagh, December ?, 1814," Weigall, *Correspondence*, 72.

173 **She told her interrogators:** Branda, *La guerre secrète*, 217.

174 **"to trouble . . . they could!":** Welvert, *Napoléon et la police*, 300–301.

30: HE HAD BEEN CALLED COWARD!

175 **He'd just sold:** Campbell, *Napoleon*, 324–25, 344. Campbell had also seen some intercepted correspondence detailing the terms of a sale of munitions and iron ore to two Italian merchants at Civitavecchia, signed by Drouot.

175 **"foreign papers . . . their triumphs":** Concerning this and all following quotations and details from Campbell's December 4 conversation with Napoleon, see Campbell, *Napoleon*, 325–38.

177 **"if the means":** Campbell, *Napoleon*, 343.

177 **"keep a lookout":** Campbell, *Napoleon*, 343.

177 **"The more I see":** "Campbell to Burghersh, December 6, 1814," in Weigall, *Correspondence*, 68.

31: A LAST GOODBYE

181 **"My Darling, it seems":** "Marie Louise to Napoleon, Schönbrunn, January 3, 1815," Palm-stierna, *My Dearest Louise*, 224–25.

32: THE SADNESS OF MY *RETIREMENT*

183 **"He has gradually":** Campbell, *Napoleon*, 349.

183 **"This was intended":** Campbell, *Napoleon*, 349–50.

184 **"diminish the sadness":** Pellet, *Napoléon à l'île d'Elbe*, 113.

33: THE (NEAR) WRECK OF THE *INCONSTANT*

185 **The squall hit:** Campbell, *Napoleon*, 348.

185 **They were brief:** Branda, *La guerre secrète* (Annexe II), provides copies of the two intercepted letters, dated December 26, 1814 (to Pauline), and December 27, 1814 (to Napoleon).

187 **Command of the *Inconstant*:** Details about the near sinking of the *Inconstant* can be found in Campbell, *Napoleon*, 353–59; Marchand, *Mémoires*, VI; Peyrusse, *Mémorial*, 268–69; MacKenzie, *The Escape from Elba*, 190–93.

187 **"some persons say":** MacKenzie, *The Escape from Elba*, 192.

187 **The narrowly avoided loss:** MacKenzie, *The Escape from Elba*, 192–93.

187 **Campbell missed the drama:** Campbell, *Napoleon*, 351–53; Branda, *La guerre secrète*, 243.

187 **"with a . . . he stated":** Campbell, *Napoleon*, 352–53.

188 **Now battle-hardened men:** MacKenzie, *The Escape from Elba*, 184, 198. Castlereagh, busy in Vienna crafting an understanding with Metternich and Talleyrand that would unite them against the threat of Russian dominance, wrote to his prime minister that the end of the American conflict was "a most conspicuous and seasonable event" and told Liverpool that between the new treaty and the emerging alliance with France and Austria, "the alarm of war is over."

188 **"were few, his evenings":** Peyrusse, *Mémorial*, 262.

34: BOURBON DIFFICULTIES

189 "as though they had": Branda, *La guerre secrète*, 218.

189 One agent reported: Branda, *La guerre secrète*, 228.

189 Talleyrand read a: "D'Hauterive to Talleyrand, 14th November, 1814," Talleyrand-Périgord, *The Correspondence of Prince Talleyrand and King Louis XVIII*, 100.

190 No single overarching: MacKenzie, *The Escape from Elba*, 160–63.

190 Beugnot, for instance: Branda, *La guerre secrète*, 213–16.

190 Louis XVIII did, however: Branda, *La guerre secrète*, 202.

190 The young Dumoulin: Laborde, *Napoleon et sa Garde*, 75; Branda, *La guerre secrète*, XXIV.

191 "To bind up": Sauvigny, *Bourbon Restoration*, 57.

191 Most often this: See, for example, "Vision de M. de la Jobardiere," Bibliothèque nationale de France (BNF), Vinck, vol. 70, 9220; "M. de la Rotomontade Apprenant le Débarquement de l'Empereur," BNF, Vinck, vol. 72, 9453. Sauvigny, *Bourbon Restoration*, 81, was also helpful.

191 "Be careful not": Carnot, *Mémoire*, 24. For amount of copies sold, see Sauvigny, *Bourbon Restoration*, 82.

192 Louis XVIII ordered: Carpenter, *Aesthetics*, 73–84. See also Dunn, *The Deaths;* Ben-Amos, *Funerals.*

192 The funeral procession: Castellane, *Journal*, 274.

192 "God has . . . disastrous dissensions": Carpenter, *Aesthetics*, 74.

192 Traveling through France: Jones, *Paris*, 263.

192 In roadside inns: Sauvigny, *Bourbon Restoration*, 83.

192 "Do you believe": Driault, *The True Visage*, 303; Fraser, *Pauline Bonaparte*, 215.

192 "I no longer take snuff": Broadley, *Napoleon in Caricature*, II, 59. It is interesting to note that Walter Scott wrote his island travelogue *The Lord of the Isles* in 1814, just as Napoleon was making Elba famous.

192 "There were many": Thibaudeau, *Mémoires*, 400.

35: NIGHTS AT THE THEATER

194 Napoleon spotted the: Details and all quotations concerning this visit come from the diary of John Cam Hobhouse, which records Macnamara's entire conversation as the latter recounted it to him. See "John Cam Hobhouse, Diary Entry, April 22, 1815," as reproduced in the late Peter Cochran's draft for an edited volume on the Hundred Days, which contains the note: "Edited from B.L.Add.Mss. 47232, and Berg Collection Volumes 2, 3 and 4: Broughton Holograph Diaries, Henry W. and Albert A. Berg Collection, The New York Public Library, Astor, Lenox and Tilden Foundations." Hobhouse dates the conversation to "the 13th or 14th of last January." One wonders about the exactitude of either of these potential dates, given that Napoleon would have been dealing with the near sinking of the *Inconstant* on January 13, which goes unmentioned in the conversation. The manuscript of Cochran's draft has generously been made available at petercochran.files.wordpress.com/2009/12/17-hundreddays .pdf. Also useful are Cochran, *Byron, Napoleon;* MacKenzie, *The Escape from Elba*, 189.

195 A smokescreen, monument: Concerning the theater, see Branda, *La guerre secrète*,99; MacKenzie, *The Escape from Elba*, 177; Pons, *Souvenirs*, 243.

195 "I'll explain that": MacKenzie, *The Escape from Elba*, 178.

195 Her parties took place: Houssaye, *1814*, 10; Vivian, *Minutes*, 10.

195 Pauline's ladies-in-waiting: MacKenzie, *The Escape from Elba*, 178.

196 "adopted a dreamier look": Pons, *Souvenirs*, 243; Fraser, *Pauline Bonaparte*, 215.

196 In the first months: Branda, *La guerre secrète*, 86.

196 Campbell made a: MacKenzie, *The Escape from Elba*, 177.

196 With the *Inconstant:* MacKenzie, *The Escape from Elba,* 194.
196 "Shall I listen": MacKenzie, *The Escape from Elba,* 194.
196 Pons answered that: MacKenzie, *The Escape from Elba,* 194.
196 "because his cooperation": MacKenzie, *The Escape from Elba,* 194.
196 It may be possible: Pons, *Souvenirs,* xi.
197 "I knew enough": Peyrusse, *Mémorial,* 268.
197 When Peyrusse saw: Peyrusse, *Mémorial,* 268–69.

36: PIETRO ST. ERNEST, OTHERWISE KNOWN AS FLEURY DU CHABOULON

198 "This is, I think": Campbell, *Napoleon,* 353.
198 But along with: Campbell, *Napoleon,* 353–58.
198 "unusually grave and dull": "Campbell to Burghersh, February 2, 1815," Weigall, *Correspondence,* 96.
199 He tried to broach: Campbell, *Napoleon,* 358.
199 "there could be no treason": Campbell, *Napoleon,* 361.
199 "duty to notify": Campbell, *Napoleon,* 362.
199 "right to interfere": Campbell, *Napoleon,* 361–62. Campbell's journal entry concerning Palmaiola contained a tidbit that would have tickled Alexandre Dumas: "Without attaching too much importance to this rock, or the facts in connection with it, it is worthy of remark that there is another island, without any inhabitants, called Monte Christo, south of Elba, and not double the distance of Pianosa, to which Napoleon's fancy or projects may also lead him . . . so that his absence from Elba could be less easily known, while any pretext remained for quitting it."
199 Campbell wasn't sure: Campbell, *Napoleon,* 359.
199 Fanny Bertrand told him: Campbell, *Napoleon,* 360.
200 "Mysterious adventurers and": Campbell, *Napoleon,* 359.
200 He was bothered: Campbell, *Napoleon,* 360.
200 "It is scarcely": Campbell, *Napoleon,* 362.
200 "ordered him not": Campbell, *Napoleon,* 260.
200 Pietro St. Ernest was: Concerning Fleury de Chaboulon's trip to Elba, see Fleury, *Mémoires,* especially 100–120. Marchand, *Mémoires,* VI, corroborates the essence of Fleury's claims about his trip to Elba. See also Branda, *La guerre secrète,* XXVI; Houssaye, *1815,* 181; MacKenzie, *The Escape from Elba,* 197–98.
201 After Cambronne became: Fleury, *Mémoires,* 104.
201 Former revolutionaries were feeling: MacKenzie, *The Escape from Elba,* 198.
202 "a general insurrection": Fleury, *Mémoires,* 115.
202 "Yes, Sire, and": Fleury, *Mémoires,* 112.
202 After the interview: Fleury, *Mémoires,* 118.
202 A few months later: King, *Vienna,* 247.
202 "disagreeable . . . remaining at Elba": Campbell, *Napoleon,* 367.
202 Either way, Campbell's: Campbell, *Napoleon,* 367.
202 "a short excursion": Campbell, *Napoleon,* 362.
202 "visit Palmaiola for my": Campbell, *Napoleon,* 362.

37: THE EAGLE PREPARES FOR FLIGHT

204 He specified that: Napoleon, *Correspondance,* XXVII, 449.
204 He told Drouot: See the full transcript of Drouot's trial in Saint-Edmé, *Repertoire.*
204 "humanly possible . . . be staying": Saint-Edmé, *Repertoire,* 398–400, 409. During his trial Drouot highlighted the fact that he'd drawn none of the pay rightfully owed to him as a

French officer during his time in exile, just as he'd rejected Napoleon's monetary gift for joining the exile.

205 **"I do not allow":** Roberts, *Napoleon*, 730.

205 **"Abandoning the sovereign":** Saint-Edmé, *Repertoire*, 409.

205 **Then he called:** Branda, *La guerre secrète*, XXVI; Napoleon, *Correspondance*, XXVII, 450.

205 **The gunners were drilled:** Branda, *La guerre secrète*, XXVI; Pellet, *Napoléon à l'île d'Elbe*, 152–53.

38: The Oil Merchant Returns

206 **"more as if":** Pellet, *Napoleon à l'île d'Elbe*, 159.

207 **"several interviews with":** Pellet, *Napoleon à l'île d'Elbe*, 152.

207 **All of the isolated:** Branda, *La guerre secrète*, XXVI; MacKenzie, *The Escape from Elba*, 210, 237; Pellet, *Napoleon à l'île d'Elbe*, 154, 158–59, 161.

39: Campbell in Florence

208 **Castlereagh, in his:** Concerning Burghersh's admonishing Campbell, writing to Castlereagh, and Castlereagh's response, see "Castlereagh to Burghersh, January ?, 1815," Weigall, *Correspondence*, 88, and "Burghersh to Castlereagh, March 3, 1815," Weigall, *Correspondence*, 108–9.

209 **"that everything is":** Campbell, *Napoleon*, 363.

209 **"I did feel":** Campbell, *Napoleon*, 363.

209 **"very absurd, contradictory":** Campbell, *Napoleon*, 365.

209 **"The troops," wrote Ricci:** Campbell, *Napoleon*, 365.

210 **"prepared to quit":** Campbell, *Napoleon*, 366.

210 **"My access to Napoleon":** Campbell, *Napoleon*, 367–68.

40: Mardi Gras

212 **Peyrusse ended his meeting:** Peyrusse, *Mémorial*, 269–70.

212 **"pay . . . but don't pay":** Peyrusse, *Mémorial*, 270.

213 **Drouot, however, was:** Saint-Edmé, *Repertoire*, 400.

213 **Peyrusse left Drouot's:** Peyrusse, *Mémorial*, 270; Nollet-Fabert, *Drouot*, 122.

213 **The night of February 22:** Pons, *Souvenirs*, 243–44.

213 **"exquisite taste":** Pons, *Souvenirs*, 243.

214 **Amazingly, no one:** MacKenzie, *The Escape from Elba*, 209.

214 **"absurd reports . . . only fools":** Gourgaud, *Talks*, 168.

214 **"One can't take a step":** Pellet, *Napoléon à l'île d'Elbe*, 162.

215 **"I begged, I offered bribes":** Pellet, *Napoléon à l'île d'Elbe*, 162.

215 **Campbell's Elban contact:** The most detailed source concerning Adye's brief return to Portoferraio comes from Adye's debriefing to Campbell of what he'd seen, repeated verbatim in Campbell, *Napoleon*, 369–70. See also Napoleon's version, as recalled to Gourgaud on Saint Helena, in Gourgaud, *Talks*, 168–69. Additional details can be found in Branda, *La guerre secrète*, XXVI; MacKenzie, *The Escape from Elba*, 210; Marchand, *Mémoires*, VI; Pellet, *Napoleon à l'île d'Elbe*, 162; Peyrusse, *Mémorial*, 271–72; Pons, *Souvenirs*, 379–82.

41: Tower of Babel

216 **"I seem . . . in Spain":** Pellet, *Napoléon à l'île d'Elbe*, 163–64.

217 **While it remained:** MacKenzie, *The Escape from Elba*, 210.

217 **But that evening:** Campbell, *Napoleon*, 370.

217 **From Antibes they would march:** The plan for the landing and march on Paris has been described in many sources. See, for instance, Hazareesingh, *The Legend of Napoleon*, 17–18; Thiry, *Le vol de l'aigle*.

217 **An Italian landing:** Historians have offered different theories as to why Napoleon chose France over Italy as the landing destination. Branda, for instance, makes the point that an Italian landing would have been unwise because the peninsula was then almost completely administered by former enemies of Napoleon: Field Marshal Bellegarde oversaw Milan; Stahremberg, Florence; General Spannochi, Livorno; Cardinal Pacca, Rome; and the cardinal's nephew, Civitavecchia. In their communications these officials referred to Napoleon as their "bad neighbor" or simply as "questo signore" (this mister). The Austrians had also beefed up their presence on the Italian peninsula, increasing a force of 50,000 in May 1814 to 150,000 by early 1815, mostly centered around Milan. MacKenzie suggests that Napoleon would have foreseen that he had little to gain by teaming "with his unstable brother-in-law at the bottom of the Italian peninsula, far from the centres of power and the classic battlefields of Europe. On the contrary, he was well aware that such a flight would confirm every suspicion of collusion and lead at once to war with Austria, France, and possibly England." Branda, *La guerre secrète*, 263–66; MacKenzie, *The Escape from Elba*, 203–4.

217 **But he'd enjoyed:** MacKenzie, *The Escape from Elba*, 191.

218 **Unknown to anyone:** Concerning the Corsican plans, see Branda, *La guerre secrète*, XXVI; du Casse, *Le général Arrighi*, 52, 89–93; Napoleon, *Correspondance*, XXXI, 37; Pons, *Souvenirs*, 382.

218 **"I have reason to believe":** Du Casse, *Le général Arrighi*, 67.

219 **She pressed a diamond:** MacKenzie, *The Escape from Elba*, 211; Marchand, *Mémoires*, VI. The necklace was later discovered in Napoleon's carriage after Waterloo by some looting Prussian soldiers.

219 **"That's not how":** Marchand, *Mémoires*, VI.

219 **"if Heaven intends":** MacKenzie, *The Escape from Elba*, 211.

219 **"doomed herself to live":** Las Cases, *Memorial*, 308–9.

219 **Before retiring:** Roberts, *Napoleon*, 730.

219 **He was worried:** Fleury, *Mémoires*, 403. Fleury remarks on Bertrand's refusing to sign a decree that would seize the property of several former enemies and arguing that Napoleon was in this case reneging on his earlier promise not to seek harsh reprisals.

219 **"there was, on my":** "Henri Bertrand to his father, undated," Bertrand, *Lettres à Fanny*, 447.

219 **"Our children . . . tender affection":** "Henri to Fanny, undated," Bertrand, *Lettres à Fanny*, 443.

220 **The letter, discovered:** Bertrand, *Lettres à Fanny*, 441.

220 **He'd pictured her:** Bertrand, *Lettres à Fanny*, 447.

42: EVERYTHING WAS QUIET AT ELBA

221 **He wrote to Castlereagh:** Campbell, *Napoleon*, 364.

221 **"throw down the gauntlet":** Campbell, *Napoleon*, 368.

221 **"to intercept, and":** Campbell, *Napoleon*, 368.

222 **"be justified by":** Campbell, *Napoleon*, 368.

222 **It had taken:** MacKenzie, *The Escape from Elba*, 218.

222 **"would neither be":** Campbell, *Napoleon*, 370.

222 **"everything was quiet":** Campbell, *Napoleon*, 369.

223 **"it might not":** Campbell, *Napoleon*, 369.

223 **Campbell figured that:** Campbell, *Napoleon*, 369–70. See also Adye's full report as cited in the notes below Campbell's entry, in Campbell, *Napoleon*, 363–64.

223 **"I think he will leave":** Campbell, *Napoleon*, 370–71.

224 **Campbell had likely also:** MacKenzie, *The Escape from Elba*, 203–4. As MacKenzie has suggested, it was an error "to see Napoleon as an enthusiast for the liberation of Italy when his whole career showed that he would cynically encourage or betray the Italian patriots as it suited him."

224 **That way if British:** Campbell, *Napoleon*, 371.

224 **Adye predicted they:** These events are recorded in Campbell's journal entry under the heading "February 15," presumably written in intervals from that date onward, and ending on the morning of February 27, as the next entry is dated February 28. The last section of this long "February" entry, presumably written aboard the *Partridge* while bound for Elba, is tantalizing in its ambiguity, and gives little detail about Campbell's actions on the key night of February 26. Campbell, *Napoleon*, 359–72.

43: INCONSTANT

225 **A soft breeze:** Pons, *Souvenirs*, 381–82.

225 **He took special care:** MacKenzie, *The Escape from Elba*, 212.

225 **"I leave you peace":** Bartlett, *Elba*, 105.

225 **Pons thought he:** Pons, *Souvenirs*, 381–82.

226 **An officer rushed:** Laborde, *Napoleon et sa Garde*, 48.

226 **Murat would wait:** MacKenzie, *The Escape from Elba*, 208.

227 **Luckily a nearby:** Pellet, *Napoléon à l'île d'Elbe*, 166.

227 **At around two:** Pellet, *Napoléon à l'île d'Elbe*, 166; MacKenzie counters the Oil Merchant by writing that the sailor's announcement came at eleven. MacKenzie, *The Escape from Elba*, 213.

227 **"tonight's ball has been":** Bartlett, *Elba*, 111.

227 **"to cede to no one":** Branda, *La guerre secrète*, Conclusion.

227 **Napoleon burned some:** MacKenzie, *The Escape from Elba*, 213–14.

227 **Mayor Traditi, struggling:** Grattan's account, in Campbell, *Napoleon*, 372–73; Pons, *Napoléon* (Bourachot edition), 7.

227 **"was sobbing all around":** Pons, *Souvenirs*, 384.

227 **"Elbans! Our august":** Peyrusse, *Mémorial*, 275; Napoleon's original letter to Lapi in Napoleon, *Correspondance*, XXVII, 451.

228 **"in violent agitation":** Peyrusse, *Mémorial*, 272.

228 **Peyrusse handed the captain:** Peyrusse, *Mémorial*, 273.

228 **Six hundred members:** Peyrusse, *Mémorial*, 275.

228 **Just under five hundred:** Marchand, *Mémoires*, VI.

228 **Even with all the:** Branda, *La guerre secrète*, XXVI.

229 **Whatever minuscule lead:** MacKenzie, *The Escape from Elba*, 217.

44: AT SEA

230 **It took until:** Napoleon, *Correspondance*, XXXI, 37–38.

230 **To look less conspicuous:** Napoleon, *Correspondance*, XXXI, 38.

231 **At midday the topsails:** Napoleon, *Correspondance*, XXXI, 37–38; MacKenzie, *The Escape from Elba*, 217–18.

231 **By early afternoon:** MacKenzie, *The Escape from Elba*, 220.

231 **Napoleon might also:** MacKenzie, *The Escape from Elba*, 220.

231 **The log from the *Partridge*:** MacKenzie, *The Escape from Elba*, 220.

231 **Merchant vessels sailed:** MacKenzie, *The Escape from Elba*, 220.

232 **"At 9 p.m.":** Campbell, *Napoleon*, 371–72.

232 **This could have been:** MacKenzie, *The Escape from Elba*, 221.

232 **"we must have been":** Campbell, *Napoleon*, 372. It is possible, though very unlikely, that Adye and Campbell did in fact recognize Napoleon's ships and simply chose not to pursue them.

232 **The ship's captain:** MacKenzie, *The Escape from Elba*, 220.

232 **"We knew enough":** Napoleon, *Correspondance*, XXXI, 38.

233 **"against deceiving himself":** MacKenzie, *The Escape from Elba*, 221.

233 **The captains of:** MacKenzie, *The Escape from Elba*, 221.

233 **The day's most baffling:** Branda, *La guerre secrète*, XXVII; MacKenzie, *The Escape from Elba*, 222; Peyrusse, *Mémorial*, 276.

233 **When the *Zéphir*:** Peyrusse, *Mémorial*, 276.

233 **He later claimed:** Napoleon, *Correspondance*, XXXI, 40.

233 **On Saint Helena:** Napoleon, *Correspondance*, XXXI, 40; Gourgaud, *Talks*, 169–70.

233 **Andrieux, for his part:** Branda, *La guerre secrète*, XXVII; MacKenzie, *The Escape from Elba*, 222–23.

234 **Peyrusse claimed that:** Peyrusse, *Mémorial*, 276. "Ali," *Napoleon*, 102, also mentions Andrieux asking after Napoleon's health.

234 **Later, the Polish:** Broughton (Hobhouse), *The Substance of Some Letters*, 54. Mariotti later claimed that if the *Zéphir* had only reached him two days earlier than it did, "I should have given such instructions that the Inconstant would either have been captured or sent to the bottom with her cargo," but Andrieux's actions indicate that Mariotti's orders, however cunning, might not have been obeyed. In early March 1815, an Italian spy would swear in a letter to his superior that he had been at a dinner in Livorno with both Campbell and Mariotti in which a French captain was also present who said that he had encountered Napoleon's ships and let them pass. See MacKenzie, *The Escape from Elba*, 223; Weil, *Les dessous du Congrès de Vienne*, 324.

234 **"a day to match":** Peyrusse, *Mémorial*, 276.

234 **"their Gallic heritage":** Marchand, *Mémoires*, VII.

234 **It was a variation:** Several biographers and historians have similarly made the point that Napoleon was adept at convincing his soldiers they would be remembered for their actions, but here I draw most specifically on Andrew Roberts, who has written that Napoleon's "constant references to the ancient world had the intended effect of giving ordinary soldiers a sense that their lives—and should it come to that, their deaths in battle—mattered, that they were an integral part of a larger whole that would resonate in French history. There are few things in the art of leadership harder to achieve than this, and no more powerful impetus to action. Napoleon taught ordinary people that they could make history, and convinced his followers they were taking part in an adventure, a pageant, an experiment, an epic whose splendour would draw the attention of posterity for centuries to come." Roberts, *Napoleon*, 134–35.

234 **"I know . . . at Portoferraio":** From Drouot's trial, in Saint-Edmé, *Repertoire*, 400. See also Branda, *La guerre secrète*, XXVI. Marchand, *Mémoires*, VII, alludes to Drouot's lack of participation by claiming that he spent the crossing seasick in his cabin.

235 **"the moon was full":** Marchand, *Mémoires*, VII.

45: CAMPBELL LANDS AT ELBA

236 **Campbell set off:** Campbell, *Napoleon*, 372.

236 **The port was quiet:** As the Oil Merchant had noted in his journal the day before, the only remnants of Napoleon's entourage were "the women, and some of the household staff." Pellet, *Napoléon à l'île d'Elbe*, 168.

236 Campbell headed toward: Alger suggests that this man was likely the father of the novelist and traveler Thomas Colley Grattan. Alger, *Napoleon's British Visitors*, 302.

237 "fired at or seized": Campbell, *Napoleon*, 372–75. Grattan's account, as recorded in Campbell's journal, is the most detailed description we have of Napoleon's last day on Elba. Some of Grattan's details may be embroidered, though Campbell noted in his journal that a few hours after talking with Grattan he talked with a Piedmontese surgeon with whom he had often dined at the Bertrands', and this surgeon's account corroborated Grattan's account of the escape. As far as Campbell's own account of returning to Portoferraio on the twenty-eighth, the details of his journal entry are corroborated by the Oil Merchant's report from February 28, in Pellet, *Napoléon à l'île d'Elbe*, 169–70.

237 "alternately smiling . . . at first": Campbell, *Napoleon*, 374–75. According to Fanny's later recollection of the same conversation, Campbell said that he knew for certain Napoleon was heading to Naples, which reassured her that he had been bluffing about the capture, because by that point she knew they were heading to France. Napoleon, *Correspondance*, XXXI, 39. See also MacKenzie, *The Escape from Elba*, 224.

238 "as one of the Commissioners": Campbell, *Napoleon*, 375.

238 Though bluffing, Campbell: MacKenzie, *The Escape from Elba*, 223. This "rash threat," writes MacKenzie, "can only be explained by the fact that Campbell was beside himself with rage, or by some undisclosed knowledge that the Allies would treat any escape as the signal for a new conflict."

238 "to prevent misery": Campbell, *Napoleon*, 376.

238 He also hoped: Campbell, *Napoleon*, 376.

239 "drawing her chair": Campbell, *Napoleon*, 376.

239 "She asked me": Campbell, *Napoleon*, 377.

239 "laid hold of": Campbell, *Napoleon*, 377.

239 "two or three minutes": Campbell, *Napoleon*, 377.

240 "more reconcilable . . . considered traitors": Campbell, *Napoleon*, 379.

241 "No part of Napoleon's": Campbell, *Napoleon*, 379.

241 "and thus made": Campbell, *Napoleon*, 379.

241 "restless and . . . that quarter": Campbell, *Napoleon*, 380–81.

241 "With the free sovereignty": Campbell, *Napoleon*, 381.

46: OUR BEAUTIFUL FRANCE

243 "We're either . . . Not quite": Laborde, *Napoleon et sa Garde*, 51-52.

243 "revived our spirits": Peyrusse, *Mémorial*, 277.

243 Napoleon teased him: Peyrusse, *Mémorial*, 277.

244 "join the other": Austin, *1815*, 18.

244 "had learned . . . badge of shame!": The proclamations can be found in Marchand, *Mémoires*, VII. For excerpts in English, see MacKenzie, *The Escape from Elba*, 228.

244 "were made by hand": Gourgaud, *Talks*, 171.

245 Drouot signed his name: Saint-Edmé, *Repertoire*, 416.

245 Napoleon later claimed: Austin, *1815*, 289.

245 "There is no precedent": Peyrusse, *Mémorial*, 278.

245 Marchand wrote that: Marchand, *Mémoires*, VII. "Never has the old saying that no man is a hero to his valet been less true than of the twenty-four-year-old Louis Marchand," writes Paul Britten Austin: *1815*, 20.

245 "Look at our": Pons, *Mémoire de Pons de l'Hérault aux puissances alliées*, 138.

245 The final evening: Pons, *Mémoire de Pons de l'Hérault aux puissances alliées*, 138.

47: The *Partridge* in Pursuit

246 **The captain, de Garat:** Campbell, *Napoleon*, 383–87. Campbell describes the meeting with de Garat in detail and the published version of his journal contains de Garat's later testimony concerning the same events. As MacKenzie points out, de Garat's testimony is confusing. He made, writes MacKenzie, the "forceful and misleading claim that the *Inconstant* and the rest of the flotilla could not have passed Capraia, because he [de Garat] was lying to the north-west of the island all Monday afternoon and north-east of it on Monday night and Tuesday morning. Since Napoleon undoubtedly sailed north of Capraia on Monday afternoon de Garat was not telling the truth. Either he had been away from his station and had let the convoy through by default, or he had been where he claimed to be and let it pass by design. But whatever his reason for deceiving Campbell his story had serious consequences." MacKenzie, *The Escape from Elba*, 226.

48: Golfe-Juan

248 **At sunrise on:** For details about the landing at Golfe-Juan, my main sources are "Ali," *Napoleon*, 103–5; Austin, *1815*, 22–28; Gourgaud, *Talks*, 170–73; Houssaye, *1815*, 206–10; Laborde, *Napoleon et sa Garde*, 70–79; MacKenzie, *The Escape from Elba*, 228–29; Marchand, *Mémoires*, VII; Napoleon, *Correspondance*, XXXI, 40–43; Peyrusse, *Mémorial*, 279–81. For descriptions of Golfe-Juan and Vallauris as they would have looked then, I have drawn on Bartoli, *Vallauris*.

248 **"I have long weighed":** Broughton (Hobhouse), *The Substance of Some Letters*, 55. Napoleon's speech is quoted by Hobhouse, who claimed to have written it verbatim from the recollection of Colonel Jerzmanowski.

249 **"Where are you off to":** Austin, *1815*, 22.

249 **The commander and:** Austin, *1815*, 23.

249 **"a great . . . this narrative":** Gourgaud, *Talks*, 170–71.

250 **Peyrusse, who for:** Peyrusse, *Mémorial*, 279.

250 **"find only friends":** Houssaye, *1815*, 209.

250 **"I heard . . . organize themselves":** Gourgaud, *Talks*, 172.

251 **The prisoners were transferred:** Campbell, *Napoleon*, 390.

251 **Filidoro, the Elban portmaster:** Filidoro lived the rest of his life as a wandering mariner, forever looking over his shoulder, surviving in this peripatetic existence for decades, and never caught by Bourbon officials. Branda, *La guerre secrète*, Conclusion.

49: Most Reluctantly I Have Felt Called Upon to Mention It

252 **The Oil Merchant finally:** Pellet, *Napoléon à l'île d'Elbe*, 170–73.

252 **He arrived at Livorno:** Branda, *La guerre secrète*, Conclusion.

252 **In Florence, Mariotti:** Branda, *La guerre secrète*, Conclusion.

252 **"It is . . . been avoided":** "Burghersh to Castlereagh, March 3, 1815," Weigall, *Correspondence*, 108–9.

50: In an Iron Cage

254 **Word of Napoleon's landing:** Sauvigny, *Bourbon Restoration*, 93.

254 **A line of:** Houssaye, *1815*, 225.

254 **No one was sure:** O'Brien, *Mrs. Adams*, 198; Lefebvre, *Napoléon*, 580.

254 **At the Tuileries:** Sauvigny, *Bourbon Restoration*, 93.

254 "It is just as well": Schom, *One Hundred Days*, 12.

254 "in an iron cage": Alexander, *Bonapartism*, 1.

255 "Let's pack it up!": *L'enjambée imperiale* (Paris, March 1815), Bibliothèque nationale de France, Estampes et Photographes, QB-370 (72)-FT; Broadley, *Napoleon in Caricature*, II, 62. See also Waresquiel, "Talleyrand au congrés de Vienne"; and the University of Warwick's rich online resource, "The Last Stand: Napoleon's 100 Days in 100 Objects," which sheds light on the history of these kinds of "enjambée" images. The Order of the Extinguishers was a creation of the satirical French newspaper *Le Nain Jaune*.

255 "temerity . . . with apprehension": Burney, *Diaries and Letters*, 301.

255 "a torpor indescribable": Burney, *Diary and Letters*, 301.

255 She knew his character: Burney, *Diary and Letters*, 301.

255 "so degraded and": Berry, *Extracts*, 43.

51: URGENT

256 "The English Commissary": Metternich, *Memoirs*, II, 254. King helpfully points out that Metternich, writing years after the event, had mistakenly remembered the letter coming from Genoa; King points to contemporary sources confirming that the letter had in fact been sent from Livorno. King, *Vienna*, 335.

256 "said to me . . . with me": Metternich, *Memoirs*, II, 254.

257 "The war": Metternich, *Memoirs*, II, 254.

257 He was speaking figuratively: King, *Vienna*, 229.

257 When Metternich told: Metternich, *Memoirs*, II, 254; "Report to Hager, March 12, 1815," Weil, *Les dessous du Congrès de Vienne*, 320. Metternich, in recalling this conversation long after the fact, made the dubious claim that he had by then already guessed that Napoleon would land in France and head straight for Paris.

257 "be seized the moment": King, *Vienna*, 230.

257 "believe that he would": "Talleyrand to Louis, March 7, 1815," Talleyrand-Périgord, *The Correspondence of Prince Talleyrand and King Louis XVIII*, 197–99.

257 "the consequences of this": "Talleyrand to Louis, March 7, 1815," Talleyrand-Périgord, *The Correspondence of Prince Talleyrand and King Louis XVIII*, 197–99; on Talleyrand's implying that they could do away with both Napoleon and Murat, see Harris, *Talleyrand*, 254.

258 "I will . . . against him": "Talleyrand to Louis, March 7, 1815," Talleyrand-Périgord, *The Correspondence of Prince Talleyrand and King Louis XVIII*, 197–99.

258 Back at Schönbrunn: Palmer, *Napoleon and Marie Louise*, 196.

258 "There was dinner": Méneval, *Memoirs of Napoleon*, 1129.

258 "At this moment when": Palmer, *Napoleon and Marie Louise*, 196; Weil, *Les dessous du Congrès de Vienne*, 303. On the reason for writing in French, see Palmer, *Napoleon and Marie Louise*, 196.

259 But speculation about: King, *Vienna*, 230.

259 "Though there was every": Castlereagh, *Correspondence*, X, 264–65.

259 "The events . . . invisible magician": Eynard, *Journal*, 21.

259 "Are we Napoleon's keepers?": "Reports to Hager, March 8 and 12, 1815," Weil, *Les dessous du Congrès de Vienne*, 298, 318. Talleyrand, in his letter to Louis XVIII, wrote that "the English, whose duty it was to watch his movements, were guilty of a negligence which they will find it difficult to excuse." Tallyrand-Périgord, *The Correspondence of Prince Talleyrand and King Louis XVIII*, 198.

259 "as if they had": King, *Vienna*, 232.

259 "the news spread": Garde-Chambonas, *Fêtes*, 507–8.

260 "All festivities ceased": Méneval, *Memoirs of Napoleon*, 1130.

260 His governess, Madame: Palmer, *Napoleon and Marie Louise*, 197; King, *Vienna*, 243–44.

260 "beyond the pale": "Déclaration des Puissances signataires du Traité de Paris, réunies au Congrès de Vienne au sujet de l'évasion de Napoléon de l'île d'Elbe, March 13, 1815," d'Angeberg, *Le Congrès*, II, 912–13.

260 To rhetorically place: Price, *Napoleon*, 252.

52: LAFFREY

262 They shouted their vivas: Concerning Laffrey, my main sources have been Austin, *1815*, 142–49; Bell, *Napoleon*, 1–4; Houssaye, *1815*, 240–46; Laborde, *Napoleon et sa Garde*, 88–94; Marchand, *Mémoires*, VII. Napoleon's words are commemorated with a plaque at Laffrey, placed there in 1843. Bell reminds us that this dramatic confrontation was in some ways "stage-managed," as "one of Napoleon's officers had met with a royalist officer before the confrontation, and the royalist had confessed that his men would probably refuse to fire on their former sovereign. Napoleon's envoy then suggested, with a crowd of royalist soldiers listening in, that Napoleon could make a personal appeal. While the emperor could not know for sure that the royalists would hold their fire, when he opened his coat on the afternoon of March 7, he did so with reasonable confidence that his gesture would have the intended effect." More details about the preparations for Laffrey can be found in Houssaye, *1815*, 240–44. Bell argues that "this stage-management is, in its own way, as important as the drama itself for understanding Napoleon's life," as it demonstrates how much he keenly understood the political value of a well-crafted public image. Bell has written that Napoleon "was a product of the first great modern age of celebrity, and he understood, viscerally, how to manage celebrity in the service of power."

53: TO CONTEMPLATE ALL OBJECTS AT A CERTAIN ANGLE

263 "the glorious chance": Campbell, *Napoleon*, 388.

263 Only after two: Austin, *1815*, 22; Campbell, *Napoleon*, 389.

263 Campbell found it: Campbell, *Napoleon*, 390.

264 He stayed in the area: Campbell, *Napoleon*, 394.

264 His ensuing journal entries: Campbell, *Napoleon*, 395–98.

264 His journal leaves: Campbell, *Napoleon*, 398.

264 His younger brother: "Hobhouse diary, March 21, 1815," Cochran, *Byron, Napoleon*, 51.

264 "inconceivable why so": "Hamburgh Mail," *Times* (London), March 23, 1815.

264 "too much . . . in Germany": "Hobhouse Diary Entry, April, 18, 1815," Cochran, *Byron, Napoleon*, 119.

265 Though Campbell's full journal: Broughton (Hobhouse), *The Substance of Some Letters*, 5.

265 "a very commonplace . . . of stature": Broughton (Hobhouse), *The Substance of Some Letters*, 5.

EPILOGUE: NAPOLEON, MARIE LOUISE, CAMPBELL, AND ELBA

267 "They let me come": Guizot, *Mémoires*, I, 57.

267 He wrote to Marie Louise: Palmer, *Napoleon and Marie Louise*, 198; Palmstierna, *My Dearest Louise*, 176.

267 He wanted her and: Palmer, *Napoleon and Marie Louise*, 198.

267 She said she would rather enter: "Hager report, April 14, 1815," Weil, *Les dessous du Congrès de Vienne*, 465.

267 **Caulaincourt returned the:** Palmstierna, *My Dearest Louise*, 176.

267 **One morning in May:** Palmer, *Napoleon and Marie Louise*, 198–99; Guedalla, *The Hundred Days*, 84.

268 **"We are all . . . be forgotten":** "Lord Liverpool to Lord Castlereagh, July 21, 1815," Castlereagh, *Correspondence*, X, 434.

268 **Though the results:** On the Napoleonic myth, see Hazareesingh, *The Legend of Napoleon* and *Saint-Napoleon;* Jourdan, *Mythes.*

268 **"had portrayed himself":** Hazareesingh, *The Legend of Napoleon*, 17.

269 **In 1836, Joseph Beaume:** Beaume's work is among the collection at Versailles, though it was also on loan for a time to the Naval and Napoleonic Museum on the boulevard John F. Kennedy in Antibes.

269 **Two years later:** Faure, *Au pays de Stendhal*, 59–61.

269 **"Bonaparte, in debarking":** Chateaubriand, *Memoirs*, 323.

269 **"walking on the same":** Faure, *Au pays de Stendhal*, 59–61.

269 **"a return which was":** Dumas, *The Count of Monte Cristo*, chapter 13.

269 **"the extraordinary episode":** Las Cases, *Memorial*, November 4, 1816.

270 **"The Emperor is":** Bertrand, *Cahiers de Sainte-Hélène*, III, 168.

270 **She finally attained:** d'Angeberg, *Le Congrès*, II, 1426.

270 **"I hope that we":** Palmer, *Napoleon and Marie Louise*, 201.

271 **Facing a firing squad:** Palmer, *Napoleon and Marie Louise*, 205.

271 **She married Neipperg:** Palmer, *Napoleon and Marie Louise*, 207–15.

271 **"speak truthfully . . . while":** Castelot, *Napoleon's Son*, 195.

271 **"The love of glory":** Englund, *Napoleon*, 149. Englund points out that the valediction of the will constituted Napoleon's final public utterance.

272 **Unlike so many:** Englund notes Marie Louise's distinction in being one of the few people close to Napoleon to produce no memoir. Englund, "Napoleon: The Unsolved Enigma," *New York Review of Books*.

272 **"was feared that my":** Campbell, *Napoleon*, 112.

272 **He rejoined the regiment:** Campbell, *Napoleon*, 112–13.

273 **He continued to be:** *Napoléon quittant l'Ile d'Elbe pendant que les gardiens sont endormis*, undated, unsigned, Bibliothèque nationale de France, Estampes et Photographes, QB-201 (156).

273 **"England had favored:** "Exposé in Justification of Marshal Ney," *Times* (London), September 6, 1815.

273 **"an excess of . . . navy of Britain":** House of Commons, *The Times* (London), April 7, 1815.

273 **"as to diplomatic agents":** "House of Commons," *Times* (London), April 7, 1815. A rebuttal came in another session of the House of Commons a few days later: Why, Mr. Elliott asked Castlereagh, had "the noble lord consented to place [Bonaparte] near to France and Italy, and after having placed him there, took no precaution for his return? . . . If he had an officer of great merit in the island, in what situation was he to be considered? Was he there in a diplomatic character, or was he in a confidential situation? If Colonel Campbell was placed there for the purpose of corresponding with the government, [he] should like to know what communications had been made to ministers." Had Campbell informed ministers that Napoleon had raised troops on the island, as was clear from his escape? And did Castlereagh pass along that information to his allies? Campbell's nephew inserted the following version of Castlereagh's speech from the same day: "With respect to the residence and situation of this personage at Elba, whatever may be my own individual opinion upon the subject of the arrangement which gave to him that jurisdiction—whatever objections I may have had to this settlement from the beginning, and the opportunities of its locality afforded for the realization of what has

unhappily since occurred—there can, I trust, exist but one feeling among liberal minds, and that is, that when this island was given to Bonaparte for his residence, that residence should comprise the portion of fair and free liberty which was then due to a person in his situation. When the island was secured to him by treaty; it was of course done with as much exercise of personal liberty as became the compact; it was never in the contemplation of the parties that he should be a prisoner within that settlement, that he should be the compulsory inmate of any tower, fortress, or citadel; they never meant that he should be so placed, or that he should be deprived of sea excursions in the vicinity of the island for the fair purposes of recreation.

The Allied Powers who concurred in the Treaty of Fontainebleau never undertook to conduct a system of espionage, either within or without the residence which they had ceded to him; it was never in their contemplation to establish a naval police to hem in, or prevent this man's committing himself, as he has done, to his fortunes. In fact, if they were so inclined, they were without the means of enforcing such a system; for the best authorities in our Government were of opinion; that it was absolutely and physically impossible to draw a line of circumvallation around Elba; and for this very conclusive reason—that, considering the variation of weather, and a variety of other circumstances, which could not be controlled, the whole British navy would be inadequate for such a purpose. I repeat that our Government never took a police establishment at Elba. Colonel Campbell was certainly there, for the purpose of occasionally communicating with our Government upon such matters as might pass under his observation both there and in Italy; where at that time we had no accredited agents: he was there at first merely as one of the conductors, according to the treaty; and I afterwards suffered him to remain between that island and Livorno for the purpose I have mentioned; but nothing more was contemplated. It would have been out of Colonel Campbell's power to have attempted anything further—he could not have done it; for the fact was that, although at first treated with familiarity by Bonaparte, his visits were subsequently disapproved of: latterly he found the greatest difficulty in obtaining an interview with him, so completely did the latter surround himself with imperial etiquette." Campbell, *Napoleon*, 105–6; "House of Commons," *Times* (London), April 20, 1815.

274 **In 1826, restless:** Note that between the terms of the governor killed by an Ashanti soldier (Charles MacCarthy, 1821–24) and the governor who died of yellow fever (Charles Turner, 1824–26) there were two brief periods where Sierra Leone was controlled by acting governors.

274 **He ruled ruthlessly:** Campbell's post-Waterloo biography is traced in Campbell, *Napoleon*, 125–50.

274 **He was buried:** Fyfe, "Circular Road Burial Ground."

274 **"I attach . . . a casino":** Napoleon, *A Selection from the Letters*, 356.

POSTSCRIPT

277 **"My great talent":** Englund, *Napoleon*, 59.

277 **"What a pity":** Leys, *The Death of Napoleon*, 2.

277 **"In man's life":** Marcus Aurelius, *Meditations*, 15.

278 **"In his 'romantic and epic dream'":** Herold, *The Mind of Napoleon*, xxxiv.

278 **He and his collaborators:** In using the term "collaborators," I draw on the work of Isser Woloch.

279 **"I walk with":** Bell, *Napoleon*, 41.

279 **"respected abroad and":** Englund, *Napoleon*, 173.

279 **To walk with gods:** Bell argues that Napoleon, "despite his taste for conquest, was no conscious advocate of total war (still less was he the bloodthirsty megalomaniac of legend). But it

was the radical intensification of war that brought him to prominence and power, and in the end, he could not contain it. He was, in turn, the product, master, and victim of total war." Bell also cites François Furet's description of Napoleon's apotheosis at Marengo as "the result of the most one-sided contract that a nation had ever made with its leader, who was forced into a commitment never to be beaten." Bell, *Total War*, 8, 227.

279 **"It may be a costly"**: Herold, *The Mind of Napoleon*, xxxix.

279 **"so well off"**: Gourgaud, *Talks*, 167–68. I've translated the French idiomatic expression "Ma foi! [literally, My faith!]," meant to sum up a statement with emphasis, as "Well!" Others might choose to translate "Ma foi!" as "Frankly!"; "Honestly!"; or "Indeed!" Napoleon also told Gourgaud "that what also induced him to return to France was that people said he had shunned death, and was a coward."

BIBLIOGRAPHY

CORRESPONDENCE, MEMOIRS,
AND OTHER PRIMARY SOURCES

d'Abrantès, Laure Junot, duchesse. *Memoirs of Napoleon, His Court, and Family.*
Bentley, 1836.

Alexander I and Grand Duchess Catherine. *Scenes of Russian Court Life: Being the*
Correspondence of Alexander I and His Sister Catherine. Translated by Henry
Havelock. Jarrolds, 1917.

"Ali" (Louis-Étienne Saint-Denis). *Napoleon from the Tuileries to St. Helena.*
Translated by Frank Potter. Harper, 1922.

d'Angeberg, comte. *Le Congrès de Vienne et les traités de 1815, précédé et suivi des*
actes diplomatiques qui s'y rattachent. Amyot, 1863, 2 vols.

Bainvel, Pierre-Marie. *Souvenirs d'un écolier: Épisode de 1815.* Pillet, 1846.

Barras, Paul. *Mémoires.* Edited by George Duruy. Hachette, 1895–96, 4 vols.

Bary, Émile. *Les cahiers d'un rhétoricien de 1815.* Hachette, 1890.

Beauharnais, Eugène de. *Mémoires et correspondance politique et militaire*
du Prince Eugène, publiés, annotés, et mis en ordre pas A. du Casse. Paris,
1860, vol. X.

Beauharnais, Hortense de. *Memoirs of Queen Hortense.* Edited by Waxhall and
Wehran. Hurst and Brackett, 1864.

Berneaud, Arsenne Thiébaut de. *A Voyage to the Isle of Elba.* Translated by William
Jerdan. Longman, Hurst, Rees, Orme, and Brown, 1814.

Berry, Mary. *Extracts from the Journals and Correspondence of Miss Berry, 1753–1852.* Edited by Lady Theresa Lewis. Longman's, 1865, vol. III.

Bertrand, Henri. *Cahiers de Sainte-Hélène.* Edited by Paul Fleuriot de Langle. Albin Michel, 1949–59, 3 vols.

———. *Lettres à Fanny: 1808–1815.* Edited by Suzanne de la Vaissière-Orfila. Albin Michel, 1979.

Beugnot, comte. *Mémoires de comte Beugnot, ancien ministre, 1783–1815.* Dentu, 1868, 2 vols.

Boigne, Louise-Eléonore-Charlotte-Adélaide d'Osmond, comtesse de. *Memoirs of the Comtesse de Boigne, 1781–1814.* Edited by Charles Nicoullaud. Heinemann, 1907.

Bright, Richard. *Travels from Vienna Through Lower Hungary; With Some Remarks on the State of Vienna During the Congress, in the Year 1814.* Constable and Longman, 1818.

Broughton, John Cam Hobhouse, Baron. *The Substance of Some Letters.* M. Thomas, 1816.

Burney, Fanny. *The Diary and Letters of Madame d'Arblay (Frances Burney): 1792–1840.* Frederick Warne, 1892, vol. III.

Byron, George Gordon. *Byron's Letters and Journals.* Edited by Leslie A. Marchand. Harvard University Press, 1975, vols. IV–V.

Calvert, Frances. *An Irish Beauty of the Regency.* Edited by Warenne Blake. John Lane, 1911.

Campbell, Sir Neil, and Archibald Neil Campbell MacLachlan. *Napoleon at Fontainebleau and Elba: Being a Journal of Occurrences in 1814–1815.* John Murray, 1869.

Carnot, Lazare. *Mémoire adressé au Roi, en juillet 1814.* Chaumerot, 1815.

Castellane, Boniface de. *Journal du maréchal de Castellane, 1804–1862.* Plon, 1895.

Castlereagh, Viscount. *Correspondence, Despatches, and Other Papers of Viscount Castlereagh.* Edited by Charles William Vane. Colburn, 1850, vols. IX–X.

Caulaincourt, Armand-Augustin-Louis de. *Mémoires du général de Caulaincourt, duc de Vicence, grand écuyer de l'Empereur.* Plon, 1933, vol. III.

Chateaubriand, François-René de. *Memoirs from Beyond the Tomb.* Translated by Robert Baldick. Penguin, 2014.

Chautard, Joseph. *De Saint-Hélène aux Invalides: Souvenirs de Santini.* Lacombe, 1854.

Constable, Archibald, ed. "Documents Relative to the Counter-Revolution in France." *Scots Magazine: A General Repository of Literature, History, and Politics for 1814.* Sands, Brymer, Murray and Cochran, 1814, vol. 76.

Constant, Benjamin. *Mémoires sur les Cent-Jours, en forme de lettres*. Béchet, 1820–1823.

———. *Political Writings*. Edited and translated by Biancamaria Fontana. Cambridge University Press, 1988.

Ebrington, Lord. *Memorandum of Two Conversations Between the Emperor Napoleon and Viscount Ebrington*. Ridgway, 1823.

Eynard, Jean-Gabriel. *Journal de Jean-Gabriel Eynard*. Plon Nourrit, 1924.

Fain, Agathon-Jean-François. *Manuscrit de mil huit cent quatorze: Trouvé dans les voitures impériales prises à Waterloo*. Perrin, 1825.

Fleury de Chaboulon. *Mémoires pour servir à l'histoire de la vie privée, du retour et du règne de Napoléon en 1815*. John Murray, 1819, vol. I.

Fontaine, Pierre-François-Léonard. *Journal, 1799–1853*. École nationale supérieure des beaux-arts, 1987, 2 vols.

Fouché, Joseph. *Mémoires de Joseph Fouché, duc d'Otrante, ministre de la police générale*. Biblio, 1824.

Garde-Chambonas, Auguste Louis Charles, comte de La. *Fêtes et souvenirs du Congrès de Vienne; Tableaux des salons, scènes anecdotiques et portraits, 1814–1815*. Apper, 1842.

Gourgaud, Gaspard. *Talks of Napoleon at St. Helena*. McClurg, 1904.

Guizot, François. *History of France from the Earliest Times to the Year 1848*. Low & Searle, 1885, 8 vols.

———. *Mémoires pour servir à l'histoire de mon temps*. Lévy, 1858, 8 vols.

Hyde de Neuville, Jean-Guillaume. *Mémoires et souvenirs*. Plon, 1890, vol. II.

Laborde, Étienne. *Napoleon et sa Garde*. Desrez, 1840.

Las Cases, Emmanuel de. *Memorial de Sainte Helene: Journal of the Private Life and Conversations of the Emperor Napoleon at Saint Helena*. Thomas Smith, 1823.

Macdonald, Étienne-Jacques-Joseph-Alexandre. *Souvenirs du Maréchal Macdonald, duc de Tarente*. Plon, 1892.

Marchand, Louis. *Mémoires de Marchand: Premier valet de chambre et exécuteur testamentaire de l'empereur*. Edited by Jean Bourguignon and Henry Lachouque. Tallandier, 2003.

Marie Louise, Empress. *The Private Diaries of the Empress Marie-Louise, Wife of Napoleon I*. Edited by Frédéric Masson. John Murray, 1922.

Maxwell, Montgomery. *My Adventures*. Henry Colburn, 1845, vol. I.

Méneval, Claude-François de. *Memoirs of Napoleon Bonaparte: The Court of the First Empire*. Collier, 1910, vol. III.

———. *Memoirs to Serve for the History of Napoleon I from 1802 to 1815*. Translated by Robert H. Sherard. Hutchison & Co., 1894, 3 vols.

————. *Napoléon et Marie Louise.* Meline, 1843–45, 3 vols.

Méneval II. *Marie-Louise et la cour d'Autriche entre les deux abdications (1814–1815).* Émile-Paul, 1909.

Metternich, Klemens von. *Memoirs.* Edited by Prince Richard Metternich. Translated by Robina Napier. R. Bentley & Son, 1880, vol. II.

Montet, baronne du. *Souvenirs de la baronne du Montet, 1785–1866.* Plon, 1904.

Moore, Thomas. *Letters and Journals of Lord Byron with Notices of His Life.* John Murray, 1830.

Napoleon I. *Correspondance de Napoléon Ier.* Plon, 1858–70, 32 vols., vols. XXVII, XXXI.

————. *Le registre de l'île d'Elbe: Lettres et ordres inédits de Napoléon Ier: 28 mai 1814–22 février 1815.* Pélissier, 1897.

————. *Lettres de Napoléon à Joséphine, pendant la première campagne d'Italie, le consulat et l'empire, et lettres de Joséphine à Napoléon et à sa fille.* Firmin Didot, 1833, 2 vols.

————. *Mémoires de Napoléon, Tome 3: L'île d'Elbe et les Cent-Jours 1814–1815.* Edited by Thierry Lentz. Tallandier, 2013.

————. *A Selection from the Letters and Despatches of the First Napoleon: With Explanatory Notes.* Edited by D. A. Bingham. Cambridge University Press, 2010.

Nesselrode, Karl Robert, Count. *Lettres et papiers, 1760–1850.* Lahure, 1904, 11 vols.

Palmstierna, C. F., ed. *My Dearest Louise: Marie-Louise and Napoleon, 1813–1814: Unpublished Letters from the Empress with Previously Published Replies from Napoleon.* Translated by E. M. Wilkinson. Methuen, 1958.

Peyrusse, Guillaume. *Lettres inédites de Guillaume Peyrusse "à son frère André," 1809–1814.* Edited by Léon Pelissier. Plon, 1894.

————. *Mémorial et archives de M. le baron Peyrusse, 1809–1815.* Labau et Lajoux, 1869.

Pons de l'Hérault, André. *Mémoire de Pons de l'Hérault aux puissances alliées.* Picard, 1899.

————. *Napoléon, empereur de l'île d'Elbe: Souvenirs et anecdotes de Pons de l'Hérault.* Présenté et annoté par Christophe Bourachot. Les éditeurs libres, 2005.

————. *Napoléon, souverain de l'île d'Elbe: Mémoires de Pons de l'Hérault.* Plon, 1934.

————. *Souvenirs et anecdotes de l'île d'Elbe.* Pélissier, 1897.

Pozzo di Borgo, Carlo Andres, comte. *Correspondance diplomatique du comte Pozzo di Borgo, 1814–1818.* Lévy, 1890.

Rebuffat, J. "Portolongone durante il primo Impero." In *Archivio storico italiano.* Pélissier, 1895, ser. IV, vol. XVI, 293–98.

Roncière, Charles de La, ed. *Napoleon's Letters to Marie Louise.* Farrar & Rinehart, 1935.

Roustam Raza. *Souvenirs de Roustam.* Edited by Paul Cottin. Ollendorf, 1911.

Saint-Edmé, B., ed. *Repertoire général des causes célèbres.* Rossier, 1834, vol. II.

Savant, Jean, ed. *La déportation de Napoléon à l'île d'Elbe: D'après les archives de l'Institut (Bibliothèque Thiers, Fonds Frédéric Masson), documents inédits présentés et annotés.* Éditions Académie Napoléon, 1952.

Schuermans, Albert. *Souverain de l'île d'Elbe: Itinéraire général de Napoléon Ier.* Jouve, 1911.

Scott, John Barber. *An Englishman at Home and Abroad.* Heath Cranton, 1930.

———. *A Visit to Paris in 1814.* Longmans, 1816.

Scott, Walter. *The Letters of Sir Walter Scott.* Edited by H. J. C. Grierson. Constable, 1932–1937, 12 vols.

Staël-Holstein, Germaine de. *Considérations sur les principaux événements de la révolution française.* Charpentier, 1845.

———. *Ten Years Exile.* Translated by Doris Beik. Saturday Review Press, 1972.

Stanhope, Philip Henry Stanhope, Earl. *Notes of Conversations with the Duke of Wellington, 1831–1851.* Longmans, Green & Co., 1888.

Talleyrand-Périgord, Charles-Maurice de. *The Correspondence of Prince Talleyrand and King Louis XVIII During the Congress of Vienna.* Edited by M. G. Pallain. Harper, 1881.

———. *Mémoires du prince de Talleyrand.* Edited by the duc de Broglie. Paris, 1891–1892, 5 vols.

Tardieu and Denesle, eds. *Notice sur l'île d'Elbe: Contenant la description de ses villes, ports, places fortes.* Tardieu-Denesle, 1814.

Thibaudeau, Antoine Claire. *Mémoires de A. C. Thibaudeau.* Plon, 1913.

Underwood, Thomas Richard. *A Narrative of Memorable Events in Paris, Preceding the Capitulation, and During the Occupancy of That City by the Allied Armies in 1814.* Longmans, 1828.

Ussher, Thomas. *Napoleon Banished: The Journeys to Elba and to St. Helena Recorded in the Letters and Journal of Two British Naval Officers: Captain Thomas Ussher and Lieutenant Nelson Mills.* Rodale, 1955.

Vivian, John Henry. *Minutes of a Conversation with Napoleon Bonaparte During His Residence at Elba.* Ridgway, 1839.

Wairy, Louis Constant. *Mémoires de Constant.* L'Advocat, 1830, vol. VI.

Waldbourg-Truchsess, Friedrich Ludwig von. *Nouvelle relation de l'itinéraire de Napoléon de Fontainebleau à l'île d'Elbe.* Pancoucke, 1815.

Weigall, Rachel, ed. *Correspondence of Lord Burghersh.* John Murray, 1912.

Weigall, Rose, ed. *The Letters of Lady Burghersh.* John Murray, 1893.

Weil, Maurice-Henri. *Les dessous du Congrès de Vienne: D'après les documents originaux des archives du Ministère impérial et royal de l'intérieur à Vienne.* Payot, 1917.

Wellesley, Arthur, Duke of Wellington. *The Dispatches of Field Marshal the Duke of Wellington During His Various Campaigns.* Edited by Lieutenant Colonel Gurwood. John Murray, 1831, vol. XII.

———. *Supplementary Despatches and Memoranda of Field Marshal Arthur, Duke of Wellington.* Edited by His Son the Duke of Wellington. John Murray, 1872, vol. XIV.

KEY SECONDARY LITERATURE

Ackroyd, Peter. *London: The Biography.* Chatto & Windus, 2000.

Alder, Ken. *Engineering the Revolution: Arms and Enlightenment in France, 1763–1815.* Princeton University Press, 1997.

Alexander, Robert. *Bonapartism and Revolutionary Tradition in France: The Fédérés of 1815.* Cambridge University Press, 1991.

———. *Napoleon.* Oxford University Press, 2001.

Alger, John. *Napoleon's British Visitors and Captors: 1801–1815.* Archibald Constable, 1901.

Arnaud, François-Hector, and Antoine Caillot, eds. *Précis historique de la campagne de 1814.* Arnaud, 1814.

Ashton, John. *English Caricature and Satire on Napoleon I.* Chatto & Windus, 1888, vol. II.

Auricchio, Laura. *The Marquis: Lafayette Reconsidered.* Vintage, 2015.

Austin, Paul Britten. *1815: The Return of Napoleon.* Greenhill Books, 2002.

Baldensperger, Fernand. *Le Mouvement des idées dans l'émigration française, 1789–1815.* Plon, 1924.

Baring-Gould, Sabine. *The Life of Napoleon Bonaparte.* Methuen, 1897.

Barthes, Roland. *Camera Lucida.* Hill & Wang, 1980.

———. *Michelet.* Translated by Richard Howard. University of California Press, 1992.

Bartlett, Vernon. *A Book About Elba*. Chatto & Windus, 1965.

Bartoli, Camille. *Vallauris: Le jour ou Napoléon y débarqua*. Étude, 2005.

Beecher, Jonathan. *Charles Fourier: The Visionary and His World*. University of California Press, 1986.

Bell, David A. *Napoleon: A Concise Biography*. Oxford University Press, 2015.

————. *Shadows of Revolution: Reflections on France, Past and Present*. Oxford University Press, 2016.

————. *Total War: Napoleon's Europe and the Birth of Warfare as We Know It*. Mariner, 2008.

Ben-Amos, Avner. *Funerals, Politics, and Memory in Modern France, 1789–1996*. Oxford University Press, 2000.

Bew, John. *Castlereagh: A Life*. Oxford University Press, 2012.

Blanning, Tim. *The Pursuit of Glory: Europe 1648–1815*. Penguin, 2008.

————. *The Romantic Revolution: A History*. Modern Library, 2012.

Bonnett, Alastair. *Unruly Places: Lost Spaces, Secret Cities, and Other Inscrutable Geographies*. Houghton Mifflin, 2014.

Boudon, Jacques-Olivier. *Napoléon et les cultes: Les religions à l'aube de XIXe siècle (1800–1815)*. Fayard, 2002.

————. *Napoléon et la dernière campagne: Les Cent-Jours, 1815*. Armand Colin, 2015.

Branda, Pierre. *La guerre secrète de Napoléon*. Perrin, 2014.

Braudel, Fernand. *The Mediterranean and the Mediterranean World in the Age of Philip II*. University of California Press, 1995, vol. I.

Braudy, Leo. *The Frenzy of Renown: Fame and Its History*. Vintage, 1997.

Brett-James, Antony. *The Hundred Days: Napoleon's Last Campaign from Eyewitness Accounts*. St. Martin's, 1964.

Broadley, A. M. *Napoleon in Caricature: 1795–1821*. John Lane, 1911, 2 vols.

Broers, Michael. *The Napoleonic Empire in Italy, 1796–1814: Cultural Imperialism in a European Context?* Palgrave Macmillan, 2005.

————. *Napoleon: Soldier of Destiny*. Faber & Faber, 2014.

Brooke, John. *King George III*. Constable, 1972.

Bruce, Evangeline. *Napoleon and Josephine: An Improbable Marriage*. Scribner, 1995.

Byrne, William R. *A Naval Biographical Dictionary*. John Murray, 1849.

Calasso, Roberto. *The Ruin of Kasch*. Translated by William Weaver. Belknap, 1994.

Calvino, Italo. *Six Memos for the Next Millennium*. Harvard University Press, 1988.

Carlyle, Thomas. *The Works of Thomas Carlyle: The French Revolution*. Chapman and Hall, 1896.

Carpenter, Scott. *Aesthetics of Fraudulence in Nineteenth-Century France: Frauds, Hoaxes, and Counterfeits*. Routledge, 2009.

Casanova, Antoine. *Napoléon et la pensée de son temps*. Boutique de l'histoire, 2008.

Casse, Albert du. *Le général Arrighi de Casanova, duc de Padoue*. Dentu, 1866, vol. II.

Castelot, André. *Napoleon's Son*. Hamish Hamilton, 1960.

Chandler, David G. *The Campaigns of Napoleon*. Simon & Schuster, 2009.

———. *Dictionary of the Napoleonic Wars*. Simon & Schuster, 1993.

Chartier, Roger. *The Cultural Origins of the French Revolution*. Translated by Lydia G. Cochrane. Duke University Press, 1991.

Chernow, Ron. *Alexander Hamilton*. Penguin Press, 2004.

Chevallier, Bernard, Roberta Martinelli, and Monica Guaraccinno. *Le Mobilier: L'inventario della residenza imperiale di Napoleone all'Elba*. Livorno, 2005.

Christophe, Robert. *Napoleon on Elba*. Translated by Len Ortzen. Macdonald, 1964.

Chuquet, Arthur. *Les cent jours: Le départ de l'île d'Elbe*. Leroux, 1920.

———. *La jeunesse de Napoléon: La Révolution*. Colin, 1898.

Claassen, J. M. *Displaced Persons: The Literature of Exile from Cicero to Boethius*. Duckworth, 1999.

Cochran, Peter. *Byron, Napoleon, J. C. Hobhouse and the Hundred Days*. Cambridge Scholars Publishing, 2015.

Cohen, Margaret. *The Novel and the Sea*. Princeton University Press, 2010.

———. *Profane Illumination: Walter Benjamin and the Paris of Surrealist Revolution*. University of California Press, 1995.

Cole, Juan. *Napoleon's Egypt: Invading the Middle East*. Palgrave Macmillan, 2007.

Collins, Irene. *The Government and the Newspaper in France, 1814–1881*. Oxford University Press, 1959.

Colmache, Charles-Maurice de. *Revelations of the Life of Prince Talleyrand*. Colburn, 1850.

Cooper, Duff. *Talleyrand*. Grove Press, 2001.

Coote, Stephen. *Napoleon and the Hundred Days*. Da Capo, 2005.

Corbin, Alain. *The Lure of the Sea: The Discovery of the Seaside in the Western World, 1750–1840*. University of California Press, 1994.

Cronin, Vincent. *Napoleon*. London, 1994.

Dallas, Gregor. *The Final Act: The Roads to Waterloo*. Henry Holt, 1997.

Darnton, Robert. *The Great Cat Massacre: And Other Episodes in French Cultural History*. Basic Books, 2009.

Davidson, Denise. *France After Revolution: Urban Life, Gender and the New Social Order*. Harvard University Press, 2007.

Davidson, Ian. *Voltaire in Exile*. Grove Press, 2006.

Davies, Peter. *The Extreme Right in France, 1789 to the Present*. Routledge, 2002.

Demerliac, Alain. *La marine du Consulat et du Premier Empire: Nomenclature des navires français de 1800 à 1815*. Ancre, 2003.

Derry, J. W. *Castlereagh*. London, 1976.

Driault, Edouard. *The True Visage of Napoleon*. Translated by W. Savage. Morancé, 1929.

Dubois, Laurent. *Avengers of the New World: The Story of the Haitian Revolution*. Belknap, 2005.

Dunn, Susan. *The Deaths of Louis XVI: Regicide and the French Political Imagination*. Princeton University Press, 2008.

Dwyer, Philip. *Citizen Emperor: Napoleon in Power*. Yale University Press, 2013.

———. *Napoleon: The Path to Power*. Yale University Press, 2008.

———. *Talleyrand: Profiles in Power*. Routledge, 2016.

Edelstein, Dan. *The Terror of Natural Right: Republicanism, the Cult of Nature, and the French Revolution*. University of Chicago Press, 2009.

Edmond, Rod, and Vanessa Smith, eds. *Islands in History and Representation*. Routledge, 2001.

Englund, Steven. *Napoleon: A Political Life*. Scribner, 2004.

Esdaile, Charles. *Napoleon's Wars: An International History*. Penguin, 2009.

Faure, Gabriel. *Au pays de Stendhal*. Rey, 1920.

Fayot, M. *Précis historique sur le duc de Reichstadt, avec son portrait*. Mansut, 1832.

Fenby, Jonathan. *France: A Modern History from the Revolution to the War with Terror*. St. Martin's, 2016.

Firmin-Didot, Georges. *Royauté ou Empire: La France en 1814*. Firmin-Didot, 1897.

Fisher, H. A. L. *Bonapartism: Six Lectures Delivered in the University of London*. Oxford Clarendon Press, 1914.

Forrest, Alan. *Conscripts and Deserters: The Army and French Society During the Revolution and Empire*. Oxford, 1989.

———. *Napoleon*. Quercus, 2011.

Forrest, Alan, Étienne François, and Karen Hagemann, eds. *War Memories: The Revolutionary and Napoleonic Wars in Modern European Culture*. Palgrave Macmillan, 2013.

Franc-Lecomte, P. *Histoire de Napoléon II, né roi de Rome, mort duc de Reichstadt*. Paris, 1832.

Fraser, Elisabeth. *Delacroix, Art and Patrimony in Post-Revolutionary France*. Cambridge University Press, 2004.

Fraser, Flora. *Pauline Bonaparte: Venus of Empire*. Knopf, 2009.

Fritzsche, Peter. *Stranded in the Present: Modern Time and the Melancholy of History*. Harvard University Press, 2004.

Gachot, Edouard. *Marie-Louise Intime*. Talandier, 1911–12.

Gaertner, Jan Felix. *Writing Exile*. Brill, 2007.

Garros, Louis, and Jean Tulard. *Napoléon au jour le jour, 1769–1821*. Tallandier, 2002.

Gengenbre, Gérard. *Napoleon: The Immortal Emperor*. Vendome, 2003.

Geyl, Pieter. *Napoleon: For and Against*. Yale University Press, 1949.

Gillis, John R. *Islands of the Mind: How the Human Imagination Created the Atlantic World*. Palgrave, 2004.

Girard, Philippe. *Toussaint Louverture: A Revolutionary Life*. Basic Books, 2016.

Godechot, Jacques, Beatrice F. Hyslop, and David L. Dowd. *The Napoleonic Era in Europe*. Holt, Rinehart & Winston, 1971.

Godlewski, Guy. *Napoléon à l'île d'Elbe, 300 jours d'exil*. Nouveau monde/ Fondation Napoléon, 2003.

Goldstein, Robert. *Censorship of Political Caricature in Nineteenth-Century France*. Kent State University Press, 1989.

Gorce, Pierre de La. *La Restauration: Louis XVIII*. Plon, 1926.

Graham, Peter. *Byron's Bulldog: The Letters of John Cam Hobhouse to Lord Byron*. Ohio State University Press, 1984.

Grove, Richard. *Green Imperialism: Colonial Expansion, Tropical Island Edens, and the Origins of Environmentalism*. Cambridge University Press, 1995.

Gruyer, Paul. *Napoleon: King of Elba*. Lippincott, 1906.

Guedalla, Philip. *The Hundred Days*. Putnam's, 1934.

Gueniffey, Patrice. *Bonaparte: 1769–1802*. Translated by Steven Rendall. Belknap, 2015.

———. *Histoires de la Révolution et de l'Empire*. Perrin, 2013.

Habermas, Jurgen. *The Structural Transformation of the Public Sphere: An Inquiry into a Category of Bourgeois Society*. Translated by Thomas Burger. MIT Press, 1993.

Hanley, Wayne. *The Genesis of Napoleonic Propaganda, 1796–1799*. Columbia University Press, 2002.

Harris, Robin. *Talleyrand: Betrayer and Saviour of France*. John Murray, 2007.

Harvey, A. D. *English Literature and the Great War with France*. Nold Jonson, 1981.

Harvey, David. *The Condition of Postmodernity: An Enquiry into the Origins of Cultural Change*. Wiley, 1990.

Hazan, Eric. *The Invention of Paris: A History in Footsteps*. Verso, 2011.

Hazareesingh, Sudhir. *The Legend of Napoleon*. Granta, 2005.

————. *The Saint-Napoleon: Celebrations of Sovereignty in Nineteenth-Century France*. Harvard University Press, 2004.

Healey, F. G. *The Literary Culture of Napoleon*. Droz, 1959.

Herold, J. Christopher. *The Mind of Napoleon: A Selection from His Written and Spoken Words*. Columbia University Press, 1955.

Hibbert, Christopher. *George III: A Personal History*. Basic Books, 2000.

————. *Napoleon: His Wives and Women*. Norton, 2002.

Hill, J. R. *The Oxford Illustrated History of the Royal Navy*. Oxford University Press, 1995.

Hobsbawm, Eric. *The Age of Revolution, 1789–1848*. Vintage, 1996.

Hobsbawm, Eric, and Terence Ranger, eds. *The Invention of Tradition*. Cambridge University Press, 1983.

Hollier, Denis. *A New History of French Literature*. Harvard University Press, 1994.

Horne, Alistair. *The Age of Napoleon*. Modern Library, 2006.

————. *The Seven Ages of Paris*. Modern Library, 2006.

Horowitz, Sarah. *Friendship and Politics in Post-Revolutionary France*. Pennsylvania State University Press, 2014.

Houssaye, Henry. *1814*. Perrin, 1888.

————. *1815: La première restauration, le retour de l'île d'Elbe, les cent jours*. Perrin, 1893.

————. *Le retour de Napoléon*. Flammarion, 1933.

Hughes, Michael. *Forging Napoleon's Grande Armée*. New York University Press, 2012.

Humbert, Jean-Marcel. *Napoléon aux Invalides: Le retour des cendres*. Albaron, 1990.

Hunt, Lynn. *The Family Romance of the French Revolution*. Routledge, 1992.

————. *Politics, Culture, and Class in the French Revolution*. University of California Press, 1984.

Hussey, Andrew. *Paris: The Secret History*. Penguin, 2007.

Jackson, Richard A. *Vive le Roi!: A History of French Coronation from Charles V to Charles X*. University of North Carolina Press, 1984.

James, C. L. R. *Black Jacobins: Toussaint L'Ouverture and the San Domingo Revolution*. Vintage, 1989.

Johnson, Paul. *Napoleon: A Life*. Penguin, 2006.

Johnston, R. M., ed. *In the Words of Napoleon: The Emperor Day by Day*. Greenhill Books, 2002.

Jones, Colin. *The Great Nation: France from Louis XIV to Napoleon*. Columbia University Press, 2002.

————. *Paris: The Biography of a City*. Penguin, 2006.

Jordan, David P. *Napoleon and the Revolution*. Palgrave, 2012.

Jourdan, Annie. *L'Empire de Napoléon*. Flammarion, 2000.

————. *Mythes et légendes de Napoléon: Un destin d'exception, entre rêve et réalité*. Privat, 2004.

————. *Napoléon: Héros, imperator, mécène*. Aubier, 1998.

Judson, Pieter. *The Habsburg Empire: A New History*. Belknap, 2016.

Kantrowicz, Ernst H. *The King's Two Bodies: A Study in Medieval Political Theology*. Princeton University Press, 1957.

Kauffmann, Jean-Paul. *The Black Room at Longwood: Napoleon's Exile on Saint Helena*. Translated by Patricia Clancy. Four Walls Eight Windows, 1999.

King, David. *Vienna, 1814: How the Conquerors of Napoleon Made Love, War, and Peace at the Congress of Vienna*. Broadway, 2009.

King, Dean, with John Hattendorf and J. Worth Estes. *A Sea of Words: A Lexicon and Companion for Patrick O'Brian's Seafaring Tales*. Henry Holt, 1997.

Kissinger, Henry. *A World Restored: Metternich, Castlereagh, and the Problems of Peace, 1812–1822*. Houghton Mifflin, 1957.

Kraehe, Enno. *Metternich's German Policy*. Princeton University Press, 2014, vol. II.

Kramer, Lloyd. *Threshold of a New World: Intellectuals and the Exile Experience in Paris, 1830–1848*. Cornell University Press, 1988.

Kroen, Sheryl. *Politics and Theater: The Crisis of Legitimacy in Restoration France, 1815–1830*. University of California Press, 2000.

Lacour-Gayet, Georges. *Talleyrand, 1754–1838*. Paris, 1928–34, 4 vols.

Laflandre-Linden, Louise. *Napoléon et l'île d'Elbe*. Castel, 1989.

Lawday, David. *Napoleon's Master: A Life of Prince Talleyrand*. Cape, 2006.

Lean, Edward Tangye. *The Napoleonists*. Oxford University Press, 1970.

Lefebvre, Georges. *Napoléon*. Translated by Henry F. Stockhold and J. E. Anderson. Routledge, 2011.

Lentz, Thierry. *Napoléon*. Le Cavalier Bleu, 2001.

————. *Nouvelle histoire du Premier Empire. IV. Les Cent-Jours, 1815*. Fayard, 2010.

Lieven, Dominic. *Russia Against Napoleon: The True Story of the Campaigns of War and Peace*. Penguin, 2011.

Lilti, Antoine. *The Invention of Celebrity*. Wiley, 2017.

Livi, Giovanni. *Napoleone all'isola d'Elba*. Treves, 1888.

Lloyd, Rosemary. *Revolutions in Writing: Readings in Nineteenth-Century French Prose*. Indiana University Press, 1996.

Longford, Elizabeth. *Wellington: The Years of the Sword*. Harper & Row, 1969.

McGuigan, Dorothy. *Metternich and the Duchess: The Public and Private Lives at the Congress of Vienna*. Doubleday, 1975.

MacKenzie, Norman. *The Escape from Elba: The Fall and Flight of Napoleon, 1814–1815*. Oxford University Press, 1982.

Madelin, Louis. *Fouché*. Plón, 1901, vol. 2.

Maloy, Frank. *The Constitutions and Other Select Documents Illustrative of the History of France, 1789–1901*. Wilson, 1904.

Mansel, Philip. *The Court of France, 1789–1830*. Cambridge University Press, 1988.

———. *The Eagle in Splendour: Inside the Court of Napoleon*. Tauris, 2015.

———. *Louis XVIII*. John Murray, 2005.

———. *Paris Between Empires: Monarchy and Revolution, 1814–1852*. St. Martin's, 2001.

Mansel, Philip, and Torsten Riotte, eds. *Monarchy and Exile: The Politics of Legitimacy from Marie de Médicis to Wilhelm II*. Palgrave, 2011.

Marcus Aurelius. *Meditations*. Translated by Martin Hammond. Penguin Classics, 2006.

Martin, Andy. *Napoleon the Novelist*. Polity, 2000.

Martinelli, Roberta, and Velia Gina Bartoli. *Napoleone: Imperatore, imprenditore e direttore dei lavori all'Isola d'Elba*. Gangemi Editore, 2014.

Masson, Frédéric. *Napoleon et sa famille: 1814–1815*. Ollendorff, 1907.

Maza, Sarah. *The Myth of the French Bourgeoisie: An Essay on the Social Imaginary*. Harvard University Press, 2003.

Mitchell, Timothy. *Colonising Egypt*. University of California Press, 1991.

Monier, A. D. B. *A Year of the Life of the Emperor Napoleon*. Longworth, 1815.

Morriss, Roger. *The Royal Dockyards During the Revolutionary and Napoleonic Wars*. Leicester University Press, 1983.

Morrissey, Robert. *The Economy of Glory: From Ancien Régime France to the Fall of Napoleon*. Translated by Teresa Lavender Fagan. University of Chicago Press, 2013.

Nagel, Susan. *Marie-Thérèse, Child of Terror: The Fate of Marie Antoinette's Daughter*. Bloomsbury, 2008.

Nicolson, Harold. *The Congress of Vienna: A Study in Allied Unity, 1812–1822*. Constable, 1946.

Nollet-Fabert, Jules. *Biographie du général Drouot*. Dumaine, 1850.

O'Brien, Michael. *Mrs. Adams in Winter: A Journey in the Last Days of Napoleon*. Farrar, Straus & Giroux, 2010.

O'Dwyer, M. M. *The Papacy in the Age of Napoleon and the Restoration: Pius VII, 1800–1823*. University Press of America, 1985.

O'Meara, Barry. *Napoleon at Saint Helena*. Scribner & Welford, 1889, vol. II.

Orieux, Jean. *Talleyrand ou Le sphinx incompris*. Flammarion, 1970.

Ozouf, Mona. *Festivals of the French Revolution*. Translated by Alan Sheridan. Harvard University Press, 1988.

Palmer, Alan. *Alexander I: Tsar of War and Peace*. Harper & Row, 1974.

————. *Bernadotte: Napoleon's Marshal, Sweden's King*. John Murray, 1991.

————. *Metternich: Councillor of Europe*. Faber, 2010.

————. *Napoleon and Marie Louise: The Emperor's Second Wife*. St. Martin's, 2001.

Paulin, Jules A. *Notice biographique sur le lieutenant-général comte Bertrand: Grand-maréchal du palais de l'Empereur*. Au Comptoir des Imprimeurs-Unis, 1847.

Pellet, Marcellin. *Napoléon à l'île d'Elbe*. Charpentier, 1889.

Perl-Rosenthal, Nathan. *Citizen Sailors: Becoming American in the Age of Revolution*. Belknap, 2015.

Petiteau, Natalie. *Napoléon, de la mythologie à l'histoire*. Seuil, 1999.

Pichot, Amédée, ed. *Napoléon à l'île d'Elbe: Chronique des événements de 1814 et 1815, d'après le Journal du colonel sir Neil Campbell, le "Journal d'un détenu," et autres documents inédits ou peu connus, pour servir à l'histoire du Premier Empire et de la Restauration*. Dentu, 1873.

Plongeron, Bernard. *Des résistances religieuses à Napoléon, 1799–1813*. Letouzey & Ané, 2006.

Pocock, Tom. *Stopping Napoleon: War and Intrigue in the Mediterranean*. John Murray, 2004.

————. *A Thirst for Glory: The Life of Admiral Sir Sidney Smith*. Thistle, 2013.

Porterfield, Todd, and Susan Siegfried. *Staging Empire: Napoleon, Ingres, and David*. Penn State University Press, 2007.

Price, Munro. *Napoleon: The End of Glory*. Oxford University Press, 2014.

————. *The Perilous Crown: France Between Revolutions, 1814–1848*. Macmillan, 2007.

Reiss, Tom. *The Black Count: Glory, Revolution, Betrayal, and the Real Count of Monte Cristo*. Broadway Books, 2013.

Roberts, Andrew. *Napoleon: A Life*. Viking, 2014.

Rosanvallon, Pierre. *The Demands of Liberty: Civil Society in France Since the Revolution*. Translated by Arthur Goldhammer. Harvard University Press, 2007.

————. *Le Monarchie Impossible: Les Chartes de 1814 et 1830*. Fayard, 1994.

Rosebery, Lord. *Napoleon: The Last Phase*. Harper, 1900.

Rowell, Diana. *Paris: The "New Rome" of Napoleon I*. Bloomsbury, 2012.

Rudé, George. *Revolutionary Europe 1783–1815*. Harper & Row, 1964.

Said, Edward. *Reflections on Exile and Other Essays*. Harvard University Press, 2004.

Saint-Amand, Imbert de. *Marie Louise, Elba, and the Hundred Days*. Scribner, 1894.

Sante, Luc. *The Other Paris*. Farrar, Straus & Giroux, 2015.

Sauvigny, Guillaume de Bertier de. *Bourbon Restoration*. University of Pennsylvania Press, 1966.

Schalansky, Judith. *Atlas of Remote Islands: Fifty Islands I Have Never Set Foot On and Never Will*. Translated by Christine Lo. Penguin, 2010.

Schama, Simon. *Citizens: A Chronicle of the French Revolution*. Vintage, 1990.

Schom, Alan. *One Hundred Days: Napoleon's Road to Waterloo*. Penguin, 1992.

Schroeder, Paul W. *The Transformation of European Politics, 1763–1848*. Oxford University Press, 1994.

Schwartz, Vanessa. *Modern France: A Very Short Introduction*. Oxford University Press, 2011.

Scott, Walter. *The Life of Napoleon Buonaparte, Emperor of the French*. Harper, 1828, vol. III.

Sebag Montefiore, Simon. *The Romanovs: 1613–1918*. Knopf, 2016.

Seidel, Michael. *Exile and the Narrative Imagination*. Yale University Press, 1986.

Semmel, Stuart. *Napoleon and the British*. Yale University Press, 2004.

Serieyx, William. *Drouot et Napoléon*. Tallandier, 1929.

Sipe, Thomas. *Beethoven's Eroica Symphony*. Cambridge University Press, 1998.

Stabler, Jane. *The Artistry of Exile: Romantic and Victorian Writers in Italy*. Oxford University Press, 2013.

Strathern, Paul. *Napoleon in Egypt*. Bantam, 2008.

Tackett, Timothy. *When the King Took Flight*. Harvard University Press, 2003.

Taine, Hippolyte. *Les origines de la France contemporaine, Tome III: Le régime moderne, Napoléon Bonaparte*. Hachette, 1899.

Thiry, Jean. *Le vol de l'aigle*. Berger-Levrault, 1942.

Tocqueville, Alexis de. *The Ancien Régime and the Revolution*. Translated and edited by Gerald Bevan. Penguin, 2008.

Troyat, Henri. *Alexander of Russia: Napoleon's Conqueror*. Translated by Joan Pinkham. Grove Press, 1982.

Tulard, Jean. *Le Grand Empire: 1814–1815*. Albin Michel, 2016.

———. *The Myth of the Saviour*. Translated by Theresa Waugh. Methuen, 1985.

———. *Napoléon et les mystères de Sainte-Hélène*. L'archipel, 2003.

———. *Paris et son administration (1800–1830)*. Comité d'histoire de la ville de Paris, 1976.

Uglow, Jenny. *In These Times: Living in Britain Through Napoleon's Wars, 1793–1815*. Farrar, Straus & Giroux, 2015.

Vasson, Jacques de. *Bertrand, le grand-maréchal de Sainte-Hélène*. Laboureur, 1935.

Waresquiel, Emmanuel de. *Cent Jours: Le tentation de l'impossible: Mars–juillet 1815*. Fayard, 2008.

————. *Talleyrand: Le prince immobile*. Fayard, 2003.

Waresquiel, Emmanuel de, and Benoît Yvert. *Histoire de la Restauration, 1814–1830*. Perrin, 2002.

Waters, Dagmar, and Tony Waters, eds. *Weber's Rationalism and Modern Society*. Palgrave, 2015.

Webster, Charles K. *The Congress of Vienna, 1814–1815*. Oxford University Press, 1918.

————. *The Foreign Policy of Castlereagh, 1812–1815*. Bell and Sons, 1931.

Weckerlin, Jean Baptiste. *Chansons populaires du pays de France*. Ménestrel, 1904.

Welvert, Eugène. *Napoléon et la police sous la première Restauration*. R. Roger & F. Chernowitz, 1913.

Williams, Helen Maria. *A Narrative of the Events Which Have Taken Place in France*. John Murray, 1815.

Wilson, A. N. *Victoria: A Life*. Penguin Press, 2014.

Wilson, Emily. *The Greatest Empire: A Life of Seneca*. Oxford University Press, 2014.

Wolff, Henry Drummond. *The Island Empire*. Bosworth, 1855.

Woloch, Isser. *The French Veteran from the Revolution to the Restoration*. University of North Carolina Press, 1979.

————. *Napoleon and His Collaborators: The Making of a Dictatorship*. Norton, 2001.

————. *The New Regime: Transformations of the French Civic Order, 1789–1820s*. Norton, 1995.

Young, Norwood. *Napoleon in Exile: Elba*. Stanley Paul, 1914.

Zamoyski, Adam. *Moscow 1812: Napoleon's Fatal March*. HarperCollins, 2004.

————. *Rites of Peace: The Fall of Napoleon and the Congress of Vienna*. Harper Perennial, 2008.

NOVELS

Broch, Hermann. *The Death of Virgil*. Pantheon, 1945.

Dumas, Alexandre. *The Count of Monte Cristo*. Penguin, 2003.

Stendhal. *The Red and the Black*. Penguin, 2002.

Leys, Simon. *The Death of Napoleon*. New York Review Books, 2006.

ARTICLES, CONFERENCE PAPERS, AND DISSERTATIONS

Bear, Jordan. "Adrift: The Time and Space of the News in Géricault's *Le Radeau de la Méduse*." In *Getting the Picture: The Visual Culture of the News*, edited by Jason Hill and Vanessa R. Schwartz. Bloomsbury, 2015.

Beer, Gillian. "The Island and the Aeroplane: The Case of Virginia Woolf." In *Nation and Narration*, edited by Homi K. Bhabha. Routledge, 1990.

Clubbe, John. "Between Emperor and Exile: Byron and Napoleon, 1814–1816." *Napoleonic Scholarship* 1, no. 1 (April 1997).

Delvaux, Steven Laurence. "Witness to Glory: Lieutenant-Général Henri-Gatien Bertrand, 1791–1815." Dissertation, Florida State University, 2005.

Dutourd, Jean. "'Le Dictionnaire des girouettes,' paru en 1815, demeure une arme pour comprendre notre temps." *Le Figaro*, June 2, 2007.

Éloi-Vial, Charles. "4, 6 et 11 avril 1814: Les trois actes d'abdication de Napoléon Ier." *Napoleonica: La Revue* (January 2014): 3–24.

Englund, Steven. "Napoleon: The Unsolved Enigma." *New York Review of Books*, March 24, 2016.

Fyfe, Christopher. "Circular Road Burial Ground." *Journal of Sierra Leone Studies*, 1958, II.

Gabriëls, Jos. "Cutting the Cake: The Congress of Vienna in British, French and German Political Caricature." *European Review of History* 24, no. 1 (2016): 131–57.

Gopnik, Adam. "The Good Soldier." *New Yorker*, November 24, 1997.

———. "Voltaire's Garden." *New Yorker*, March 7, 2005.

Gray, D. S. "An Audience of One: Sir Neil Campbell on Napoleon." *History Today* 24, no. 9 (September 1974).

Hicks, Peter. "Napoleon on Elba: An Exile of Consent." *Napoleonica*, no. 19 (January 2014): 53–67.

MacDonogh, Katharine. "A Sympathetic Ear: Napoleon, Elba and the British." *History Today* 44, no. 2 (1994).

McFadden, Robert D. "Long After Napoleon's Conquests, a Tale of Intrigue Leads to Court." *New York Times*, April 6, 2001.

Sainte-Beuve, C.-A. "Essai sur Talleyrand par Sir Henry Lytton Bulwer." *Nouveaux Lundis*, XII. Michel Levy, 1870.

Smith, Zadie. "Two Paths for the Novel." *New York Review of Books*, December 20, 2008.

Thompson, J. M. "Napoleon's Journey to Elba in 1814. Part I. By Land." *American Historical Review* 55, no. 1 (October 1949): 1–21.

Tozzi, Christopher. "Soldiers Without a Country: Foreign Veterans in the Transition from Empire to Restoration." *Journal of Military History* 80, no. 1 (January 2016): 93–120.

Wagner, Anne M. "Outrages: Sculpture and Kingship in France After 1789." In *The Consumption of Culture: 1600–1800: Image, Object, Text*, edited by Ann Bermingham and John Brewer. Routledge, 1995.

Waresquiel, Emmanuel de. "Talleyrand au congrés de Vienne et les caricatures du *Nain jaune*." Delivered at the "200ème anniversaire du congrés de Vienne, Talleyrand l'indispensable," organisé par l'association les amis de Talleyrand, Hotel de Talleyrand, 8 et 9 juin, 2015.

INDEX

—————